ONE MIND

ONE MIND

A Psychiatrist's Spiritual Teachings

Thomas Hora, M.D.

The PAGL Foundation
Old Lyme, CT

Published by the PAGL Foundation
P.O. Box 4001, Old Lyme, CT 06371

Copyright © 2001 by The PAGL Foundation
Edited in 2014

Printed in the United States of America

Library of Congress Cataloging-in-Publication Data

Hora, Thomas.
        One Mind : A Psychiatrist's Spiritual Teachings / Thomas Hora.
            p.   cm.
        ISBN 1-931052-01-8
        1. Psychiatry and religion.   I. Title.

RC455.4.R4 H674 2001
616.89-dc21

                                                                00-065205

In the multitude of dreams and many words,
there are diverse vanities: but "hear" thou God.
— Ecclesiastes 5:7

Awake thou that sleepest, and arise from the dead,
and Christ shall give thee light.
— Ephesians 5:14

Contents

Preface

One Mind is a collection of class sessions in Metapsychiatry, the spiritual teaching which flowed into the world through the consciousness of Thomas Hora, M.D. The chapters that were compiled to form this book were transcribed from tapes of dialogues between Dr. Hora and his students that took place over a period of ten years. These dialogues are examples of the Metapsychiatric approach in which diverse human problems are examined and the spiritual remedies to them are revealed. Through the use of issue-oriented, Socratic dialogue, these group sessions allowed Dr. Hora's students to bring their difficulties and struggles to his expanded awareness for his metaphysical discernments and his guidance to a vision of perfect life.

The goal of Metapsychiatry's therapeutic work is to help us realize that there is no existence apart from God, which is synonymous with enlightenment. Metapsychiatry identifies the meanings of our suffering and endeavors to bring healing and fulfillment to those who are receptive. The teaching views the human journey as a glorious opportunity in which to examine all aspects of our tangible, material experience ("what seems to be") in order to uncover and reveal to us the existence of the intangible, spiritual truth of our being ("what really is").

Through a method of juxtaposing ideas, we can come to know the one true Mind, which is God, the only Reality, in a palpable way that has a beneficial effect on our lives. A benefit of this juxtapositional process (which is formulated in Metapsychiatry's "Two Intelligent Questions") is that it always directs our attention back to the Allness of God and to our real identities as spiritual. This reorientation not only corrects our mistaken notions and the misperceptions that are manifesting as our problems, painful experiences, or illnesses, it makes health and healing solutions possible. Dr. Hora uses this method advantageously in the dialogues that follow to clarify and contrast ideas in order to see their true nature and their impact on our lives.

"All problems are psychological, and all solutions are spiritual," one of Dr. Hora's oft-quoted axioms, is itself constructed to demonstrate the value of the juxtapositional arrangement. The first part of the axiom speaks to "what seems to be," while the second reveals "what really is." This axiom is an unequivocal statement about the powerful dynamic of thoughts and their tendency to attract corresponding experiences into our lives. It also points us to the redeeming idea of freedom from our suffering through spiritual understanding.

*   *   *

Thomas Hora, M.D., the founder and guiding light of Metapsychiatry until his passing in 1995, was a renowned psychiatrist who was inspired to go beyond conventional medical practices to find healing of sickness, mental disorders, problems and difficulties. Having observed that traditional forms of treatment did not always make a patient well, Dr. Hora explored spiritually enlightened teachings in depth to uncover the knowledge that lay within them that could bring wholeness and healing to those who sought his help. Dr. Hora discovered a system of thought and a methodology to accomplish this holy process. The fruit of his quest is the teaching he called "Metapsychiatry" (literally, "beyond psychiatry").

Thomas Hora was born in 1914 in northern Hungary and received his medical degrees from the Royal Hungarian University in Budapest and from Charles University in Prague. In 1945, he immigrated with his German wife to the United States where he subsequently received his psychoanalytic training from the Postgraduate Center for Mental Health in New York, and went on to establish private practices in New York City and Bedford, New York. His practice in New York spanned close to fifty years.

In the years until 1967, Dr. Hora was active in psychiatric circles in the United States and in Europe, delivering over forty lectures and publishing an equal number of articles. In 1958, in recognition of his contribution to the field, he received the first Karen Horney Award for the Advancement of Psychoanalysis. During these years, his spiritual search was in full bloom. After 1967, Dr. Hora withdrew from participation in professional societies and focused all of his time and attention on his evolving Metapsychiatric practice. He gradually transcended a traditional psychiatric approach, since his work clearly demonstrated that the solutions to all problems--mental, physical, and experiential--are to be found in the realm of the spiritual. The thrust of Dr. Hora's healing work moved from a human context to one whose paramount reality was the essentially divine nature of his patients (or, as he called them, "students"). His work, being transdenominational, drew students from throughout the world--Catholics, Protestants, Jews, Buddhists, and non-religious individuals—many of whom studied with him for fifteen to twenty years or more. In addition, he supervised the work of therapists and counselors; some of his students are now counselors and teachers. Dr. Hora worked until a week before his passing. He left a legacy of grateful students, several books (some posthumously published), a dozen booklets on various subjects, and hundreds of class and seminar tapes.

Metapsychiatry springs from the spiritual teachings of Jesus, the wisdom of Zen Masters and Hebrew prophets, and from the insights of mystics, seekers, and philosophers throughout the ages, infusing them with fresh understanding. In Dr. Hora's own words, "Metapsychiatry came into the world to put soul into psychiatry, and to breathe the life of Spirit into the 'valley of dry bones'" (Ezekiel 37:1-6).

* * *

The dialogues of this book do not need to be read sequentially, as each stands on its own. (Dr. Hora entitled these dialogues to identify the principal issue addressed in each.) Since these classes were comprised of students with whom Dr. Hora worked regularly, there might be references to certain concepts, which the new reader of Metapsychiatry may not completely understand and which are explained more fully in earlier books. Editorial brackets are inserted in a few places where elucidation seemed needed. Extraneous remarks from the students have been eliminated where they distracted from the flow of dialogue and Dr. Hora's inspired responses.

While the written word does not allow the reader to experience the good natured laughter that punctuated Dr. Hora's lively classes or the warm glow of his smiles or the compassion Dr. Hora exuded, it does allow the reader to consider the brilliant perceptions of this keen observer of the human condition and to be lifted up to a new reality by the enlightened wisdom that is so powerfully articulated by this teaching.

- Susan von Reichenbach
April 2000

Acknowledgments

As this book is published posthumously, his students would like to express their gratitude to Dr. Thomas Hora (who liked to say, "I'm really not even here!") with these words from the Tao:

> *The perfect man has no self,*
> *The holy man has no merit,*
> *The sage has no reputation.*

A special thanks goes to Jim and Gaye Pigott, whose generosity made the publication of this work possible. Gratitude also goes to Susan von Reichenbach, who lovingly edited the manuscript; to Susan Ayers, who carefully transcribed the class sessions; to Sarita Van Vleck, who did the preliminary preparation; to James Kuslan, who typed the final manuscript; to Ruth Robins, who coordinated the project; to Bruce Kerievsky, who helped in a variety of ways; to Michael Leach, who guided it to publication; and to PAGL Foundation Board of Directors for its encouragement and support.

Dialogue No. 1

One Mind

Dr. Hora: We look around and we see millions of people, and everyone seems to have a mind of his own, and most everyone's mind is at loggerheads with most everyone else's mind. There are only a few of us here today, and yet we all seem to have our own minds. Now when we try to communicate with one another, we find that this one thinks differently from that one. The "meeting of two minds" always involves some tension or interaction. Even under favorable circumstances it seems very difficult for minds to meet and to establish harmony, so the impression is very powerful that this world consists of billions of separate minds that cannot find harmony with one another. And if there is harmony, it usually does not last long. There is a tremendous diversity of individual minds, and this makes life very complicated and very difficult. Beyond that, every individual mind has a desire to assert itself as superior to every other mind, so what we have in the world is a constant battle of minds. There is a battle of the sexes, and there is a battle of minds going on all the time—and this makes life rather stressful. People inflict tremendous suffering on each other with their minds. But the Bible says that there is only One Mind, the Mind of Christ, and besides this Mind, there is no other mind. How can we understand this statement? Is it possible? Meditation is a way we can come to understand the existence of the One Mind.

*Student: Does this have to do with the idea of not thinking? In other words, we do not really think. We listen—we listen, even if it seems as though we are thinking?

Dr. Hora: Yes.

Student: I'm always trying to think, but I realize in meditation that we do not think. We are just receptive to thoughts from the divine Mind, from God to us.

---

*Each dialogue in the book is between Dr. Hora and ten to fifteen students. The word Student in the text refers to any one of them.

1

Dr. Hora: Yes, but logically it does not make any sense that there would be only One Mind. If it is so plain, then how is it that there seem to be billions of minds now on the planet Earth? How can the Bible claim that there is only One Mind? Isn't it absurd to hope ever to realize that fact? What would happen to us if we successfully realized in meditation that there is only One Mind?

Student: It seems frightening, but the idea of ourselves as persons would be dissolved.

Student: A workman was at our house recently, and he happened to tell me that he studies voodoo. Doesn't voodoo imply mind control?

Dr. Hora: Voodoo, of course, and many other cults affirm the belief that not only do we have a mind but that this mind is so powerful that it could project through time and space and influence other minds, either favorably or unfavorably—mostly unfavorably. And there are systems that believe that one can heal people by projecting thoughts onto them, wanting people to get well. There are still other systems that recommend the use of mental powers in the form of visualizations and imaginings. The individuals who embrace these systems believe that whatever they wish strongly enough will come true. The idea is to use the "personal mind" to get what you want. It's very tempting. And there are also people who believe that one can use mental powers to cure cancer. But of course Metapsychiatry views these approaches as forms of hypnotism, and hypnotism is a form of mental despotism that can result in all sorts of disturbances, like megalomania and manic-depressive psychosis. All sorts of problems can come from the belief in a "personal mind" power. Once someone believes that he has a superior mind, then there is no living with him anymore. For such an individual, everyone has to be dominated and subjugated. This is the case with cults. There is an individual, a charismatic personality, who believes that he has special mental powers. Others are attracted and submit to him because they are hypnotized by the idea that he has special powers and they want to participate in his powers. We then have a cult with a leader and followers and all the various complications of brainwashing and mind control and all sorts of insanities to which the human race is given. But the Bible says that none of these things really exist: there is only One Mind, the Christ-Consciousness, the divine Mind, infinite Love-Intelligence. Paul explains it this way: "There are diversities of gifts, but one spirit" (1 Corinthians 12:4).

This means there is an infinite variety of ways that this One Mind expresses Itself through individuals, but there is only the activity of the One Mind. In meditation, we seek to become aware of these truths. Now what happens when we become aware that it is really so, that there is only One Mind—all-powerful, infinite, omnipresent, eternal, all-knowing and all-loving, which expresses itself through every individual in the universe in a unique way? What would happen to the world if this truth were universally understood?

Student: All conflict between individual minds would cease.

Dr. Hora: That's right. The millennium would arrive. What is the millennium?

Student: The millennium refers to the idea of heaven on earth (Revelation 20:1-6).

Dr. Hora: Right. Heaven on earth means that jealousy, rivalry, competition, power struggles, anger, fear, greed, deception, cunning, foxiness—all these would disappear and there would just be divine Intelligence flowing through the world. In meditation, we seek to understand the One Mind; and, in proportion to our ability to receive this understanding into consciousness, we become transformed into "beneficial presences" in the world because we can see reality in its true light. We would no longer see many minds at war with one another, trying to gain advantage; instead we would see infinite wisdom and love manifesting themselves everywhere in an infinite variety of ways. That is how meditation could transform every one of us. This is what the world needs.

Student: Meditation seems to be just thinking the words, as opposed to really understanding something.

Dr. Hora: Yes. How do we move from words to real understanding? If we start meditating, and we settle down in a comfortable chair and become quiet, what will happen?

Student: Garbage thoughts start bubbling up.

Dr. Hora: What kind of garbage thoughts?

Student: It seems the whole dream of human pictures in which we are living starts appearing before us.

Dr. Hora: In what form does the garbage come to us?

Student: It is anything that makes me aware of myself as a person with a personal mind.

Dr. Hora: To be precise, the garbage thoughts consist of thinking about what others are thinking about what we are thinking—in other words, interaction thoughts—which means that the illusion of the personal mind feels threatened and is excited and preoccupied with the contents of the personal minds of other people. So, when we start meditation, our attention is focused on the interaction between the illusory personal minds with which we have recently had some contact. These nonexistent personal minds are constantly battling with each other. Now how can we be liberated from this painful mental preoccupation with what other people are thinking or not thinking or did say or would say or how to cope with that mentality or how to get back at this mind or how to win in that situation? What is the remedy to these ruminations? It's hell. It's absolute hell to think about what others are thinking about.

Student: Well, we could think about the One Mind—is that what we do? I guess we have to recognize that we are thinking about others.

Dr. Hora: All right. So you move from thinking about interaction of minds to thinking about the One Mind. Well, that's already progress. Now what happens when you decide, "I'm not going to think about what he said or she said; I'm going to think about the One Mind." What will happen? It will be very hard to sustain it.

Student: Because we are still "thinking"?

Dr. Hora: Yes. But even if you would want to think about the One Mind and nothing else, it would be very difficult because the other thoughts would keep coming back and intruding themselves.

Student: But we could turn our attention from the interpersonal, interaction thoughts to Omniaction.

Dr. Hora: All right. Now at this point we have arrived at the Transcendental Meditation of the Maharishi where we are focusing mental attention on the One Mind. But all these other garbage thoughts keep wanting to distract us. Our mantra is the One Mind. However, we persist, in spite of all distractions, in reminding ourselves that there is only One Mind. And as we are faithful to that thought, we notice that the garbage thoughts gradually begin to fade out, because we are less and less interested in them. We cannot "serve two masters": we cannot maintain the thought of the One Mind and at the same time pay attention to the garbage thoughts. That is the basic principle of the Maharishi's Transcendental Meditation—the One Mind transcends the many minds. When we focus on the One Mind, the many minds gradually leave us.

Student: After first really distracting us.

Dr. Hora: Right, but we keep faithfully to the idea of One Mind. We are still thinking, but already the agitation of the garbage thoughts is gradually fading away and we are becoming increasingly tranquilized, more and more quiet. And here we go into real meditation where we do not have to think any longer about the One Mind. Then the soul takes over, and instead of thinking about the One Mind, the soul begins to be aware of God's presence as Consciousness. We reach a point of complete quietude, where there are no more thoughts, and we do not have to think about the One Mind—there is only a state of awareness which the Buddhists call "emptiness." In this emptiness, God rushes in with a message or an idea, and we can then hear the soundless voice of God, speaking to whatever need happens to be before us at the time when we are meditating. And this soundless voice, this message from God, gives us an awareness of PAGL [PAGL is an acronym for Peace, Assurance, Gratitude, Love, and Its Presence in consciousness informs us that we are in tune with the One Mind.] Armed with this awareness of PAGL, we can get up and face life in an effective way, assured that whatever problems we have had will eventually be solved. We can be healed—whatever has bothered us will be healed in that emptiness. The Bible speaks of the "desert place." In this place, there is usually a healing message—and more than that, we become increasingly aware of the fact that there is only One Mind, and we find that we are not depressed anymore by the multitude of minds and that they no longer threaten us. Whenever someone tries to exercise control over our awareness—either through deception or arrogance or pressuring or cheating or lying—we are aware that this is not real, that it is not really happening, that this cannot touch us because God is the only Mind and whatever comes from the divine Mind is always loving, always honest, always intelligent and benevolent. So even if we are facing a con artist, it doesn't disturb us because we know this "mind" is not real. Now, these are the blessings of meditation.

Student: When one is focusing on the One Mind, is it appropriate to try to focus on some divine quality, like beauty, and then let one's thoughts flow to things beautiful and harmonious that come into consciousness, or is that just a pleasant distraction?

Dr. Hora: Yes. The issue in practical living is not beauty or harmony, but the battle of minds. This is the greatest problem we face every day. We can see beauty; we can see harmony; we can listen to music; we can watch the sunset; we can gaze at flowers. But these activities will not have sufficient power to liberate us from the very painful experience of being at loggerheads, most of the time, with other human beings. Only the right realization of the One Mind will give us peace and enable us to look at the battleground and see that everything, everywhere, is peaceful. There's a bloody battle going on all the time if we judge by appearances. But when we judge with "enlightened judgment," we can discern that everything, everywhere, is peaceful and good and intelligent and harmonious. There is no conflict; there is no strife—there is only One Mind, and this Mind is in control of the whole universe. Right where strife seems to be, there is harmony because the One Mind is in charge [regardless of appearances to the contrary].

Student: Are meditation and ceaseless prayer the same?

Dr. Hora: Not exactly. Ceaseless prayer takes place on a conceptual level. We think about God; we think about spiritual values. We are affirming and clinging mentally to these ideas. That is ceaseless prayer. In meditation, we go beyond concepts and words into pure awareness. Now the faculty of awareness is not a mind faculty; it is a soul faculty. It is the soul that has the faculty of awareness. So we moved from sense existence to soul existence.

Student: Ceaseless prayer, then, is a preparation.

Dr. Hora: ". . . Prepare ye the way of the Lord, make straight in the desert a highway for our God. Every valley shall be exalted, and every mountain and hill shall be made low: and the crooked shall be made straight, and the rough places plain" (Isaiah 40:3-4). What does this mean?

Student: It means that self-confirmation will be brought down, and sin will be abolished.

Dr. Hora: It means that there are no crooked minds in God's kingdom. Everyone is forthright and loving. And what about "the rough places"?

Student: Real life is not contention and interpersonal friction.

Dr. Hora: It is beautiful poetry.

Student: But there are wolves out in the human world, and we have to be intelligent enough to know how to respond to a cunning individual who might be out to devour us. How do we "unsee" what seems to be foxiness or deviousness, especially in the business world, where it seems to be a norm? And how can we maintain efficient, effective, harmonious living, being "in the world" and "not of it," under these human conditions? In light of all that was said today, meditation is a way to understand the existence of the One Mind, which will protect us and keep us from being hypnotized and locking horns with "personal minds." It seems you have to be a wolf, too—even when you do not want to be sucked into it. How can you be straight in a crooked world?

Dr. Hora: Good question.

Student: Where I work there is an individual who acts very important and seems to think that he is superior. But I notice that what happens to me is that I want to be important and superior, too. I was exhausted today, and in trying to understand my fatigue, I realized that I was interacting mentally because I wanted the same things he does. So we both have the same invalid thoughts in consciousness, and that accounts for the tension. But, if we would meditate and understand there is only One Mind, then this conflict would not happen.

Dr. Hora: There are individuals who can go among a group of wolves, and they will not be hurt by them—the wolves will just snuggle up to them like pets. And there are individuals who can walk among rattlesnakes, and the snakes will not bite them; and there are individuals who can put their hands into a tiger's mouth, and the tiger will not hurt them. What is their secret?

Student: They really have assurance.

Dr. Hora: Yes. They are not vulnerable to evil because they know something. You see, when we come to know the One Mind, no one can hurt us with "his" mind because we no longer believe in the power of an illusory mind. This understanding allows us to confront such individuals with the utmost assurance. They will have no way of taking advantage of us.

Student: What if we notice that we are being influenced by deviousness?

Dr. Hora: It means that we believe in the reality of such a mind, and as long as there is this belief, there will be vulnerability. Therefore, we cannot say, "I won't believe anymore that wolves can't hurt me." We would be very foolish to say this. To say "I don't believe" means that we believe. We have to know something, to have realized that there is an overriding Reality whose truth replaces our belief or unbelief. We neither believe nor disbelieve—we know something. And it is this knowing that makes us invulnerable to any illusory powers of illusory minds. The problem is the belief: if we can be healed of the belief, then we will see that there is nothing to see.

Student: Isn't there a "meaning" to the experience of separate minds? Isn't it always that we invite friction and conflict?

Dr. Hora: It is not we who are inviting it; it is the universal belief that is inviting it. For example, if we believe that there are vicious minds, then we are going to experience vicious minds.

Student: Let's return to the example that was mentioned earlier where two individuals each wanted to be important and the result was a power struggle. When we realize that we are in a power struggle and we want to be important, we could turn to the thought that God is all important. This idea would ameliorate the power struggle by lifting us out of interpersonal thinking and putting us in contact with the One Mind. It seems that this is a step that would help us.

Dr. Hora: But we need to go beyond even that step and seek to be healed of the belief [in the existence] of many minds. How can we be healed of this belief in many minds? In meditation, as we seek to realize that there is only One Mind, the belief will gradually disappear. There is an old saying, "Seeing is believing." But what we are saying is, "Believing is seeing." When the belief disappears, the seeing disappears—and we will see that there is nothing to see. There are no personal minds, no crooked minds, no vicious minds, no con artists. There is only One Mind, and what we suffer from is the collective belief in the existence of personal minds.

Student: When all these different garbage thoughts come to us, is it because we believe that they are able to gain entry into our consciousness? Should we disbelieve them?

Dr. Hora: Disbelieving is not enough. We have to reach a point where we really know that there is no such thing. Then there is no more believing nor disbelieving—there is seeing that there is nothing to see. When we see that there is nothing to see, then we have realized that what we saw before was just an illusion. We have been healed of the belief, and thereby we become invulnerable.

Dialogue No. 2

The Dynamics of Liberation

Student: Dr. Hora, during the process of the purification and spiritualization of consciousness, it seems that the mind is supposed to die to the past. But, if the mind is made up of the past, how can that mind "die" to the past, so that there is no past? Is it that same mind or another mind that is meant to die? What happens?

Dr. Hora: How many minds are there?

Student: There is no mind.

Dr. Hora: Where have you read this?

Student: In a Zen book.

Dr. Hora: In a Zen book, yes. Exactly how is this idea expressed?

Student: You must die to the past if you want to be free. You must die to all the past, to everything that ever was.

Dr. Hora: That's very true. Could you explain what it means?

Student: In the Zen context, one is speaking of infinity where there is no beginning and no end; therefore, we are living in the now. There is no past.

Dr. Hora: It reminds me of a Zen Master who said to his student, "The past is gone; the future is not yet, and the present you are not aware of."

Student: We're not aware of the now, even though now is what's now. We're not there; we're so often preoccupied . . .

Dr. Hora: With what "should" be and what "should not" be, with what we want and what we do not want and with what was and what should not have been. Is it possible to abolish the past and live an ahistorical existence? There is a Western philosopher who said, "They that are not aware of the past are condemned to repeat it." So where does this idea get us?

Student: What kind of awareness or understanding about the past do we need?

Dr. Hora: The Zen Master says none at all, but the Western philosopher infers that it is important to know the past or else you will keep repeating it. How can we reconcile these two seemingly contradictory ideas?

Student: We have to learn from the past. We can recognize our errors—our false, invalid states of consciousness that got us into trouble—and turn in another direction.

Dr. Hora: Yes. The Zen Master says that the past has to die. And the Western philosopher says that he who does not remember the past is condemned to repeat it. What are we going to do with the past? The Zen Master seems to be saying to ignore it, and this Western philosopher is saying we don't dare ignore it because we will keep repeating and reliving it. What does Metapsychiatry say? "What we do not remember, we cannot forget." That is what Metapsychiatry says about healing the past. Do we all understand it?

Student: No.

Dr. Hora: Can anyone explain it?

Student: If we have repressed our errors, if we refuse to face them, then they are going to haunt us always, and we will have no chance of correcting our course.

Dr. Hora: Now Socrates said, "An unexamined life is a life not worth living." An unexamined past will haunt us all our lives [in one way or another]. On the other hand, an examined past, when clung to, will also make us miserable. Therefore, the past must be fully understood at some point before it can be forgotten. This means it must be fully remembered before it can be fully forgotten. Do you understand?

Student: Not really.

Dr. Hora: God inspired us to bring up this idea so that we could benefit from it. How does God know these things?

Student: Does he? You're pulling my leg!

Dr. Hora: No, you're pulling your own leg—on the tennis courts!

Student: As a matter of fact, I went through all kinds of statements before I last played tennis. "I'm here for God." "There's no competition." "Just enjoy it." And even so, I pulled my leg! What is the meaning of this? I have no idea. I did everything right, and I still pulled my leg.

Dr. Hora: Now, what is the lesson in this? The message is that incantations do not work. What is the difference between incantations and contemplative meditation on the truth?

Student: Please explain these words.

Dr. Hora: Incantations refer to the reciting of certain words [hoping they will magically produce the outcome we want]—nice, pretty words from Metapsychiatry. Jesus called them "vain repetitions." Now contemplative meditation—what is that?

Student: It is sitting quietly and waiting for truth to be revealed and understood on whatever issues we are concerned about.

Dr. Hora: Yes, it occurs when we are seeking the clarity and the relevance of certain knowledge to a particular situation. Now one of the most difficult things is affirmations. There are certain religious groups that recommend that we resort to affirmations, and incantations are just affirmations of certain statements about the truth. It is interesting that for some people it works when they make these affirmations, but for many others it does not work.

Student: When we are affirming something, it is still on a mental plane. Few of us seem to be able to move into the spiritual.

Dr. Hora: What does it mean to "move into the spiritual"?

Student: To transcend, to progress into a higher state of consciousness.

Dr. Hora: You see, there are two kinds of people in prayer: there are the thinkers, and there are the contemplatives. The thinkers cannot pray—their prayers do not work—they are not heard. God does not hear a thinker, but a contemplative will find that his prayers are effective. What is the difference?

Student: In contemplation, our will would not be present. We would not be full of wanting; we would not be reciting words to get something that we had in mind. Instead we would be aware of God's presence, and the motivation for prayer would not come from fear or lack; it would come from a desire to draw close to God, to appreciate God at that moment.

Dr. Hora: And thinking?

Student: Thinking is entirely different—thinking blocks God, and thinking blocks receiving. Thinking is manipulative and tries to influence; it is usually centered on ourselves or other selves. "Thinking" leaves God altogether out of the picture.

Dr. Hora: Thinking can be centered on God, but in the wrong way.

Student: If you are thinking in prayer, you're turning to self to figure out an answer; and if you're contemplating in meditation, you're turning to God for the answer.

Dr. Hora: Yes, that is correct. We could say it this way: the contemplative seeks clarity and understanding; the thinker seeks mastery—he wants to master the problem with his own mind. The thinker has an arrogant approach to prayer, and the contemplative has a humble, receptive approach to prayer. God doesn't hear the prayers of a thinker, and it can be very frustrating, because thinkers are usually very diligent students of Metapsychiatry who do not get very far. They know the words; they know the books inside out, but God doesn't hear them because they are not really addressing themselves to God, but to their "own" mind power. It is such a subtle thing, but it is very crucial to grasp this difference, as it can make all the difference.

Student: Would this be the meaning of having difficulty meditating?

Dr. Hora: That is possible, yes. Thinkers cannot pray effectively, and they cannot meditate.

Student: Is there any hope for them?

Dr. Hora: Yes, they have to become contemplatives, seekers after clarity and understanding. The Bible says that the principal thing in life is wisdom. "Therefore, get wisdom: and with all thy getting, get understanding" (Proverbs 4:7). So the contemplative seeks the wisdom and the understanding that flow from the divine Mind.

Student: I would like to know how to be healed of this interest in thinking and knowing—in other words, in being a knower and wanting mastery as opposed to being a seeker who receives understanding.

Dr. Hora: You just face the fact that being a seeker is better than being a knower. The Bible says, "I have set before you life and death, blessing and cursing; therefore, choose life, that ye may live" (Deuteronomy 30:19). So when we choose to be seekers— contemplatives—we are choosing life.

Student: Do we choose, or are we just aware? Do we have a choice?

Dr. Hora: When it has been made clear to you what is good, you can choose to turn your interest toward being a seeker rather than a knower or a thinker. Now let us come back to the original question that opened this session—about the past. We said that the past has to die, and the mind also has to die. What does this mean?

Student: The personal mind has to die.

Dr. Hora: What does that mean?

Student: It refers to the mind that the ego knows, to the contents of consciousness which confirm the sense of a personal identity with a personal past.

Dr. Hora: Yes. We said, "What we cannot remember, we cannot forget." In order for the past to be let go, it must be remembered. If we can remember the past, it means that all our repressed memories have been examined carefully and found to be existentially invalid; with this realization, we can forgive. We can have compassion for ourselves and for others from our past, and then the past can "die." Otherwise it cannot die; and it is important for the past to die in the right way in order that we may be freed enough to turn our attention to God wholeheartedly, unencumbered by repressed memories. Then we discover that the past never was; the future is not yet, and reality is now. How does the Bible explain this process? We have mentioned the words of the Zen Master, of the Western philosopher, and of the Greek philosopher Socrates, as well as the Metapsychiatric position on this subject. And now, would you like to know what the Bible has to say about it? The Bible says: "That which has been is now, and that which is to be has already been, and God requireth that which is past" (Ecclesiastes 3:15). Do we understand this mystical saying? What does it mean? If the past is not remembered, then it is being lived now, and it will be lived in the future. Right? Therefore, the solution is to give it back to God. But we cannot give it back to God unless we have it, and we only have it when we have remembered it fully. When we have remembered the past fully, then we can give it back to God, and, then, we are free—we are "newborn of the spirit"(John 3: 7). Is that clear?

Student: What is a valid way of remembering? If we try very hard to remember something, it seems to slip away.

Dr. Hora: Yes. So what is the valid process of remembering?

Student: What is it that we need to remember? Is it a way of life or a way of thinking or the incidents of an individual life?

Dr. Hora: We wish to remember everything that has been forgotten. How do we remember the things that were forgotten or repressed? The psychoanalytic word is repressed. How do we remember these? Clearly, we cannot will ourselves *to* remember them, because we will *not to* remember them.

Student: Sometimes when we are on the verge of being healed of a problem, we remember how it has affected us in the past, how that error has come up in very specific instances in our past.

Dr. Hora: Yes, we are progressing in our study of God, and as we come closer and closer to appreciating God as Omniactive

Love-Intelligence and the good of God as PAGL [PAGL is an acronym for Peace, Assurance, Gratitude, Love, and Its Presence in consciousness informs us that we are in tune with the One Mind.], we become strengthened by the proximity of God, and this gives us a certain kind of courage and humility to face up to unbearable memories of the past. This is one aspect of the process. The other one is the process of examining the meaning of our outcropping problems. As long as there are repressed memories, we experience repetitive problems; and every time we discover the meaning of a particular problem, a little more of the repressed past is revealed. And little by little we can see clearly the whole fabric of the past. We learn to remember—in order to forget.

Student: What would be the meaning of repeated rememberings and rememberings and rememberings? Are we resisting whatever might bring healing? One can be haunted by certain memories even though one understands them and recognizes them—there is still a repeated haunting quality, usually accompanied by guilt. Maybe guilt is the culprit.

Dr. Hora: Nobody is feeling guilty in Metapsychiatry. Guilt does not exist. It has been outlawed!

Student: It's been outlawed, all right, but it's still hard to get rid of it.

Student: How is the Metapsychiatric process of healing different from the psychoanalytic one?

Dr. Hora: In psychoanalysis, the patient has no one to lean on but the therapist, and that dynamic leads to a troublesome complication called "transference neurosis," which means that you are accusing the therapist of being like your mother or father or brother—you hallucinate that he is "this way" or "that way." The process is very difficult, and without God, healing is impossible.

Student: What does it mean to give the past to God?

Dr. Hora: The Bible says: "God requireth that which is past." This means: Stop dwelling on the past and turn your attention to "the good of God which is spiritual blessedness." Then you let it die and are freed of the burden of the past.

Student: Dr. Hora, is the process of healing the past involved with learning a lesson from a present problem? Is it that some of the bits and pieces that are repressed come up in our present experiences, and we can see them in the context of the "meaning" that is discerned?

Dr. Hora: Yes, that's right.

Student: That's why you never ask about the past.

Dr. Hora: It is not necessary. You see, you cannot force it out. It has to come out by itself.

Student: But sometimes it does come out without even talking about it. It becomes clear as we progress spiritually.

Dr. Hora: Yes.

Student: Would you repeat the principle one more time?

Dr. Hora: "What we cannot remember, we cannot forget."

Student: So, this principle really addresses the problem of suffering.

Dr. Hora: It addresses the *"dynamics of liberation."* In order to be liberated from the influence of past experiences, we have, first, to remember the past and, next, to forget it, to let go of it. Then we can turn wholeheartedly to God—otherwise we are hampered.

Student: And yet what seems to happen is that we turn first to God without examining our suffering.

Dr. Hora: Yes.

Student: And, then, a healing comes.

Dr. Hora: To the extent that we are capable [of receiving it]. For instance, if we are full of bitterness and hatred, and we turn to God, how far can we really turn to God? Can you be loving if you are bitter and hateful? And if you blame somebody in your heart for the past, how can you be loving and joyous? Many people try hard to turn to God, but the past interferes with it. On the other hand, the sincerity of their devotion can strengthen them sufficiently to be able to face up to things from the past that they did not dare to face up to before. There is a dynamic interplay between memories, the so-called lifting of repressions and our ability to move toward being "reborn of the spirit"(John 3: 7). When the past has died, one is free to love; otherwise, it is difficult to love. Then, one can "glow."

Student: There is a kind of awe-inspiring purity that is required to become free and loving, and at times it seems unattainable.

Dr. Hora: It is recommended—it is not required.

Student: What is this purity that seems so impossible?

Dr. Hora: The Bible says: "Blessed are the pure in heart, for they shall see God" (Matthew 5:8). We purify our language, and we purify our concepts; we purify our ways of approaching the knowledge of God. We purify our motivations, and we move toward God-realization. Metapsychiatry is defined as "an epistemological method of God-realization." Do you know what the word epistemological means?

Student: Right-seeing or knowing?

Dr. Hora: It is "the science of right-knowing". In order to know something "aright," we have to find a purity of language that is able to communicate ideas in their purest form, so that the knowledge of these ideas will be unadulterated, not contaminated by misunderstandings. We are very careful about our words, and we are very careful about clarity in communication.

Dialogue No. 3

A Sermon in the Flesh

Dr. Hora: "Man shall not live by bread alone, but by every word that proceedeth out of the mouth of God" (Matthew 4:4). But God has no mouth. How does God talk without a mouth?

Student: Through inspiration, which takes form as ideas.

Dr. Hora: Could you explain it?

Student: If we say, "It dawned on me," this could possibly be a way of explaining how God speaks to us. When an idea occurs, we often say, "It just dawned on me," which is a demonstration of God coming into expression through ideas.

Dr. Hora: What language does God use? Aramaic? Hebrew? Does God speak English?

Student: He doesn't speak any language to me.

Dr. Hora: There is a scene described in the Bible (Acts 2) that is called the Pentecostal descent of the Holy Spirit. The scene describes people from all parts of the world who came together, and the Holy Spirit descended upon them. Everyone was speaking in his own language from various parts of the world, but, no matter what language was spoken, everyone understood what was being said. There was an automatic, built-in translation process. Imagine what we would have to have in the United Nations so that everyone could understand one another. How is this possible?

Student: I'd like to know.

Dr. Hora: Here we are gathered together all speaking English, and we often do not understand one another. What is the mystery of communication?

Student: The language is secondary or incidental to the consciousness.

Dr. Hora: What is the mystery of successful communication?

Student: A loving consciousness.

Dr. Hora: Yes, love. Individuals who are in a loving consciousness can communicate with one another. Without love, there is no communication. There are only noises being made, and nobody really understands anything. Have you ever tried to speak to someone who is angry? He either cannot hear you, or he hears something entirely different from what you are saying.

Student: Isn't it also a matter of paying attention? For example, you could be speaking or listening, but your mind might be elsewhere and therefore you are not paying attention to what is being said.

Dr. Hora: Well, who is it that pays attention when attention is being paid?

Student: If it's the right attention, it would be our spirit—spirit would listen.

Dr. Hora: Only love can pay attention. The more love there is, the more communication is possible; the less love, the less communication is possible. Now in the Pentecostal event, there must have been a great deal of love to enable strangers from all parts of the world to understand one another. God is Love; therefore God can speak to everybody, regardless of the language in which any of us has been brought up. Everyone, everywhere in the whole universe, understands God in his own language; we can "hear" God speaking English to us. But what do we really hear? We hear a soundless Voice.

Student: And it's not in our hearing, in the sense of human hearing. It must be something else.

Dr. Hora: What is hearing? Can the ears hear?

Student: The ear itself cannot hear; there is something within the ear that hears.

Dr. Hora: Someone once told me, "I like to play the piano, but I don't read notes. People think that I'm playing by ear, but I'm not playing by ear—I'm listening with my soul, and I play music by my soul. The soul is playing the music, and I hear the music with my soul, and it's beautiful." And that is true—the ear cannot hear. What are the ears? The ears are a statement that says: God can hear. Hearing is a spiritual faculty. The nose, the eyes, the head, the neck, the body, the arms, every little part of the body is saying something about God. The body is not really the body; the body is thought saying something about God. Every part of the body is saying [revealing] something about God. That is what the statement "Man is an image and likeness of God" means. You see, thoughts can appear either as language or as words written down or as events, or they can take form. When thoughts appear in visible form, we see what? Phenomena—phenomena are thoughts appearing in visible form. So what do we see when we look at each other? We see thoughts speaking. Every part of the body is speaking and saying: God is love, God is intelligence, God is sight, God is hearing, God is communication, God is strength, God is action, God is activity, God is skill. What we think is a material body is really nothing material—it is just language. The body is a language—a composite of many, many thoughts. It is a sermon describing God—that is what the body is—a sermon in flesh. The flesh is a language speaking about God. Isn't that marvelous? And when we say God speaks to us, what do we mean? We mean that divine ideas "obtain" in consciousness. We become aware of receiving intelligent, loving, creative ideas, and these ideas are messages from God. We call them angels. What is an angel?

Student: An inspired idea.

Dr. Hora: Yes, an inspired idea—which we have imagined with gossamer wings. Everything, the whole universe, is nothing else but thoughts speaking about God.

Student: What is intuition?

Dr. Hora: Intuition is the human counterfeit of inspiration. Do you understand what makes it a human counterfeit?

Student: We claim it for ourselves?

Dr. Hora: We do, yes, and what else?

Student: It's based on feelings.

Dr. Hora: Yes, right, but what else?

Student: We can intuit something good or something bad.

Dr. Hora: Right. That [its dualistic nature] proves that it is counterfeit, because God could never tell us anything bad.

Student: In other words, when we are in tune with divine Intelligence, we're a part of it, and that is how we receive messages. We are a part of this divine Intelligence, partaking of it.

Dr. Hora: Yes, God speaks to us in a soundless voice of inspired ideas which "obtain" [are received] in consciousness. First we become aware of these ideas, and these ideas germinate in consciousness. Then they are transformed into words, and the words are given expression as concepts.

Student: Our words? Whose words are they?

Dr. Hora: These are all God's; everything belongs to God— even your piano belongs to God. This is a creative process—like when a child is born. First there is a mutual fantasy between a man and a woman, and then this fantasy is translated into asexual communion. In this communion, the idea—the fantasy—is trans-

formed into something that is visible to the naked eye. Eventually
it comes out, and what we have here are two thoughts, those between a man and a woman, which have joined together and now
appear in visible form. This is what a child is—thoughts. As the
child grows, it gradually becomes a statement. Under favorable
conditions, a child becomes a statement about God. Under unfavorable conditions, this same child can become a statement about
the fantasies of the parents. Then Metapsychiatry could come into
the picture and endeavor to help this grownup individual realize
that he is not really what he thinks he is, but he is what God thinks.
Only God's thoughts constitute our true being. We are what God
is thinking about us, and everything about us is saying what God
is. Jesus said, "Therefore was I born, and came into the world, that
I may bear witness to the truth . . ." of what God is (John 18:37).
Our total being is "bearing witness" to the nature of God, and
every one of us is different and unique; yet we are all saying the
same thing—God is great.

Student: I understand it when you say that God is Consciousness,
but how do we view consciousness? We speak about "my" consciousness, "your" consciousness, "individual" consciousness . . .

Dr. Hora: Yes.

Student: Does that mean that there is a singular consciousness,
conscious of itself as consciousness?

Dr. Hora: Yes.

Student: And is that God?

Dr. Hora: Every individual consciousness is an aspect of the
Cosmic Consciousness which is God. We are all individualized
aspects of God.

Student: Are the consciousnesses numerically distinct, or is
there One Consciousness that sort of shapes itself in many different ways?

Dr. Hora: Numerically distinct? What do you mean?

Student: Well, physically it appears that we are numerically
apart, distinct, different from one another.

Dr. Hora: Yes, we are; even spiritually we are uniquely distinct—an infinite variety of individual aspects of the One Infinite
Consciousness. Mind boggling, isn't it?

Student: What is the One Consciousness that takes different
forms? It's not as though here is the One Consciousness and out
there are the billions of distinct imitations.

Dr. Hora: There is no spatial arrangement, and there are no numerical distinctions.

Student: Is that the One Mind?

Dr. Hora: Yes.

Student: And we are not separate or separated from it?

Dr. Hora: Impossible. It can only be an illusion.

Student: I don't know the right way to ask this, Dr. Hora, but what accounts for our individuality? What is the meaning of our having individual expression if we are all really of One Mind?

Dr. Hora: Individuality is also a thought that informs us: "God is infinite." There is an infinite variety of individualities. These are like the leaves on a tree: every leaf is different from every other leaf, and yet they are all maple leaves or all oak leaves. But they are individuals; they are unique. Every leaf is unique, and this is just a symbolic way of saying, "God is infinite." The tree is also speaking of God, just as every particle of our bodies is a statement about the nature of God. So, be it a tree or grass or our ears, everything is language and speaking about God. "All things were made by him; and without him was not anything made" that seems to have been made (John 1:3).

Student: It's easy to confuse personality with individuality.

Dr. Hora: Very easy. God knows nothing about personality. You see, personalities are never unique.

Student: Carbon copies.

Dr. Hora: Right. When we say that "everything and everyone is here for God," it is not just a cliché. It is a very basic statement of truth, and it is very helpful to contemplate it, especially if we are tempted to judge others or to harbor critical thoughts. If we remind ourselves that "everything and everyone is here for God," then suddenly this erases our judgmental thoughts, and what happens next? Do we become nice guys? No, but we can relax. We find peace, and we become fearless—because as long as we view someone in an unfavorable light, we are afraid; and being afraid is a waste of energy. We might even go further in our mistaken notion and want to change somebody—that is also a waste of energy. Nobody has ever changed anybody. Would you believe that?

Student: It seems that people do have an influence on one another though. Maybe I'm bragging, but as a teacher, one does have some influence in the young lives of students.

Dr. Hora: That's what you think. Nobody can change anybody. Does this surprise you? Can anybody explain why it is impossible for one human being to change another human being?

Student: It seems that our parents have miseducated us, and we have changed from expressing whatever God created us to expressing when we took on our parents' fantasies. So wouldn't we consider that a change?

Dr. Hora: No, that's not change—that's just an appearance of change. Now suppose you meet someone who has been very badly influenced by his parents and his childhood experiences. As a result of it, he has certain character flaws. The harder you would want to change him, the worse it becomes. It is absolutely impossible for you to change him, and he would resist all human efforts to do so. This dynamic is going on all the time in psychiatrists' offices. The psychiatrists are trying to change the patients, and the patients are resisting. Then a psychiatrist can get very frustrated and might use shock treatment to break the resistance. The shock treatments do not work, so then the psychiatrist might prescribe pills or injections—chemicals—and these do not work either. The patient gets worse because one human being is trying to change another human being. One illusion tries to disillusion another illusion. It's impossible, but is there no hope?

Student: What is the meaning of this desire to want to change anyone in the first place?

Dr. Hora: That is a very good question. It is called megalomania. Do you know what that means?

Student: Having delusions of grandeur.

Dr. Hora: Man cannot change another. There is only one thing in the whole universe that has the power to change. What is it? It is the illumination of the Truth that can set us free. Only the Truth has the power to change people. A psychiatrist does not have this power—the Truth has the power to change us. How does the Truth change us?

Student: By inspired ideas?

Dr. Hora: No, the Truth changes us into what we really are, so there is no change whatsoever.

Student: It is the Truth that sees what we really are. What happens to what we really aren't when the Truth sees what we really are?

Dr. Hora: That which we really aren't becomes what it really is—nothing. What happens to $2 + 2 = 5$ when the Truth is recognized?

Student: It disappears.

Dr. Hora: It disappears—it never was. The power to transform is in the Truth, not in any person. Jesus never healed anyone. Did you know that? The Bible says that Jesus healed people, but he never healed anybody. His understanding of the Truth was so absolute that when he came into contact with a sick man, this sick man was suddenly awakened to a glimpse of what he really was—a statement about God. That is what we all are—statements about God—and this statement about perfection has to be perfect. Jesus never healed anyone, but the Truth which glowed from his awareness did—that Truth could heal people absolutely.

Student: So it's useless to try to say something to help people?

Dr. Hora: Jesus said: "But when ye pray, use not vain repetitions, as the heathens do: for they think that they shall be heard for their much speaking" (Matthew 6:7). Words cannot heal, but words can shed light on the Truth. And if someone is interested, he can catch a glimpse of this Truth, and then he will be healed. That is how it happens. If an individual is not interested, he will not see the Truth, and he will not be healed. There were people whom even Jesus could not heal, because they were not interested in the Truth.

Student: If an individual is not receptive, speaking the Truth does not make any difference, does it?

Dr. Hora: The Bible says: "For this people's heart is waxed gross, and their ears are dull of hearing, and their eyes they have closed; lest at any time they should see with their eyes, and hear with their ears, and should understand with their heart, and should be converted, and I should heal them" (Matthew 13:15). See? And then the Bible says: "Prepare ye the way of the Lord, make straight in the desert a highway for our God. Every valley shall be exalted, and every mountain and hill shall be made low: and the crooked shall be made straight, and the rough places plain" (Isaiah 40:3, 4). What does that mean? "Prepare ye the way of the Lord"?

Student: Prepare your consciousness for Truth and Love to enter. Those are metaphors of different kinds of erroneous thoughts.

Dr. Hora: Yes, so what we can do is to open up our receptivity to the Truth. With the help of suffering and a little bit of wisdom, we can become increasingly receptive and catch a glimpse of the Truth and be healed.

Student: When an enlightened consciousness beholds another consciousness, and a healing takes place, how do we understand that within the context of your statement that one cannot change another?

Dr. Hora: It's not you who does the changing—it is the Truth that communicates itself from one consciousness to another. Now sometimes it can happen at a distance too, provided there is sufficient receptivity. Very often the most beneficial things happen when people call my office from a distance. If someone is so eager for health that he goes to the expense of a long distance telephone call, he is really receptive, and then the communication is meaningful. Healings are more frequent in this manner than when help is comfortably available.

Student: How do you know if a person is resisting or not and if there is hope—if you should hang in there, and maybe sooner or later the person might glimpse the Truth?

Dr. Hora: No one is ever refused here, and when the resistance is so great that someone drops away, it just means that he or she is not yet ready. As long as someone keeps coming, it means that some degree of receptivity must still be there. No one is asked to come, and no one is refused either—and no one is influenced one way or another. There are just two kinds of individuals: those who are driven and those who are drawn. That's all.

Student: You mean they are driven to come here?

Dr. Hora: Yes.

Student: Is it wisdom or suffering that drives them?

Dr. Hora: Suffering drives people. Sometimes a mother pressures a son or a daughter to come. This does not work very well.

Student: Could you recommend a prayer that would be helpful in that sort of situation?

Dr. Hora: The mother needs to pray for herself not to pressure her children.

Student: So the mother has to be free of wanting?

Dr. Hora: The mother has to be free of influencing. But a mother can learn to pay attention to being influential by being a model of spiritual excellence. Motherhood is primarily a modeling job, but not many mothers know that—and fatherhood likewise. We have to be models because children always imitate their parents. Psychologists have invented a phrase about parents having to provide the children with "role models." You know what a "role model" is? It is what you pretend to be—it is playing a role in life—which means that you are bringing up a phony.

Student: When we talk about being models of spiritual excellence, it sounds like we are speaking God's language. We don't say anything; it is formless.

Dr. Hora: Yes. We are teaching with our lives. Our mode of being-in-the-world is the teacher, and that is the best way. For instance, if you believe that it would be good for a child to eat spinach, you would have to sit down with a big bowl of spinach and eat it yourself and not say a word to the child about it—you would just eat the spinach.

Student: But you have to love the spinach.

Dr. Hora: Yes, but don't tell the child, "You should eat spinach." Never tell a child what he should do; let him watch you eat the spinach and see you enjoy it. He will eat spinach too, if you don't tell him to eat it. If you tell him, he won't do it.

Student: Then it's really important to know what values to appreciate, if we as parents are to set an example by the way we live our lives.

Dr. Hora: Yes.

Student: In the school where I work, it seems that both the children and the parents want a strong authority figure. It seems as if they want someone to assert authority over them because it is somehow reassuring. Is the same idea, about being a model of spiritual excellence, applicable here?

Dr. Hora: Yes, authority is very important—but not human authority—the authority of spiritual values. People think that authority is personal. Personal authority says, "There is no God. I am God; you have to listen to me. I am God; I am the authority," and that, of course, is very confusing. Children will rebel against all personal authority because it is a form of personal control. Real authority is not found in a human person—it emanates as qualities of the truth in consciousness: the love of order, the love of attentiveness, the love of joy, the love of intelligence, all of which are communicated indirectly. That is authority, and it is very desirable. Jesus said, "I am the way, the truth and the life" (John 14:6). And also, "All power is given unto me in heaven and in earth" (Matthew 28:18), in other words, from above.

Student: Jesus spoke with authority.

Dr. Hora: Yes. It is described in the Bible that he spoke "as one having authority" (Matthew 7:29). And that "authority" was not a personal assertion of the ego: it was the consciousness of divine values. That is the "authority" against which there is no objection and no rebellion and which does not enslave, belittle, or diminish others. It just elevates consciousness and results in harmony.

Hype

Student: Dr. Hora, what is it about the recent Challenger space shuttle accident that makes it such a shocking tragedy? What is a valid way to look at something like this?

Dr. Hora: It was a shocking tragedy for the whole nation. It created a sense of insecurity, fear, and doubt about our abilities to keep up. But you are not asking the real question. The First Intelligent Question asks, "What is the meaning of what seems to be?" No one has asked this question.

Student: The newspapers are asking, "Why did it happen?" It happened because the gas tank exploded, and that's why it's supposed to have happened.

Dr. Hora: "He who seeks reasons only finds excuses." So what is the "meaning"? Can anyone guess?

Student: The one thing that was clear about this particular situation was all the excitement.

Dr. Hora: Yes. The national obsession with "hype." What is hype? Creating excitement, bragging and exaggerating—flaunting everything in the eyes of the world and magnifying the human experience—that is hype. Whenever personal experience and personal hype are worshiped, the "Four Horsemen" [envy, jealousy, rivalry, malice] start galloping, and invariably some¬thing bad happens. We always make the same mistake. The media are sensationalistic and personalistic—very boastful, self-confirmatory, and often attract tragedies. For weeks we observed the school teacher's excitement and happiness, and it was painful to watch. This happiness is not real happiness. Mostly we believe that happiness is fame and excitement, but this is the devil's happiness—it is immature and childish. We forget about God; we worship our own experiences, and God is out of the picture. But without God, nothing can be harmonious or safe or good.

Student: The news said that we were seeking to understand space, but the idea that it was an adventure was also stressed. Is going on a great adventure as troublesome as excitement?

Dr. Hora: Certainly. The emphasis was on personal experience. Inviting civilians was a gimmick to promote the space pro¬gram. These values are immature. We get hurt over and over again, and we do not learn because we do not have the maturity to go about life in a reverent, loving, humble, and effective way.

Student: You say that we keep making the same mistakes and are not learning from them. The only way that we, as a nation, could learn from them would be to ask, "What is the meaning?"

Dr. Hora: Yes. We are not learning because we are always looking for reasons. We want to figure out what went wrong with the machines. Machines are only mental, but this is not known. We think machines are high-tech, but high-tech is mental—[the manifestation of] a certain kind of intelligence. It is all mind. If the mind is immature, filled with invalid ideas and completely separated from God, then these tragedies are repeated, and there is no learning. The real tragedy is that we are not learning.

Student: Many countries are envious of America.

Dr. Hora: Envy rules the world, and envy is hurting us because we are constantly provoking it with our behavior. Hype is inviting envy, jealousy, rivalry, and malice—the Four Horse¬men are galloping.

Student: Is that the meaning of terrorism?

Dr. Hora: Of course.

Student: We don't exactly have a low profile.

Dr. Hora: A low profile would not be enough. We have to have a spiritual profile. Have you ever seen a spiritual profile? How would we describe the spiritual profile of a nation?

Student: It's hard enough to describe it on an individual basis.

Student: But the values would be the same.

Student: And the world wouldn't find that threatening?

Dr. Hora: No, I don't think so. We are very immature as a nation.

Student: But there is some maturity; how do we explain it?

Dr. Hora: The Founding Fathers of this country were very mature individuals, and their foresight is what has kept us going all these years—a good foundation was laid. But the nation at large is not really mature; the values we have embraced are invalid. Bragging is existentially invalid, very contagious and always troublesome.

Student: What would it take for the nation as a whole to mature?

Dr. Hora: There is a story about a king who was a great braggart, and he had all kinds of fortunes, and everything went well with him. He was always so proud of himself. Now he had a court philosopher advising him, and one day this philosopher said to him, "I am really worried about you because you are just bragging all the time about how everything goes well with you. This is not good. You must do something to become more humble." And so the king said, "All right, what should I do?" And the philosopher said, "Get rid of something that is most precious to you." The king said, "This ring is the most precious thing that I have." The philosopher responded, "Throw it into the sea!" The king obeyed him and threw it into the sea. The philosopher thought, "Maybe now he will be more humble." Then one day they were walking around, and after a while the king said to the philosopher, "I feel lonely; come and have dinner with me tonight." The philosopher agreed, and they had dinner together. A big fish was brought in, beautifully prepared; the fish was served and when it was carved, the ring was found inside the fish! The philosopher got panicky and said, "I will not stay under the same roof with you for another moment!" And he got up and left. See how that is? This is an ancient Greek story, and there is much truth in it: Good can be dangerous if it is seen as a personal attribute and not in the context of God. We are only safe if we see life and live life consciously in the context of God.

Student: The space program seems to be based on belief in what we call "personal mind power" and the human capability to build things and to succeed, but we haven't considered God in this picture.

Dr. Hora: Yes, if one thinks in this way, then bragging is inevitable because one is taking credit for every success.

Student: Is research like this valid?

Dr. Hora: Yes, if it is understood in the context of God. God is infinite, creative Intelligence, and all valid ideas come from the divine Mind. But if we take credit for these ideas ourselves, then we are saying, "There is no God—I am God. My mind has accomplished this."

Student: It is interesting that our record of space travel has been so good and that this is the first time that a civilian was part of the crew. Perhaps trained astronauts have a more mature interest.

Dr. Hora: Inviting a teacher was based on an invalid motivation—she was being used as advertisement. Whenever a motivation is invalid, there can be no success because every success depends on the validity of the motivation with which a task is approached.

Student: If her motivation had been different, might it not have turned out so tragically?

Dr. Hora: She was a victim of an advertising campaign. A young woman wants excitement and fame; she was bubbling over all the time and enjoying the interviews and being on television. The nation fell for it.

Student: Does malicious thought have power? Was the public envious?

Dr. Hora: Envy was a very powerful presence in this situation. If the original premise was false and existentially invalid, how could it be successful?

Student: If we take personal credit for having figured out how to put the shuttle into space, then we slip out of wisdom and things can go wrong—we tend not to notice certain things.

Dr. Hora: Whenever self-confirmation takes over, it creates a gap between God and man. How can things work well that way? Every self-confirmatory motivation is an assertion of man's separateness from God—which removes us from the context of God—and then we are surprised that bad things happen. So it is ignorance, immaturity, and lack of integrity [that are the culprits]. Maybe when human beings get tired of looking for a cause, they will start asking some different questions.

Student: I was wondering if curiosity was another aspect of the problem? There seem to be many benefits from research into space, but it seems to be predominantly an issue of curiosity.

Dr. Hora: All scientific research is based on curiosity. There is no research of any other kind, so that aspect would not be unusual. Curiosity about how nature works, and things in the physical universe, is not bad. But if we are curious about a spiritual being, a child of God, that is a trespass. It is all right for science to be motivated by curiosity; that kind of curiosity would not be a problem. But we can never ignore God, and we cannot pursue invalid motivations in life with impunity. So in Metapsychiatry we say, "Self-confirmation is self-destruction, and self-destruction is self-confirmation."

Student: Concerning curiosity: When we are really interested in exploring things, isn't that a part of seeking? One might not be seeking in the right direction, but perhaps it could lead to it and be helpful.

Dr. Hora: Yes, right.

Student: Is that what happens when physicists write books like The Tao of Physics? They outgrow themselves and go to a higher level of understanding . . .

Dr. Hora: And discover that Love is the motivating power of the universe.

Student: Are scientists like that seeking to understand the koan "Nothing is as it seems to be, and neither is it otherwise"— which has to do with the juxtaposition of matter with nondimensional reality?

Dr. Hora: Yes, that's right.

Student: If we have humility, is it still possible to be envied? Dr. Hora: Yes.

Student: Doesn't humility make us immune to envy?

Dr. Hora: We are immune if we are humble. Envy could be present; it would come to our attention, but it would not come into our experience.

Student: But, it would still be there.

Dr. Hora: Right.

Student: One could view it with compassion: "understanding the lack of understanding."

Dr. Hora: Of course, humility is a tremendous defense against all the "Four Horsemen."

Student: What is Metapsychiatry's definition of humility?

Dr. Hora: There are two definitions. Human humility is "a willingness to be embarrassed." Spiritual humility is realized in Christ's words: "Of mine own self, I can do nothing.... It is the Father who dwelleth in me that doeth the works" (John 5:30; 14:10). Human humility is better than nothing; but spiritual humility provides us with a tremendous freedom and assurance which Jesus gave us when he said: "Behold I give you power to tread on serpents and on scorpions and over all the power of the enemy, and nothing shall by any means hurt you" (Luke 10:19). If we have spiritual humility, it gives us immunity.

Student: We were saying that the country was founded on valid ideas.

Dr. Hora: Yes, these valid values and enlightened ideas have sustained us, and they still do to a large extent.

Student: So what is a spiritual profile for a country? We said earlier that what we need is a spiritual profile.

Dr. Hora: First of all the statement "In God we trust," which is printed on our coins and notes, must be greatly appreciated. The presence of God has to be considered extremely important. I remember a young couple who came to see me once in despair because they were engaged to be married and the boy had been indicted for arson. They were terribly afraid that the young man might have to go to jail for who knew how long. They did not know much about Metapsychiatry and even less about God. But when they went to court, the girl, who was sitting in the audience while the boy was standing in front of the judge, lifted up her eyes and saw an inscription above the judge that said, "In God we trust." This shocked her because she had never thought of God before, and at this moment she reached out for that thought so powerfully that everything else disappeared for her. She didn't know where she was or what was going on—she was just completely absorbed in that statement, "In God we trust." And guess what happened? The case was dismissed, and they walked happily home. Unwittingly she had prayed effectively for this boy. She told me the story afterwards. In a pinch we turn to God and, if we are sincere, God never lets us down. But when we pray, we have to pray as this girl did—with such intensity of devotion and interest that the whole world disappears and we are completely filled with the thought of God. No other thought can exist in consciousness at that time—that is the most effective way to pray—we abolish the world, and God becomes the only reality. And even if it happens just for a split second or a few minutes, it will be effective in some way. She wasn't praying that the boy should be released or that he should get only two years instead of ten years. She completely forgot about him and became wholly absorbed in that one statement: "In God we trust." She was not asking God to do anything. She wasn't trying to use God in that situation. She just immersed herself in God and forgot everything else. That is the secret, because we cannot tell God what he should do—that is not prayer—that is manipulation. Inadvertently this girl realized her complete oneness with God to the exclusion of everything else. This single-minded attentiveness to the presence of God constitutes effective prayer. She lost sight of everything—the judge, the courtroom, her fiancé, even herself—and all she was aware of was the statement "In God we trust." This was a girl who had never prayed before in her life, practically a teenager, who had no religious education whatsoever. This story illustrates that there is such power in the truth.

Student: There is mention in the Bible of having faith the size of a "mustard seed," just that little bit (Matthew 17:20). But I always seem to get stuck on the problem because its appearance seems so much more powerful than the idea of God.

Student: Most of the time we think, "I have to pray about this situation, or I have to pray about that problem." Is this the wrong approach, right from the start? Don't we need to realize that there really is no problem, there is only God?

Dr. Hora: We just simply understand that prayer is the endeavor to become fully conscious of the reality of God. If we learn to pray in this way, then there are no limitations to the possibilities for our fulfillment or happiness or healing or blessedness—all this is possible. "Be still, and know that I am God" (Psalm 46:10). To "be still" means that all other concerns have to disappear.

Student: This is the healthy motive because we are seeking to understand reality.

Beyond Words

Student: Dr. Hora, if we have a problem with wanting to be in control and are told that we cannot be in control and that we need to learn about God, how can the transition occur—letting go of the thing that we think is so important to control?

Dr. Hora: That is an interesting question. How do we get there from here? When we get tired of beating our heads against a wall, then we might begin to contemplate whether there really is a God and whether we could bring ourselves into alignment with what God wants; and then we can discover that indeed God is in control. What happens when we discover it? There are no more spasms, no more headaches and high blood pressure, and no more ulcers. Suddenly there is peace and trusting. Life becomes less and less strenuous, and we discover a new power, which is called wisdom. Wisdom has the power to control everything. God comes to us in the form of wisdom, and this wisdom has a way of dealing with everything effortlessly, efficiently, and effectively.

Student: You used the word "suddenly." Is it sudden?

Dr. Hora: "In the twinkling of an eye." It is interesting to consider how wisdom operates. How does wisdom operate in us? Very quietly, without any hype, in subtle ways. It is just amazing to watch wisdom in operation. Have you ever seen wisdom operate?

Student: Sometimes an idea will dawn on us from nowhere.

Dr. Hora: That's right. If one considers the fact that wisdom is God, then we can directly observe God in action. Usually when we think of God, we think of some ten-foot-tall person who will "do" something. But God is very subtle. God works in us and in the world in most subtle ways—mostly as love and wisdom.

Student: If we want to be in control, then we are probably in constant fear of losing control. But then we could try to see that "Perfect Love casteth out fear" (1 John 4:18). What is perfect Love?

Dr. Hora: You don't know?

33

Student: It's God. Perfect Love, I guess, would be God. But which comes first, the chicken or the egg? Do you need to know God first in order to know Love?

Dr. Hora: You need to know Metapsychiatry to know "perfect Love." We are blessed with a certain definition of Love which makes divine Love accessible, even to human comprehension. Do we all know this definition of perfect Love?

Student: "Nonpersonal, nonconditional benevolence."

Dr. Hora: That's right. Translated into human language, perfect Love is nonpersonal, nonconditional benevolence. I spoke to a young lady from a Jewish family once, and she was raving about her father—how he has loved her all her life, how he is "the best father anybody could ever have." "He is just God in my life," she said. "He loves me so much that he does everything for me, and he always did—except I'm not allowed to marry a Christian. I must marry a Jewish boy; and I can't find a Jewish boy, but I have a Christian boyfriend." Parental love is mostly conditional; therefore it is a troublemaker.

Student: I have seen fathers who so "loved" their children that if they married out of the faith, they would disown them and pretend that they were dead. That's love?

Dr. Hora: That is conditional love, and sometimes there are even more absurd conditions. Human love is conditional; divine Love is unconditional, and enlightened human love is nonconditional. It says, "I love you just the way you are; I make no conditions; you don't have to like spinach, and you don't have to wear your hair in a certain way." Conditional love is more harmful than neglect. If we are neglected, at least we are free to make our own mistakes and learn from them. But if we are loved conditionally, it enslaves us. Conditional love is disabling; nonconditional love is empowering. So when we have loving parents, we are in danger; it is a dangerous thing to be loved by human parents.

Student: But we all crave it, all of our lives.

Dr. Hora: Yes. Most of us grow up disabled in some way because our parents "loved" us.

Student: Or not.

Dr. Hora: If they do not love us, then we are free.

Student: So the way to become free of this dependence on conditional love is to discover nonconditional love, which we realize by seeing wisdom-in-action, as you have just described? Can we come to know God as a reality in this way?

Dr. Hora: Right, and also to understand what real love is—that it is nonconditional. It is very illuminating. When I spoke to this young woman who was raving about her father's love, I explained to her that she has been experiencing conditional love. Real love is nonconditional. It was shocking to her to realize that there is something better than what her father had been offering her all these years.

Student: Often parents have the idea that perhaps there would be more harmony if two people of like religions married—maybe because they would have more in common. I am wondering about the validity of a parent, or a boss, having an idea that they think would be good for another individual. In the case of a child, doesn't the parent have certain rights?

Dr. Hora: Can't you have your cake and eat it, too?

Student: How do you give guidance to a teenager or someone going into college?

Dr. Hora: There are two ways to give guidance. One is by pushing a string and the other is by pulling a string. Have you ever tried to push a string?

Student: What is pushing a string?

Dr. Hora: Try pushing a string.

Student: You can't.

Dr. Hora: Right. In giving guidance, that is what many parents are doing. They are pushing their children in certain directions—they are not guiding them. They are pushing them, and it works just like pushing a string.

Student: What is pulling?

Dr. Hora: Being an example to be followed.

Student: I think I have been a string!

Dr. Hora: We all have been because we all have had unenlightened parents who love conditionally and "guide" us by pushing.

Student: So the right kind of guidance would come out of unconditional love?

Dr. Hora: Out of nonconditional love—only God can love unconditionally. We do not make conditions. Nonconditional love says, "I will love you, even if you marry out of the faith."

Student: Conditional love comes about from "should" thinking. The parents think that for your own good you should do this or that.

Dr. Hora: "Should" thinking is an aspect of conditional love, but conditional love comes about through ignorance. Ignorance has many faces. There are a million ways to be ignorant, and only one way to be "gnorant." Do you know what "gnorant" means? It means "to know."

Student: The Bible says: "For if a man think himself to be something, when he is nothing, he deceiveth himself" (Galatians 6:3). It seems we would first have to understand this idea in order for there to be nonconditional love and no fear. If we understand that we are nothing, then we could not make these conditions; and if we are nothing, then there is nothing to fear.

Student: It occurred to me today, "You are nothing, but you are everything." If we are made in the "image" of God, we are also "all."

Dr. Hora: Yes.

Student: It is frightening to hear that we are nothing.

Student: But it is not frightening—we can go back to what Dr. Hora said at the beginning of the hour, which is that we are able to see God working quietly through love and through wisdom, and this helps us to realize that we are "nothing" and not to be scared by it. We are emanations of the "All."

Dr. Hora: Yes. We must not get stuck on the word "nothing" because it could be misinterpreted as nihilism. When St. Paul says we are "nothing," he knows that we are "no thing." We understand that "nothing" does not mean nothingness: it means nonmateriality—spiritual living. We are "living souls." A "living soul" is not a thing—it is a nondimensional reality. Unenlightened people want to assert their "somethingness," and that is what we call "self-confirmatory ideation." When we are self-confirmatory we are saying, "I'm not nothing; I'm not a nobody. I am somebody, and I am something, and I really am!"

Student: And we invest a lot of importance in that idea because if we are something or somebody, we think that others are something or somebody needing to be controlled. So the idea of "nothing" is a humbling idea that lets God be everything through us.

Student: Isn't the passion of self-confirmation based on the fear that we are nothing, a nobody?

Dr. Hora: It is hard to make a positive statement about what we really are.

Student: But if we are each an image of God, is that not a positive statement?

Dr. Hora: Millions of people say this, and it doesn't do them any good. It is just a meaningless phrase.

Student: I mean in the context of Metapsychiatry.

Dr. Hora: We seldom use the phrases "image" and "likeness" or "child of God." We are trying to get beyond these words to the point of realization where we can see that intangible quality which is our reality. Whenever we name the intangible, we set up a barrier to realization. Words can be stumbling blocks to realization. We need to be very careful; only under extreme pressure do we resort to these words to communicate.

Student: I have a question about the working of divine wisdom. Even when we are endeavoring to be sincere, we can still fall victim to self-deception; but if we do maintain a certain level of sincerity, can we be confident that this wisdom will reveal our errors to us and bring them to light before we reach the point where they can do us real harm?

Dr. Hora: What exactly do you have in mind that will do us harm?

Student: I guess it is a question about recognizing God's presence in time. For example, I just saw that I was about to make a certain mistake which, had I not caught it in time, could have brought about certain unpleasant consequences. But having seen it when I did, it cost me nothing to fix it. So is that actually the activity of God's presence as wisdom?

Dr. Hora: Of course, and you were receptive. Some people, who are not receptive, do not have the requisite humility to be receptive. It can be pointed out to them a thousand times, and nothing will happen—they will continue making the same mistake. The prerequisite to enable us to benefit from some aspect of Truth, which is pointed out to us or which we are able to discern, is humility. Humility is the basis of receptivity. If one has humility and receptivity, healing can occur.

Student: I have another question. It may seem that we are dependent on having someone come along at the right time and point a mistake out to us. But isn't it actually God's wisdom working that is the source of the correction, and isn't it just a question of recognizing it when it comes to us?

Dr. Hora: Yes. There is no wisdom but God's wisdom. God is always working in everybody's life, but it is not perceived because of a lack of humility and receptivity.

Student: So this divine wisdom is always working to correct our mistakes, even before we make them. It is just a question of maintaining receptivity in order to be able to "see" its presence.

Dr. Hora: That's right.

Student: But we need the humility first, in order to be receptive.

Student: So is an aspect of humility knowing that when something good happens, it is the "good of God" and that "I" didn't "do" it?

Dr. Hora: If it is really seen, yes. But religion teaches a way of behaving, a certain kind of conduct where we give credit and say the right words, but we don't really see that whatever good happened is the "good of God" manifesting. This is where religion can become a stumbling block on our way to God-realization.

Student: We might think that we finally got God to do some⁻thing for us.

Dr. Hora: Right.

Student: How is it that the English language is so insufficient to express the truth? Is there any language more able to express it?

Dr. Hora: No, all languages have a tendency to give the illusion that if we know the words, we already know what it is all about. It is the same when we say, "God is Truth." This is not the truth—it is just a statement about the truth. Or there is the statement that we are an "image and likeness of God," which may be true, but these words only point to the truth. And then we stop at the words because if we know the words, it gives us the illusion that we already know the reality behind these words—and we do not. This is an aspect of intellectualism that makes it such a difficult problem.

Student: That is why we have the Prayer of Beholding. Dr. Hora: Could you tell us more about that?

Student: This prayer does not have any words. It is a direct awareness, beyond words, which is the highest form of prayer.

Dr. Hora: That's right, but it is not easily realized.*

Student: In the Bible there is a statement about power given to Adam when he named the animals.

Dr. Hora: Yes, Adam was given the privilege of naming the animals. What do you think that could mean?

Student: A name is symbolic of the nature of a creature, but it also seems to give one power, if he or she can name the problem.

Dr. Hora: Yes, that is why doctors like to name illnesses. They diagnose, and this facility gives them a tremendous power. If one

* "In the realm of beholding, there is neither self nor other; there is only the awareness of God's perfect Reality revealing all life forms in absolute perfection and beauty. . . . Everything everywhere is already perfect" (Dr. Hora).

can say, "You are schizophrenic," one has a tremendous power over another individual. You gave him a name; you are God. And if that poor fellow believes that name, he is lost. Diagnosing is very dangerous.

Student: Is it because words are human? They can only describe human things?

Dr. Hora: Yes. When Adam was given the privilege of giving names to animals, what happened? All the animals became "human." The trouble with animals is that they are human. Adam could not have given animal names to animals—he was a human being. He could only give human names to animals: you are a fox; you are a beast; you are a bull; you are a skunk. All these names express certain human characteristics, and ever since that time, animals are "human."

Student: Is that the nature of labels too, that once somebody is labeled, he tries to live up to it? So the tiger has to be tigerish, the fox has to be foxy. . . .

Student: And the schizophrenic has to be a schizophrenic. We become our labels. Is using words as a diagnosis really a form of hypnotism? Sometimes words can really help to clarify, for example, the words "living soul," or other terms that we use to help us understand spiritual truths.

Dr. Hora: We have to be careful with talking about the "living soul" too glibly, because immediately we try to give form to that which is nondimensional. If we have a word for something, we start imagining its form. If we give a name to something non-dimensional, then the mind will immediately give it dimensionality of some kind, and we will start imagining that the "living soul" is some kind of diaphanous form or something else like that—we get stuck in imagining something that has form or is formless. But the "living soul" has no form, and it is not formless, which is mind-boggling because the human mind is incapable of under-standing anything nondimensional. Modern artists have tried for years and years to paint pictures that would represent nondimen-sional reality, and the result is called abstract expressionism. They tried, but what did they achieve? Formlessness. Formlessness is the furthest one can go in artistic representation. No one will ever paint a picture of anything nondimensional. It is an impossibility.

Student: Can music bring us a little closer?

Dr. Hora: I don't think so. It doesn't matter whether a painting is representational or abstract—what matters is what it is pointing toward, what value it is pointing in the direction of. Every word, every statement, every work of art is a finger pointing beyond itself, and beyond itself is the realm of the non-dimensional. So if a piece of art is valuable, it is because it is pointing toward something valuable, something real. And similarly, so it is with words—the nondimensional cannot be named. And if we name it, which of necessity we have to, we must be mindful of the fact that the name does not do it justice. In meditation and in the Prayer of Beholding, we have to get beyond the words, like "living soul." Because we know those words, it does not mean that we know what the "living soul" is—we just know the name for it. In order to know what the "living soul" is, we must penetrate into the realm of the nondimensional in consciousness. Then we will have a little bit of understanding of what it really is. Anyone can say the word "Christ," but very few individuals really know what Christ means. Most of us think it is the surname of Jesus. So words have to be transcended in order for realization to take place. It is good that we can say "living soul," because if we did not have the language to express the idea, we would be even further away from understanding. But let us be aware of the fact that now that we know these words, it does not mean that we really know what the "living soul" is; and if we dare to admit that we do not know, then we may come to know. That is why the Zen Master says, "Knowing comes from not knowing. He who knows does not know." It is interesting that these ancient, spiritual seekers have discovered these truths.

Student: Is it impossible to learn if you think you already know it all?

Dr. Hora: Yes—knowers are difficult to teach, and they find it difficult to learn.

Student: What is happening in consciousness when we are quiet and an idea occurs and then becomes a word and then an action? Now was it the divine wisdom that occurred first? Can the human mind grasp wisdom, or is it consciousness that is grasping the idea?

Dr. Hora: The human mind can watch wisdom in amazement.

Student: Does the wisdom do the action?

Dr. Hora: Wisdom does everything. "I can of mine own self do nothing" (John 5:30). It is the wisdom of God in me that does the work. So we cannot ever take credit for anything; but we can be awestruck and amazed, watching wisdom operate.

Student: Is that the explanation of the word "fear" in the expression "fear of the Lord"? "The fear of the Lord is the beginning of wisdom" (Psalm 111:10).

Dr. Hora: The "fear of the Lord" is an entirely different fear. Most fear is self-concern. But the "fear of the Lord" is a concern with God, something that keeps us mindful of God. When we are concerned with God, we are interested in knowing God, and we are awestruck by the immensity and wisdom and love and greatness of God—the reality of God—which shows that we are "no thing" because God is everything.

Dialogue No. 6

The Mystery of Ignorance

Student: I would like to understand how there can be intelligence and fear present at the same time. Everything that points to intelligence works out harmoniously, and yet I notice that I still struggle with fear. I need to be fearless, but I can't seem to become fearless. When I catch the fear, I remind myself that I am "here for God," and I am not here for myself. But I am not really free of fear; it is still there. I have been reading the chapter on fearlessness and listening to class tapes, and it is becoming clearer. I realize fear is about self-concern, but that is not enough. Something isn't clicking, so that I can really let go of the fear.

Dr. Hora: Is this fear about a job interview?

Student: The job interview went well, in spite of myself.

Dr. Hora: There was no fear there?

Student: No fear. It was harmonious; everything worked out beautifully. At the end of the week, the job will be mine.

Dr. Hora: Wonderful.

Student: Yes, there was perfect harmony.

Dr. Hora: God is with you.

Student: I can see that, and I am very grateful.

Dr. Hora: So what more is there to complain about?

Student: Fear—my body temperature is constantly manifesting fear; it is just there. Although I can function and there is harmony and I can do the work, the fear is still there.

Dr. Hora: You are afraid that your parents will find out.

Student: This is true. I already mentioned it to one individual, and he said, "Don't let anybody rob you of your joy."

Dr. Hora: That must have been a Metapsychiatrically sophisticated individual.

Student: What is a child to do when faced with the parents' wishes? How can I become fearless of their wishes? As soon as they know about my life, somehow they have a way of attacking it, and it robs me of my joy. It hits me unawares, and that is what really scares me. Apparently I am not sufficiently immune to their influence.

Dr. Hora: Whenever we are afraid, we either want something or we do not want something. That is all there is to it—it is very simple. Is it possible to neither want nor not want? We want our parents to love and approve of us, and we don't want them to disapprove of us. So we live in constant fear about whether they will approve or disapprove. We want approval, and we do not want disapproval.

Student: How does one transcend that? It seems so natural to want your parents to love you.

Dr. Hora: Yes, it is natural, that is true; but then we are not "natural." Did you know that we are not natural? If we were natural there would be no problems. We would be in harmony with Reality. A worm is natural; a snake is natural—they have no problems. Animals are natural, but we are not natural. What are we?

Student: Ignorant.

Dr. Hora: That's natural. Ignorance is natural, but it does not work. We are neither natural nor supernatural—we are spiritual. Therefore we can only prosper and live harmoniously if we have understood what it means to be a spiritual being, rather than a natural person or a supernatural psychic. What does it mean to be a spiritual being?

Student: Of our own selves, we can do nothing.

Dr. Hora: How is that?

Student: It looks as though we have a brain; physically it appears that we have what we need to live a life: we have a heart; we have organs to keep our bodies alive, and we have a head to come up with the right ideas at the right time.

Dr. Hora: Is that so?

Student: But this does not describe a spiritual being. If we want to understand that we are spiritual, we have to give up the idea that we can live our own lives, that we can do things on our own, that we are this "doing," achieving person.

Dr. Hora: How will that help us to know what a spiritual being is?

Student: Good things can come into our lives, and we can have understanding of things, and we can be loving. But it isn't we who are understanding and loving and making the good happen.

Dr. Hora: Who is it?

Student: Love-Intelligence. It is God.

Dr. Hora: Who is He or She?

Student: God is Goodness; It is Intelligence; It is Love. What we are isn't self-evident when we say we are spiritual beings.

Dr. Hora: How do we know that this is really true?

Student: For most of us, it comes by learning to understand our problems.

Dr. Hora: That is what psychologists say too.

Student: It seems that we are what we think, and what we think is what we experience. There are intellectual thoughts and emotional thoughts, and I guess there could be spiritual thoughts too. But that is where I stop, because if there are all these different types of thoughts, how can we say that we are just made up of spiritual thoughts? What happens to the other thoughts? Maybe the other thoughts are needed, in juxtaposition, to reveal to us the truth that we are spiritual beings. But that is as far as I get.

Dr. Hora: That is not far enough.

Student: I don't know how to get further than that, to really know that we are just spiritual beings. How can we know that, when all these other thoughts are present in consciousness?

Dr. Hora: In the booklet A Hierarchy of Values, there is a whole dialogue on the question, "How do we know that we are spiritual?"

Student: The strange part here is that we have raised this question so many times.

Dr. Hora: And we still don't know.

Student: There is an answer, and it is offered in the booklet. But apparently we still lose sight of it.

Dr. Hora: Yes, the greatest mystery in life is ignorance.

Student: At least we should know the words by now—that man is the only living organism that has the faculty of spiritual discernment, the ability to discern spiritual qualities and values. Isn't that what constitutes a spiritual being?

Dr. Hora: That is proof of his spirituality; [it is evidence] that man is a spiritual being, because he has the capacity to know spiritual values, spiritual ideas, and spiritual qualities. No other life form has this conscious capacity. It is what entitles us to claim that we are spiritual beings. Not even a dolphin, which is a most intelligent life form, is able to distinguish between spiritual values and other kinds of values. Dolphins are very loving, but they do not know that they are loving. And man can be very cruel, but he knows that he can be.

Student: But not everybody is aware that he knows spiritual values; individuals might be loving, but they might not be aware of it.

Dr. Hora: We did not say that everybody is aware; we said that everybody has the capacity to know. The Bible says: "He that hath ears to hear, let him hear" (Matthew 11:15). But there are many people who say, "I'm not interested in spiritual values; I am interested in money, sex, and power," and that about covers a large part of natural man's interests.

Student: We were talking about spiritual discernment. This seems like a beautiful way to discover the difference between human love, which is probably present in most parents, and spiritual love. We can see how troublesome human love can be.

Dr. Hora: What makes it troublesome?

Student: It is conditional.

Dr. Hora: Yes, human love is conditional, and therefore it is not really love. Spiritual love is nonconditional. Is this clear? It is good to know this difference.

Student: What is good will? Is it a human quality or a spiritual quality?

Dr. Hora: Human good will is conditional; spiritual good will is nonconditional. Do we know the Metapsychiatric definition of spiritual Love, of perfect Love?

Student: The love of being loving.

Dr. Hora: The love of being loving is a quality of a realized individual. But what is our definition of spiritual Love?

Student: "Nonpersonal, nonconditional benevolence."

Dr. Hora: Nonpersonal, nonconditional benevolence, yes. Benevolence is good will. So enlightened people do not love with their own love; they love with God's love.

Student: Do we need to learn to love parents nonconditionally even when they are loving us conditionally?

Dr. Hora: Yes, exactly, and this is called transcendent regard. What is transcendent regard?

Student: Seeing persons as places where God reveals Itself.

Dr. Hora: Yes, but what does transcendent mean?

Student: To go beyond.

Dr. Hora: Yes.

Student: And to "let be"—to see a disturbing situation and be able to rise above it.

Student: And not to experience it.

Dr. Hora: When we neither agree nor disagree, neither approve nor disapprove, we can rise above the human perspective on life and see from a higher perspective, which is the spiritual perspective. Then there will be no fear, no problems—this is transcendent regard. In Metapsychiatry, we are learning to view everyone with transcendent regard under all circumstances.

Student: Is transcendent regard called love?

Dr. Hora: It is love; it is the spiritualized viewpoint on life, on individuals, and on circumstances. So we never have to agree, and we never have to disagree with anything or anyone.

Student: When we see behavior that is troublesome, do we just see it as the manifestation of invalid ideas and ignorance?

Dr. Hora: Exactly, that is all.

Student: So we must not take it personally; what we see is just invalid ideas taking form.

Dr. Hora: Yes, of course. Unenlightened people love conditionally—some conditions are crazier than others—but it is still just conditional love which is universal in the human species.

Student: Then the fear I experience is just a conditioned way of thinking. Here is an opportunity to become "unconditioned" from this way of reacting to my parents' conditional love.

Dr. Hora: Yes.

Student: And learning to respond to whatever issues are being presented and not to react when the fear is present will help me to recognize what the fear is.

Dr. Hora: Yes. You are concerned about yourself and what others will think of you.

Student: So if I can see that dynamic, and also see the existential issues, then eventually I would lose the fear because I would lose interest in getting approval.

Dr. Hora: That's right.

Student: And that understanding would gradually be changing my perspective and my whole focus to include God and God's unconditional love.

Dr. Hora: We are only interested in loving nonconditionally under all circumstances.

Student: What happens to wanting and not wanting?

Dr. Hora: It would fall away because we respect people's right to be "wrong," and we take no issue with it.

Student: But if an individual is acting from a transcendent viewpoint, isn't it appreciated and accepted in the world?

Dr. Hora: We are not concerned about that.

Student: I know, but I am wondering: Can a "beneficial presence" have problems being a beneficial presence, avoiding the entanglements that are often considered part of being a social being?

Dr. Hora: A "beneficial presence" has no entanglements. One is "in" the world, but not "of" it.

Student: I understand, but what about other people?

Dr. Hora: What about other people? Can you wrestle with fog?

Student: I think what is meant by this question is that if we don't go along with gossiping and socializing, one might be misunderstood and get the reputation of being aloof.

Dr. Hora: A "beneficial presence" is not aloof.

Student: I know, but one might be seen to be aloof, if one doesn't join in.

Dr. Hora: A "beneficial presence" is not concerned with how he is seen. He neither renounces society nor courts society. Sometimes it is hard to conceive of this.

Student: If you live in a place like the one where I live, it is very hard.

Dr. Hora: You cannot blame it on that.

Student: Dr. Hora, you mentioned that ignorance is the greatest mystery. Is it a mystery because we are human?

Dr. Hora: We are not really human—we just seem to be. And ignorance is really nothing—it is just an illusion. God is infinite Mind. The whole universe is filled with the presence of this infinite Intelligence called Mind. How can there be ignorance in the universe of Mind? And yet it seems that ignorance is ubiquitous. So God is not a mystery; Love is not a mystery; Goodness is not a mystery; Wisdom is not a mystery; Joy is not a mystery. Ignorance is the great mystery. How can we account for all this ignorance?

Student: I thought we accounted for it the way we account for the darkness, that we couldn't really know the light without the darkness.

Dr. Hora: That is the purpose of darkness, and we define darkness as "the absence of light." But in the universe of Mind, there is no absence of Intelligence or of Love or of Life or of Truth, and yet there seems to be so much ignorance and suffering in the world. This is the great mystery.

Student: But the mystery is self-confirmation, and the ignorance is man's eternal thinking that life is self-confirmation. Isn't it the self-confirmation that keeps us in ignorance?

Dr. Hora: No, ignorance keeps us in self-confirmatory ideation.

Student: Ignorance is first?

Dr. Hora: Yes.

Student: And we reverse it—we make a mystery out of God and a reality out of ignorance.

Dr. Hora: Yes.

Student: It is easier for us to see it that way.

Dr. Hora: We are all emanations of the divine Mind, which is all-knowing, supreme Intelligence. How can there be ignorant people?

Student: There can't be.

Dr. Hora: It is like saying some sun rays are really darkness—this ignorance is a great mystery.

Student: But you say it is all just appearances, that we are not really ignorant.

Dr. Hora: It is easier for us to say that.

Student: Didn't you say that ignorance is a mystery? Are we saying that there really is ignorance?

Dr. Hora: Ignorance is an experience, and all humanity is experiencing the evil of ignorance.

Student: What will it take for us to understand that we are not persons?

Dr. Hora: It takes one of two things: suffering or wisdom.

Student: It seems that the whole issue is always personhood. As long as we see ourselves as persons in the world, then suffering is inevitable.

Student: When we were talking earlier about how we can know that we are spiritual beings, the answer was that we have the ability to discern spiritual qualities and values. Is that also the answer to the question, How do we know that we are not persons?

Dr. Hora: Not really, because someone could say that persons have this faculty—I am sure many theologians would say that persons are spiritual. But then you are sinking into that quagmire called semantic darkness.

Student: If we have the ability to discern spiritual qualities, don't we also have the ability to discern other thoughts?

Dr. Hora: That is the great mystery. We can see that which does not exist, and that is our problem. It seems very real to us— not only do we see that which does not exist, but we can also experience and feel it. So it is very easy to say, "I can feel it; therefore, it must be real."

Student: It is helpful to understand the difference between feeling, experiencing, and realizing...

Dr. Hora: We have to go "beyond the dream."

Student: First we have to have the conviction that it is a dream, to recognize it, and then to go beyond it.

Dr. Hora: Yes.

Student: Seeing the dream doesn't seem like the worst part. We need to regret what we have not understood and go beyond it. It seems necessary to come to a point where we see all these erroneous ideas. I seem to see more than ever that what I feel is only what I think.

Dr. Hora: If we have reached a thorough understanding of the principle "Nothing comes into experience uninvited," then we can see that the experience is a dream that the thought has invited. It is just a thought, transmuted into an experience. An experience is a very tangible thing, and it seems very real. But when one discovers the "meaning" [or mental equivalent] of an experience, one sees that it was just a dream.

Student: Wasn't that dream serving a purpose?

Dr. Hora: Yes, dreams not only have meanings; they also have a purpose.

Student: To demonstrate certain erroneous thoughts in consciousness.

Dr. Hora: Yes, problems have a purpose, and the purpose of problems is to help us understand the specific nature of the darkness we are experiencing. Thus, darkness makes it possible to see the light. It is this juxtaposition of darkness to reveal light that we call "cognitive dialectics."

Student: Does the word "dream" indicate that it is unreal?

Dr. Hora: Are dreams real?

Student: What is a dream?

Dr. Hora: A dream is a thought in the form of an image or a feeling or an emotion or a sensation or a friendship.

Student: Or a broken leg.

Dr. Hora: Or anything else.

Student: I'd like to get back to that profound question of ignorance.

Dr. Hora: Yes? Interested in it?

Student: Yes, we said clearly that there cannot be ignorance.

Dr. Hora: There is no place for ignorance because the universe of Mind has no provision whatsoever for ignorance. Everyone is supremely intelligent.

Student: And yet there appears to be ignorance.

Dr. Hora: There seems to be ignorance, yes. "Nothing is as it seems to be, but neither is it otherwise" (Zen koan).

Student: Is it possible for a young man, especially when he is beginning to meet girls, to understand nonpersonal, nonconditional love?

Dr. Hora: It is possible, but there would be no interest in it. We have said here many times: it is not difficult to become enlightened—it is just difficult to become interested in it. Did you know that?

Student: This must have something to do with the mystery of ignorance.

Dr. Hora: Yes, possibly. Could you talk about that a little?

Student: Interest has something to do with our values.

Dr. Hora: Yes, whatever we value is what we are interested in.

Student: It appears that there are things that we value of which we are unaware—we cherish and hate and fear things, and we do not always recognize them. Therefore, we are ignorant—we do not know—and that condition seems to be inevitable.

Dr. Hora: Inevitable, but not necessary.

Student: But God has nothing to do with ignorance.

Dr. Hora: He ignores ignorance completely. Who can reveal to us the great mystery of ignorance?

Student: Ignorance concerns the "knower" who would like to know, and thinks he knows when he doesn't. There seems to be a paradox: one has to be in a place of "not knowing" in order to know.

Student: Is that what meekness is, knowing that you don't know?

Dr. Hora: No, meekness is "shouldlessness."

Student: What is ignorance?

Dr. Hora: We have said that ignorance is "the ignoring of that which is available to be known."

Student: Isn't it the "dread of nothingness" that keeps us stuck in ignorance? If there is no realization of God, then the "dread of nothingness" would keep us in self-confirmatory preoccupations. Reaching a willingness to admit to "not knowing" seems to be the only way we are ever going to come to know.

Dr. Hora: Yes, that reminds us of the Zen Master who said, "Knowing comes from not knowing."

Student: But in the "not knowing," there is the dread.

Dr. Hora: In the "not knowing," there is the dread and many other things. So have we revealed the mystery of ignorance?

Student: We have never before discussed that there was a "mystery of ignorance," and somehow it makes that which is spiritual seem powerful and that no other thing can interfere with it. Ignorance is the problem.

Dr. Hora: Ignorance is always the problem.

Student: There is another trap. Even if we do not "ignore that which is available to be known," we can fall into the trap of trying to master that which is available to be known. We can read and meditate and study, but we are still trying to master it.

Dr. Hora: The desire to master spiritual knowledge is another form of ignorance.

Student: Dr. Hora, is overcoming ignorance a part of the evolution of consciousness?

Dr. Hora: It has to be, yes. Jesus said: "This is the condemnation, that light is come into the world, but men love darkness rather than light, because their deeds are evil" (John 3:19). What could he have meant?

Student: We don't want to see our evil thoughts; darkness can cover them up. We don't want to face them.

Student: We don't want to be embarrassed.

Student: It does seem to indicate that man, by nature, is bad.

Dr. Hora: No, the "deeds are evil," which means that operationalism is a source of much evil. "Men love darkness." When we love darkness, what does it mean?

Student: Does it all boil down to self-confirmation?

Dr. Hora: No, self-confirmation is just a symptom of ignorance.

Student: When "men love darkness," does it mean that man does not want to be aware of his ignorance?

Dr. Hora: He is not aware of it, and sometimes he is too embarrassed to become aware of it. All ignorance starts from "judging by appearances." Mankind has a tendency to see everything only through the senses; he judges by appearances and misinterprets everything and builds up a "sea of mental garbage," which results in the love of experiential living. Unenlightened individuals believe that the good of life consists of having pleasant and exciting experiences. And experiential life seems to be what we are interested in; it seems substantial to us. We are all confused about reality. Metapsychiatry says that all experiences are dreams. So the question is, "What else is there besides experiential life?" Another name for experiential life is sense-existence. Jesus tells us that real life is soul-existence, not sense-existence. Now are we interested in exchanging sense-existence for soul-existence? Not on your life, right?! It is difficult. So there is the mystery. We love what is not good for us. Experiential life is both good and bad—it consists of pleasure and pain. But soul-existence is neither pleasurable nor painful. What is it?

Student: It is spiritual blessedness.

Dialogue No. 7

The Gift of Knowledge and Speech

Student: Dr. Hora, in order to be receptive do we have to come to a realization that we really do not know anything? Is being a "knower" an obstacle to receptivity?

Dr. Hora: The "knower" has difficulty becoming receptive; and then we have the "thinker" and the "thief" and the "hitchhiker" and the "dreamer." All these types of students have difficulty being receptive.

Student: We may realize we do not know, but as we learn the truth, do we know then?

Dr. Hora: Well, is it possible to know the truth?

Student: Jesus said: "Ye shall know the truth, and the truth shall make you free" (John 8:32).

Dr. Hora: Yes. What does it mean to "know the truth"? Is it possible to know the truth? When Buddha became enlightened, he stood up and said, "I have overcome, and I have gained absolute knowledge of everything." What is this absolute knowledge that one can come to know?

Student: It is the knowledge of what is real, as opposed to a knowledge about appearances and unreality.

Dr. Hora: Please explain that.

Student: It is similar to mathematics—if we know what real mathematics is and understand mathematical relationships, then we can recognize error immediately as being nonsense.

Dr. Hora: Yes, but that is an analogy that is not adequate to explain knowing the truth.

Student: I used to think that it meant that if we became enlightened, we would know everything that is written in every book without reading it, and if someone would ask any question, we would just know the answer.

Dr. Hora: You would become a supercomputer with an infinite database.

Student: Right, and what page number the answer was on . . .

Dr. Hora: With random access memory.

Student: If we take it on a small scale with a particular individual problem, we can see that we are all confused, that things don't make any sense, and we are looking here and there and everywhere, trying this and trying that. But when the truth is seen about that particular issue, all of a sudden things fall into place and the dynamics of it become clear. So it seems that if our context of existence were real, based on God, then everything would always make sense, and perhaps that is what Christ was referring to. We could look at a situation, and we would just have that underlying understanding about it, seeing it in the proper perspective, and valid ideas would flow freely into consciousness.

Dr. Hora: Yes. The difficulty lies in the fact that the word "knowing" has many interpretations. What is real knowing? There are many kinds of superficial knowing: we know the alphabet; we know computers; we know geography. But it is important to face the fact that there are many levels of knowing which give us the experience that we know something. But when we are confronted with the ultimate Reality—and we seek to really know the Truth—this knowledge is different from any other kind of knowledge that exists in the world, because this knowledge is not in the world—it is out of this world. When Buddha speaks about knowledge and Jesus speaks about knowledge, they sound different, but they are speaking about the same knowledge of the Truth. What is this Truth which, when we really know it, gives us absolute freedom?

Student: That God is real, that God is Love-Intelligence which is always available, and that this is the reality of the situation.

Dr. Hora: Well, you are close, but not close enough. Jesus explained it very well when he said that he knew that he could not know anything of his own self, that it was the Father in him who knows. And this is the ultimate Truth—to discover that of our own selves, we cannot know anything. All knowledge is vested in the divine Mind, and we can only know what this divine Mind is giving us to know. This is real knowledge; other kinds of knowledge are just information—scientific, psychological, theological. Real knowledge is the knowledge which the divine Mind knows and in which we can partake by the grace of God, provided we are sufficiently receptive. From moment to moment, God is providing inspired wisdom to those who are interested. The Bible says, "He that hath an ear, let him hear" (Revelation 2:11). So ultimate knowledge is not a human capacity; it is the self-expression of the divine Mind appearing in human consciousness. The truth is that we can never know anything of our own selves, but we can come to know everything through the grace of God. The divine Mind is omniscient, all-knowing, and human consciousness can be a medium through which this knowledge is able to manifest itself in the world. So that's the way it is when it comes to really knowing something. The Zen Master says, "Knowing comes from not knowing." He who knows, does not know; and he who does not know will know. There are individuals who would like to believe that they have "a good head on their shoulders," and they can figure out everything there is to know—they "use their heads." These individuals have a tendency to get migraine headaches. There are the "thieves" who want to steal knowledge and accumulate information. They usually have little cards and write it all down or put it in the "filing cabinets" of their minds or into the computer memory. These are the thieves. And then there are the "dreamers" who dream about knowing; and there are the "hitchhikers" who do not care about knowing anything—they just want to socialize.

Student: Do we have to realize that we don't know and that of "our own self," we can know nothing?

Dr. Hora: Yes, all knowledge resides in the divine Mind.

Student: Maybe I had this last hope that if we acknowledge that we don't know and then study Metapsychiatry, we would know again.

Dr. Hora: Acknowledging is not enough—realizing is necessary.

Student: Yes, and it has dawned on me that once we realize that it is only for good, we will never be the "knower" again.

Dr. Hora: Hopefully.

Student: Is it true that no matter how long one is a student of Metapsychiatry, one never gets to know anything personally?

Dr. Hora: Individuals who do not acknowledge the existence of God are really without hope because they will always try to find knowledge in their brain. The brain does not know anything. So it is absolutely necessary to come to understand that there is a God, and this God is infinite Mind and is the source of all wisdom, knowledge, life, energy, and love, and that is all there is.

Student: But we cannot will to see this.

Dr. Hora: There is no law against willing it. But it would be very frustrating, and one could wind up with a headache.

Student: The problem is to know that God is, even in the slightest way to realize it.

Dr. Hora: Yes, that is very desirable. Understanding the six types of students is very helpful, because if we are to remove the obstacles to true knowledge, we have to be able to identify these obstacles. How can we remove a stumbling block unless we can see it?

Student: Dr. Hora, is it possible to be more than one of these types of students at the same time?

Dr. Hora: If one is very ambitious, yes, it is possible to be a "dreamer" and a "hitchhiker," or a "knower" and a "thinker," or a "thief."

Student: We said we have to see a stumbling block in order to remove it. We do this by being constantly attentive to our thoughts and motivations. I have had numerous experiences where it seems as if I have seen a stumbling block just in time to prevent it from creating problems; but then I find myself being concerned—it is hard to be sure that one is always being sufficiently attentive, and it is possible that we won't catch one of these obstacles in time. So is there some way that we can bring these things to our attention, before they manifest as problems in our experience?

Dr. Hora: The best way to become aware of these stumbling blocks is in meditation because, in meditation, we focus our attention on the thoughts that preoccupy our attention. And we will find that suddenly we have a thought like, "I have to write this down, so I won't forget it," or "I have to file this way," or "I'll figure this out later." The "thinker" says, "I will think about it tomorrow." The "thief" wants to write everything down, and the "knower" will say, "I already know this" and will not ask a question. When this is pointed out, the "knower" will say, "What question? I already know everything. I know ahead of time what you are going to say." That is a "knower"; he doesn't know anything. The "dreamer," of course, is fantasizing about being enlightened. And the "hitchhiker" is thinking, "Does Dr. Hora like me or not?" Utter a deep truth, and he will be thinking, "I wonder if he likes me."

Student: Are you also saying that sometimes it is hard to recognize a problem because it is so shallow?

Dr. Hora: It is embarrassing, isn't it? We don't like to see it, but it is good to be willing to be embarrassed. It is important because without humility, no learning is possible.

Student: So, our mistakes can always be redeemed as long as there is a willingness to be embarrassed?

Dr. Hora: Yes, a "knower," a "thief," or a "hitchhiker" can always become a sincere "seeker" after he has suffered enough frustrations.

Student: So it doesn't really matter how far you have strayed from the path.

Dr. Hora: We have to return to it to become sincere seekers, because only a sincere seeker will ever learn and understand anything.*

Student: What we seem to be saying also is that the only safeguard against self-deception is ceaseless meditation.

Dr. Hora: Yes, right. Radical sincerity is required, because it is very easy to deceive ourselves.

Student: When we are afraid to face up to thoughts like anger or hatefulness, is it that we are not willing to be embarrassed?

Dr. Hora: It is always embarrassing to admit that we are ignorant. We would prefer to be called guilty, not ignorant. No one likes to admit to ignorance. This is one of the difficulties.

Student: If we feel guilty about something, does it mean that we were too proud to admit that we were ignorant?

Dr. Hora: Guilt is a devious way of confirming oneself. When we say, "I feel guilty," we are confirming ourselves. But when we say, "I am ignorant," we are facing up to an unpleasant truth.

Student: But it is also liberating, because we can't be blamed for our ignorance.

Dr. Hora: However, if one lives in a culture where knowing is at a premium, it will be difficult to admit to ignorance.

Student: Is knowing the highest premium, more important than anything else?

Dr. Hora: In our culture? No, not necessarily. Some people think being sexy is more important, or being popular or being liked.

Student: Can one want to be a "knower" for love?

Dr. Hora: Yes, but it makes no difference; the tragedy is that no one loves a "knower." What is it about "knowers" that no one likes?

Student: They make other people feel insufficient, inadequate.

Dr. Hora: Yes.

Student: There is a children's phrase, being a "know-it-all," that

---

* [At a later date, Dr. Hora expanded the six types of students to become seven, to include the "finder." Only the "seeker" and the "finder" are existentially valid.—Ed.]

refers to a particularly unpleasant type of individual.

Dr. Hora: Yes, a "know-it-all" is usually unsympathetic and disliked by others. Therefore, many "knowers" have developed a mannerism of claiming, "But, I don't know," after having talked knowledgeably about some subject. Teenagers are not so sophisticated as to lie about not knowing while believing that they know. But the less sophisticated teenager will often say, "You know," which means, "I know, and I want you to know that I know." Individuals cherish certain values, and then these values determine their mode of being-in-the-world, their functioning. Some individuals claim to "not know," and some claim to know, but it is all the same. Now how does an enlightened individual communicate? Can we learn to do this—to communicate in such a way that others would have the impression that we are enlightened?

Student: The enlightened man wouldn't even be thinking about whether somebody else thought he was enlightened or not.

Dr. Hora: God gave us the gift of speech and the ability to communicate ideas; these are a gift of God. Now what did God intend when he gave us this faculty?

Student: That the truth should be known, moment by moment.

Dr. Hora: No. Most people communicate in order to obscure the truth and create confusion and to control the minds of others. Have you ever listened to a politician or an aggressive salesman talk? The gift of God is often distorted and abused, and most of the time we are really very sinful in our ways of communicating. Now the philosopher Heidegger said that language is a light whose purpose is to shed light wherever there is darkness; and the motivation to talk must be to benefit someone who is in darkness, so that he might see. Jesus said, "I am come into this world, that they which see not might see; and that they which see might be made blind" (John 9:39). Isn't that strange, that such a loving man would say such a thing? How is it possible? Does anybody know what he meant?

Student: Wasn't it to cure the "knowers"?

Dr. Hora: That's right. When an ignorant individual is confronted with a light, he has an experience of being blinded because it suddenly dawns on him that he cannot really see— there is this new clarity. It happens sometimes when a very knowledgeable psychiatrist or psychologist or theologian starts reading Metapsychiatry. Such an individual can have a great shock because for years and years he believed that he could see; and now he has read something which sheds light on the same issues which he thought he could see and which illuminates them from a different perspective. At this point, he has a realization that he wasn't seeing. It is a great shock. So here is a situation where this book helps those who do not see—it helps them to see. And those who think they see are helped to realize that they do not see. And it wouldn't be a surprise if some of them would exclaim, "My God, I've been blind all these years!" It happens.

Student: So this "blindness" refers to a revelation of ignorance.

Dr. Hora: Yes. Before we can see, we have to discover that we really don't see. As long as we believe that we can see, we don't really see—we only think we see.

Student: Does this truth apply to knowing only spiritual things, or does it apply to other things in life as well? I ask because the "knower" is very often proud of his intellectual knowledge of things outside of spirituality.

Dr. Hora: Jesus came to help us to see Reality. There are not two realities: there is only one Reality, and that Reality is spiritual. We can know the price of butter, but that knowing does not mean that we really see; we are just participating in a dream with mankind. But Jesus said, "I am come that they that do not see might see, and they that see, might become blind." Heidegger said that if a blind man does not know that he is blind, he is in great danger; but if a blind man believes that he can see, he is in an even greater danger—that of destroying himself. It is most dangerous if we do not see, and we believe that we can see. But if a blind man knows that he cannot see, he will begin to see, and he will be safe. So a miseducated individual is like a blind man who believes that he can see—he is in great danger. Language is a light which God gave us to help each other to see better, to clarify issues, and it has to be motivated by love. If our speech is not motivated by love, it becomes intrusive and is a mischief maker and troublesome.

Student: When we speak, then, either we are clarifying or we are influencing. It is either one or the other, isn't it?

Dr. Hora: Yes. Influencing is a sin of trespass, and language is very much used for that purpose; it is dreadful. But how does an enlightened individual communicate? He communicates by being motivated through love to shed light, and that kind of communication is very helpful and effective and very much appreciated. All other forms of communication create discord and trouble in life. So it is of great value to learn to speak in such a way as to really say something. Usually we don't speak in order to say something; we speak in order to do something. There seems to be a lot of verbal warfare among individuals. We speak in order to hurt each other with words, to pressure each other or intimidate each other or coerce each other or destroy each other. It is amazing how many uses language has, and how few people really know how to use this gift of God—this gift of language, this gift of speech.

Student: We have to be really careful, then, not to trick ourselves, because we could be expert in a particular field and start telling everyone how to proceed and think that we are being helpful and beneficial, when we are really being tyrannical.

Dr. Hora: Of course. It happens all the time, especially if the motivation is self-confirmatory—"I am telling you." We can go into a store to ask a question of a salesman; he will answer that question, but in such a way that we feel he is convinced that we are idiots. It comes across very clearly at times, doesn't it?

Student: It is really so, because the salesman is an expert, and he usually does know more than we do about the particular product he is selling, but he might convey that in such a way that it is really an attack. So I guess the way to know if we are being loving or just tricking ourselves is to see if a situation ends up being clarified or is just more confused, no matter how much we might think we know about it.

Dr. Hora: Yes.

Student: But that doesn't seem to be a reliable guide, because we can think that something is clearer and yet we can be involved in intimidation.

Dr. Hora: Oh, yes.

Student: We talk about love and shedding light. Is this what God intends?

Dr. Hora: Yes, God said: "Let there be light" (Genesis 1:3). And he gave us the faculty of speech to shed light.

Student: We said earlier that we can of our own selves know nothing; but we can of our own selves also speak nothing.

Dr. Hora: Yes.

Student: What does the seeming urge to say something mean? Is it to make small talk?

Dr. Hora: There can be a million motivations for talking.

Student: Would the important thing be to examine our motivation?

Dr. Hora: Yes, as a matter of fact, it is so difficult to communicate verbally with love and clarity that we have recommended that everyone who would like to talk about Metapsychiatry do so nonverbally. Because if we have not yet reached that level of understanding where we can communicate clearly and with love, it is better that we do not talk. There was an Indian teacher of God whose name was Meher Baba, and this man understood the difficulty of verbal communication so well that he decided at a certain point in his life that he would never speak again. And he devised a way of talking about God without words, by using a tablet with the alphabet. Instead of saying words, he pointed at letters, and people had to put together the words according to the way he pointed—and he had fantastic results. He has followers throughout the world, and books have been written about him by his disciples. There is profound knowledge in his teaching. In forty years of teaching, Meher Baba never uttered a word. He never wrote anything except his signature, and yet he communicated effectively. After a while, he even abandoned the cumbersome communication through this alphabet table and only used sign language.

Student: Was that to protect himself from any impulse to speak with self-confirmatory motivation?

Dr. Hora: I don't think so. He was beyond self-confirmation. Apparently he believed that words are easily misinterpreted. If we know words, we have a false impression that we already understand because we know the words. He tried to bypass this difficulty in communicating spiritual truth, and he managed to do that. It is still a mystery how he was able to do it, but, nevertheless, there is a record that it was done effectively. He still has thousands of followers through the world—even though he has passed on.

Student: Is it a religious idea that if you know the words, you have the Truth?

Dr. Hora: No, it is the perversity of the human mind. One of the initial quotations in the book Beyond the Dream is as follows: "In the multitude of dreams and many words, there are diverse vanities: but hear thou God" (Ecclesiastes 5:7). So we talk a lot, and we dream a lot, and we are very vain until we learn to seek God with radical sincerity. We cherish words because they give us the easiest way to communicate, but it can be difficult if we are being misunderstood or misinterpreted or if it creates a belief in individuals that they already know. One could repeat a biblical sentence, for instance, know the words and have the illusion of already understanding them, but on the contrary one is further away from understanding than before one heard them. So the language that is a great blessing is also a stumbling block—unless we learn to use it the way God intended it to be used.

Student: If love is the only valid motivation for speaking, then it would seem that speech is an opportunity for us to teach ourselves to be loving. I'm wondering if we could make this more specific. How we can teach ourselves to be loving, to come to know what love is, when we speak?

Dr. Hora: One of our many definitions of love is "responding to manifest needs." The world manifestly needs understanding and clarity. If we learn to speak and to write in such a way as to shed light on darkness, we will be expressing divine Love.

Dialogue No. 8

Basket Weaving

Student: Dr. Hora, when I'm studying, how can I lose interest in the desire to go into the kitchen, every hour on the hour, and eat? I think I understand the meaning—I realize it's selfconfirmatory—maybe it's just wanting to feel good?

Dr. Hora: If the food is good, then yes. If the food is bad, then maybe you want to feel bad. But it also could be that you are longing to be loved.

Student: I see—that is clear. Well then, I guess the question is, How does one lose interest in wanting to be loved?

Dr. Hora: That's a good question. Is that possible? Doesn't everyone want to be loved? No, not everyone wants to be loved. Some individuals want to be rich or powerful or important or right or first. There are many things we suffer from, and these are always what we want or what we do not want. But compulsive eating and running to the refrigerator is like running to a "big mamma."

Student: Is it the physical aspect of eating that makes it so attractive to us in terms of affection? Is that the way in which it is like counterfeit love?

Dr. Hora: Being fed is a childhood experience of love. We get used to thinking that if we are being fed, it means that we are being loved; and we long for affection. Many people have this hunger for affection.

Student: So is it helpful at the point of moving toward the refrigerator to stop and see if we can recognize the motivating thought?

Dr. Hora: Well, even before we start moving toward the refrigerator, we can learn to be aware of our thoughts; and we might discover that we are thinking about wishing to experience affection or love from someone, to be loved in some way. Most of the time, it is affection that we crave. Of course, that is conditional love; everyone is suffering from having been brought up with conditional love. Some mothers say, "Eat, eat." And if we eat,

63

then we are a good girl or boy and being loved, especially if we like Mommy's cooking. These things will not go away until we understand that we are not here to be loved by others or to be disliked by others. This is just a dream of interaction thinking. When we crave affection, there is always an interaction thought: there is a self and an other in the picture. It is a dream, and we have to go beyond the dream. What is "beyond the dream?" Is there life beyond the dream? Sometimes it seems as though there is no life, that we will die unless we are loved by another or unless we get what we want. But awakening from the dream is like a resurrection to a new life, and this is called being "born again." In order to be born again we have to understand what the Bible says: "My grace is sufficient unto you" (2 Corinthians 12:9). We do not have to ask anyone else. Is God affectionate? No, God is not affectionate—God is unconditional goodness, and that is a different kind of love. Sometimes it is embarrassing to admit to what we want, and we would prefer not to know it and not to let anyone else know it because it is always childish— and it is embarrassing to be childish. But we have to be willing to be embarrassed. And then we can wake up.

Student: This problem of wanting to be loved seems to be from the moment of birth on. It just dawned on me that when I was in college, we watched a program that was actually funny, where the phenomenon called bonding was shown. People were playing around with little monkeys and put a beer can in with them, and the next thing you know, the monkeys would not let go of them. They would follow them around. There have been studies done where children who were not physically handled do not develop properly. And we know that allegedly so much of misbehavior stems from this problem. It seems to be the number one problem. Even as we grow older, we look for signs of God's love. So the problem is, how do we know that we are loved? From the moment we are born, we are looking for someone or something to fulfill us.

Dr. Hora: How do we know that we are not monkeys? Can we tell that we are not infants? Sometimes it is hard, but it is possible to tell. We are neither monkeys nor infants. We are not natural— what we see in nature does not really apply to us.

Student: What I meant was, it seems like a particularly difficult problem to snap out of this idea of wanting to be loved.

Dr. Hora: Yes, but snap out of it we must, sooner or later. If not, we may be reborn as monkeys. And then we will hug a can! There are many people who do that—they hug the can.

Student: The whole issue of stimulation as a child is interesting; those studies seem to give psychological proof that children who were not given nurturing love grew up very troubled. From a psychological point of view, do we need stimulation to grow up human, at least to a certain point? But then don't we have to go beyond needing the physical confirmation that we are real and that we are loved? It seems as though it is an idea that has been ingrained through many lifetimes.

Dr. Hora: Yes. Would life be possible without being hugged? Have you seen those bumper stickers that say, "Have you hugged your child today?" It is important to hug your child; it is important to love children and nurture them and constantly confirm them as acceptable and desirable—this is necessary. But the Bible says: "When I was a child, I spoke as a child, I understood as a child, I thought as a child: but when I became a man, I put away childish things" (1 Corinthians 13:11) and discovered that I am a spiritual being, entirely different from anything that can be found in nature. There is no other life form in nature that is required to make the transition to being "born again of the spirit." This is what Jesus tried to explain to Nicodemus, who was seventy years old. Nicodemus had come to Jesus one night to ask about life, and Jesus said: "Except a man be born again, he cannot see the kingdom of God." And Nicodemus said, "How can a man be born when he is old? Can he enter the second time into his mother's womb and be born?" Jesus did not argue with him. He said: "Verily, verily I say unto you, except a man be born of water and of the Spirit, he cannot enter into the kingdom of God" (John 3:3-5). What does that mean, to "be born of water" and to "be born of Spirit?" We have to be born twice in a lifetime?

Student: Maybe the first birth is a physical baptism, but the one of spirit is the inner transformation.

Dr. Hora: Every child is born of water. In the womb a child is enveloped with a bag of water; and when the birth takes place, the waters burst, and then the child is born out "of water"— intrauterine life is under water. Now the "second birth" is a spiritual birth; it is a realization that we are spiritual beings. So first we have to be born of water, and then we have to be "reborn" of the Spirit. Metapsychiatry is the obstetrician that helps us to be reborn of the Spirit. Now what happens when we are successfully reborn of the

Spirit?

Student: Well, there is peace, and all those false cravings that we found on the human level subside, and we are free to manifest spiritual qualities. There are no more limitations; false cravings consume a lot of energy. We have a chance to realize that false appetites are never really satisfied; we can never get to the point where we are full.

Dr. Hora: The door on that refrigerator never stays shut! The more you are hugged, the more you want to be hugged. Yes, that is a very important point; it is like eternal damnation. The human condition is full of frustration and futility. "In this world ye shall have tribulation" (John 16:33). We have to become reborn of the Spirit, which means we have to come to understand that we are spiritual beings. How do we recognize a spiritual being when we see one?

Student: We would know them by the fruits. They would manifest goodness and harmony. We would recognize a peaceful presence.

Dr. Hora: Yes. Can it be faked?

Student: I think we try to be peaceful presences, and maybe sincerely, but if we fake, eventually the truth will out. A lot of us yearn to be peaceful presences.

Dr. Hora: There is a story about a Zen Master who had a young student, and this is how he taught him: the Master gave the student a basket and said, "Go to the river, fill up this basket with water and bring it back." The student ran to the river and ran back, and every time he came back, there was no water in the basket. This kept going on and on, a hundred times, and finally the student said, "Why are you sending me to the river? You cannot carry water in a basket!" The Zen Master answered, "Well, you see that is true!" And supposedly the student became enlightened then and there. This is a koan. What does this basket koan say?

Student: I think it means that he should have used a pail.

Dr. Hora: No, that is not what it is saying.

Student: I am trying to understand it in the context of what was said before, that we have to be the real thing, or it does not work. We cannot pretend enlightenment.

Dr. Hora: That's right, exactly. Anybody who would try to fake it, or would have an operational or behavioristic impulse toward enlightenment, would be like someone who tries to carry water in a basket. It cannot be done.

Student: How can we tell when we're pretending? It seems that when one is on the path, life is always going from good to better, so it is easy to deceive oneself. There is a lot of ignorance being shed, but true enlightenment is a horse of a different color.

Dr. Hora: Well, the water runs out, and all you have left is the basket. What does the water stand for? Peace, assurance, gratitude, love, freedom, wisdom, joy, beauty, harmony, dignity. One of the members of this group says, "While I am here, it is wonderful; I know everything, and I can see it, and I can understand it. But, by the time I get to the subway station, it is all gone." This is the water running out the basket, isn't it?

Student: Could it also reveal wanting? We cannot want it either. It is a gift to which we have to be receptive, rather than something we can acquire. Wanting it could get in the way.

Dr. Hora: That's true. We cannot want it, and we cannot not want it.

Student: That's really a paradox.

Student: So the way we can recognize whether we are pretending or not is by the quality of our being? If we are not filled with spiritual qualities, is it an indication that somewhere we are still covering up something that we have not understood? Can an individual be peaceful and still be ignorant about certain things?

Dr. Hora: How long will you stay peaceful? Until you get home to the refrigerator? You need a tighter basket! We are all just baskets. Every time we get together here, we fill these baskets with spiritual truth, spiritual qualities and values and divine ideas, and the hope is that one of these days, they will not get lost on the way home. They will become permanently a part of us— essential aspects. And then the baskets will not be made of twine but of these spiritual values. The baskets themselves will become transformed, so that nothing will get lost. And we will live in permanent PAGL [PAGL is an acronym for Peace, Assurance, Gratitude, Love, and Its Presence in consciousness informs us that we are in tune with the One Mind], in the land of PAGL. It is important to outgrow operationalism, behaviorism, knowledgeableness, stealing, calculative thinking, daydreaming, and hitchhiking. Our "baskets" are woven of these human tendencies, and as long as we have these kinds of baskets, everything inside—the understanding and learning and reading and hearing—does not stay very long; it just leaks out. A student of Metapsychiatry was once afflicted by an epidemic of leaks. His car started leaking—the crankcase was leaking, the transmission started leaking, and the brake fluid leaked out of the car. Then the washing machine started leaking, and there was a leak in the basement. Next the roof began leaking—one after another, not all at once, but one after another— and we were puzzled. What was the meaning of all these leaks? And that is what it was, that everything he learned here, he was losing quickly. God has mysterious ways of teaching us.

Student: Even if we don't fully understand everything, if we appreciate that which we learn here, will it not help to carry us through?

Dr. Hora: We are learning to improve our baskets—to have a good basket that is free from operationalism, behaviorism, and all these various factors. Eventually it becomes leakproof. What we are learning and reading leaks out very fast until such time as we appreciate it sufficiently that it is able to stay with us and actually transform our seeing and being and the quality of our lives. We become "leakproof," as consciousness becomes spiritualized. The First Principle becomes our guideline to intelligent living, and nothing else is taken seriously. It is a nice koan about the baskets, isn't it?

Student: I have a problem that I would like to ask about. I have always had trouble making decisions, and I have to make a certain decision by Friday. I'm wasting so much time because I'm making it more complicated than it is; and if I don't make the decision, it won't even make that much difference. The decision is really for my own good. How can I discern what is operational thinking, and how can I get out of it? It is taking so much time, and it is a repeated problem in my life. When I come to something that I deem important, I make it too important. I have trouble making decisions.

Dr. Hora: Who can help with this problem?

Student: Maybe it's a sign of wanting to be important, if one has to wrestle with trying to make a decision.

Dr. Hora: Now let's ask a question. What is the meaning of wrestling with decisions?

Student: Is it making sure that one is right?

Dr. Hora: Not necessarily, but it could be.

Student: Is it "wanting" and "not wanting" and not asking what God wants?

Dr. Hora: Wanting what? What do we want?

Student: A certain outcome.

Dr. Hora: We want to believe that we can figure things out in our heads. This kind of wanting leads to obsessive ruminations which can be very painful and disturbing. We cannot sleep, and we rack our brains to figure it out. There is a desire in us to believe that we can think in the brain and that we can squeeze the brain to come out with some intelligent solution that will benefit us. Again we suffer from what we want. So what is one to do?

Student: Once we get to the point where we accept that we cannot produce ideas, the next step is to acknowledge that thoughts and ideas come to us from two sources, from either the "sea of mental garbage" or from divine Mind. So if we start listening to discern the ideas that are coming to us which give us PAGL, because the presence of PAGL is the barometer by which we can measure whether or not an idea is valid, it is not we who make decisions—it is just thoughts that urge us in one direction or another. So we listen for ideas to see which ideas give us peace.

Dr. Hora: Very good. So we do not make decisions. It is presumptuous for man to believe that he can make decisions. And of course, it is very troublesome; many people suffer big headaches from trying to make decisions. So we cannot really make decisions, but if we are receptive, we are guided. In all humility, we acknowledge that we need some intelligent idea, and we wait and watch—and ideas obtain in consciousness. And they are always the right ideas. We approach life situations in humility, being mindful of what Jesus said: "Of my own self I can do nothing... It is the Father in me who doeth the works" (John 5:30; 14:10). But often we say, "Yes, but I have a deadline, and I cannot wait for God to take his time. Maybe he will tell me too late." Now the question is, Is God slow? Is God dragging his feet?

Student: If we are not willing to learn a lesson, then it certainly would appear so.

Dr. Hora: What is the lesson?

Student: The first lesson is to see that we cannot produce thoughts, and this understanding somehow lifts us. If we could even consider this truth, it would be a blessing in and of itself, because it would set us on course.

Dr. Hora: Yes, in other words, God is instantly available, but we are not. It takes a long time for us to listen.

Student: One time we said here that the hardest principle is "God helps those who let him" [Fifth Principle of Metapsychiatry].

Dr. Hora: Right, we don't like to "let him." We would like to use our own heads, and that makes for the impression that God is slow too. He is dragging his feet. We have a deadline, and we cannot wait.

Student: The deadline only puts more pressure on us, and that makes it even harder to give up the idea that we have to find a solution.

Dr. Hora: Yes. So what is needed is to learn to be receptive to the divine ideas that are constantly available. God is forever and constantly sending us intelligent ideas, which in turn make choices, instead of "decisions," possible. We can make intelligent choices—we cannot make decisions. "Choose this day whom ye shall serve; for whomsoever ye lend yourself servants to be, his servants ye are indeed" (Joshua 24:15). The title of today's session is "Basket Weaving." Let us watch ourselves tonight and see how far we can go before the basket is empty.

Student: Is the goal authenticity? Do the ideas that we are learning actually become an authentic part of us? Is there a contrast between behavior, operationalism, and authenticity?

Dr. Hora: Authenticity and genuineness are our second birth— being reborn of the Spirit. "Enter ye in the joy of the Lord," and stay there! Don't lose it. It is easy to lose it. If you don't use it, you lose it.

Student: It's a mystery. What is the meaning of losing it? The Truth is all-powerful, so how can it possibly be lost?

Dr. Hora: Good question—because of the basket. What does the basket stand for?

Student: Consciousness.

Dr. Hora: Yes, a leaky consciousness. What makes consciousness leaky to spiritual treasures?

Student: Focusing on worldly values.

Dr. Hora: Right, and being influenced. By the time we get downstairs to the street corner, we see all kinds of interesting people. And we get fascinated by the human picture, and everything goes unless we are mindful and treasure the spiritual knowledge we are learning, and understand that we have to become a different kind of basket—a spiritual basket that is leak proof.

Dialogue No. 9

Receptivity

Student: I bought the book Beyond the Dream, and I opened it at random and right in front of me was a little paragraph that clarified a problem that I have lived with for years. Is this how God helps us? We are lifted up in a moment, and everything is fine. What is it? It is like an invisible hand. How does this happen?

Dr. Hora: There are fifty-eight chapters in Beyond the Dream and over three hundred pages. We buy this book, open it up, and find exactly what we need right away. If it only happened once, we could say it is a coincidence; but, it happens quite frequently. Remember the story of the student who opened the Bible and read: "Thou art a whore." She closed the Bible and thought, "This could not be for me." And then she got on the subway and opened a little pocket Bible to the passage: "Thou art a whore." How do we explain this? It is not a coincidence. There must be some principle behind it because it happens too often.

Student: It also happens when we are faced with something that we need to know, in order to help us be healed or to lift us above an invalid thought. This has happened to me for years. I know it is not a coincidence or chance. I'd like to know how such a thing happens. It seems mysterious, and I would like to understand it.

Dr. Hora: Most people would laugh it off and say this is superstition. If there is no God, then we would have to classify it as a chance event.

Student: It seems that this intelligence is always available to us, but we have to be receptive to it.

Dr. Hora: Yes, the secret is receptivity. The Bible says: "To them that received him gave he the power to be the sons of God" (John 1:12). What does that mean, "to be the sons of God" or the daughters of God? It means to be in communication with the Father. In the course of studying Metapsychiatry, we acquire a great deal of receptivity to spiritual truth. God is the Cosmic Principle of Love-Intelligence, which is constantly flowing into consciousness, and when we have "an ear to hear" and are receptive, our needs are supplied in one form or another. The real need is for the right idea in any situation. No matter what the problem may be, the need is to get the right idea. The Bible is full of right ideas; Metapsychiatric literature is full of right ideas. The great blessing in studying Metapsychiatry is that we develop ever greater receptivity to spiritual truth. "Natural man" has no receptivity. The Bible says: "Natural man receiveth not the things of the spirit of God, for they are foolishness to him; neither can he know them, for they are spiritually discerned" (1 Corinthians 2:14). When we become students of Metapsychiatry, we are not "natural man" anymore; we become transformed into spiritually receptive consciousness.

Student: Last week, we were asked the question, "How do we refuse to consider a thought that we know is not going to be life enhancing or helpful?" And Dr. Hora said that the secret was Metapsychiatric study. It is interesting that when I was considering this, something clicked. I just saw the value of this study contrasted to what the world gives us. My perspective changed, and it was fabulous.

Dr. Hora: It is not possible to study this wonderful truth without a transformation taking place in our consciousness. It is imperceptible; we are not aware of it, and yet it is happening. We are transformed from "natural man" into spiritualized consciousness which is receptive. "God so loved the world that he gave his only begotten son, that whosoever understandeth his teachings should not perish, but have everlasting life" (John 3:16). So we can expect to live forever. What is "everlasting life?" There is a Zen story about a student who was dying, and the Master said to him, "The essence of your mind is not born, so it will never die." So, we are immortal. What did he mean? Is this a way to comfort a dying man? Yes, it is. How is that?

Student: If we are a part of divine consciousness, then that part cannot be destroyed.

Dr. Hora: That's right. What are we really? The Buddhists speak of mind, but this is unclear because when we speak of mind, we think of the brain, and certainly the brain is not immortal.

Student: Is consciousness or awareness immortal?

Dr. Hora: In the letter to the Hebrews, Paul writes very clearly, never born, never dying. ("Neither beginning of days, nor end of life . . ." (Hebrews 7:3) ". . . hid with Christ in God" (Colossians

3:3). This is the "living soul." So we are living souls—emanations from the divine Mind, nondimensional units of awareness, which were never born and will never die. This is the Christ-consciousness that every one of us is, and therefore our true essential identity is immortal. It cannot die, and this truth is comforting. Now Jesus said: "I am the resurrection and the life and he that understandeth me, though he were dead, yet shall he live" (John 11:25). It is similar to what the Zen Master was saying—the living soul, which we all are, is immortal because it is not born, and it does not die, and it is "hid with Christ in God." What does that mean? Why is it hiding? What is it hiding?

Student: Maybe it means that it is not like a physical thing that we can see with our eyes: it is spiritual.

Dr. Hora: Right. To us it seems to be hidden, but it is not hidden—it is just not known. But it can be known. The enlightened Zen Masters know this, and Jesus endeavored to reveal it to us. Now, what is the practical import of knowing this? Is it just a religious shibboleth, or does it have practical value to know what the Zen Master calls the "unborn?" How do we come to know the "unborn?" How do you know "the face which you had before your parents were born?" The Zen Masters say, "Show me the face which you had before your parents were born." This is one of those mysterious koans. St. Paul writes in Hebrews, "Without father, without mother, without descent, having neither beginning of days, nor end of life . . ." (Hebrews 7:3) ". . . hid with Christ in God" (Colossians 3:3). This is the "living soul" or Melchizedek. Melchizedek was a high priest. What is so special about him? He was never born, and he never died—he just appeared on the scene. Paul speaks of Jesus as "a high priest after the order of Melchizedek" (Hebrews 5:6).

Student: In order for this to be comforting, don't we have to come first to know ourselves as spiritual? If we are attached to the body and if we think of ourselves as encased in it, then we cannot be receptive.

Dr. Hora: Right, you are a "natural man." See what a disadvantage it is to be a "natural man?" We do not understand these things. But through study, our consciousness becomes spiritualized. We become increasingly receptive to spiritual truth. God becomes increasingly real to us, and we begin to suspect that we are not what we seem to be—and neither are we something else. There is in all of us a nondimensional unit of awareness that is immortal, supremely intelligent, loving, and fearless. Now every time we catch a little glimpse of this truth, beyond theory, something happens—a healing takes place somewhere in our lives. It can be physical or emotional or occur in other aspects of living, like work or family. A little healing takes place because we lose a few molecules of physicality—they disappear. Little by little, we are learning to see the unseen. As the Bible recommends: "We look not upon the things that are seen, but upon the things that are not seen" (2 Corinthians 4:18). Every time we seek a healing, we move from the "seen" to the "not seen." When we catch a glimpse of the Reality of the not seen, there is a healing.

Student: When we are quiet and we are receptive to an idea, that instant when awareness is aware in consciousness, is that the eternal? Or is that how we get acquainted with what we really are?

Dr. Hora: The truth is eternal, and nothing can destroy it. Ignorance can, however, obscure it. God can only be obscured from our awareness. We can lose sight of God, but that does not mean that God has been destroyed. Not even an atomic bomb can destroy God. Neither can a "living soul" be killed by an atomic bomb. Atomic bombs can only destroy dimensional things. They cannot destroy anything that is nondimensional. Therefore, Reality cannot be destroyed because Reality is non-dimensional. St. Paul said: "Things that are seen are not made of the things which do appear" (Hebrews 11:3). What could that mean?

Student: He is speaking of seeing what is real. The things that appear are illusion; so what one sees with light and shadow are illusion. What one really sees is Reality.

Dr. Hora: "Things that are seen are not made of the things that do appear."

Student: And what we can see is really thought, but it seems as though it is something tangible.

Dr. Hora: We think this chair is made of wood and steel and that this body is made of skin and bones, but this is not really true. They are made of thoughts. The phenomenal world is made of thoughts appearing as dimensional form.

Student: There are valid thoughts and invalid thoughts, and they all keep appearing?

Dr. Hora: No.

Student: What is the difference?

Dr. Hora: Valid thoughts are permanent. Only invalid thoughts are impermanent. The Bible says: "Whatsoever God doeth, it shall be forever; nothing can be put to it nor anything taken from it" (Ecclesiastes 3:14).

Student: So people are invalid thoughts?

Dr. Hora: Not the people, but the appearance of people—we are counterfeit symbolic structures. Symbolic structures are dimensional forms that point beyond themselves. We appear as "natural man," but we are not really natural: we are spiritual. So the "natural man" is a symbolic dimensionality that indicates the existence of the real man, who is nondimensional, indestructible, immortal awareness, made of love and of intelligence. That is what we really are. This kind of understanding is the "pearl of great price." It has great value because it lifts us out of the miserable condition which Jesus called "the world." The world is a place of constant tribulation. Now what is it made of? According to some speculative theoreticians, the world is made of elements: fire, water, earth, and air. But this is not really true. It seems this way only if our approach is chemical, geological, or material. The world is really made of thoughts. What kind of thoughts? Interaction thoughts.

Student: It is difficult to understand how the physical world takes on existence through interaction of thoughts.

Dr. Hora: It doesn't "take on existence"; it takes on the appearance—that is, the dream. And we are studying to go beyond the dream.

Student: What we see is such a powerful illusion. What would it take for it to occur to us that it really is not so?

Dr. Hora: It would take satori. There is a story of a Zen monk who, when he became enlightened, broke out into laughter and could not stop for two days. When he discovered that all this is a dream—and a really ridiculous dream—he broke out into laughter and couldn't stop; it nearly killed him. So, therefore, we are warned against seriousness, right? What is seriousness?

Student: When we think "what seems to be" is real.

Dr. Hora: Yes, that's right. When we take interaction seriously, as a reality, we become very serious.

Student: But sometimes certain things can seem to be frightening, like certain behavior . . .

Dr. Hora: And illnesses and accidents.

Student: In the moment, they can be very frightening and mesmerizing, and we take them seriously.

Dr. Hora: Yes, and then we are lost. The moment we take something seriously, the situation becomes aggravated. Of course, we are not advocating flippancy and silliness.

Student: So is the alternative to ask ourselves, What is the meaning of the appearance?

Dr. Hora: That always helps, but what is the alternative to seriousness?

Student: Joy.

Dr. Hora: That's right—joy, gratitude, and a spiritual outlook on life.

Student: Frequently, seriousness seems to come from too much thinking and trying to figure things out.

Dr. Hora: Some of us become frightened by appearances or have an aggravated reaction. And then there are others who use seriousness, almost consciously and habitually, to intimidate others in order to control them. It is a very ugly trait. Some individuals are trained to be intimidating, both with their facial expressions and with the intonation of their voices. Intimidation is part and parcel of their ideology, their whole mode of being in-the-world.

Student: It seems that when we are serious, we are not loving; and when the atmosphere is not loving, people get tongue-tied. It is very sad.

Student: When we are confronted by coercion and intimidation and provocation, it is difficult to resist being affected by it.

Dr. Hora: You can learn to laugh it to scorn. The best, most effective way to deal with seriousness is by laughing it to scorn. It falls apart.

Student: I guess if we treasure something, then we are serious about it. So if something happens to threaten it, we can become frightened because something is happening to our treasure.

Dr. Hora: Yes. In Metapsychiatry we say, "Where our treasure is, there will our problems be also."

Student: How do we "untreasure" something?

Dr. Hora: By shifting our attention to the real treasure: PAGL is our real treasure. "Lay not up for yourselves treasures on earth, where moth and rust doth corrupt, and thieves break in and steal, but lay up for yourselves treasures in heaven" (Matthew 6:19) where these things do not happen.

Student: What is the meaning of treasuring our children? It seems as if God presents them to us to treasure.

Dr. Hora: God gives us children to be custodians and educators of them.

Student: I didn't know that.

Dr. Hora: Parents look at their children as possessions, naturally. "Natural man" thinks this way: "I have children. They are my children, my treasure." Then the parents begin to treasure them as property. Then, of course, there is a problem because we forget that children belong to God and are "here for God," not for us. They are individual spiritual consciousnesses, and the parents' job is constantly to give them back to God. Remember the story of Abraham and Isaac? Abraham made the mistake of becoming possessive of his only son, and then God required him to slaughter him as a sacrifice. He must have gone through hell, but he had to comply. And just in the last moment, the child was saved. This story is a parable, and it has a meaning. It means we must not turn our children into personal possessions. They belong to God. The same goes for a wife or a husband. Would we be willing to give them over to God? It is very dangerous to look at each other possessively, because this is not real. It is a fantasy. Everything and everyone belongs to God, and to know it makes all the difference. "Ye shall know the truth and the truth shall make you free" (John 8:32). We will spare ourselves a lot of agony in life if we keep remembering that. We do not own our spouses; we do not own our children. We do not own anything. We are owned by God—we all belong to God.

Student: Could you elaborate on the statement, Beware of what you cherish, what you hate, and what you fear?

Dr. Hora: The original idea comes from Emerson: "Beware of what you pray for because you may surely get it." In Metapsychiatry, we say that three things will give us trouble in life—what we cherish, what we hate, and what we fear—because these things indicate that we have developed a mistaken viewpoint on certain aspects of life. So we have to be mindful of them. This is good to know, so we can guard against this natural tendency. "Natural man" has a natural tendency to turn everything into a personal possession.

Student: Is this also true with spiritual qualities? If we understood that we belong to God, then would we never invite envy?

Dr. Hora: There will always be envy—even Jesus was envied a great deal—but we can acquire immunity against envy. We can be aware that we are being envied, so that it cannot touch us. Jesus was once preaching in a synagogue, and the people were not hearing what he was saying. They were asking each other and murmuring among themselves how this man came to know so many things (John 7: 12-15). They were not interested in what he was saying; they were envying the fact that he had some knowledge that they did not have. "Natural man" is always thinking, "What does he have that I have not?" This is the natural way for "natural man" to think. There is envy, jealousy, rivalry, and malice—the world is full of the "Four Horsemen." That is why it is a place of tribulation to them who have not yet overcome it. But if we rise above the world into spiritual consciousness, then these things cannot touch us. Einstein said: "Arrows of hate have been shot at me many times, but they never touched me because they came from a world with which I have nothing in common." He overcame the world, and envious arrows of hate could not touch him. He had immunity from these things.

Glowing

Student: Dr. Hora, how does one stop worrying? It seems never-ending. I realize the problem is "should thinking," but this doesn't seem to help. Yesterday was a beautiful day. Today when I got to work, it started out perfectly, but then an old friend came back—worry. What happens if today won't be as perfect? What happens if I can't live up to yesterday? What will be tomorrow? I couldn't ward off these thoughts. I got hooked, and by the end of the day, I was completely joyless. There is something I need to understand, so I can be stronger and not get so involved with worry.

Dr. Hora: Should one day be as another day? Is that what you are saying?

Student: I'm speaking about worrying. One day I can be worry-free and joyful, and the next day, worry is the main issue.

Dr. Hora: What is worry? Worry is thinking about what "should not" be. That's all.

Student: How do we lose interest in it?

Dr. Hora: How do we lose interest in worry?

Student: It is a self-confirmatory thought, an "old friend." I have also noticed that I can gain a certain understanding and let go of fear and worrying for the time being, but the next day it is back. It seems as if I have to worry in order to be on guard. It is a self-confirmatory way of functioning.

Dr. Hora: It is a way of malfunctioning.

Student: But, if I'm not worrying, who else will be in charge? When we don't know that there is God, then someone has to worry.

Student: Otherwise it seems as though we are falling down on the job.

Student: We have to make sure that everything is okay. I guess there is no trust in God.

Dr. Hora: Life without God does not make any sense.

Student: It is joyless.

Dr. Hora: There are ways of creating moods, as with mood-

79

altering drugs—we take things into our own hands. If there is no God, then we are on our own, and that is not easy.

Student: Dr. Hora, I thought anxiety went along with worry and fear, and I was surprised to read in Beyond the Dream that anxiety is described as "a heightened state of alertness," that its presence is an indication that we are eager to do well.

Student: But isn't anxiety usually associated with fear?

Dr. Hora: There are degrees of anxiety that are incapacitating and degrees of anxiousness that make you more alert and responsive. It is a matter of degree.

Student: What kind of anxiousness leads to increased alertness?

Dr. Hora: If we would not be anxious to come here today, we would miss the bus and not be here.

Student: Isn't that eagerness or interest?

Dr. Hora: Eagerness is just another word for anxiousness. To be anxious means to want something. If we want something too much, we become jittery and confused. If we are interested in something, we are anxious to get there. We could say that anxiety is something that makes us more alert. But if it is too intense, it becomes disruptive and undesirable. A little anxiety can't hurt you, but too much can. Worrying, of course, doesn't make any sense at all. Will worry bring harmony into our lives? No, it makes things worse. What will ensure a good day? A rabbit's foot? No... glowing. The secret of a good day is to face it with glowing. If we travel in a bus or in the subway, how many glowing faces do we see? Not too many. Most people are serious most of the time; they are not glowing. If someone takes the bus in the morning and goes to work with a serious face, what can he expect? Things will go from bad to worse naturally.

Student: But how do you glow?

Dr. Hora: This a good Student: How do we glow? It is a secret. Glowing is "the pearl of great price." Jesus is never depicted as glowing. Did you ever notice that? In all pictures he is depicted as sad, serious, even angry.

Student: How is that? The Buddha is not depicted that way at all.

Dr. Hora: This is a tragedy of the Christian faith—this misinterpretation of Jesus as a tragic figure.

Student: But he is always shown as being crucified

Dr. Hora: In other pictures too, he is depicted as a very serious man.

Student: Is it because, at that time, God was conceived to be very severe?

Dr. Hora: Yes, but Jesus came to present to the world a God of love, joy, freedom, and liberation.

Student: All the Christian religions interpret the crucifixion as a very serious situation.

Student: And that Jesus "died for our sins."

Student: Is there any meaning in the statement "He died for our sins"?

Dr. Hora: Yes, it is very helpful when you are trying to glow. We have to become a new kind of Christian and understand Jesus in a new way.

Student: We're not the ones who are glowing; it is God glowing through us.

Dr. Hora: That's right. How do we "do" that?

Student: We "do" it in consciousness, by being more aware of the reality of God than we are of our worries or any other invalid idea that we are holding on to. It is as if we had a scale and the "weight" on God's side suddenly became heavier. The only important thing, then, would just be glowing.

Dr. Hora: That's right. God is on one scale, and what is on the other scale?

Student: The "sea of mental garbage"—our whole life until this point.

Dr. Hora: Self-confirmation, sadness, seriousness, depression, anger, jealousy, interaction thinking is all on one scale—and on the other scale is the good of God. We do not "do" it; we just understand something. This understanding brings the love of God into a "glow" in your life.

Student: I was riding in the car recently, and I was quite worried about something and had been praying to find peace. I would take some idea from the Eleven Principles or the Four Ws and try to relate it to the situation, and that was very helpful. The fear and worry passed, and I did become peaceful. But I became aware that I was initiating all of this; I was talking to myself silently; I was doing it. Really, it was not glowing. It was just something I was making happen. It seemed eventually that it wasn't really good enough, because I had not stopped to listen for anything—I was listening to me. So I thought, "Just be quiet and still, and let's see if God has anything to say." And it was just wonderful! I became aware of PAGL [PAGL is an acronym for Peace, Assurance,

Gratitude, Love, and Its Presence in consciousness informs us that we are in tune with the One Mind]. Not talking about it and not thinking about it, it was marvelous. It was very still and very quiet, and suddenly I just knew everything was fine. There were no doubts; it was like getting a glimpse of Reality—where we know that everything is always at the standpoint of perfection. I knew I didn't have to continue.

Dr. Hora: You moved from prayer into meditation.

Student: And it is wonderful because now I know what that glimpse is.

Student: Dr. Hora, when something does seem to be serious— when a loved one is hurt, for example—how can we glow when what we are seeing seems to be bad?

Dr. Hora: How can we glow when we see a loved one suffering?

Student: It seems the question to ask in a situation like that is, "What is needed?" A loved one certainly does not need for us not to be glowing then. It is more important, especially for the one who is suffering, that we do not take it seriously and that we are able to see through whatever appearance there seems to be.

Dr. Hora: Nothing is worse than becoming alarmed or sympathetic or serious, and showing it on our faces, because we are then agreeing with the devil. The devil works this way: the devil is either seducing or provoking or intimidating. The devil wants us to become serious, frightened, worried, upset, and tempted. So we must understand that whenever we yield to the influences of the devil, we are not helping things—we may even be making things worse. These are the aggressive suggestions that come to our attention in life, and it is the devil's operation. That is what happened to Jesus. Who invented a "sad sack" Jesus, a failure, a tragic figure? There never was such a man. Jesus was a triumphantly enlightened, glowing, brilliant individual. Who threw the monkey wrench into Christianity? It is the devil working through the religions and the various preachers. It does not help to yield to the aggressive suggestions of the devil. So we must counteract them.

Student: It is helpful for me to realize that intimidation is the devil's work.

Dr. Hora: Of course, and we refuse to be intimidated.

Student: But we are impressed.

Student: Where does guilt come in?

Dr. Hora: Guilt is seduction. In what way is guilt seduction?

Student: Guilt is seductive because it makes you think that you have power to control things, so that they are your responsibility.

Dr. Hora: Yes, the devil says, "You are an autonomous person, and you are to blame for whatever happens." And we answer, "Yes! I am to blame. I feel guilty"—which means, "I am a person, and I have my own power to cause evil." Therefore, by accepting guilt we are confirming ourselves as autonomous persons, apart from God, who can "do" something. If we cannot do any good, at least we can do something bad.

Student: This kind of thinking is very hard to overcome for many people who have had it ingrained in them from way back in Sunday school.

Dr. Hora: Self-confirmation is very hard to overcome, especially if we don't know what it is. If we do know what it is and how to overcome it, then it is not hard. The first step is to stop talking about ourselves; the second step is to stop talking about others; the third step is to stop talking altogether; and the fourth step is to glow for God.

Student: Dr. Hora, is interaction based simply on those three things that we just talked about—provocation, intimidation, seduction? Is that the basis of it?

Dr. Hora: The basis of all interaction thinking is self-confirmatory ideation: it is thinking of oneself in relation to another self. So when we say, there is no interaction anywhere, or when we say, stop talking about yourselves, and stop talking about others, this eliminates interaction—and at the same time it eliminates self-confirmatory ideation. And when there is neither self nor other, what is left?

Student: Only that which really is.

Dr. Hora: What is that?

Student: One could say that there is only divine Reality.

Dr. Hora: Yes, there is only God. God's presence fills the whole universe. We are individual aspects of this infinite consciousness, or cosmic Mind, which is God, and there is nothing else. So we have eliminated everyone. Now what is the good of that?

Student: We can be peaceful and see PAGL, and then we can glow. Because if we have eliminated self and other, then what else is there? There is nothing left but light.

Student: It must be a wonderful freedom to be done with all that seems to be.

Dr. Hora: Then we can be conscious of all that really is. What is "what really is"? Life really is; truth really is; love really is; intelligence really is; goodness really is; beauty really is; harmony, perfection, joy, health—these things really are, and everything else just seems to be.

Student: It seems that the context we use to identify ourselves is the real prison, and whenever we see that as being reality, we are trapped.

Dr. Hora: How do you identify yourself?

Student: Unfortunately, today I identify with mother.

Dr. Hora: Back to mother again! Mother knows best, and mother is always right. What is this force which binds us to mother? Most everybody has some trouble with mother. There is a mystery about our attachment to our mothers. More often than not, it is hostile.

Student: May I say something in defense of mothers?

Dr. Hora: We do not imply that we blame mother.

Student: What occurred to me is that I think a parent develops a false sense of responsibility—a mother, for example, thinks she should respond in a particular way to her child.

Dr. Hora: What is the mystery about mother fixations?

Student: We seem to think that it is the mother who gave us life. For a while, we are even attached with an umbilical cord. It seems that the father goes out into the world, and the mother is the nurturing one.

Dr. Hora: That is cause-and-effect reasoning.

Student: We think our lives depend on our parents.

Dr. Hora: I know a young lady, a very intelligent, beautiful woman, who had a psychotic mother who was constantly rejecting and cursing her and always suggesting to her that no matter what she did in life, she would always fail. Now this poor unfortunate woman cannot get rid of her mother. She even lives in another part of the country. The mother is a hostile, very malignant woman, and the daughter is living out the curse that this mother seems to have planted in her consciousness. Even though we have clarified all the details of this malignant relationship, she is unable to shake it off. She can see all the tragic faults, what the mother is and was, and one would think that once this was understood that she would just get rid of the memory and be free. It is clear that the mother was not good for her, that she didn't love her daughter. In fact, she hated her and considered her a rival; and yet the daughter is clinging to her and cannot be free. This is called a mother fixation, and more people have mother fixations than you would expect. Everyone blames the mother and curses the mother and psychoanalyzes the mother. Very few people can get free of their mothers—even the religious people have a problem. Jesus said: "I am come to set apart mother and daughter, sister and brother" (Matthew 10:35). It is very hard to become separated from mother. In the American culture, the father does not play much of a role and is not so much of a problem. The best parents are the neglectful parents— those are the easiest kind to become free of. Jung spoke of "separation individuation"—we cannot become individuals until we have succeeded in completely severing our ties with mother. But how do we do it? It is impossible. What makes mother so important?

Student: We need her love.

Dr. Hora: Her love? We need her hate just as much.

Student: We need her self-confirmation.

Dr. Hora: That is what it is. The problem is not mother. The problem is that the mother figure is the most convenient identity to confirm our ego. No one in the world is as important for self-confirmatory utilization as the mother. The secret is we need the mother to justify our self-confirmatory ideation. We are using our memory of our mothers as an excuse to think about ourselves. Until such time as we are healed of self-confirmatory desires, we will always be fixated on mother. So we are using the poor mothers. They are not to blame; they just became very important to us as a source of self-confirmatory ideation.

Student: Do we also transfer it onto others? If we don't get it from mother, can we get it from, say, the psychiatrist?

Dr. Hora: You can have as many substitute mothers as you like So that is the mystery of mother. Poor mothers are always being blamed. Generations of psychoanalysts have worked very hard on creating hostile feelings toward mother, but the more hostile we feel toward our mothers, the more we are attached to them. If we love her, it's no good; if we hate her, it's also no good.

Student: Is that even if she is dead?

Dr. Hora: She lives forever. All mothers are immortal in the minds of their sons and daughters. But when self-confirmatory desires are abandoned, then mother has a chance to find peace either here on earth or in the grave. Our mothers do not have any peace from their offspring because they are either loved or hated. We can only release them by abandoning the desire to confirm ourselves. So let us not complain about rejection, and let us not reject mother because that's nonsense. We cannot reject mother; the more we try, the more we get entangled with her. We cannot cling to mother; we cannot love her, and we cannot hate her. We can just outgrow the desire for self-confirmation, and we are free.

Student: What is the best way?

Dr. Hora: The best way is to stop talking about oneself. The second step is to stop talking about others; the third step is hardly to talk at all.

Student: Is that the meaning of my friend's finding peace by my leaving her?

Dr. Hora: Of course, she was a mother substitute.

Student: I took a mother substitute, someone else's mother, and I felt she needed me and that I was taking care of her and saving her. In the meanwhile she got very sick—my thoughts were hurting her and myself. Finally I was able to leave her, and she became very healthy. She is ninety-seven years old and was almost dead. Now, she is healthy and well, peaceful and quiet.

Student: Since you went away.

Student: It's still hard for me to laugh about it.

Dr. Hora: See what Metapsychiatry can do?

Student: So this would also be the meaning of our becoming more like our mother? I see that with myself—looking physically like my mother—and I can't stand it. You could begin to hate yourself. It is like being trapped in self-confirmation.

Dr. Hora: Yes, exactly. That is the basic problem.

Student: And to perpetuate it more, do we marry our mothers?

Dr. Hora: Yes, definitely. A woman marries her mother—and a man likewise. We have a matriarchal society, but the basic problem is self-confirmation. We welcome anybody who will confirm us either positively or negatively; that is all we are interested in.

Student: It seems that we invite people into our experience whose main interest is also to confirm themselves.

Dr. Hora: Oh yes, that is not a rarity. So someone could ask, "What else is there in life?"

Student: If we lost interest in self-confirmation, would we still be inviting the same type of individual into our experience? Or would we be able to observe it without it bothering us?

Dr. Hora: No, we would be inviting a divine individual, a wonderful, divine character into our experience. We could ask this question, "What is the mystery of some people not being able to get married?" There are some men who cannot find the right woman, and there are many women who cannot find a man. They are good-looking, intelligent, educated; they have everything, but they cannot seem to get married. What is the mystery? In Texas they have an explanation for this—when a woman can't find a husband, they say to her, "You ain't the man your mamma was." What does this mean?

Student: Mother is the man in one's life. I can see clearly that my attachment to my mother would never allow another individual to get between us. When there was a young man who was important in my life, I chose my mother over that individual because it was more important to make her happy.

Dr. Hora: You can't find a man who will confirm you as wonderfully as your mother. If there is a mother fixation, there is no place for anyone else in your life.

Student: Is there any special reason that so many marriages break up? What is the significance to that?

Dr. Hora: It is not surprising. We do not know what marriage is. If we were to interview a thousand people and ask them what a marriage is, we would get the strangest answers. It is hard to tell who is better off—those who get married or those who do not get married. Metapsychiatry distinguishes three types of marriages: the coercive, the cooperative, and the joint participatory. There are coercive marriages, where one partner is always coercing the other. This is wonderful self-confirmation—to be a victim of coercion is very exciting. Then there are cooperative marriages, and they don't work—there is no excitement in them. And then there is participatory marriage where two spiritually mature individuals coexist harmoniously in the universe of Mind. There is no confirmation there; there is just the joy of the Lord, that is participatory marriage.

Student: The emphasis here is on spiritual maturity. What does that really mean?

Dr. Hora: Spiritual maturity is, first, when we never talk about ourselves; second, when we do not talk about others; third, when we hardly talk at all; and fourth, when we are glowing for God.

Dialogue No. 11

Self-Esteem

Student: Dr. Hora, could we talk about self-esteem? It seems easy to think of getting self-esteem from how well we perform. But Metapsychiatry says that self-esteem is our inherent birthright, and that it comes from a spiritual source; it has nothing to do with our performance. I am attempting to understand this, but there is a nagging question, Does it make a difference whether I do something sloppily or not or whether I lie in bed and eat, as opposed to getting up and working? Obviously it is not a spiritual value to indulge myself, but does what we do, and how well we do it, make any difference in terms of our spiritual development?

Dr. Hora: This is a very interesting issue. Many individuals derive a sense of self-esteem from how well they perform at work, in art, in science, or from winning scholarships and prizes. Almost everyone seeks to derive self-esteem from what they do and how they do it. Performance is one of the most frequent means of gaining self-esteem. There are other forms of seeking self-esteem, mainly through interpersonal relationships and getting someone to admire us or feed us compliments. If we go to a restaurant and the waiters jump all around us and make us feel important, we get a sense of self-esteem. Or if we are down and out, we can take a drink for self-esteem. But these are all transitory illusions, and they usually fade out and result in a letdown. If today we were very productive and intelligent and performed well at work, we might come home and have a great sense of self-esteem. But what if tomorrow we do not manage to keep up the standard? It never occurs to us that this is a very precarious way to go about having self-esteem. After a while we can get so fed up and angry that we become negative on self-esteem derived from performance and begin to derive pleasure from malperformance. For instance, if someone is deriving self-esteem from being neat and orderly, he could come disorderly with a vengeance and try to derive self-esteem from being a slob. So this whole idea of performance, which is also fostered by our educational system, is a precarious idea through which we seek self-esteem. But what would happen to our performance if we suddenly discovered that self-esteem is spiritual and that we do not have to earn it? It is our birthright through divine Love. God so loves us that he gives us self-esteem for free. We do not have to earn it—it is called grace. What will happen to our performance? If we already have self-esteem, why bother to perform? Will we become bums? What will our motivation be for excellence if we already have self-esteem?

Student: If one knows that one's self-esteem is from God, performance is a fruit and is not used to confirm oneself. Performance comes automatically in the right way and in the right areas.

Student: Our role in life is to demonstrate the qualities of God. It is helpful to think of it in terms of music and playing the piano. If the motivation is to play as well as one possibly can and to work at the highest degree of one's ability, then playing the piano is a demonstration of spiritual qualities—like beauty and harmony. If the motivation is to manifest spiritual qualities—not for self-esteem, but for God-confirmation—then it seems valid.

Dr. Hora: Is it reasonable to expect somebody to perform well automatically, just for the love of God?

Student: Perhaps, but that word "automatic" is a little difficult for me. I think it is conceivable, yes, and we have to understand excellence as a spiritual quality. But then so much of what goes on in the world would not seem too important. I saw a mailman today, and he was singing as he did his work. He was radiating joy and all those wonderful qualities, and I thought, "Well, does it make any difference if one is a mailman or a college professor or a businessman or anything else?" Probably not—as long as we do it well. But is there any sense to those Puritan ideas that say we have to search to make the best use of our talents? To me, all that involves work, and it isn't "automatic."

Dr. Hora: Our performance is not an ego trip anymore; it is a form of worshiping God. What a glorious freedom that we do not have to perform for self-esteem. Self-esteem is spiritual. It is not psychological; it is not operational, and it is not interperonal. It is spiritual, born of divine Love.

Student: I am a little confused by the term itself, "self-esteem." I thought that there was no self, that there is no self or other. How can we speak of "self"-esteem when there is no self?

Dr. Hora: Can anyone answer this question? It sounds as if a monkey wrench has been thrown into everything that has been said until now. But don't worry, there is a self which is, and there is a self which is not.

Student: You are speaking of the spiritual self.

Dr. Hora: There is no other kind, really; it just seems that way. Self-esteem is very important to the whole world—and it is spiritual, born of divine Love. When we understand it, everything is effortless, efficient, orderly, pure, harmonious, aesthetic, and very good. The Bible says: "God saw everything that he made and behold it was very good" (Genesis 1:3 1). Did he do it for self-esteem? No, he did it for the joy of it. When we understand that self-esteem is spiritual, born of divine Love, then life becomes a joy: it is effortless, and whatever we touch turns out well.

Student: What is the difference between neatness as a spiritual quality and compulsive neatness?

Dr. Hora: When we are compulsively neat, we do not know that we are loved by God. What is this compulsive behavior? It is a struggle to perform in order to get recognition. This builds up psychological self-esteem, which is here today and gone to-morrow—it is very fleeting. Psychological self-esteem is just an illusion.

Student: What does that mean, "psychological self-esteem"?

Dr. Hora: It is personal, self-confirmatory thinking.

Student: I understand now why I experience this tremendous letdown after I do something well. I realize that it is not valid to praise myself for it, and when it all turns to ashes, it seems meaningless because I have not understood what the real value of it was.

Student: I just heard a piano concerto, and the pianist was very gifted. The performance transcended everyday experience. I wonder what the secret is?

Dr. Hora: Maybe he was not performing; maybe he was just playing music.

Student: There is an expression, "making music." I have watched certain musicians, and there is such joy when they play! They laugh with each other, and they "make music."

Dr. Hora: They are not concerned with "performance."

Student: They forget about themselves.

Dr. Hora: There are people who have sex, and there are people who make love. What is the difference? There are many men who become impotent because they believe they have to "perform" in the sexual act, and the result is impotency and a terrible loss of self-esteem. Similarly, if our outlook on life is in terms of a performance where we have to prove that we are worthwhile in order to gain self-esteem from what we have done, then life becomes a difficult situation. There are people who suffer stage fright because they were taught to perform on stage or to address an audience and make a speech. If we have to "perform," then there will be fear and anxiety. But if we go to communicate ideas rather than to perform, then there will be peace, freedom, and stage presence. What is the difference between stage fright and stage presence?

Student: As long as we think we have to perform, then spontaneous creativity has no place. The performer who is interested in communicating ideas is open, moment by moment, to creative ideas, and in that spontaneity, he is going to be a presence, whereas someone who has stage fright is going to be watching himself perform in order to make sure he is going to have the audience's eye. Consequently he will always be commenting on everything he is doing.

Dr. Hora: Yes, in Metapsychiatry the very idea of performance would be classified as operationalism. Operationalism is problematic.

Student: There would be no transcendence because the self is watching the self. That is actually what happens—one is watching oneself do these things.

Dr. Hora: We see how one single word can poison a whole life. The word "perform" can ruin everything in our life. Meeting people, in business or socially, becomes a performance. As the saying goes, "How am I doing?" Performance is a dangerous word.

Student: Self-consciousness is performing all the time—"What will they think of me?"

Dr. Hora: Right, exactly. In German, there is a word for it, gemacht, which means artificial behavior. We are victims of language; also it is assumed, from childhood on, that "perform" is a respectable word. It is used everywhere. How can there be anything wrong with such a nice word? Everyone is using it, and the word is poison.

Student: Are self-consciousness and self-confirmatory thinking the same?

Dr. Hora: Yes, and they are very painful.

Student: What is the difference between the self observing the self and just being aware of what we are doing? Is there some quality of observation? Who is doing the observing?

Dr. Hora: Who is doing the observing when there is no self-consciousness?

Student: The transcendent observer.

Dr. Hora: That is correct. Do we understand it?

Student: The transcendent observer is an aspect of consciousness which is aware, which can observe and behold. Its presence is one of the things that distinguishes us from lower life forms— we have the ability to transcend our own actions and to be aware of thoughts.

Student: Please contrast that with self-consciousness.

Dr. Hora: Self-consciousness is psychological—watching your own performance, being an audience to yourself.

Student: It is thinking about what others are thinking about what we are thinking.

Dr. Hora: Yes, it is judging our "self."

Student: Approval and disapproval are going on.

Dr. Hora: And that is very uncomfortable. But the transcendent observer does not judge, does not criticize, does not blame, does not evaluate; it is just aware.

Student: The psychological self knows only judgment because it is comparing.

Dr. Hora: Yes, it is always judgmental and critical.

Student: It is also a "killjoy."

Dr. Hora: Yes, of course.

Student: Does the transcendent observer tell us what is right and what is wrong; would it ever judge?

Dr. Hora: The transcendent observer does not judge; therefore it cannot say what is right and what is wrong. It can however bring into our awareness what is valid and what is not valid, which is not the same as right and wrong.

Student: Right and wrong is still judgmental.

Dr. Hora: Yes. In Metapsychiatry we never speak about who is right and who is wrong, or what is right and what is wrong, or what "should" be or what "should not" be. We always ask, "Is it existentially valid or not?" We say operationalism is existentially not valid. Spiritual self-esteem is valid because it is a quality of truth, and truth is liberating. Indeed there is a glorious sense of freedom and PAGL when we understand that self-esteem does not have to be earned—it is ours by virtue of divine Love.

Student: It seems so easy and so good. What makes claiming this birthright so difficult?

Dr. Hora: It is a mystery. It is there, and yet so few of us see it.

Student: Yes, we could say to someone, "You can have this." And they might say, "Sure, of course, give it to me."

Dr. Hora: Who can give it to us?

Student: God, I guess, but we have to recognize it. Now logically, it seems like the best thing in the world.

Dr. Hora: Yes, it is the "pearl of great price." Spiritual self-esteem comes by the grace of God.

Student: Some people spend their whole lives looking for approval, and they are closed to spontaneous ideas of any kind.

Dr. Hora: Yes, so how do we explain that such a self-evident, glorious fact as spiritual self-esteem is so little known in the world? This is a great mystery.

Student: Is it that we like to judge others and take it upon ourselves to say whether somebody is worthy or not?

Dr. Hora: That would be cause-and-effect reasoning. The great mystery of life is not the good of God, but ignorance. Ignorance is the greatest mystery of life.

Student: And nobody knows it.

Student: Misinformation seems to be worse than ignorance.

Dr. Hora: That is positive ignorance. What is the mystery of ignorance? Where does it come from, and where is it going? How is it possible for millions of individuals to live in ignorance when the truth is so simple and readily available and so wonderful and liberating and healing?

Student: Would it be cause-and-effect reasoning to say that ignorance is passed on from one generation to another?

Dr. Hora: That is not cause-and-effect: that is just an observation that ignorance goes from one generation to another. It is a historical fact. It has always been, and it will always be. Jesus said: "The poor will always be with you" (Matthew 26:11). But poverty is not involuntary.

Student: For a few or for everybody?

Dr. Hora: Everybody. This seems shocking? Ignorance has its source in "judging by appearances." Jesus said: "Judge not according to the appearance, but judge righteous judgment" (John 7:24). The tendency in the human race is to "judge by appearances" and to arrive at invalid conclusions and interpretations of life. For instance, if someone is chopping wood, we look at him, and it occurs to us that he is performing a certain act. We "judge by appearances" and arrive at a false interpretation and suffer the consequences. The next time we want some firewood, we will go into a performance and start chopping wood as a performer and have all sorts of difficulties. If chopping wood is a performance, we will find that the ax is not sharp enough, or the wood is too hard, and it doesn't stand up. "Judging by appearances" gives rise to misinterpretations and they, in turn, are shared. This darkness spreads and spreads until it becomes a "sea of mental garbage." In this "sea of mental garbage," we can find all kinds of invalid ideas, such as "Poverty afflicts people innocently," or "Illness befalls people innocently." We are "sitting ducks in the devil's shooting gallery." All kinds of invalid ideas come, and then we suffer from this ignorance.

Student: It seems to boil down to seeing the right way. Because we're looking at this fellow chopping wood, and we're thinking a certain thought about it, we have projected that thought onto the situation. But if we could see what was really going on, the spiritual aspect . . .

Dr. Hora: Yes, but the eyes cannot see the truth. We cannot see truth with our eyes.

Student: From a spiritual perspective, what exactly is going on with this individual who is chopping wood?

Dr. Hora: Well he seems to be "doing" something. But from a spiritual perspective, he is expressing intelligence, power, usefulness, joy, and harmony. There is a Zen story about two happy monks. Everyone marveled about their joyousness and happiness and asked, "What is your secret?" And the monks answered, "Don't you see how glorious it is? All day long . . . chopping wood and fetching water!" Do we understand it? If activity is not a performance, it is a joy, no matter what it is. The idea of performance makes it a chore.

Student: Getting back to the idea of poverty . . . If we "judged by appearances," many individuals might seem to be poor when they are really not poor, because they are doing what they are doing joyously. Is that possible?

Dr. Hora: They may be economically impoverished, but poverty is not involuntary.

Student: Could you expand on that? It sounds like a Zen koan.

Dr. Hora: Jesus said: "For whosoever hath, to him shall be given, and he shall have more abundance: but whosoever hath not, from him shall be taken away even that he hath" (Matthew

13:12).

Student: You told a story a long time ago about one of our friends who had a coin in her pocket. She knew that every time she took that coin out to spend it, it was going to be replaced, and her financial situation just got better and better. In her consciousness she thought of herself as one who "hath," and that thought was manifested in her daily living.

Dr. Hora: Yes, this is affluence.

Student: Are we talking about physical possessions when we talk about poverty?

Dr. Hora: Any kind of poverty.

Student: When we say involuntary does it mean that it is by choice? I don't understand the words.

Dr. Hora: "Not involuntary"—there is a special meaning in putting it this way. Poverty is not involuntary; sickness is not involuntary.

Student: If something is "not involuntary," doesn't that mean it is voluntary?

Dr. Hora: No. This is unusual language. Suppose that somebody has an accident. We cannot say he wanted to have an accident—that the accident was voluntary. But we can say that this accident was "not involuntary."

Student: We are saying, "Nothing comes into experience uninvited" [Seventh Principle of Metapsychiatry]. I can understand it when we speak about an individual accident, when something in our consciousness has invited it . . .

Dr. Hora: The individual did not invite the accident. Some invalid thought in his consciousness invited it; therefore it is "not involuntary." It is neither voluntary nor involuntary: it is "not involuntary."

Student: Is there such a thing as a mass consciousness, as, for instance, the whole population inviting famine?

Dr. Hora: Yes, it is called "collective consciousness."

Student: "As thou seest so thou beest." Is that what Christ was talking about—the way that we see will then manifest and become the way that we perceive? So if we perceive ourselves as impoverished, then it will be so?

Dr. Hora: Yes, definitely. Poverty is "not involuntary."

Student: "That which I feared the most has come upon me." I am afraid of falling, and sure enough, I fell. Once we fall, is it acted out and over with?

Dr. Hora: As long as the invalid thought is present, there will always be the tendency to fall. Who is it that is falling? Falling is not involuntary. It is neither voluntary nor involuntary—it is "not involuntary."

God Is

Student: Dr. Hora, when we can see that certain ideas about our identity are incorrect and harmful, what allows them to persist? What gives those thoughts their staying power?

Dr. Hora: Could you give us an example?

Student: I clearly see that the way in which I see myself is invalid—it is harmful—and I see how it prevents me from fulfillment and makes life very difficult; and yet this self-identity persists.

Student: I was just thinking that I have exactly the same problem.

Dr. Hora: Could you explain it to us?

Student: I still haven't resolved it. I don't understand the meaning of it, but it seems that we are very loath to give up our ways of seeing ourselves. It is our identity, and we don't like to change it.

Student: Is it simply that we don't clearly see an alternative?

Dr. Hora: No. There is a story about a philosopher at the Chinese court. The emperor was complaining to the philosopher about a problem he had with a certain attachment in his life, and he couldn't get rid of it. The emperor was walking in the garden with the philosopher, and suddenly the philosopher jumped up into a tree, climbed up into the branches and stayed there. The emperor became very annoyed and said, "What are you doing? Come down, and let's go for a walk!" And the philosopher said, "I can't come down. The tree won't let me." What is the lesson in this story?

Student: It seems that invalid thoughts are holding us. But they are not holding onto us—we are holding onto them.

Dr. Hora: What makes it so difficult to let go of these invalid ideas?

Student: Is it because they seem to be our thoughts, and we identify with them?

Dr. Hora: What are we learning from our parents when we grow up? What are they teaching us?

Student: To be a person.

Dr. Hora: That's right. Every child learns a special way to confirm himself, and that is the education that parents give to their children. We get used to confirming ourselves in this manner, and we cherish our particular ways of confirming ourselves.

Student: So even if we see that we are suffering from these invalid ideas, we still get enough of a self-confirmatory charge out of them to keep us holding on.

Dr. Hora: Yes. Recently an Indian delegate to the United Nations was asked, "Why do you wear a diamond in your nose?" And she answered, "Because I don't like rubies." She had learned from childhood on that wearing a diamond stud in the nose is a way to confirm oneself. Who told her to do this? The parents told her that this is what you are, that wearing this stud in your nose gives you your identity! So we begin to cherish our special ways of confirming ourselves. Some parents teach the craziest things to their children, and then the children are stuck with them and cannot change or give them up. Suppose someone said to this Indian lady, "You must not wear this stud in your nose, not even a ruby—nothing at all!" She could get panicky and say, "Then I am nothing. You are taking away my sense of identity as a person." The particular ways that we have learned from our parents to confirm ourselves become our sense of identity, and to give them up would mean to face the possibility of nothingness, of being nobody—and that is frightening.

Student: Aren't most of these thoughts unconscious?

Dr. Hora: So what is the difference?

Student: How do we recognize these thoughts in order to become free of them?

Dr. Hora: We consult a Metapsychiatric teacher, and then we recognize them. If we had asked this Indian delegate, "Why are you wearing this? All right, you don't like rubies, but why are you wearing diamonds in your nose?" She might answer, "It is fashionable; it makes me look good; it's nice."

Student: "Why" is an invalid question.

Dr. Hora: Of course, but people do ask these invalid questions. She doesn't know that it has a self-confirmatory meaning for her. And if she went to various other specialists, none of them would know either. They would accept her rationalization that she is wearing a diamond in her nose because this is the custom in India—it is fashionable. But the real truth is that it is a self-confirmatory idea which gives her a sense of identity, and she wouldn't dare go out

on the street without this stud in her nose, because then she would
feel lost and like a nobody. We all have learned in childhood, from
our parents, a special way of confirming ourselves. Some children
are learning to be brilliant; some children are learning to be stupid; some are learning to be criminals or failures; some children
are even learning to be poor, and they have a fear of giving up
their poverty and putting on better clothes or maybe of earning
more money. Poverty is very important to them—it gives them a
sense of identity. It is even worse than a ring in the nose because
if we have a ring in our nose, we can still enjoy life if we have
money. But what if we are poor or sick? We learn to be sick—it
is not so easy to be sick because God did not teach us this, but
we learn it. It is an idea of self-confirmation in accordance with
parental fantasies. We go through life using that which we have
learned from our parents and assuming this is what we are. It is
very important to us that we live that way.

Student: Do we have to become more aware of the actual thought
as it arises before we are able to turn to God? We might see more
of the manifestation of ignorance than seeing the thought itself.
For example, we might just see financial problems rather than
the thought, "I am poor." Would it be necessary to see the actual
thought before we are able to learn our lesson and turn to the
Second Intelligent Question ["What is what really is?"]?

Dr. Hora: Two things must be seen. First of all, it must be seen
that we are using this idea for self-confirmatory purposes, and
we have to see it with the help of somebody showing it to us. We
can go through life poor—and blame economic or employment
conditions and think, "It is natural that I am poor because my job
doesn't pay me enough money." We can rationalize this and never
really know that poverty is important to us as a badge of identi-
fication. We must wake up from this dream of self-confirmation
through poverty, recognize the source of it and say, "How can
I be so crazy as to confirm myself in this particular way?" We
could see that indeed we learned this at home from someone. We
may already see that this is self-confirmatory and that poverty
has great value for us because it provides a sense of identity. The
Metapsychiatric teacher then brings it to our attention that this is
a mistake. We could say, "If poverty is a mistake for me, then the
solution is to be rich." Will that work? No. What will work? This
problem is very frequent with homosexuals or transvestites. There
are men who have a compulsion to wear women's clothes, and it

is very important for them to do this. When they go into therapy, it is pointed out to them that this is a way of confirming themselves because they have learned this in childhood. They may see it, but they will say, "I cannot wear men's clothes. I know that what I have to do is put on men's clothes instead of women's clothes." But that is not really the solution. What is the solution? The issue is not to do the opposite—the poor girl trying to be rich, the woman with the ring in her nose trying to put something else in her nose. The answer is to recognize that it is not necessary for us to entertain self-confirmatory ideas—we have to lose interest in self-confirmation. How do we lose interest in self-confirmation? It is very simple if we realize that we are not in this world to say, "I am." Everyone is saying, "I am." Someone says it with poverty; someone else says it with riches; someone else says it with rings in the nose; someone else says it with having expensive cars or with femininity or masculinity. Everyone is saying, "I am." The special ways we say "I am," we have learned in childhood from our parents. But, it never occurs to any of us to consider that it is invalid for anyone to say, "I am." What else could we say? In Metapsychiatry, we learn that the important thing is to say, "God is." When we understand this, then we lose interest in saying, "I am," and this is liberation. What happens when we learn to say, "God is," instead of saying, "I am"?

Student: Your voice changes?

Dr. Hora: Whatever was changes. The poor girl will not be interested in poverty; the childish girl will not be interested in childishness; the good girl will not be interested in goodness; and the bad girl will not be interested in badness. All interest will be focused on that which really is—God really Is, and that is all that there is. Once we are willing to say the right affirmation, then we are healed of the childhood conditioning. The way we learn to say "I am" determines our entire individual destiny. All our experiences are determined by the particular way we have learned to say, "I am." Is there a healthy way to say, "I am"? Can our parents teach us how to be healthy? Absolutely not. There is no healthy way anyone can say, "I am."

Student: If personhood is really an illusion, then it is impossible to be a separate person apart from God; and, if we try to live that way, it will be a mess.

Dr. Hora: So there is no way that we can make a self-confirmatory statement and be healthy.

Student: What's really amazing is that I have been wrestling with the same kind of thing, an idea that I seem to be unable to give up. But just seeing that it is self-confirmatory, even without knowing what the alternative is, all of a sudden it was nothing. Self-confirmation is only fun if we think that it is working. Once we know that it is self-confirmation, we know that it is a big show of nothing, and we can't do it anymore.

Dr. Hora: Yes. How does this work in practice? We cannot go around all the time saying, "God is, God is." The final chapter of Beyond the Dream is called "The Prayer of At-one-ment." According to the Bible, Moses climbed up on Mount Sinai and had an encounter with God. God revealed himself to Moses in the burning bush, and then Moses asked, "What is your name?" And he heard God say: "I am that I am." Then Moses came down from the mountain and revealed to the children of Israel that God said, "My name is I am that I am." It is in the Bible like this, and for thousands of years, people have read this and cannot make any sense out of it. What does it mean, "I am that I am"? There are all kinds of theological speculations of what it could mean. Year after year in churches and synagogues, people have tried to make some sense out of this. And Moses, having heard this, assumed that God was talking about himself in some way, and he didn't understand it. But when God said to him, "You must go to negotiate with Pharaoh to release the children of Israel from bondage," he was afraid and said, "I cannot go." Moses balked at the task and used an excuse, "I am slow of speech; I am not very articulate; send somebody else." That was his way of saying, "I am": "I am slow of speech." He was afraid to go. This reveals that he misunderstood what God said to him. When Moses was making excuses, God said to him: "Who made your mouth? You go, and I will be with your mouth." And he went, and indeed he was able to talk. He took his brother along to help him. He saw himself as apart from God. He understood that Moses is here, and God is there on top of the mountain—and there is a separation. For forty years he related himself to God as another, which means he never became enlightened. This is the "meaning" of his not entering the Promised Land. What was the mistake? There is only one conclusion—he "misheard" God. What did God say? It stands to reason that God said: "I am the only I am." If Moses had heard correctly, he would have understood that if God is the only "I AM," then no human being can legitimately make the statement,

"I am." There is no such thing. If God is the only "I AM," then
there is no one in the entire universe who is entitled to say, "I am."
The right understanding of this can help us to practice the Prayer
of At-one-ment, because then we cannot say, "I am." We can say,
"God is the only I AM. My 'I am' is not 'I' who 'am'; my 'I am'
is God." In that moment we realize at-one-ment—we do not exist
apart from God. We are an inseparable, integral aspect of God,
which is the only "I AM." Moses did not make it to the Promised
Land. This has a meaning, and now we can understand that he
made a mistake. And if we understand the mistake, we have the
great blessing of understanding at-one-ment. Now what are the
consequences of learning the Prayer of At-one-ment? What are
the practical consequences of understanding that God is the only
"I AM"? Does this have practical, healing consequences?

Student: It can heal whatever self-confirmatory problem we are
dealing with.

Dr. Hora: How will this healing come about?

Student: We would be able to let go of our personal identities and
of the self-confirmatory thoughts which manifest as our problems.

Student: We would be free.

Dr. Hora: In practice we have outlined the practical approach to
"I-am-lessness." What is "I-am-lessness," and how do we practice
it? We do not speak about ourselves, and we do not speak about
others, and we start glowing for God. The "I-AM-ness" of God
becomes manifest through every individual who understands this.

Student: Do we talk about information?

Dr. Hora: We just respond to issues. And who is it that is responding to issues? Love-Intelligence—it is nonpersonal.

Student: I usually think of self-confirmation in terms of wanting
to stand out in some way or to be different. For example, parents
want their children not to be like everyone else. Of course, for me
it takes the form of a certain kind of defiance, but here it seems
that even conformity—wanting to be like everyone else— is a
form of self-confirmation.

Dr. Hora: Yes, and self-effacement is also self-confirmatory.

Student: If an Indian woman puts a jewel in her nose in an effort
to be like all the other Indian women, she is being self-confirmatory. But when we get up in the morning, and we simply wear
what is acceptable clothing or fix our hair a simple way, is all of it
going to be self-confirmatory? Or is it only if we take an interest
in it, of a particular kind, that it becomes self-confirmatory? When

is it not self-confirmatory?

Dr. Hora: The only non-self-confirmatory expression any individual is capable of is glowing. Besides that, everything else is self-confirmatory—conformity is self-confirmatory, and nonconformity is also self-confirmatory. Only glowing is not self-confirmatory, because it is God-confirmatory.

Student: When we choose the kind of clothes we are going to wear, is that self-confirmatory?

Dr. Hora: Of course.

Student: Inevitably and always?

Dr. Hora: Unavoidably. What is the difference between inevitably and unavoidably? Who is a linguist here?

Student: Unavoidably refers to our human nature and means that we are not going to avoid something, but inevitably means that there would be no possibility of our avoiding it. And it isn't really inevitable, because we could glow.

Dr. Hora: Yes. Unavoidably describes something that we do not want to avoid; inevitably describes something that might happen to us without reflecting on it. If we stumble on the street, it is inevitable—it is an "accident," so to speak—but it is not unavoidable, because if we were more alert, we could have avoided it. There is a subtle, semantic difference between these expressions. The enlightened mode of being-in-the-world is completely God-confirmatory—this is the essence of the enlightened mode of being-in-the-world.

Student: When we are talking about issues, are we talking about self-confirmation?

Dr. Hora: Self-confirmation can be an issue for clarification. It serves God because it helps people to discover the Allness of God, to realize that nothing else can be said but "God Is." That is an all-encompassing statement of truth.

Student: What is the meaning of the statement made earlier that it never occurs to us to ask if something is self-confirmatory?

Dr. Hora: It might reveal a "meaning," rather than just a cause.

Student: What is the meaning of our not ever asking that?

Dr. Hora: We prefer to "not know." Suppose someone has a habit of promoting himself—he will never ask, "What is the meaning of my self-promoting habit?" He would rather not know; it is very important to him.

Student: To ask the question means that we are thinking about giving it up.

Dr. Hora: Yes, we are already questioning the validity of it, but that doesn't come spontaneously—it requires some guidance. Most people are bragging their heads off, and they never realize that there is something wrong with it.

Student: Before we can even ask the question, we have to know that we are bragging.

Student: If five years ago someone had told me that a troublesome car was about boasting, I would not have understood. We need a guide even to suggest that it might be the case.

Dr. Hora: There is positive boasting, and there is negative boasting. Some people are boasting with what they have, and some are boasting with what they do not have—and it is the same.

Student: If we see that a problem keeps coming up—and we see that this is another invalid thought taking form—how can we avoid operationalism?

Dr. Hora: What is the meaning of operationalism?

Student: Fixing the problem.

Dr. Hora: No, that is the effect of operationalism. The meaning of operationalism is, "I can do it," which is another "I am" statement.

Student: What is the "it" that I can do in this statement?

Dr. Hora: "I can do it; I can fix the car." We can try to do it this way or that way, but the idea is that "I" can do it. No one can fix anything. Intelligence can, but Intelligence is God. Intelligence can fix the car. Without Intelligence, the car will never get fixed.

Student: When we think we are doing it, we think we are very powerful people, and the more powerful we think we are, the less we acknowledge God. We like to think that we are "doing" it.

Dr. Hora: Yes, we are interfering with Intelligence, taking over the situation, So, we don't say, "I am." We say, "Love-Intelligence Is." Love-Intelligence is the Metapsychiatric name for God.

Dialogue No. 13

Epistemology

Student: Dr. Hora, I keep forgetting what the word epistemological means. Does it identify the difference between philosophy, religion, and Metapsychiatry? Is that why I keep forgetting?

Dr. Hora: We do not ask why, right? The meaning is that it is a difficult word, and not many people really know what it means—but it is good to know. What does the word epistemology mean?

Student: The study of knowing.

Dr. Hora: The science of knowing. In our education, we are only being taught the knowledge of science, but in Metapsychiatry we are interested in the science of knowledge, and that is a remarkable thing. Epistemology is the science of knowledge. What do we really know?—and what do we just seem to know? And how can we know what is possible to know? Without realizing it, teenagers and hippies are involved a great deal with epistemological problems. What is the evidence of that? They keep saying, "You know, you know," and they don't know! It is a very interesting phenomenon. Miseducated or uneducated individuals keep saying, "You know." Apparently they are aware of a problem with knowing, because they realize how little they really know. It really means, "I would like you to know that I know."

Student: Doesn't it also concern the issue of assurance? If there is doubt that we know, then we are looking for someone to confirm that what we say is so.

Dr. Hora: Yes, and it is very sad too. Metapsychiatry is really the only system of study I know of where the science of knowledge is of primary interest. We are always wondering whether we really know what we seem to know. And then the question is, How could we really know? Most of the time, we just know about things.

Student: How is spiritual seeking to understand God different from knowing how to bake a cake or from some other skill—like learning how to play the piano? We have to learn things all the time how to do things—how to speak a language, for instance—

but when it comes to understanding a spiritual truth, it seems very different.

Dr. Hora: Yes. Real knowing is existential. If we know how to bake a cake or how to play the piano, it isn't going to heal us of our headaches—it may just give us one. This is not existential knowledge; it is operational knowledge, technical knowledge—it is information. But to know God is existential knowledge, which means it affects our existence. The quality of our life is altered to the extent that we really know God.

Student: That faculty must be in everyone because we are all "living souls."

Dr. Hora: Of course. But apart from Metapsychiatry, not many understand the difference between knowledge as information and knowledge as transformation. We go to church and are taught to believe in Jesus Christ, that he died for us, shed his blood, and we are washed clean. We say, "Yes, I believe; I accept." But that does not mean that we know. Believing, agreeing, disagreeing, accepting, rejecting—this is not knowledge. What is it? It is just self-deception. Now Jesus knew the difference. He said: "Ye shall know the truth, and the truth shall make you free" (John 8:32). The true knowledge of the truth will make us free, which means it will heal us; it will lift us out of the dream of interaction thinking and will transform us into a spiritualized consciousness, which is our true identity. Only existential knowledge is true knowledge—everything else is fake, and epistemology illuminates the difference. If we are facing a problem in life and we seek healing, then we seek to know something existentially, because only the existential knowledge can heal—information cannot heal. Knowing how to bake a cake will not heal any illness, and knowing about God is not going to heal us. Only the real knowledge which Jesus spoke of will. He knew that knowing the truth means true knowledge. If we have true knowledge, that will heal us. If we seek healing, we are really praying, meditating, and studying in the hope that we will catch a glimpse of true knowledge, because the knowledge of the truth is that true knowledge which heals. It is very rare and hard to come by. In Metapsychiatry we have been blessed by certain concepts which make it possible to know. For instance, the process of "cognitive dialectics" makes it possible to reach true knowledge by juxtaposition to error—the Two Intelligent Questions are designed to make it possible to come to know what we really need to know in order to be healed. This true knowledge can come about only in the process of juxtaposition. The cognitive dialectic system is an epistemological principle that makes the attainment of true knowledge possible. So we are quite a unique system of study.

Student: I'm wondering if it is really possible to present this in a scientific way. I read a book recently by a modern physicist who is looking for enlightenment. He wrote about the criterion of knowledge and how we know that something is true. He set forth some conditions—that this knowledge has to be life-enhancing and lead to well-being and so forth. And the way he expressed it, it sounded like our Principle of Existential Validation. But then, when he gave examples of it, he wrote about people who reported mystical experiences of sudden ecstasy and being dazzled by the light. But these examples sounded like emotionalism.

Dr. Hora: He is talking about experiences. A student of Metapsychiatry was scheduled to undergo cancer surgery. Over the weekend, she went into the hospital. She was put to sleep, and the surgeon opened her up and found nothing—because, while waiting to get on with the operation, she was healed through the right knowledge. This is proof positive that when right-knowing is realized, a healing happens. This is a beautiful illustration of what we are talking about. Many individuals are searching in this direction—all the various spiritual schools—but they do not know three things: they do not know phenomenology; they do not know the cognitive dialectic process; and they do not know the difference between experiencing and realizing. If we do not know these three things, then we are just floundering. Practically all spiritual systems and schools speak about religious experiences and try to find the truth in an experience—having visions and ecstasy. But experiences are dreams, and we cannot find reality in a dream, so we get stuck at the point of trying to validate the truth as an experience.

Student: One of the things that seems helpful is understanding that true knowledge is knowledge that is everlasting. If you know how to bake a cake or be a good craftsman, those things might pass when this body passes, but true knowledge would never pass—one would have it for eternity.

Dr. Hora: Yes. Knowledge is unalterable, indestructible, immortal, eternal, and immutable. Truth and Reality are defined as that which is immutable—everything else is mutable. Truth and Reality are immutable, so this is one criterion for coming to know Reality. For practical purposes on the human level, the right knowledge immediately validates itself as healing. That is why Jesus healed people. He wasn't going into medical practice, but by healing people, he was demonstrating the Truth of God. That way even the most primitive, uneducated individual could catch a glimpse of God. Of course, the individual may have remained superstitious or thought that these are miracles or hocus-pocus. Jesus may have seemed like a magician to many individuals, because the healing was like magic. And here is this student of Metapsychiatry, diagnosed by medical authorities as having cancer of the breast, scheduled for an operation, and they find nothing. The whole thing vanished into thin air. This is proof positive of the validity of right-knowing; without right-knowing, this would not be possible.

Student: In that situation it seems very helpful to understand that "the physical is mental"—then the process of juxtaposition can take place.

Student: When we say that the tumor or cancer disappeared, are we saying that it was never there?

Dr. Hora: Sure. It was a dream, an interaction thought.

Student: Are we actually saying that it was never there, that it was a thought and had no material substance?

Dr. Hora: Yes. This student of Metapsychiatry was not only healed of the cancer but was also healed of the meaning of this cancer, which was lesbianism. So not only was she healed of that clinical evidence, but we discovered the meaning of it before she went to the operation. She was a practicing lesbian, and she saw that this kind of interaction thinking was the essential substance of that cancer—and she was healed of that too.

Student: But wouldn't that have had to occur for the other to occur? She couldn't have been healed of the cancer unless she saw the nature of the interaction thought.

Dr. Hora: That's right. It is a beautiful healing, a beautiful transformation of her entire mode of being-in-the-world.

Student: And the whole interest in lesbianism just disappeared?

Dr. Hora: Yes. She could see the folly and understood that lesbianism is just a form of interaction. Interaction thinking was the problem.

Student: Can healing of a symptom occur without the healing of one's mode of being-in-the-world?

Dr. Hora: No, it requires a radical transformation. Once you

catch a glimpse of the truth-of-being, your mode of being-in-the
-world is transformed.

Student: That is the real focus of the healing.

Dr. Hora: Right. So we did not work to make the cancer disappear; we worked on helping her to lose interest in interaction
thinking. That is what constitutes a healing.

Student: That is the difference between the Metapsychiatric
approach and certain kinds of religious practitioners who would
focus on the symptom.

Dr. Hora: Right. We focus on the meaning of the symptom, not
on the clinical appearance.

Student: But to her, wasn't that an "experience," the fact that
she woke up and was healed?

Dr. Hora: It was a "realization" that interaction thinking is invalid and harmful and isolates people from God. Whenever we
are involved in interaction thinking, we have separated ourselves
from God, which is a dangerous condition to be in.

Student: Is there a difference between interaction thinking and
self-confirmatory ideation, or are they just two sides of the same
thing?

Dr. Hora: They are intertwined. Certainly when we think about
interaction, we think about self in relation to another. There is also
the narcissistic form of thinking, where the other is not visible
but the self is being constantly affirmed—and that is pure self-
confirmatory ideation. But the two really belong together.

Student: But that is also a form of interaction because you want
others to admire you.

Dr. Hora: In a way, that is right, sure. When we are bragging
and talking about ourselves, we want others to know how wonderful we are—"I want you to know how much I know." Right? That
is very frequent.

Student: So it is really hard to conceive of one without the other.

Dr. Hora: Yes. But whenever it happens, there is a separation
of man from God, and that is the problem. When we talk about
ourselves and when we talk about others, God is not in the picture.

Student: What is the purest motivation to know the truth? Is
there a purer motivation than to seek healing and liberation?

Dr. Hora: Yes. When we seek a healing, we are driven. When
we have been healed and have caught a glimpse of the glory of
enlightenment, then we are drawn. When we are drawn, when
we have discovered PAGL [PAGL is an acronym for Peace,

Assurance, Gratitude, Love, and Its Presence in consciousness informs us that we are in tune with the One Mind] as the supreme good of life, then our motivation becomes very pure.

Student: Just to love understanding?

Dr. Hora: Yes—being "here for God," not as a religious duty but as a supreme privilege—then the motivation is pure.

Student: It usually starts with being driven?

Dr. Hora: Yes, most of us are driven initially. If someone believes that enlightenment will come as an "experience," he will never become enlightened. And most books that deal with this issue speak about religious and spiritual experiences, without realizing that this is a contradiction. Epistemology places great importance on the right terms and concepts, on correct semantics. Semantics is the study of words—using the right words to communicate the right ideas.

Student: When we understand something existentially, are we always able to talk about it? Does it necessarily mean that we are able to communicate something about it and explain it to somebody?

Dr. Hora: Only if sincerely solicited—otherwise we are unable to talk.

Student: But then would one be able to say something?

Dr. Hora: Only if sincerely solicited, right?

Student: I see. Is it also the case that someone may be able to talk about something when, in fact, there is not complete understanding?

Dr. Hora: Sure, that's not rare. "Who is this that darkeneth counsel with words without knowledge?" (Job 38:2). I always liked this saying—spreading darkness "with words without knowledge." "Understanding is a wellspring of life unto him that hath it: but the instruction of fools is folly" (Proverbs 16:22).

Student: There can be communication without interaction.

Dr. Hora: Certainly, that is the real communication—it is called dialogue. In dialogue we are communicating without interaction. What makes dialogue different from all other forms of communication?

Student: Whoever is involved will be focusing on what the truth is.

Dr. Hora: That's right—and not on each other—and that is very rare.

Student: When we say that the truth communicates itself existentially, does that mean it is beyond words? We can have a dialogue, and the motivation can be love; but then there can be another aspect to it, where the truth is being communicated without words. Is that the way realization happens, when the communication is from God to us?

Dr. Hora: In every realization, it is God who enters into consciousness through an inspired idea. We cannot produce understanding or true knowledge—we can just be receptive to it—and when we reach a certain level of receptivity, it happens.

Student: Sometimes people can be glowing with pride. It reminds me of television programs where people talk about different ideas and are very charming, charismatic, but they are very focused on interaction thinking.

Dr. Hora: Yes, that is a very good way to distinguish what is dialogue and what is not. People on television do not communicate in a dialogic fashion. They are usually trying to influence public opinion in one way or another, by making themselves attractive, by making impressions or by being emphatic about things. On television we rarely see someone who is purely communicating ideas, which is very pleasant to listen to. Most of the time someone is either selling himself or herself or something else—the motivation is rarely pure.

Student: So are we aware of an abrasive influence?

Dr. Hora: If someone is abrasive, he is trying to influence people.

Student: They have learned that technique.

Dr. Hora: Yes, the technique of "how to win friends and influence people." A few years ago individuals were not aware of the invalidity of this title. It was accepted and spread like wildfire. No one noticed that every word in that title is invalid and an outrage.

Student: That is what made it so attractive.

Dr. Hora: Individuals were very ignorant in those years, psychologically unsophisticated. I don't think any one could get away with such a title today.

Student: We have worse books now.

Dr. Hora: Oh, yes, but that book was notorious, and it sold millions of copies.

Student: What is charisma?

Dr. Hora: An appeal, a certain kind of psychological appeal, which some people exude which attracts other people to them. A charismatic speaker, leader, or politician is someone who can elicit interest and attracts people's attention to himself.

Student: What is it that makes an individual that way?

Dr. Hora: Hitler had tremendous charisma. There are people who have this faculty of influencing others to agree with them or to become enthusiastic about their ideas or their personalities, and they exploit it.

Student: It sounds as though interest and attraction combine into interaction.

Dr. Hora: Yes, definitely. Jesus was not a charismatic leader—nobody fell in love with Jesus. He did not create a mass movement; he communicated existentially valid ideas, and most people were not interested.

Student: He was unable to heal the unreceptive.

Dr. Hora: Right. He did not use charismatic techniques.

Student: Dr. Hora, in Beyond the Dream there is a statement that puzzles me—it seems to be saying that the term "self-confirmatory ideation" has not been discovered, that it is not understood by psychology or other disciplines which might be genuinely seeking enlightenment, because of their unwillingness to acknowledge forthrightly the existence of God. Does this have something to do with epistemology?

Dr. Hora: No, that is not what is written there. What is written is that self-confirmatory ideation is not an elegant term. It is a little clumsy, but it is very important to come to appreciate it. If we say ego instead of self-confirmatory ideation, it becomes a cliché and belongs to psychology. This particular term, even though it is clumsy, has great value in terms of understanding a universal problem of mankind. It is worth contemplating it and perhaps seeing that it has value.

Student: Does it point to God?

Dr. Hora: No, it points to a universal problem of man in general. It is a universal inclination of unenlightened man to confirm himself as real, because he doubts it. We are all doubting the reality of our existence; we suspect that we are not really here. And to relieve this anxiety, we resort to self-confirmatory ideation.

Student: You are referring again to the appearance, that we suspect that this appearance has no reality?

Dr. Hora: Yes, and that drives us to keep confirming ourselves, if not in words, then in thoughts.

Student: Is that from our fear of death?

Dr. Hora: No, it has nothing to do with death—it has to do with the fear that maybe we are not what we seem to be, that we are not physical persons. Everybody suspects it, whether he knows it or not.

Student: It is difficult for me to understand that we all suspect that we are not real.

Dr. Hora: Well, the very fact that there is a compulsion to pro¬mote ourselves proves that we are afraid that we would turn into nothing unless we promoted ourselves. We think that no one would notice us, and we would disappear. There is this fear in everyone—it is called "existential dread"—the fear of nonbeing.

Student: And it is universal?

Dr. Hora: It is universal.

Student: When we are working in an important position, we feel very important, as if we are somebody. When we aren't working anymore, suddenly we feel like a nobody and get very upset and worried and try to confirm ourselves in many different ways. People who retire go through that.

Dr. Hora: And go to a bar, and get drunk, and start bragging, and get someone to beat us up—and then we really feel like we are somebody! Isn't it ridiculous?

Student: The whole world is ridiculous.

Dr. Hora: That is called "the human mockery."

Student: Realization seems to have something to do with a receptivity to knowing that we are nothing. Doesn't there have to be a willingness to know that?

Dr. Hora: No, we just have to understand the meaning of the tendency toward self-confirmation and then discover who we really are, because it isn't true that we are nothing. We are neither nothing nor something—we are nondimensional entities of Love-Intelligence. And who wants that? You couldn't sell it!

Student: We can't confirm an awareness; there is no confirmation about it.

Dr. Hora: Yes we can, because we are aware that we are aware.

Student: And that confirms it? Is that self-confirmatory?

Dr. Hora: That is God-confirmatory, because God is infinite Awareness, and we are individualized entities of this infinite Awareness. And we have the gift of being aware of being aware.

Student: That is how we learn probably, because if we couldn't be aware of it, then we couldn't "confirm" it as real. So that confirmation is good.

Dr. Hora: Yes, it is built-in: awareness is aware of being aware.

Student: It seems that this has to do with existential validation—when we really know something, then we know that we know.

Dr. Hora: Yes, and if we don't know it, we just believe that we know it—coming back to epistemology.

Student: What does entity mean? Substance?

Dr. Hora: Spiritual substance. Every individual being throughout the universe is an aspect of one, infinite Consciousness called God, and everyone is unique and therefore an entity within itself. Every snowflake is different from every other snowflake, and every raindrop is different from every other raindrop; every leaf on a maple tree, where there are ten million leaves, is different from every other leaf. How many maple trees are there in the world, and how many leaves are on these maple trees? Every one is an entity in itself—unique. So if someone says, "You are a nonentity," don't believe him.

Student: It seems that there are many people who say to themselves, "If God exists, then I do not; therefore I do not want God to exist."

Dr. Hora: That's right. Here again, it is important to have the right understanding of God. If we have a mistaken notion, we can run into all kinds of anxieties and confusing, theological speculations which do not heal. The Bible says: "For my people have committed two evils; they have forsaken me the fountain of living waters, and hewed them out cisterns, broken cisterns, that can hold no water" (Jeremiah 2:13). Isn't that interesting? What does that mean?

Student: The people made systems for knowing which have nothing in them—no knowledge.

Dr. Hora: Not valid—they are useless. A cistern that holds no water is useless, and it takes a lot of work to hew out a cistern from a rock. Theology, psychology, and philosophy are studied a great deal, and it is for naught because they do not understand "what really is"; it cannot validate itself and therefore remains a belief. And beliefs are intolerant of other beliefs; so there is always strife among believers. The world is in a mess because of beliefs. Beware of believers.

Student: So intolerance exists because with every belief there is always the suspicion that it might not be true—there is doubt.

Dr. Hora: That's right, and people feel threatened by other kinds of beliefs which they do not believe. This is why there is anti-Semitism—the Shiite Muslims hate the Sunni Muslims, and the

Orthodox Jews hate the Reformed Jews, and the Catholics hate the Protestants. Wherever there is intolerance and strife, we can be sure that people are suffering from beliefs.

Student: There seems to be a connection between the words "belief" and "attachment": we become attached to what we believe in and believe our belief is the best.

Dr. Hora: We feel threatened by other beliefs. Only knowledge can give assurance. If we really know something, we are not intolerant of anyone. Nothing threatens us, because we cannot be shaken. Belief systems do not constitute a threat to those who have the right understanding; but if we are just believers, we feel threatened.

Dialogue No. 14

The Right Orientation

Student: Dr. Hora, this is not necessarily a topic for discussion, but I wanted to thank the group for the help I was given with my problem two weeks ago, when I talked about having been served with a subpoena. I was very worried about it, and I felt much better after the group discussion. When I went down to the court the next day and spoke with the judge, as soon as I said I was an ordained clergy and a pastoral counselor, she said, "Well, of course, you can't release any information without signature." Later she said, "Just go home. Leave your number with us, and we will get in touch with you." They haven't called, so I assume it is all over.

Dr. Hora: We had nothing to do with it.

Student: Divine Mind?

Dr. Hora: Of course, that's what it is, and it is important to know that. "All things were made by him, and without him nothing was made that seems to be made" (John 1:3). So let's give credit where credit is due, or else we might be in danger of pride; and "pride goeth before a fall," and we don't want to fall.

Student: I would like to make a comment. I acknowledge that we do not have personal power, but sometimes, just out of a sense of gratitude to the members of the group, it is nice to make a statement like that, because so many times I have been helped by stories or comments that I have heard here. I did not know at the time how to anticipate in the future just how they would help me. Members of the group have said things, just at the moment when I needed it, and I am very grateful for that. So it is God's wisdom and creative intelligence coming through the members.

Dr. Hora: That reminds me of something. We are very grateful to God, and we are interested in God's ways of working. I received a little printout, and you might be interested in this—it is all about God. God is like Coca-Cola—He's the real thing.

God is like Pan Am—He makes the going great.

God is like General Electric—He lights your path.

116

God is like Bayer Aspirin—He works wonders.

God is like Hallmark Cards—He cares enough to send the very best.

God is like Tide—He gets the stain out that others have left behind.

God is like VO5 Hairspray—He holds through all kinds of weather.

God is like Dial Soap—Aren't you glad you know him? Don't you wish everybody did?

God is like Sears—He has everything.

God is like Alka Seltzer—Try Him; you'll like Him.

God is like Scotch Tape—You can't see Him, but you know He's there.

Now you've learned about God, and some people think that there is no God! "When two or more gather in my name I shall be among them" (Matthew 18:20). In this group, we do not really look to each other for help. This is not like any other group where people learn to help each other. We are not helping each other. We are seekers endeavoring to see the presence of God, and in this seeing is the redemptive power that heals our problems. So let us not have the mistaken idea that we are cultivating relationships with each other, and that because we are such nice people we help each other and we benefit from the interchange between one person and another person. I don't know if there is such a group anywhere else in the world, but there are no persons here—there is only the emerging visibility of the Presence, or the Invisible. St. Paul said: "We look not upon the things that are seen, but upon the things that are not seen" (2 Corinthians 4:18). So it is this invisible "Scotch Tape"—you can't see Him, but He is here. God is here. In order for God to become more visible, it is necessary to gather in his name. When two or three or more "gather in my name . . ." What does it mean, "in my name"?

Student: As sincere seekers.

Dr. Hora: We have the same interest: we seek to behold the reality, the power, and the presence of God. In this sincere motivation, this sincere desire to see God's presence, therein lies the beneficial effect in these situations. So while we all love being loving, we don't really look to each other for help. Human persons cannot help; nobody can. But the discernment of the presence of God solves everything, heals everything, inspires wisdom and joy, and that is the main thing. Ordinarily people lean on each other for everything. We only lean on the sustaining infinite Mind. God is infinite Mind, and whatever is needed can be received from this sustaining power, which is infinite Love-Intelligence. In a group like this, the visibility of God is increased somewhat because nobody gets away with anything. Nobody can indulge himself in interaction thinking or in self-confirmatory ideation, so the world is really overcome. In order for God to become visible, the world has to be transcended.

Student: Other groups are correctly named when they are called "support groups."

Dr. Hora: Yes, they support each other.

Student: The challenge seems to be being able to turn to God when we are not desperate. For me, it seems that I turn to God last after trying to do everything I can for myself, after trying to figure out what to do.

Dr. Hora: For some people, it is good to be desperate all the time. It results in ceaseless prayer, and ceaseless prayer will get you enlightened—you will see the light. It is very easy to be desperate; life offers us these opportunities every step of the way. "Problems are lessons designed for our edification" [Eighth Principle of Metapsychiatry]. If we are sincerely interested in learning and improving our spiritual faculties of discernment, then we are on the right path.

Student: What is it when it seems as though two mental tracks are operating? I can clearly see which are my ideas—which are usually really stupid—and which are God-inspired ideas.

Dr. Hora: You can see that?

Student: Very often.

Dr. Hora: That's good.

Student: For instance, it seemed like a good idea to take a trip this summer. I looked through all these brochures, and I knew I was going to make a decision. I also knew that whatever decision I made, it was not going to work out, because I knew it was going to be something that I was choosing.

Dr. Hora: Right.

Student: I knew that the motivation was incorrect. Then this other brochure came—it was someplace that I never would have chosen, but it seemed right. And it worked out right in terms of some other things that I had to do this summer; the dates worked out, and it seemed that it was an inspired idea. And I knew if I went by one of my own ideas, I just knew from past experience, that everything would have been really terrible. So it is like two tracks are operating at the same time.

Dr. Hora: Yes. It is a very good idea before we even consider something—a trip or activity or a task—to become very quiet and sincerely proclaim: "I can of mine own self do nothing . . . but the Father that dwelleth in me, He doeth the works" (John 5:30; 14:10). Then you can go on—the right ideas will come, the right opportunities will open up, and you will be peaceful. There will be no anxiety about the next step. That is a good way to live and move and swim in the ocean of Love-Intelligence.

Student: Dr. Hora, did you say it is easy to be desperate because it is so self-confirmatory?

Dr. Hora: Yes. Life offers us many opportunities for despair—especially if we are interactive and self-confirmatory—all the time—crisis after crisis, problem after problem.

Student: I have been desperate for a few weeks at my place of employment, and I see the interaction and self-confirmation. You have told me just to drop the mode of being-in-the-world, of "knowing" and "not knowing," but I find that I can't. I am influenced by the interaction; and I see the self-confirmation and the temptation, and it just continues. And yet perhaps the desperation is what will help to break that, to drop it, but, I am unable to. Do you have any suggestions?

Dr. Hora: Yes. Do you remember Nasrudin? There is an extremely instructive story relevant to "knowing" and "not knowing." Nasrudin was invited to give a lecture at a conference, and he consented. He got up and said, "Highly honored guests, dear friends, do you know what I am going to talk about?" And they said, "Yes, we know, we know." He answered, "Well, if you know, then I don't have to be here," and he turned around and left. The people were very surprised. The next day they brought him back and asked him again to give his talk. So he started all over again saying, "Do you know what I am going to talk about?" This time the audience had wised up and they said, "No! We don't know." So Nasrudin said, "If you don't know, then what's the use of talking?" And he turned around and left. They were puzzled, and they called him back a third time. And he came and said, "Dear audience, do you know what I am going to talk about?" Some of them said yes, and some of them said no. Nasrudin looked around and said, "Well, if some of you know, and others don't know, then let those who know talk to those who don't know," and he left.

Nobody understood what was going on. What was the purpose? Was he mocking these people? What do you think he was trying to do?

Student: To get beyond "knowing" and "not knowing"?

Dr. Hora: Exactly. He tried to awaken the audience to the realization that we do not come to a conference to "know" or to "not know." The basic, valid idea about a conference is learning and expanding our understanding of whatever subject the conference is all about. If we go to a lecture or a group and we think, "I wonder whether I know what he is going to talk about," or "I wonder whether I will be uncomfortable if I find that I don't know anything," this is no way to attend a conference—these are invalid issues. If we cherish these ideas, then our mode of being in-the-world is invalid and we are not getting anywhere. Anyone who is concerned about "knowing" or "not knowing" is not learning anything—it is impossible because his attention is derailed; he is not on track. In order to be on track for progress, we have to be sincere seekers, interested in understanding the truth. Only a sincere seeker will benefit from attending a conference, or a group session, or a private session, or even from reading a book. You have no idea how many people read Beyond the Dream and get nothing out of it, absolutely nothing. They don't read the book; they read their own thoughts into the book. Learning is not possible unless there is a sincere desire to understand something. There are many people who are extremely grateful for Metapsychiatry's books, but there are many who can't understand what's the big deal about them and say, "I knew it all the time; there is nothing new there." Or "It's off the wall!" Some people think they know it, and some people think they don't know it. If we are caught up on the horns of this duality, then there is stagnation. That is what Nasrudin was trying to explain. It was beautiful. One could ask, "Why didn't he come straight out and say that?" What would have happened if Nasrudin had gotten up and said, "The purpose of this conference is for everybody to pay attention and to learn something so that they will understand." What would have happened?

Student: They would have fallen asleep.

Dr. Hora: It would have been ineffective. Do you see the logic and the rationale of the Zen Masters' "trickiness" with the koan system and the mondo system? Seemingly illogical statements are made, and people get frustrated. Jesus used parables. And when his disciples asked him why he spoke to the majority of people

in parables, he said that it was not given to them to understand
but that it has been given to you disciples to understand straight
talk. For the disciples were already motivated to receive understanding, and the vast majority of people were not interested in
understanding. They were wondering, "Who is this guy, and why
does he have a red beard, and where did he come from, and where
is he going?" All these other interests closed their minds. It would
have been futile for Jesus to talk to them in a "straight way." He
had to challenge their intellectual capacities, to create situations
where they would want to rack their brains in order to change
their approach and realize that something was needed other than
just knowing and not knowing. In clinics such as the one you work
in, most people are just interested in showing what they know and
showing what others do not know.

Student: That reminds me that in school during a lesson, there
are kids who raise their hands and answer before they have heard
the question.

Dr. Hora: What do they want?

Student: They want to show how smart they are.

Dr. Hora: Right. They want recognition for their smartness

Student: When you spoke earlier of being derailed, did you
mean losing our focus?

Dr. Hora: Right, it suddenly came to you. Yes, we are out of
focus if we have an invalid idea about what is needed, and nothing
makes any sense at all. In chapter 24 of Beyond the Dream, titled
"The Bureaucrat and the Therapist," I describe how different the
focus is between the woman who comes to the agency seeking help
for herself and her child and the bureaucratic social worker who is
seeking career advancement for herself. The two try to communicate, but they do not get anywhere. The bureaucrat is preoccupied
with career advancement, so people who turn to this individual for
effective support are not helped. The whole Communist system
in Russia has broken down on this very basis—everybody has a
different concern, and effective communication is not possible.
Do you know the story of the Tower of Babel? [Genesis 11: 1-9]
The people got an idea to build a big tower to put God out of
business; they used different expressions, and the whole thing was
a big flop. It started out like a joint venture, but pretty soon there
was confusion and no possibility of communicating with one another. And that is happening in institutions more than in private
life. In psychotherapeutic and social agencies and in schools, it is

very prevalent; frustrations are great, and anxieties are mounting. People are increasingly anxious, and they try to dominate each other to alleviate the anxiety, and problems are mounting. On the other hand, if everyone would understand that "everything and everyone is here for God," there would be harmonious coexistence and effective work processes and success. This happens occasionally—especially in the beginning. In an organization, group, or agency that is starting out, if there is at least one leader who has a certain constructive concept, it starts out in a very promising way. But pretty soon warfare breaks out, and people start coming late and leaving early; they take sick days, and they go play squash. Everything falls apart. This is the human condition. Now the Bible says that God confounded the builders of the tower—they could not understand each other. One asked for a hammer, and he got something else. They could not work together because they did not understand each other and misinterpreted what was being said. It is the story of the human race. So, "knowing" and "not knowing" is not the question, and it is not the answer either.

Student: Dr. Hora, if our understanding is really expanded, does it ever shrink back to where it was? Do we go forward and backward?

Dr. Hora: Understanding is not a rubber band. True understanding is of God, and if we have understood something in truth, then we have been transformed. Our consciousness has expanded with wisdom and love, and it will not snap back. You will have become a "new man." The Bible says: "If any man is in Christ, he is a new creature: old things are passed away; and, behold, all things are become new" (2 Corinthians 5:17). Every time you really understand something of divine Reality as it pertains to the human condition, you are a "new man"; you are not a rubber band. The rubber-band syndrome happens if we lie to ourselves. Some knowers will say, "I understand." But it is a lie. They do not understand. We like to deceive ourselves—often. There has to be real understanding, which has a transforming effect on our consciousness and consequently on our perspective on life; and, with it, our mode of being-in-the-world changes. This is real understanding, not phony understanding. We have to be very careful not to say, "I understand," if we don't really understand.

Student: But if you think you understand, let's say intellectually, you wouldn't keep coming here to class sessions unless there was something that you were attracted to that seemed valid. So it seems that there is a lot that we know or know of, but to make the transition from knowing intellectually sounds very good. What finally brings about a change from an intellectual knowing to a realization?

Dr. Hora: Do you understand this question?

Student: How do you get past "knowing" and "not knowing"?

Dr. Hora: That's right; there is communication. How to get past "knowing" and "not knowing"? What would Nasrudin say?

Student: For me, the meaning of the Nasrudin story was being interested.

Dr. Hora: Suppose that you're interested in "knowing" and "not knowing."

Student: I think I heard that unless you are a sincere seeker of the truth, you cannot hear the truth.

Dr. Hora: Of course, you heard right. You cannot just say that you have to be interested—you have to be interested in the valid issues. "Knowing" and "not knowing" are not valid issues.

Student: I can see that when I first read a book, I am looking for what is going to make me feel good. Then, when I am finally able to read, to seek wisdom or to seek the truth, it is as if I am reading another book entirely—it is all different.

Dr. Hora: Yes, how many times have people said, "I have read your book for the past twenty years, and, suddenly, I opened it up in the middle of the night—a certain chapter stood out—and it was as if I'd never read that chapter before.

Student: Because finally you are sincerely searching for the truth . . .

Dr. Hora: Interested to understand something. When we speak of interest, we have to speak of what it is that we are really interested in. It is not enough just to say that we are interested.

Student: That must relate also to the idea of letting your false interests go.

Dr. Hora: The first step is to recognize that you have a hang-up on something that is blocking your progress. When we have a hang-up on something, we cannot make progress, and we do not really understand. Of course, we say we understand, but we don't really. We have a rubber-band understanding.

Student: Dr. Hora, isn't the hang-up just being concerned with myself?

Dr. Hora: There are all kinds of hang-ups. Every invalid idea that becomes a hang-up has the quality of self-confirmation. It stands to reason, "What else is there besides me? I am me, and there is nothing else." There was a man who said, "Dr. Hora, when I am with you, I am you." This is self-confirmation. When he is not with me anymore, who is he then? He returns to himself.

Student: Dr. Hora, sometimes we believe that we really put a lot of effort into understanding and become very frustrated, almost as if we are saying, "See, I am putting a lot of effort into this; how come it's not happening, not working?" So I say, I don't pretend to know. I'm trying to know, and I am really stuck here and can't get beyond it . . .

Dr. Hora: And He isn't helping me.

Student: Right.

Dr. Hora: He with capital H. If we have a Catholic or Orthodox Jewish upbringing, we blame everything on God, because God blames everything on us. If we cannot understand something, we think, "I am sincerely trying, and He doesn't help me; it's His fault." It is a hang-up on God—we can even have a hang-up on God.

Student: Another impediment is when I don't understand something right away. It is self-confirmatory because I am thinking I want to understand, that I should understand.

Dr. Hora: Religions advocate having a hang-up on Christ, and what could be wrong with that? It is not valid. Some of the evangelistic people say, "Get hooked on Jesus, and that will solve your problems." No, we cannot get hooked on God because then we would become fanatic religionists, and that would be an invalid mode of being-in-the-world. There is only one way—the straight and narrow—to be interested in understanding the truth-of-being. This is not a hang-up; this is an orientation. It is called "the straight and narrow." "Strait is the gate and narrow is the way which leadeth unto life, and few there be that find it . . . for wide is the gate, and broad is the way, that leadeth to destruction, and many there be which go in thereat" (Matthew 7:14 and 13). So let's be careful—no hang-up is ever valid. Every hang-up, even a hang-up on God, becomes a stumbling block and a misdirection in the quest for enlightenment. You don't get enlightened with the help of a hang-up of any kind. You get enlightened in the "straight and narrow" way of sincerely seeking to understand the truth-of-being.

Student: But Dr. Hora, we are all hung up on something. Why are we having such a hard time?

Dr. Hora: Speak for yourself.

Student: I am hung up on something.

Dr. Hora: No doubt about it.

Student: Most people look at the "narrow path" from a behavioral viewpoint—if I behave in a perfect way . . . , I don't drink, and I don't smoke—but I know you don't mean that.

Dr. Hora: No. Being a sincere seeker after the understanding of the truth-of-being is not a hang-up—it is an orientation, an existential orientation.

Student: Is there a difference between an orientation in life and a mode of being? Are they synonymous?

Dr. Hora: The mode of being is determined by our orientation. If our orientation is invalid, then we have a misdirected mode of being-in-the-world. Many people get hung up on self-promotion. Some advertisers say that they are experts in self-promotion.

Student: Through prayer and meditation, one can begin the day in the right spirit, then lose it after a couple of hours. I find that I can go to work and not be focused on the activity for a while; and then I get bogged down with phone calls and this or that, or I am hypersensitive to other people's thoughts and pick them up.

Student: Is that just an excuse then? Is it just a complaint?

Dr. Hora: Yes, of course it is. Circumstances are being blamed.

Student: So the real interest is in self-confirmation, because if we were interested in God-confirmation, we wouldn't lose track of it as the day goes by. We are using everything for self-confirmation.

Dr. Hora: You are trying to reason out a cause—a cause-and-effect relationship about losing sight. But there is no cause and effect—this reasoning is not valid—it is a hang-up on cause and effect reasoning. Simply, we have to understand that unless we are wholeheartedly concerned with understanding the truth-of-being, nothing will work. No amount of rationalization will help. What do we mean by the truth-of-being?

Student: Understanding what really is.

Student: What is our purpose?

Dr. Hora: Now when Moses spoke to God the first time he said: "Who are you, God, and whom shall I say I spoke to when the rest of the people will ask?" What did God say? "I am that I am." What does this mean? It means: "I am the Being that really is." Being could also be spoken of as the life force. When we seek to understand the truth-of-being, we seek to understand our identities in the context of this infinite Being which is God. Is this clear? That is what we mean when we seek to understand the truth-of-being. "I am the Being that really is"—that is what God said to Moses—"I am that I am." We are individual beings in the context of the infinity of divine Being. Every one of us is a divine entity, but we do not know it; and that is the great mystery.

Dialogue No. 15

Pain and Gratitude

Student: Would you please clarify the difference between "Who am I?" and "What am I?" In answering "Who am I?" could one say, "I am spirit"?

Dr. Hora: I am an image and likeness of God. I am a transparency for God. I am an aspect of infinite Mind. Who am I is an inquiry into identity. What am I is an inquiry into substance. Who am I? I am part of God. What am I? I am spiritual: I am made of spirit, of nondimensional substance. I am a divine consciousness. The substance of our being is not flesh and blood. What are we made of? We are made of thoughts—God's thoughts. So that is the substance. Where am I is an inquiry into location. Where is life? Life is in God—real life. I live and move and have my being in omniactive divine Mind. And What is our purpose in life? People suffer from not understanding who they are, what they are, where they are, and what their purpose is in life. Our purpose is to be beneficial presences in the world. [These four questions and responses constitute the Prayer of the Four Ws.]

Student: How do we know that we are spiritual? We are God's thoughts, but we can be aware of both valid and invalid thoughts.

Dr. Hora: If we are involved with invalid thoughts, we suffer all kinds of discordant experiences. If we are involved with valid thoughts, we prosper: we are healthy, we are peaceful, we have a sense of assurance, we are grateful, and we are loving. It is possible to know, although it is a well-kept secret. The world does not know these things, but it is really very simple. God says: "I am all there is, and besides me there is nothing."

Student: Evidently it is difficult to get over the idea that we think our own thoughts or that we are products of our own thoughts.

Dr. Hora: Is this difficult?

Student: Yes, to say to someone: "You are God's thoughts . . ."

Dr. Hora: Yes, of course, they have to study Metapsychiatry, and then it will become clear. There is a Zen koan that says, "Before

I took up the study of Zen, mountains were mountains, and rivers were rivers." Everything was very simple, plain, and natural. "But when I took up the study of Zen, mountains were not mountains anymore, and rivers were not rivers anymore." Everything became more and more complicated. That is what some people say about Metapsychiatry—it's complicated. The koan goes on to say, "But when I became enlightened, suddenly mountains were mountains again, and rivers were rivers." Do we all understand this koan?

Student: I think so. Originally when he saw a mountain or a river, he was looking at appearances; and then when he was seeing mountains and rivers at the end, he was seeing what was real.

Dr. Hora: Right, he saw that these were just appearances.

Student: I have a question having to do with phenomena. A few days ago, I got stung by a wasp. Now here is a phenomenon, a wasp. I reached to close the window and didn't see it, and I got stung. I remembered that in one of our books, a situation was described where a lady was stung by a bee, and she just relaxed and saw it as a phenomenon. I worked with that, and there was no problem—it was just fine. Nevertheless there is an experience of a wasp sting. I know that I have to ask the meaning; but, first, I would like to understand: when we say "Nothing comes into experience uninvited" [Seventh Principle of Metapsychiatry], are we talking about the event or just our experience of the event? In this case there was a phenomenon, a wasp, and there was an experience, a sting. Do we just ask, "What is the meaning of the sting?" Or do we have to understand the phenomenon too? If certain thoughts were not present, would it mean that there would not be the phenomenon of a wasp at all or that I just would not have gotten stung? Do we invite phenomena too? Is it like the Chinese saying, "Birds can fly over our heads, but we do not have to let them nest in our hair"? Do our thoughts invite an experience or a phenomenon?

Dr. Hora: Many people are getting mugged every day in the city. You got mugged by a wasp. Now we are not asking the question, What is the meaning of so many muggers? One could ask that question, but it is not relevant to you. But you can ask, What is the meaning of my experience? Whether it is a wasp or a snake or a mosquito, I have had this experience of being attacked by some unloving creature. So then you have to relax and not get angry at this poor wasp. You don't get involved with the thought, "I don't want this"—this thought is not relevant. It is an experience, and the experience is a thought that has invited the experience. Sometimes we have certain thoughts—we are afraid that someone might hurt us, or we are angry at someone or about something unpleasant—and suddenly these thoughts turn into an experience. So besides taking a neutral position about the event and not getting involved with the mugger, we are involved with trying to purify our consciousness of thoughts about interaction—hostile, hurtful interaction thoughts. The best way to do this is to contemplate these words: "In divine Reality, there are no muggers, and there are no muggees. All of God's ideas coexist harmoniously, and I am grateful to know that God is infinite Love." We lose sight of the whole thing; it vanishes out of consciousness. And if it is not in consciousness, it has nowhere to be, and then we are healed. Nothing can exist in the body—or out of the body—that is not in consciousness. So whenever we need to be healed of something, it must be healed in consciousness by discarding the invalid thought and replacing it with a valid thought, and the experience will quickly vanish. Consciousness has to be brought back to an awareness of perfect harmony in God. God is our life, and there is no other life but that, and that life is perfect, always. So that is the way to deal with unpleasant experiences.

Student: Dr. Hora, we say that certain things can come to our attention, but they do not have to come into our experience. I am wondering, in connection with the previous question of having been stung by a wasp, is one approach to say that some particular thing has come to my attention, but it doesn't have to be part of my experience? Reminding ourselves might help to calm us down, or if we have the experience of being stung by a wasp, is it advisable to look for a meaning and acknowledge that this indeed must represent an attack thought? Does something like being stung by a wasp always carry a serious meaning, or can it be something about which you can choose to respond as though it were just an experience? Does every little thing that happens have a significant, underlying meaning, or can one choose to endow it with a meaning?

Dr. Hora: What is the difference between an enlightened student of Metapsychiatry and a stoic?

Student: A stoic suffers in silence.

Dr. Hora: Yes, a stoic toughens himself against pain. Well, is that enlightened?

Student: No.

Dr. Hora: The case that I described in Beyond the Dream, about the lady who got stung, was about a stoic. She thought, "I'm not going to bother with this; I have some other things to do." That's what she did, and it worked. But, she didn't become more enlightened. There was a problem, and there was an opportunity to learn something. "Problems are lessons designed for our edification" [Eighth Principle of Metapsychiatry]. She learned not to pay attention to the pain and turned her attention to something more socially constructive, and it worked very nicely. But it did not increase her immunity against further "muggings."

Student: What is the significance of the fact that this story is helpful? I was stung by a bee this week too, and I went through exactly the same process—I recalled the story word for word. I didn't realize that it wasn't the enlightened response. What is the meaning of the fact that the story seems to carry with it an ability to calm people down? The story has a certain power.

Dr. Hora: Yes. We would all like to have certain practical solutions to our problems—this is an operational approach. Of course it is much simpler to disregard the pain and keep busy with some other project, and just let it vanish. But we will not have really learned anything; we will have just learned to be tough. It is like saying, "I'm not going to deal with this." It is better than crying or running to the doctor for liniment.

Student: Dr. Hora, you are describing a situation where somebody "toughs" it out and is a stoic and forces himself or herself not to think of the problem yet willfully and operationally takes care of the problem. But you sometimes mention a different approach, which does not involve seeking the meaning and understanding, and that is shifting our attention away from the invalid thought to a valid thought. If we are involved with an unpleasant experience and we are unable to discern the meaning, I thought it was a valid idea to shift our attention and attempt to move away from whatever the invalid thoughts might be, even if we do not know what they are—pick up a spiritual book and shift attention from thinking about invalid ideas to some spiritual ideas that we know to be valid. There is no learning of a meaning there, but I thought that approach was a good idea. Is it not?

Dr. Hora: One tries to distract oneself, but then we have not taken advantage of the opportunity to eliminate from consciousness certain habits of thought. For instance, suppose this lady would have sat down and started meditating on the meaning of the experience and theoretically she could have had the thought, "My neighbors are bugging me." Then she might say, "This may be the meaning of this experience—I must refrain from thinking of my neighbors as bugging me, even if they seem to be bugging me, because they are not bugs." The Bible says: "Love thy neighbor as thyself" (Leviticus 19:18). So this would have opened up a new way of looking at her situation that would have been even more helpful than just distracting her thoughts. She did not learn anything. So if you would find in your meditation that these were the kind of thoughts you were entertaining, then you become a better neighbor from then on.

Student: So in order for that kind of experience to have a beneficial effect, we need to be able to discern the meaning?

Dr. Hora: Right. We are studying meditation—that is what meditation is for—we seek to become aware of certain hidden thoughts which are present in our consciousness, and then we eliminate them by recalling something pertinent that the Bible says: "Love thy neighbor as thyself."

Student: Yesterday I saw a woman that I had known casually for twenty-five years. I always noticed a certain joy and happiness about her. Everyone else around me seemed to be having so many problems with children and all sorts of things, but whenever I saw her, she had a joyful way of speaking and expression. Then I didn't see her for twelve years, until I saw her about three months ago. There she was again with that same joy. Her conversation is always about how grateful she is—I don't mean in an inauthentic way—that is the way she thinks about things. Then I saw her again yesterday—it was just amazing. I have never seen her in any of these groups, yet she said to me, "I keep saying, 'Thank you, God.'" I think she is sort of religious. She doesn't know anything about meanings; she doesn't know that reality is nondimensional; she doesn't know about any of the ideas that we are endeavoring to understand. What is it that is having such a wonderful effect? She is sort of bypassing the knowledge and ending up with the joy. How can somebody be so happy all the time over thirty-five years? It can't be an accident.

Dr. Hora: She must know something.

Student: I was reminded of her when we were talking about distracting oneself as opposed to reaching for something valid. What is it that an individual like that can know without having studied?

Dr. Hora: Maybe she has studied. How do you know?

Student: Are some people just naturally grateful?

Dr. Hora: No, it is not normal.

Student: It isn't normal to be joyful and grateful and happy and loving and generous?

Dr. Hora: That does not come without study, commitment, and spiritual awareness. It is not normal to be that way, but it is good. You see, you appreciate her; but maybe there are people who think she is nuts.

Student: If the idea of reincarnation is right and if someone learned gratitude in a past life, could it carry over?

Dr. Hora: I don't think so . . .

Student: We were talking about turning from invalid ideas to valid ideas. Sometimes I find that it seems like a Catch-22 situation—if I meditate on the meaning of a problem, often the ultimate answer is that I am not attending to Metapsychiatry's First Principle: "Thou shalt have no other interests before the good of God, which is spiritual blessedness." The First Principle recommends entertaining valid ideas, and there you are again, having bypassed understanding the meaning of a problem or experience.

Dr. Hora: You won't be able to sustain it because that hidden meaning will bug you.

Student: But if, over and over again, the meaning is revealed that you are not paying attention to the First Principle . . .

Dr. Hora: If you do not know what it is that prevents you from paying attention to the First Principle, you will not be able to pay attention to the First Principle. Suppose you are obsessed with the idea that the moon should not be made of green cheese—you don't want the moon to be made of green cheese—you will not be able to sustain the First Principle. Usually when we get involved with something that we either want or don't want, we develop an obsession; and we are usually obsessed with some irrational idea. The essence of an obsession is, I want it, or, I don't want it, and we cannot stop thinking about it. The First Principle is of no real interest to us except intellectually, and we cannot sustain it.

Student: When a phenomenon occurs—such as the ceiling falling down—which seems to come from nowhere, then of course we do not ignore the meaning and simply turn our attention to valid thoughts. But there are other ways that we conduct our lives, which may be patently invalid, in which case we no longer seek deep meanings; we just realize that we are engaged in "wanting" or "not wanting."

Dr. Hora: Yes, that is very important. Always when we face some problem, we must ask ourselves, What do I want? or What don't I want? All problems are rooted in that habit of thought.

Student: It's not enough just to be aware that the problem is "wanting" or "not wanting." Do we need to know what it is that we want or don't want in order to be able to understand?

Dr. Hora: Yes. The danger is that we may become too intellectual about it. Intellectualism makes everything sterile—with no effect. There is no existential relevancy to intellectual knowledge.

Student: So it is not enough to say to oneself that my problem is I want something or that I must not want something. We have to know what the something is?

Dr. Hora: Right.

Student: Regarding the question concerning at what point it is that we might look for meanings and at what point it is that we might see that a particular situation has come to our attention but not into our experience, I wonder about living in New York City, where we are exposed to so much human suffering.

Dr. Hora: Well, if we are faced with what you have described as the generalized problem of the multimillion occupants of a certain territory, then the enlightened response is to pray for them. When we pray for them, we are neither saying that we want this to be or we don't want this to be—we are acknowledging that it is not the will of God that his creation suffer. We seek to correct our thoughts and to acknowledge that in the universe of Mind, which is God-created reality, there is no suffering—there is no interaction between drug dealers and drug users and the police; there are no crimes or jealousy or rivalries, no rich or poor, no AIDS or diseases. We seek to clarify for ourselves that these are phenomena of evil and that God has never created this evil—it is not the will of God. This is "what seems to be" going on, and it doesn't have to go on. By establishing in our consciousness the truth of God's perfect creation, we are effectively contributing to the healing of the problem without getting sick over it, or bemoaning it, or cursing it, or hating it, or running out in the streets throwing away all our money in order to help people individually. It doesn't help. The soup kitchens alleviate the problem a little bit, but they are not going to heal it— only the power of God can bring about a healing of the situation. Every individual who can heal it in his own consciousness contributes to the eventual healing of the problem. Whenever we face a problem which is not directly our own problem, we pray—we pray for the world, and we pray for New York City.

Student: I am still working on this idea that we are not naturally grateful. I would like to probe that more deeply. There seem to be relatively few people on the spiritual path, but there seem to be a great number of people who are manifesting spiritual qualities. How can I understand that no one is inherently grateful when I see the manifestation of certain spiritual qualities?

Dr. Hora: When we think of the spiritual qualities of unenlightened people, we see that there are very many people who are naturally inclined toward helpfulness, toward honesty, toward constructive participation in life. These are spiritual qualities that people interpret as [the characteristics of] being a nice person. Everybody wants to be a nice person because it is an intelligent way to be. There is an impulse of helpfulness and generosity present, and these appear spontaneously. But I have never seen anyone express gratitude without having been taught to. How can you be grateful to God if "He" is invisible? "He" is not a person, and "He" doesn't say to be grateful. We have to learn to be grateful. It is not really a very difficult problem. Very often people who are at all well brought up are grateful because they learned to say "thank you." It is easy to be grateful to another person—between persons, there can be a great deal of gratitude—it can be heartfelt, or it can be a display of good manners, or it can be just an aspect of education. We are nice people, and we can be grateful and express gratitude toward people who are nice to us or whom we like. But that is not what we are talking about here when we speak of gratitude. We are speaking of a higher order of gratitude—it is the acknowledgment not only of the existence of God but also of the essential nature of God, which is goodness. We are learning the hard way how important it is to maintain a constant consciousness of the fact that God is Infinite Good; and when we are aware of this goodness, and it becomes real to us through various blessings that we have observed in our lives and in the lives of others, then we are grateful. We are grateful to God for the good of God.

Student: That is very helpful—it takes it to a higher level. I have another question, back on a lower level. Let's say a child learns that being grateful is a pretty good deal because the more grateful you are the more you get, and that works all through life. That is a principle, but it is playing out on a human level. Could the child take it to a higher level and say that the reason the principle works on the human level is because there is something called gratitude? Then we would have to ask, "Where does all goodness come from?"

Dr. Hora: The danger here is that one may become religious. Religious people talk a lot about gratitude because that is part of their religious training. But the lady who was described earlier is more than religious—she is existentially grateful. There are many religious people who will say they are grateful, but there is no evidence—they are not "glowing." Most religious people are not glowing, especially not the Catholics. Most Catholics are unable to be grateful because they are trained to feel guilty. This is a self-defeating, theological dogma. A guilty individual cannot be grateful; he is just preoccupied with himself and tries to escape from condemnation. If an individual is grateful in an existential way, this individual knows something. This gratitude has been learned; it did not just happen. The concept of God must be existentially valid; then gratitude manifests itself in glowing and health and a joy that is natural rather than artificial.

Student: How about children? We see children glow; they are intelligent and vibrant.

Dr. Hora: They are aware of being loved, not by God but by Mommy; this is still on an anthropomorphic level. "Mountains are mountains and rivers are rivers" to them. We have to go through that process before we are grateful for the real God.

Student: Let's take the child who has been beaten up and is sorrowful and contrast this with a child who is blossoming. Is there any difference in the ability of these two individuals to make the transition to the higher level?

Dr. Hora: It is hard to tell who will be impelled to seek the higher truth—rather than the interactional experience with the parents. It is interesting that abused children have just as much chance to find God as loved children. Maybe the abused child has even more of a chance than the child who was loved and pampered and had a pleasant upbringing.

Student: Dr. Hora, what about the abused child who has been indoctrinated in religion?

Dr. Hora: That is just compounding the abuse.

Student: How do we get beyond the religious view of gratitude?

Dr. Hora: By suffering. The religious mouthing of gratitude is not going to have an existential impact—you will just become a nice person.

Student: We really have to see the religious idea of gratitude as an invalid thought.

Dr. Hora: Well, as inadequate for healing or spiritual blessedness. In Metapsychiatry we say, "Gratitude is the door to joy." In religion gratitude is a way of trying to bribe God—it is like saying, "Don't punish me. I am sufficiently miserable already, but I'm grateful."

Student: So in this context, if one were to be with an individual who was not grateful, it would be of absolutely no value to tell him to be grateful.

Dr. Hora: Very little, right.

Student: Because that is something every individual has to learn for himself.

Dr. Hora: You have to have a valid idea of God, that God is not a person, that God doesn't give a damn whether you are grateful or not. The truth lies in your interest in understanding gratitude in terms of a valid idea of God as a Cosmic Principle, and that gratitude makes you more receptive to divinely inspired ideas. Then you see that you are grateful for knowing that God is good, and then you start to glow. This lady had the secret; and she is probably responsive to a sincere student because there is something of that student in her, and that is beautiful. She probably has the right understanding of gratitude.

Student: I have been coming here for some time, and suffering does not end. When I am going through it, is there any way to use it? Can it be more transforming if you have a little knowledge, even though to you it seems like sitting in a fire? A lot of times the ideas we learn about here are not enough because they do not immediately transform the situation; so I still suffer. Suffering is self-confirmation, so how do I know it isn't just self-confirmation?

Dr. Hora: When you start to feel that you are suffering, the first thing to do is to ask, "What do I want?" You have to search for a thought that says "I want" or "I don't want."

Student: And if we come up with something and suffering continues, is it because we don't have the proper understanding of "what really is"? We may have it verbally, but it doesn't knock the suffering out. Sometimes, I continue to suffer anyway . . .

Dr. Hora: Because you have not shifted your thoughts to the existentially valid biblical counterfact to "wanting" and "not wanting," which is: "My grace is sufficient unto you" (2 Corinthians 12:9). God says that. What do you make of that?

Student: Honestly I will say that, and many times, when that idea has come, but until I can understand it, it is like a koan. I am still sitting there with unresolved issues, and I am suffering. Then I say the counterfact slowly, and I just suffer more.

Student: What is happening there? I am in the same boat. He is saying the words, but he doesn't believe them? Is it that he hasn't realized it?

Dr. Hora: It is just a biblical quotation that is intellectually acknowledged but existentially rejected.

Student: What does "existentially rejected" mean?

Dr. Hora: It is like saying, "Just because it is written in the Bible that God said, 'My grace is sufficient unto you,' so what? What does that have to do with me? It is nothing that touches me. It doesn't replace in my thoughts the thoughts of what I want and do not want. It is no consolation." Suppose that you want to win the lottery and you hear, "My grace is sufficient unto you." This biblical passage doesn't touch you, and you are not healed. We have to be willing to give up any thought that starts with the words, "I want" or "I don't want."

Heaven

Student: Dr. Hora, I recognized something in someone else that I didn't like, and I realized that what I didn't like in that other individual was something that I was very much involved with myself. It seems to me that it is important, first, to see the fault as ignorance, to depersonalize it, and, second, to give up the idea of blaming. There are certain things that took place that I could be very angry about, but how could I be angry if I participated in it? So now the question is, Where do I go from here? I am grateful that I can see it as ignorance; I can see that not staying on that level of thinking is liberating.

Dr. Hora: You will have to be more specific.

Student: No, I can't be. I've been sick for two days over it.

Dr. Hora: Otherwise, we will not really understand what you are saying.

Student: To summarize it, I was angry with someone about something that he constantly does, and then I realized that I do the same thing. So it is the old story: What Peter says about Paul is true about Peter. When that hit me, I realized that it is the same ignorance taking place in both of us.

Dr. Hora: Yes. He is very critical of people? Is that it?

Student: Well, he is very critical of women.

Dr. Hora: Are you critical of women too? Of course you are.

Student: No, I am not critical of women; I am critical of men. That is one of the meanings with the man who reports to me and lashes out at me. I was being very critical of his performance on the job. When the connection hit, I was very disturbed. It is not healthy.

Dr. Hora: It is par for the course.

Student: What is the meaning of critical thinking?

Dr. Hora: It is called faultfinding, and it is psychological. Psychology is the art of faultfinding. There is a universal tendency in man to try to find fault with other people. It makes us feel good, and everyone wants to feel good. If we can feel good by making somebody else feel bad, that is double pleasure.

Student: I don't know about the pleasure, but I do know about the pain.

Student: Is it related to envy? You envy the person, and then if you can find something wrong with him, you feel better.

Dr. Hora: Certainly envy, jealousy, rivalry, malice could be part of such tendencies. The more ignorant we are, the more we are inclined to put people down.

Student: Dr. Hora, is it related to "should-thinking"?

Dr. Hora: It could be—they "should" be otherwise.

Student: "The way I think is right."

Dr. Hora: It could be. It is an ignorance that is very harmful, full of trouble and problems. What blesses one curses the other.

Student: Dr. Hora, I have a question about the difference between dialogue and just stating opinions.

Dr. Hora: Spouting opinions . . .

Student: Yes, but I am not sure how I need to phrase it for clarification. Often when I am involved in a situation where people are criticizing others and I am tempted to get hooked in an interactional way, I would love to be able to change into a dialogic mode of discourse. I know I am phrasing it operationally, because I am probably thinking that way. But sometimes one is asked to give an opinion or to participate in criticism, and the act of silence seems to enrage the other person. It seems that I am unable to get away with not answering. I would like to be able to remain silent.

Dr. Hora: So what should a nice girl do in such a situation, right?

Student: I'm not after being nice. Jesus wasn't nice.

Student: Is it possible to change an interaction into a dialogue?

Dr. Hora: We are not interested in changing anything. As a matter of fact, we respect people's right to be critical and judgmental, anything they wish to be. We respect people's right to be wrong. As Jesus would say, "What is it to you?" So if we are in the company of people who are critical and nasty and charming, what are we to do? Nothing—absolutely nothing. It is called transcendent regard.

Student: It would be a lot more peaceful, and I wouldn't invite cruel phone calls.

Dr. Hora: What does Metapsychiatry recommend we do when we get such a phone call?

Student: Hang up!

Student: Hear the sound of one hand clapping?

Dr. Hora: The Zen Master would say: "Go wash your mouth out with soap." What do we mean by that?

Student: Misusing a koan.

Dr. Hora: No, it was not a koan; it was a tape recorder. What does a tape recorder do?

Student: Clichés.

Dr. Hora: It turns a valuable truth into a cliché. What is a cliché?

Student: Something that is true, but, because it has been said so many times and in so many different ways, it has lost its meaning.

Dr. Hora: It is a trivialization of a profound truth. So when you take the Buddha's name in vain, the Zen Master would say, "Go wash your mouth out with soap." Unless we can say something meaningfully relevant, we do not say anything. Furthermore, one hand cannot clap. We speak of "the sound of one hand." Can one hand make a sound?

Student: No.

Dr. Hora: Oh, yes. Can one hand make a sound?

Student: Like the wind maybe.

Student: Maybe it is symbolic for presence, a presence that is not involved with interaction.

Dr. Hora: What is "the sound of one hand"?

Student: Is it "the soundless music of life"?

Dr. Hora: Something like that. The sound of one hand is the sound of silence—meaningful, present, attentive, compassionate silence.

Student: So, when any one of us is on the phone, we don't hang up.

Dr. Hora: When you hang up, what kind of sound is there? Two hands clapping—two hands can clap—but one hand cannot clap, and it is good because whenever there is the sound of two hands clapping, what do we have? Interacting ad infinitum. But the sound of one hand is powerful.

Student: Just knowing the definition of compassion is helpful— compassion is "understanding the lack of understanding."

Dr. Hora: Yes, silence can be very eloquent.

Student: It seems that there could be a critical silence too, so we would have to know the difference.

Student: If we get a phone call from someone and we want to be loved, and approved of, and instead we are being criticized, it can be difficult.

Dr. Hora: Then, we are in trouble.

Student: Because we can't stop the wanting or even recognize it.

Dr. Hora: I remember a story of a wife whose husband had a fit of hysterical rage. He was abusing her in the worst possible way, ugly language and accusing her of all kinds of things and yelling and screaming at her. She remained silent. After a while, her husband stopped yelling and screaming and broke down and started to cry, sobbing. The whole thing was over. It was "the sound of one hand" bringing it powerfully home to him that he was making a fool of himself.

Student: Dr. Hora, there is a story about a Zen monk who took care of a child that the townspeople accused him of fathering, and, when he was accused, all he said was, "Is that so?" Finally, after a few years, the truth came out that he was not the father, and his response was the same, "Is that so?" No interaction.

Dr. Hora: He remained unruffled. Yes, that is a good story. I saw a cartoon once in the Wall Street Journal. A big boss of a corporation was walking into his office one morning, and on the way he passed by the receptionist who made an ugly face at him. And he said, "Any other messages?"

Student: If I can truly be compassionate, does it have any blessing on the family?

Dr. Hora: Compassion is always a blessing. We cannot expect anything, but whenever we are sincerely compassionate, something good happens.

Student: One can be attached to another individual positively or negatively, so it would also dispel attachments.

Dr. Hora: If we are compassionate, we are attached to love and mercy and understanding, and we would not provoke anyone. What is chauvinism?

Student: Male supremacy.

Dr. Hora: Yes, a male chauvinist.

Student: "Deutschland über Alles."

Dr. Hora: Yes, that's right. Chauvinism comes from a Frenchman whose name was Chauvin. He was so very, very French that he was intolerant of all other nationalities. The idea caught on like wildfire. There is national intolerance and criticism of other nations, as well as gender chauvinism. Naturally it is intolerant, faultfinding, and full of critical thinking. Chauvinistic thinking is very troublesome in the world and also in individual lives—it invites great violence into experience.

Student: This happens in religions also.

Dr. Hora: As a matter of fact, in religions you will find almost anything, including religious intolerance.

Student: Anti-Semitism.

Dr. Hora: It is high time for the nations of the world to outgrow naïve religion, nationalism, chauvinism—and all kinds of "isms."

Student: I was thinking that the root of the problem is perhaps in comparisons. We tend to rank people in groups and compare them.

Dr. Hora: Comparative thinking is the source of chauvinism, and it can be an outgrowth of misguided patriotism.

Student: After we are born we join a religion, and our religion is the best one; and our school is the best school; and the ball team that we pick is the best.

Dr. Hora: "We are the best." "We are the world." The rock stars are singing, "We are the world." What is "the world"?

Student: Each one's individual thoughts?

Student: All that which is not spiritual.

Student: Interaction.

Dr. Hora: "The world" is made of interaction thinking. As a matter of fact, before interaction thinking came into vogue, there was no world.

Student: Is interaction thinking a recent phenomenon?

Dr. Hora: Yes, it is quite recent. It started in the Stone Age, probably when sticks and stones were discovered! When we say "the world," what is the first thought that comes to mind?

Student: Appearances.

Student: Physicality.

Student: People.

Student: The human condition.

Student: Feelings.

Dr. Hora: The word "world."

Student: Other people.

Student: Countries.

Student: Material things.

Dr. Hora: Essentially, when most people are asked to describe what is the world, they say that it is the planet Earth. But that is not the "world"—that is a piece of matter. The "world" really is interaction thoughts. Without interaction thoughts, there is no world. Suppose everyone suddenly gave up interaction thinking?

What would happen?

Student: The world would disappear.

Dr. Hora: Yes, that's true. What would there be then? There would be harmonious coexistence of all of God's creation in the infinitude of Love-Intelligence. Then it would come to pass as it is written in the Lord's Prayer: "Thy Kingdom come, Thy will be done, on earth as it is in heaven." Suddenly the world would turn into heaven. It is so simple—"heaven on earth" is possible. All that is required is for interaction thinking to disappear. When there will be no more human relationships, heaven will happen in the world—the world will change into a heaven. God's kingdom can come on earth the moment that interaction thinking disappears. So it is a possibility that the world could be saved.

Student: What's puzzling me is, Would the world still exist? We use these words metaphorically too—we speak of "heaven on earth." Are you speaking of the concept of being in the world, in the world purified?

Dr. Hora: Jesus said that we have to "overcome the world." And when the world is overcome, we find ourselves in heaven. We now have a very clear concept of heaven. Most people think it is a geographical location, somewhere in outer space. Heaven is harmonious coexistence of all of God's creation in the infinitude of Love-Intelligence. The moment we become sincerely interested in living in heaven, it is here.

Student: On an individual basis, each one of us can live in it?

Dr. Hora: Yes, each one of us, right now.

Student: That's comforting.

Student: You don't have to worry about everyone else?

Student: I thought it could only come about when everyone would be at the same state of consciousness.

Student: We can learn to understand it individually.

Dr. Hora: We can hasten the process.

Student: It might snowball.

Dr. Hora: Yes.

Student: What is the meaning of this planet being so blessed with life and beauty? We don't know of any other planet like this one.

Dr. Hora: Looks like God is playing favorites with our planet.

Student: We don't know; there may be other planets.

Dr. Hora: In our exploration of the universe, we have not been very far—just in the immediate solar system. Who knows what goes on? There may be planets where there is already paradise, where people have attained harmonious coexistence. There was a beautiful Star Trek feature in which people were so advanced that they only took on physical forms in order to be accessible to communicate with earthlings, but otherwise, at will, they would dematerialize. It was very beautifully done. They showed war, killing, and the interactions in which unenlightened nations are involved—their violence and hatred.

Student: They weren't threatened, and I guess they were compassionate because they knew they could turn to light any time. They knew that they didn't really die. Can we understand compassion when we don't know that the body is just perceptualized thought? Is it possible to have compassion when one doesn't understand?

Dr. Hora: To some degree, yes. If we have already advanced beyond that way of thinking, then there is infinite compassion. But we could muster enough compassion to be immune to criticism. What is the secret of attaining such immunity? In Texas they've known about it all the time. They say, "You ain't never was nothin'!" If we know this, we become invulnerable.

Student: Does transcendent regard help too?

Dr. Hora: Transcendent regard makes it possible to see everyone as a nondimensional entity of Love-Intelligence.

Student: If we don't see it, can we affirm that the individual is a manifestation of Love-Intelligence?

Student: That idea takes us back to the beginning of this session; we can fast ["mind-fast"] from thinking critical thoughts and affirm that everyone is a manifestation of Love-Intelligence.

Dr. Hora: "Prayer and fasting."

Student: Is it good to know whether we are being seduced or provoked or intimidated? Is that necessary in this process? I find that if someone is seductive or intimidating, it doesn't bother me; but when I am being provoked, it drives me wild. What is provocation?

Dr. Hora: Provocation is endeavoring to elicit an irritable reaction in someone. It is good to know the nuances and be aware of them. Are we being seduced, or are we being provoked? If we can specify the experience we are exposed to, we can refuse it.

Student: What is intimidation?

Dr. Hora: Inducing fear.

Student: And seduction?

Dr. Hora: Inviting someone . . .

Student: To butter up somebody for further misuse?

Dr. Hora: There are various forms of seduction.

Student: Is it operationalism to seduce another to do what you want him to?

Dr. Hora: That's called manipulation. It is beyond the three prongs of the "devil's pitchfork," which are seduction, provocation, and intimidation.

Student: Dr. Hora, when someone seems to demand an opinion from us, and it doesn't seem easy simply to say nothing, is that a form of provocation?

Dr. Hora: No, that is seduction.

Student: Seduction because we are being flattered into giving an opinion?

Dr. Hora: Exactly. A student of Metapsychiatry will never spout opinions, no matter how much pressure there is to venture a personal opinion. First of all, we know we are not persons. Second, opinions are foolishness because offering them presumes that our brain is a thought factory that can produce an original thought, which is our own property, called, "my opinion." So we never hear a student of Metapsychiatry spout an opinion. I have never heard anyone say, "In my personal opinion." No one here says that. Everyone understands this very quickly. In Metapsychiatry no one feels guilty, and no one has personal opinions.

Student: When people ask us for our opinion, many times they are not really interested. Someone may be looking for an argument or be interested in getting into a debate or in being right, so it seems even more silly to give an opinion.

Student: I usually wait it out.

Dr. Hora: The Zen Master says: "Above all, cherish no opinions." He thought it necessary to warn the students. The only problem we have in Metapsychiatry is operationalism—some people learn Metapsychiatry in order to operate on other people.

Student: The hardest concepts for me are to see "formlessness" and to understand that we are not really persons.

Dr. Hora: Formlessness is not synonymous with nondimensionality. When form loses its form, it becomes formless, but it is still in the realm of dimensionality.

Student: If you were to take this chair apart, it would be formless.

Dr. Hora: Yes, it would be a formless chair, but it would still have dimensions. Formlessness is also dimensional. We have to see "form and formlessness," on the one hand, in juxtaposition with nondimensionality, on the other hand.

Student: Then, how do we understand the koan: "Form is formlessness and formlessness is form"?

Dr. Hora: Form and formlessness are the same thing.

Student: It is still material.

Dr. Hora: It is still material—it is still dimensional.

Student: What is the significance of it? What is the message?

Dr. Hora: In Zen Buddhism there is no concept of nondimensionality. There is the concept of emptiness, sunyata.

Student: Is that what the koan is pointing to?

Dr. Hora: The aim of koans is to boggle the mind. If a Zen Master can get you ruminating for six years on, "Form is formlessness and formlessness is form," eventually you may hit upon the fact that it is all the same. The alternative to "form and formlessness" cannot be found in the material, dualistic world. Then you are forced into nonduality, where there is neither form nor formlessness—there is emptiness, the void. But that is an infelicitous term because emptiness implies nothing: it means no God. God is not nothing—It is fullness of Love-Intelligence. Love-Intelligence does not have any form, neither is it formlessness, nor is it emptiness. It is not emptiness—It is fullness. Fullness of what? Nondimensional Reality

Dialogue No. 17

The Herodian Thought

Student: Dr. Hora, could you clarify the difference between judging something as valid or invalid and judging something as good or evil?

Dr. Hora: Jesus recommended that we "judge righteous judgment"—"righteous judgment" means we have to be aware of what is existentially valid and what is not existentially valid. So Jesus was an existentialist. An existentialist is someone who can distinguish between what is existentially valid and what is not valid. Judging good and evil is a moral judgment, not an existential one.

Student: Is an enlightened individual automatically moral?

Dr. Hora: Actually more than moral—an enlightened individual understands that to be immoral is existentially invalid; therefore it is harmful and dangerous. An enlightened individual goes beyond the Ten Commandments. The Ten Commandments were necessary for primitive people who had no values at all and who did not know what was right and what was wrong. To talk to them about existential validity would not have made any sense; they would not have understood it. A primitive mind sees everything in terms of punishment and of how much it can get away with. So the Ten Commandments represent a primitive moral code designed for very primitive minds. Now the Sermon on the Mount is already designed for individuals who have abilities of abstract thought and a higher awareness. The Bible says: "The law was given to us by Moses, but love and grace by Jesus Christ" (John 1:17). In Metapsychiatry we go beyond the Ten Commandments and the Sermon on the Mount to distinguish between what is existentially valid and what is not valid. This is necessary if we are to understand God as Love. If God is Love, then God cannot be a policeman. The Ten Commandments are concerned with obedience and disobedience—God is still a policeman, a disciplinarian, a judge, a legal authority who punishes evildoers. Once we are to understand God as infinite Love Intelligence, then we need to understand existential validation, because if we are unethical or immoral or cruel or not in keeping with what is existentially valid, we are hurting ourselves. So we don't need a God who is a policeman. That is the great value of the Principle of Existential Validation. We can say that you can do all the evil you want—as long as you are willing to pay the price. No one is going to get after you. You destroy yourself, not only with your actions, not only with your attitudes, not only with your behavior, not only with what you speak, but by what you think—even your thoughts can destroy you, and your fantasies can destroy you—not because God is a punitive agency but because "that's the way the cookie crumbles." As the Chinese fortune cookie says, "Fast climbers come to sudden falls." Isn't that interesting?

Student: We've talked about this before. It seems as though there are certain individuals who appear to be fast climbers, and they just seem to keep on climbing and climbing.

Dr. Hora: Yes, we don't see them fall. The devil is always whispering, "It is possible to get away with it. Look at this guy, and look at that guy—they are getting away with it!" Nevertheless, no one gets away with anything.

Student: We speak of judging the validity of something by its "fruits." What thoughts would a fast climber look at in consciousness, in order to know if what he was doing was valid or invalid?

Dr. Hora: Well, who are we to tell him, or anyone, this?

Student: This is not a valid question?

Dr. Hora: Surely not.

Student: But, if we say that no one gets away with anything, how would one know that he is not getting away with it?

Dr. Hora: He may not know. He may just think that he ate something, or it is the climate . . .

Student: . . . Or think that it is contagious, or that everybody gets cancer . . .

Dr. Hora: Yes.

Student: Perhaps what that question was driving at is that it seems by any observable standard that there are some "fast climbers" who remain successful throughout their lives.

Dr. Hora: Yes, but what do you call successful? What does success mean? Having a lot of money? Having influence, having power, having a Rolls Royce? These are external signs of economic and perhaps even social success, but is that really success?

Student: I guess success, to me, would be PAGL consciousness.

Dr. Hora: Success—there is no such thing. We either reach or do not reach a sufficient understanding of Reality to find "the peace of God which passeth all understanding." This is not success—it is fulfillment. Success is measured by all kinds of standards of the world which have no existential relevancy. We speak of fulfillment; we are in this life to fulfill what God wants. God wants us to come to understand fully and completely, so that we may bear witness to divine Reality—that is fulfillment. This can be accompanied by some measure of economic blessing or not, but the outward signs of success are not existentially relevant. Spiritual development is the only relevant criterion for a life well lived.

Student: Are there individuals who live this life in an existentially valid way, yet know nothing about being a spiritual seeker?

Dr. Hora: I don't think so.

Student: There is some element of self-confirmation in their life that is hidden?

Dr. Hora: Yes, invariably. The Bible says: "Seek and ask and knock" (Matthew 7:7). We are required to seek the understanding. It does not come by itself—we have to seek it. We have to study; we have to pray; we have to have an abiding interest in gaining this wisdom, this understanding, this fulfillment. "Blessed are they that hunger and thirst after right understanding, for they shall be filled" (Matthew 5:6). That is real life, and everything else is just counterfeit life.

Student: Are there individuals who somehow find a valid way of living without being explicitly on the spiritual path? There are stories of musicians who live to a ripe old age, for instance, and are very invigorated by their life in music and find it very fulfilling. But there is nothing said about them being spiritual seekers. So is that kind of thing possible, or is there more to it than meets the eye?

Dr. Hora: Always.

Student: So that would not be enough?

Dr. Hora: There is something about music that is spiritual, and it certainly appeals to the soul of man. And we have observed that real musicians live a long life—they seem to be living in a transcendent dimension of consciousness—but we do not know everything about these individuals.

Student: Regarding the morality, let's look at the issue of taxes. It is a very complicated, fuzzy thing; one can interpret the law this way or that way and make out the return one way or another. What is the enlightened, moral way to face that? Do we take advantage of everything that is within the law, and then let the government decide whether it is right or wrong?

Dr. Hora: Well, there is no other way to go because it has become so complex. So we are just willing to pay whatever it is necessary to pay.

Student: And if they come back and say we interpreted it wrongly?

Dr. Hora: Then we pay the remaining. But suppose that someone would think, "Well, these IRS people are really unfair; so I am going to be unfair with them, and I'm going to get away with it because I have a good, clever accountant." Whenever we get away with something in life, we hurt ourselves.

Student: How is that individual hurting himself, if he is breaking Caesar's law rather than God's?

Dr. Hora: He is damaging his own self-esteem. Deep in his heart, he will feel that in some way he is crooked and immoral, and that will ultimately hurt him.

Student: It would also be saying, "I am deprived and I need to cheat to get more."

Dr. Hora: Yes.

Student: And it could also be that he would know what was right, and he would not do what was right even though he knew it. Is that part of the trouble?

Dr. Hora: Yes.

Student: Dr. Hora, I have a question about love and "letting be." It seems that "letting be" is an essential part of real Love.

Dr. Hora: Yes.

Student: But when we are aware that certain individuals whom we care about have certain ignorant ideas about something, and we know that it is harmful to them and that they are suffering from them, it doesn't seem so easy not to be affected and just to "let be." What is the key to immunity in that kind of situation? If we are not immune, we are not only hurting ourselves, but we are adding to the ignorance of another individual.

Dr. Hora: Yes, those are very painful situations. Suppose a loved one would act contrary to moral law or behave in an existentially invalid way, and there would be no way he would listen to us. We see he is hurting himself, but he refuses to face up to it—and we love him or her. All we have to do is just secretly pray— that is all—and let him continue until the consequences catch up with him. Then, he will become receptive to a better idea.

Student: What would be a valid prayer in that kind of situation?

Dr. Hora: It would be the endeavor to behold that individual with transcendent regard; that in itself is a valid prayer and often very effective.

Student: A mother who was a student of Metapsychiatry had a daughter who was involved with drugs and prostitution. The mother did not try to influence her, and gradually the daughter became interested. The mother was beneficial to the daughter by separating the appearance of invalid interest from the daughter's true nature.

Dr. Hora: Yes, and she herself was a model of spiritual uprightness.

Student: This example seems a little different. If there is a situation where an individual sees everything in life as a control issue or a power issue, if that is his or her perspective, then any kind of speaking, about even the simplest thing, can become a power struggle—over nothing. So I guess what I am asking is how not to get drawn into it. I may not even care about the thing that we are discussing, but because of the perspective this individual has, I get drawn into it, and I find myself discussing something that I don't even care about.

Dr. Hora: That is a mistake that can be corrected.

Student: Right, but I keep falling into it, and so I don't see what I need to see.

Dr. Hora: We could see that when we fall into it, we bang our nose against the power madness or the controllingness, and then we catch a cold. So this is a very good lesson to let be; we must "let be"—letting be means that we are careful not to give the impression that we would like to control the controlling fellow. To influence is a mistake. Very often we are really trying to influence other individuals, even in the most innocuous way, and they of course are afraid of being influenced, and it provokes a negative reaction. There are phobic people who are scared to death of being controlled by others or of not being able to control others, and anyone who tries to influence them, even in a most innocuous, harmless way, can provoke a panic reaction in them. If the elevator does not run smoothly, this is a cause for panic: you are in an elevator, and you are not in control—you push the button, and the elevator is in control—and you are being controlled. So there are many people who are afraid to ride in elevators. They say, "I am afraid of elevators," but what they are afraid of is not being in control.

Student: So if the situation should arise where it seems as if that dynamic of control is occurring, the real question to ask of oneself is, "What is it that I want that would lead me to get involved in such discussions?" Obviously there must be something that I want; otherwise I could just listen and not say a word and not be affected.

Dr. Hora: We could talk about issues, but we must be careful to "not influence."

Student: I guess when I speak, I am trying to influence; but if I am not going to influence, why say anything?

Dr. Hora: "Why" is an invalid question. Most people find it very difficult to talk in such a way as to be free of any tendency to persuade, to argue, to convince, to proselytize, or to influence others.

Student: But influencing could be just having a point of view—even that could be influencing.

Dr. Hora: The moment we want something, we are influencing.

Student: Is it valid to have a point of view?

Dr. Hora: No. What is a point of view? It is another word for opinion. And what is an opinion? It is a claim of personal knowledge. If we have an opinion or a point of view, and we say so, we imply that we want the other individual to accept our point of view. In that moment we are exerting an influence. This is how it happens that people with a point of view invariably wind up in contention with other people. It goes like this, "That is your point of view; but my point of view is this, and his point of view is that," and pretty soon there is a contentious debate—and nothing is ever cleared up in a debate. People leave with their own point of view in their pockets, and no one has convinced anyone else—they just go away tired. So it is existentially invalid to have a point of view.

Student: It seems that the more spiritually mature we are, the more time we would actually spend being silent.

Dr. Hora: Silence is very good, when it is appropriate.

Student: But that can be influencing, also.

Dr. Hora: Oh, yes.

Student: Then it is not really silence.

Dr. Hora: Yes, but if we have no points of view and no opinions, we are constantly getting impressions, and we can talk about ideas that keep occurring from moment to moment or impressions we have—responses that are elicited about issues. There is no influencing there.

Student: But it seems that we are rarely sincerely asked to respond to an issue.

Dr. Hora: Then of course we are very comfortable and grateful to remain silent. Do you know the story about Mrs. Schwartz? Mrs. Schwartz was sitting in the dining room and slurping chicken soup—it was a very delicious chicken soup—and a neighbor came running in, very excited, and said, "Mrs. Schwartz, your husband just dropped dead at the business." And Mrs. Schwartz just kept slurping the chicken soup as if she didn't hear. And the neighbor said, "Mrs. Schwartz, didn't you hear what I said?" And her reply was, "I heard, I heard. Wait until I finish this chicken soup. Then will you hear a woman scream!" That's a point of view.

Student: The whole area of communication is interesting. I would like to understand it better. Before we speak, is it a good idea to question our motive? Do we need to be careful before we say something and to think about the way it could be taken?

Dr. Hora: Well, of course that is a wise thing to do, but it is a calculative approach to communication.

Student: That is why I asked the question; it does seem calculative. Is there a better way?

Dr. Hora: Yes, being free of the desire to influence people to agree with us, or to accept our point of view or to like us for having said something, is better. But if we want to provoke someone or make someone feel stupid, then this will not work. We have to learn to be issue-oriented in such a way as to give not the slightest indication of influencing.

Student: So we wouldn't have to think about what we were going to say. We would just have to be free of the desire to influence?

Dr. Hora: Yes. Once we are free of the desire to influence, then we are free to communicate.

Student: What about a desire for harmony?

Student: Even wanting harmony can come across as an influence.

Dr. Hora: Always troublesome.

Student: Well that is really true, but if we are really healed of that desire, then what we say would be just fine.

Student: Could we say it would be innocent?

Dr. Hora: Absolutely—innocent, but not naïve.

Student: How does that happen?

Dr. Hora: We go to group sessions and learn about these things, and that will spare us many unpleasant communication break-downs. Communications very frequently break down.

Student: I find myself in a situation, for instance, where I might be at a movie with friends, and afterwards they like to provoke a discussion about the film.

Dr. Hora: They want you to agree with them.

Student: Yes, and I can't be silent because that is a provocation in itself—it shows that I am not interested or feel superior or something. I haven't yet understood in what way one can simply respond to the film.

Student: Could we just say, "Is that so?"

Dr. Hora: It is very applicable. One could also say, "I see the point." That is all.

Student: Is an impression the same thing as an observation?

Dr. Hora: No, an observation is when we are using our mind. When we say, "I observe that you want me to disagree with you," we have used our mind. When we say, "I have an impression," we are not using our mind—our mind was being invaded by some ideas—and we are totally innocent.

Student: The transcendent observer doesn't use his mind.

Dr. Hora: The transcendent observer, of course, does not say, "I observe" or "I don't observe"—it says hardly anything. But it can say, "I see the point." That is innocuous, unprovocative, and very often it brings peace to the situation. It is even better than "Is that so?" because there is a little hook of irony in there.

Student: We walk out of here tonight with valid ideas, to be absolutely moral, ethical, not to cherish any opinions, and after we've left, something happens, and we don't follow what we have learned.

Dr. Hora: We forget.

Student: We don't forget; we just don't do it.

Dr. Hora: Which means . . .

Student: We haven't suffered enough?

Dr. Hora: It means we cherish the illusion of personal knowledge.

Student: So we have to suffer enough to know that it just doesn't work. Is that the only way?

Dr. Hora: That's correct. What else will help? You could tie a knot in your handkerchief to remember not to cherish opinions and never to spout opinions.

Student: What is the difference between an opinion and talking about truth? There have been a few times when I thought I was talking about truth, and then I saw that I wanted to influence. Is that what makes an opinion—wanting to influence someone with an idea?

Dr. Hora: Yes. That is why children hate Hora so much.

Student: Children?

Dr. Hora: Children of parents who are students of Meta-psychiatry—they all hate Hora. I heard a story of one mother who is a student of Metapsychiatry who overheard two of her little daughters talking, and one of them said, "Look at it this way, at least we can be happy that Hora is not our father."

Student: That really happened?

Dr. Hora: I would not lie to you. Those parents are preaching and using Metapsychiatry to control and influence the children; and the children don't like to be controlled and tyrannized with words of wisdom from Hora, so they hate Hora. You can have the most delicious chicken soup in front of you, and if you are forced to eat it, you won't like it. No one likes to be coerced.

Student: Is it ever appropriate to initiate something?

Dr. Hora: When there is a fire.

Student: Let me give you an example. We were sitting around last weekend, and it just occurred to me that it would be good to make a particular telephone call to an individual that I hadn't talked to in a long time. I initiated it, made the call, and it seemed to be a very timely, appropriate thing to do. Now I questioned my motive at the time—am I initiating something to serve some of my own needs, or am I responding to something that is right to do? How does one discern the difference between willfully initiating and responding to a divine idea?

Dr. Hora: We always have to scrutinize our motives. When the motive is right, there is PAGL [PAGL is an acronym for Peace, Assurance, Gratitude, Love, and Its Presence in consciousness informs us that we are in tune with the One Mind], and the telephone company "knows" it, because they immediately make the connection.

Student: I have noticed that when I make a telephone call, and the line is busy, that every time I insist, there is something that happens.

Dr. Hora: That's right.

Student: Can you use that as an indication?

Student: Is it valid to see it that way?

Dr. Hora: It depends on whether it appeals to you or not. If you would like to disprove the validity of it, you will succeed.

Student: But it can actually become a valid sign that the call was invalid.

Dr. Hora: Some years ago I was told that one of the students of Metapsychiatry had had an operation and was in the hospital on his death bed, because the operation had been unsuccessful. I was moved to make a telephone call to this hospital, and there was an immediate connection. I spoke to this student for a few moments, and he was very weak and very despondent. He said that the operation was unsuccessful and that they wanted to open him up again the next morning. He said that he did not have the strength to survive. So we just had these few words, and then we hung up. And I was led to pray for him a little and to meditate over his situation, and then we went to sleep. And the next morning around 11:00, I received a call from him, and he said, "You know what happened? A miracle happened! The surgeons came to take me to the operating room in the morning, but I was having breakfast in bed, and they were amazed. They asked, 'Are you all right?' I was perfectly all right! They examined me and found that there is no need for another operation—everything cleared up overnight." And then he said, "You know, it is amazing—there was no telephone in this room before you called. But just a few minutes before you called, a telephone had been installed at the other patient's night table for him. And then the telephone rang, and it was for me!" The connection—you see how that works? This was a most fantastic demonstration.

Student: When you do call someone, as in this example or in such a circumstance, what do you say that would be helpful?

Dr. Hora: Nothing, you just listen—it is not to influence. I did not make this call in order to perform a miracle. I just wanted to talk to him and hear what he had to say.

Student: Just listen?

Dr. Hora: That's all. No magic mumbo-jumbo was performed— I didn't even tell him to get well.

Student: Try to think of how to cheer up sick people, and that can really become a form of influencing.

Dr. Hora: No, just establish communication, and that in itself has a certain value. This man was on his deathbed, and suddenly someone is interested and calls him. I was impelled to make that call.

Student: You also knew "who" that individual was—aside from who he thought he was. Isn't that what can heal?

Dr. Hora: Yes. The healing was taking place even at the moment I was dialing to call him, because it was God that inspired me to do this—and the rest was just an unfolding of the healing process. I didn't know that this would happen, but it was just marvelous to hear about it.

Student: Is it the receptivity to inspired ideas, that openness, which allows healing to take place?

Dr. Hora: Yes, that is how we explain it—receptivity and responsiveness—this is our explanation. Who can tell what God is doing? But there was PAGL; there was no hesitation to call, and the telephone company cooperated miraculously.

Student: A pure instrument of God—a perfect example.

Student: Going back to my call this last weekend: if I had called, and the individual had not been at home or if the line had been busy, would that have been a signal that it was the wrong motivation?

Dr. Hora: Yes, lay off it for a while.

Student: Wrong motivation.

Dr. Hora: No, that would just be an interpretation of your motivation. You have to know ahead of time what the motivation is without deceiving yourself.

Student: I see, scrutinize your motivation.

Dr. Hora: Scrutinize your motives, and if there is PAGL, then it is all right; but if there is some anxiety or tension, don't make a move without PAGL. When our motivation is valid and pure, there is PAGL—and it is smooth, and it works out. We have to learn to be aware of our motivation, always to scrutinize our motivation. We want to go to the hardware store? We examine our motivation. We want to do this, want to do that—turn left, turn right—we have always to be aware of our motivation. If the wrong man does the right thing, then the right thing works the wrong way—that is the whole story.

Student: Are we always talking about want when we are talking about motivation?

Dr. Hora: Well, we could want or we would like or we are interested or we are inspired to act—to take action. When God gives us an idea, then there is action taking place, and that is called spontaneity.

Student: Dr. Hora, sometimes someone will call and invite me someplace, and I have to say yes or no.

Dr. Hora: So you say yes or no.

Student: That is very difficult; there is no time to question our motivation about accepting the invitation or refusing it.

Dr. Hora: So you say, "Give me a break!"

Student: "Give me time" to see whether I have PAGL or anxiety.

Dr. Hora: Right.

Student: Dr. Hora, we were speaking earlier about talking and influencing. I've been trying to keep my mouth shut, practicing for what may be my next job. I have been warned that if I take this job, it will be fine, but that it is best not to talk about it. So I have been trying to practice this and not to talk about it until it is final, because it is not final yet.

Dr. Hora: It is hard.

Student: Everyone who has seen me in the last few weeks knows, because I do talk about it, but I don't understand what it means that I do. Is it just the urging of self-confirmation that refuses to pay attention to an idea like "keep your mouth shut"?

Dr. Hora: What is happening when we talk prematurely and tell people about some intimate concern or plan of ours? It is most likely that something will get spoiled and that a monkey wrench will get thrown into it. This wisdom has been known for a long time. For instance, writers are advised never to tell people that they are writing a book because it will never get written.

Student: Is that superstition?

Dr. Hora: No, it is really true. There is such a thing as "Herodian thought." What is Herodian thought? After Jesus was born, he was hidden from Herod, the king [who wanted to destroy him—see Matthew 2]. The Herodian thought is malicious envy— which is not difficult to encounter—and if we are blabbermouths, we will just hurt ourselves by talking.

Student: Can other people's envy prevent a book from being written?

Dr. Hora: If you are a blabbermouth, you will be influenced subliminally to mess yourself up.

Dialogue No. 18

Envy

Dr. Hora: Envy is so ubiquitous that it doesn't need an invitation. The world seems to be filled with envy, jealousy, rivalry, and malice. This is "the sea of mental garbage." We cannot hide from envy, so the question is, How can we find immunity? In our culture envy is particularly rampant because we are an upwardly mobile society. There is much conspicuous consumption, and there is the freedom to compete and to be in rivalry with everyone else—no one is going to stop it. What is needed is to acquire immunity. Einstein said, "I am free of these arrows of hate and envy, because they come from a world with which I have nothing in common." He was very much envied because he was so brilliant.

Student: It seems difficult to accept that there are malicious thoughts. I find it disturbing.

Dr. Hora: How can we acquire immunity to voodoo, witchcraft, and gossip and from influencing and claims of personal mind power? There are two problems: how to be free of the inclination toward envying—this is perhaps the bigger problem—and how to have immunity to being envied. How are they connected? The more envious we are, the more susceptible we are to the ill effects of being envied because we believe in it. Of course, we cannot just say, "I won't believe in it"; that would not help.

Student: I can clearly see that I believe that envious thoughts can hurt me. This is very disturbing because I believe it, and every time it comes, I am amazed at its effect.

Dr. Hora: Who can outline a procedure whereby we could be liberated from this problem and acquire immunity? The homosexual epidemic is called Acquired Immune Deficiency Syndrome (AIDS). It is interesting that it has cropped up among homosexuals because homosexuality is a condition that is completely based on envy. It is called love, but it is just envy. What is sexual attraction? Sexual attraction is based on envying the body parts of another.

Student: Even between opposite sexes?

159

Dr. Hora: Yes. Men envy what women seem to have, and women envy what men seem to have. As the saying goes, "What has he got that I ain't got?" And that is the "natural" way to be— it is covered over and called "love" and "sexual attraction." Now there is an epidemic of men becoming women and of women undergoing surgery to become men. This is called a transsexual operation, and it is all about envy. Everyone envies everyone else—and that goes for money or cars or boats or clothes or hair or for whatever he has—envy tends to completely dominate the unenlightened mind.

Student: Dr. Hora, in homosexuality, when two men live together, does one pretend to be a woman? What is it they envy?

Dr. Hora: Whatever the other seems to have. What is fetishism? There are men who become sexually aroused by looking at earlobes or shoes or gloves. We can get hooked on envying something so powerfully that it becomes eroticized. What do we mean by eroticized? We mean it becomes an object of sexual arousal—then we are hooked on it. It is called love, but what is it? It is envy turned into an eroticized object. Now if we can fall in love with an earlobe, we can fall in love with a head or buttocks. It is interesting that many people envy the body parts of others, and out of that is being spun a fantasy that leads to sexual arousal, and people have the impression they have fallen in love. A whole romantic fantasy is built around a single body part. That is what envy does.

Student: We were talking about body parts, but is it also possible for someone to envy someone else's intelligence? Is it the same thing?

Dr. Hora: Yes, it is the same thing.

Student: Or their seeming power . . .

Dr. Hora: Yes, power is very often an object of envy. There is a lot of self-deception in the world. Are we really interested in acquiring immunity from envy, so that we might not be harmed by people who envy us and that we might not suffer the hell of being envious? It is a hellish thing to be envious. It is interesting that envy primarily affects the teeth. We observed years ago that envious people have a lot of trouble with their teeth. So how can we be healed of this universal problem?

Student: Well, first we have to identify envy for what it really is. If we can see it as part of the human condition, then it makes it easier to understand. We do not have to be afraid of envy because that is just the way the human condition is—and we do not have to take it personally or think that we are victims of someone else's thoughts. They cannot hurt us—unless we are interested in wanting something from them. But if we do want something, then we are hooked.

Dr. Hora: Yes. How does envy start? By comparison thinking. All comparison thinking has to be nipped in the bud. We have to guard against this tendency and realize that there is no basis for comparison. Every one of us is a unique manifestation of infinite, divine Love-Intelligence, and there are no two individualities alike. Therefore it makes no sense to compare, and if we do compare, we fail to bring into manifestation our uniqueness and to find fulfillment in life. So the first step is to become aware of the tendency to compare and to refrain from it; then there will be no envying on our part. But there will still be envy all around us. How do we cope with that?

Student: Maybe we need to go beyond interaction thoughts because if we are aware of envy, then we are in that whole mode of thinking about what others are thinking about "me." So we can recognize it as an interaction mode and rise above it.

Dr. Hora: Yes, that is good. Another aspect of this is to allow people to be envious—to be aware of it and to acknowledge that anyone has a perfect right to envy us till they are green in the face—it is none of our business. Whatever we allow, we are immune to. If we think someone should not envy us, or we don't like it, then we are involved in the interaction scheme of the situation, and we are vulnerable. We are vulnerable to envy and voodoo and witchcraft, and we begin to stumble over our own feet and to make mistakes and get into accidents and all kinds of things.

Student: We say we suffer from our own thoughts, not from someone else's thoughts; so the stumbling isn't the manifestation of someone else's malicious thought, but of our disapproving thought?

Dr. Hora: Yes. It is our own disapproving thoughts that make us vulnerable to envy.

Student: We don't have to compare because we are all unique in the eyes of God. But it is hard to understand that concept, to know that we are unique. I guess we are interested in society and in material values.

Student: It seems that one of the problems is that we think we are unique persons, but there is no good in being a unique person if another unique person has what we want. However, we can say, "I am unique," and understand it as something nondimensional. That doesn't seem so hard.

Dr. Hora: Yes, very good. We do not speak of unique personalities—there is no such thing—it is just wearing certain psychological makeup like everyone else. But we are unique manifestations of divine Love-Intelligence. And the more we appreciate that, the more we reach fulfillment in this life because God is fulfilling himself in everyone of us in a unique way.

Student: Dr. Hora, I also think that when we come to appreciate PAGL, we begin to realize that without it material life is nothing, absolutely nothing. So as we grow and mature with spiritual wisdom, we begin to recognize that PAGL [PAGL is an acronym for Peace, Assurance, Gratitude, Love, and Its Presence in consciousness informs us that we are in tune with the One Mind] is the true value in life.

Dr. Hora: Yes, and if we are envious, there is no PAGL. If we are susceptible to being envied, there is also no PAGL—there is anxiety. We feel threatened by people who envy us.

Student: Is that true of any ignorant thought, if we fight it or judge it or condemn it, then we will be affected by it? Can we have immunity to any ignorant thought if we let it be?

Dr. Hora: Yes, like a transcendent observer: it is important not to approve and not to disapprove, not to agree and not to disagree, not to accept and not to reject.

Student: That can be provocative too, can't it? If we are critical or fighting some thought, without another individual even realizing it, that can provoke him to continue.

Dr. Hora: Yes, and try harder to get a rise.

Student: There is a situation like that where I work. A colleague seems to be power hungry, and no one is capable of doing anything well around him because there is constant personal criticism. I have been wondering how to become immune to it, but because I am so disapproving of it, I get involved more often than not.

Dr. Hora: Right, no immunity there. "Letting be" is immunity, strangely enough.

Student: Seeing it, but letting them be.

Student: Then the inability to let be would indicate that the whole fight is really just a self-confirmatory way of being.

Student: Interaction, total interaction.

Student: Today I saw two little boys being envious of some little girls. I tend to think that they shouldn't be that way, but anyone has a right to entertain any thought. It seems sad though; it is a shame that these boys are growing up with envious thoughts.

Dr. Hora: The point is not what they are envying but that they are envying. There are children in the school where you work, and you observe that some of them envy the bodies of little girls. We don't say, "You shouldn't envy the girls' bodies—you should envy the boys' bodies!" No, we just try to help them see that if they envy anything, then they are suffering—they are hurting themselves. Of course, they may not listen. But we respect people's right not to listen, and that helps sometimes too.

Student: When we read something that is written by an individual who has something worthwhile to say, what is it that makes us inspired by it instead of thinking, "I wish I could be that way?" How can we be inspired if envy is so much with us? What is there about what we are seeing or reading that allows us to be inspired?

Dr. Hora: As long as we envy, we are not accessible to inspiration, and we cannot really appreciate things of true value.

Student: If we find that we are inspired by something, then what is it that is being presented that is allowing us to be inspired?

Dr. Hora: We have discovered some spiritual values.

Student: Are we inspired also because we didn't see what was presented in a personal way? It seems easier not to be envious of composers, for example, because they are making music, and we can appreciate it because they have made use of certain principles and disciplines. But it seems that when someone writes a book or does something unusually creative, it is as if they did it. Then we are envious of them and wish we could do it too—or we wonder how they could do it and we cannot. It is hard to understand that it came from God.

Dr. Hora: Yes. Without God, there is no way of outgrowing envy. Unless we can see God in a work of art or a beautiful flower, we will always think, "Why the hell can't I do this?"

Student: We have to see God in order not to be envious. How else could we understand what it means to be unique?

Dr. Hora: What is besting?

Student: To one up.

Dr. Hora: Yes, showing that we know more or better, which is a form of envy bordering on rivalry.

Student: There is so much unconscious envy. Do we always have to be "mind-fasting?"

Dr. Hora: Well, that is not bad, "mind-fasting." We have to be aware of our motivation at all times. What impels us to say something? Is it a desire to shed light or to clarify—to contribute—or to show that we know? And if it is a desire to show that we know, we are in trouble.

Student: Dr. Hora, it seems that an individual who suffers from envy has a lack of self-esteem because he or she is always looking at another and comparing. How do we begin to build a sense of self-esteem? How can we lose the low opinion we have of ourselves?

Dr. Hora: It is a hopeless effort. There is no way anyone can build up self-esteem for himself or for anyone else.

Student: We have to recognize that then?

Dr. Hora: No, we have to ask the question, What is self-esteem?

Student: Recognizing that we are created by God.

Dr. Hora: The only kind of self-esteem is that which God gives us. People who try to acquire self-esteem wind up as egomaniacs. If we are aware of our spiritual self-esteem, we can relax.

Student: But it seems as if it is taken away from us; it seems as if the fantasies that our parents held for us have taken it away . . .

Dr. Hora: Only the human illusion of self-esteem. Our parents cannot give it to us, and they cannot take it away from us because that is just a counterfeit self-esteem: it is ego. Real self-esteem is spiritual—born of divine Love—and it does not have to be acquired or deserved. It is given to us by the grace of God.

Student: How do we recognize it?

Dr. Hora: By studying Metapsychiatry, we can come to recognize it.

Student: I'd like to understand how to see that intelligent ideas are not coming from a person.

Dr. Hora: Intelligent ideas are coming through an individual consciousness. The brain cannot produce intelligent ideas—not even unintelligent ideas—the brain is not a thought factory.

Student: Some individuals seem better able to become aware of intelligent ideas than others, but that may be just another way of personalizing intelligence—that someone else could become aware of intelligent ideas while I am busy being distracted by ignorance—but I guess this is just another comparison thought

Dr. Hora: Yes.

Student: Dr. Hora, what is the difference between envy and jealousy?

Dr. Hora: Envy is wanting to have what someone else has, and jealousy is wanting to be what someone else is.

Student: And rivalry?

Dr. Hora: Rivalry is wanting to be better than someone else— it is besting. And malice is ill will. When the "Four Horsemen" deteriorate [if envy, jealousy, and rivalry are unchecked and allowed to progress], they become malicious. In the play Othello, murder took place, based on malicious jealousy. People create problems for themselves when comparison thinking gets out of hand.

Student: Many games that children play are based on rivalry because the opponent wins or loses. There really is no valid basis for these games, is there?

Dr. Hora: Rivalry is competition gone awry.

Student: But some games can be a way of learning something well. I play games with children sometimes. We learn how the game works, and it seems that there is an issue-oriented way of playing the game.

Dr. Hora: Yes, however, when it becomes interactive, it deteriorates into malicious rivalry.

Student: I remember as a kid always losing, and finally I just didn't play games anymore. It just occurred to me now that they are two sides of the same coin—that the one who is the winner of the games keeps playing the games and the one who is the loser, who stopped playing games, is also still playing the game, but in a very apathetic way.

Dr. Hora: Yes, we can decide to frustrate the winner by not playing.

Student: Is there such a thing as healthy competition?

Dr. Hora: Yes, if it is not allowed to deteriorate into rivalry. Rivalry is essentially personalized, interactive competition where the issue is winning. Healthy competition is nonpersonal, where the issue is about attaining greater skill in something—it is not an interactive situation but a situation oriented toward maximizing a certain skill. Competitive skiing, for instance, is not interactive; one is competing against time for skill. That is healthy competition because it maximizes the skill. But it can very easily become personal, and at that moment, it is not competition anymore—it is rivalry.

Student: In America, do we suffer more from envy and jealousy than in other countries, like Russia, for example?

Dr. Hora: I think so. You see, the Russian people are so oppressed, and there are such limited possibilities for advancing over others, that there is nothing to envy; there is just a common bond in suffering. Whenever people are afflicted by some collective problem, they band together and suddenly love each other and are good to each other. Rivalry disappears, and even envy disappears. There is nothing to envy—everyone is just sharing the burden of suffering. So from this standpoint, they seem to have fewer problems, but of course the potentialities of human creativity are stifled. Here we have this freedom, this expansive social order which brings out the best and the worst in us.

Student: Do we have more mental illness as a consequence of that?

Dr. Hora: Yes, most likely. But suffice it to say, envy is inevitable but not necessary.

Dialogue No. 19

Awareness

Student: I would like clarification regarding awareness. Is it good enough just to be aware? For instance, if there is a problem, we ask ourselves what the meaning is; but if we could be aware of our thoughts all the time, it seems that would be ideal. What do we need to understand to become more aware all the time?

Dr. Hora: Do we all understand the question?

Student: Awareness can have several meanings. We can be aware of our thoughts, and we can be aware of the presence of God—

Dr. Hora: Or we can be aware of a stomachache and disgust. We can be aware of many things. So it is not enough just to be aware; we also have to know what is valid and what is not valid, what is worthwhile to be aware of and what is not worthwhile to be aware of. Gaining an awareness of God, and of spiritual values, would assure us of peace, assurance, gratitude, love, freedom, and health. But if we are aware of certain fantasies, erotic fantasies, for example, then we get sick. Awareness, of course, is important, but we also have the God-given dominion over what we shall pay attention to.

Student: So there is a difference between awareness and what we are paying attention to; we can be aware of a stomachache, but that is not going to help?

Dr. Hora: Yes. There are valid and invalid ideas to be aware of—that's what it means to be "stewards of consciousness." God gave us dominion, which means we have the power to choose what thoughts we shall pay attention to. Most people do not realize that the thoughts they cherish or pay attention to will determine their experiences. Thoughts are very dangerous. The enlightened way of life is to be constantly monitoring our thoughts, rejecting illness-producing thoughts and turning our attention to spiritual values. We gain a broad-minded perspective on life. Now most people get sucked into interaction thoughts—they are always "thinking about what other people are thinking about what they are thinking." If we let our hair down and become sloppy mentally, we find that we are thinking about relationships with other people, and this is the root of the problem. This kind of narrow-minded outlook on life is the source of any kind of illness—from a simple cold to cancer and including accidents and high blood pressure—anything can come from interaction thinking. That is the normal way to be. The normal way to be is to be involved mentally in thoughts of interaction.

Student: Sometimes it is so automatic that we are not even aware of it.

Dr. Hora: Here comes awareness. Metapsychiatry, following Jesus, says, "Be aware." "Be sober, be vigilant; because your adversary the devil, as a roaring lion, walketh about, seeking whom he may devour" (1 Peter 5:8). What is this devil? It is just interaction thought. It means that anyone who is in the habit of interaction thinking—working on his relationships with people, how to get along with people—is a victim of a constricted outlook on life. In Metapsychiatry we learn to open up our mental horizon and to see life in the context of God—not in the context of human relationships, but in the context of God—and there we find freedom and PAGL [PAGL is an acronym for Peace, Assurance, Gratitude, Love, and Its Presence in consciousness informs us that we are in tune with the One Mind] and healing. The whole thing is really very simple—it is a matter of learning to be aware of what is valid, of what is broad-minded and of what is narrow-minded. Narrow-minded people think about their relationships and about cause and effect. That is all—all the time. This is considered the normal way to be. Millions of people suffer all kinds of diseases and symptoms and aches and pains. It is very interesting: in Metapsychiatry we have discovered that every symptom is the body's way of telling us about the interaction thoughts we are entertaining. Every symptom clearly reveals the interaction thoughts with which we are preoccupied, so it is very easy to discern the meaning of problems.

Student: Is that what it means when we ask, "Who am I sick against now?"

Dr. Hora: Yes, that is right. We can ask, "What is the meaning of my experience?" "Who am I sick against?" "What is the body talking about now?" If we ask these questions, we can discover the meaning of our problems.

Student: Sometimes I can see that I am resentful about a person or that I want a person to like me. I see the thoughts, and then I make an affirmation. What is an affirmation, as opposed to just seeking to broaden the perspective or the context? It seems that I start with an affirmation that the individual is a unique expression of God, and then I wait to realize that.

Dr. Hora: Affirmations are not very helpful, because essentially they are superstitious and operational. We recite certain words in the hope that they will have some effect and influence God to solve our problem. We have to recognize and become aware that we are thinking about our relationship to someone else. The moment we become aware of this, we must cut it out. It is a narrow-minded, harmful way to be mentally preoccupied.

Student: Oftentimes I recognize invalid thoughts, but I don't know where to go from there. When you say just stop it, I don't seem to be able to stop it. Do we have to turn attention to something else?

Dr. Hora: We can stop it. First we kick ourselves and then say, "I am being narrow-minded and interactional in my thoughts. Let me see if I can expand my horizon and see the situation in the context of God."

Student: If we stop thinking about our relationships with others, wouldn't that be rejecting them?

Dr. Hora: Rejection is just another interaction thought. We don't reject anyone—we just abolish the context. We are not rejecting people: when we reject people, or we love people, or we like people, or we dislike them, that is interaction thinking. It is nowhere, and it is harmful.

Student: We say we must switch the context. If we are aware of the interaction context—which is self and other—maybe the only real switch we can make is from an invalid context to a divine context. We cannot say, "Well now I will think nice thoughts about this person," because we will still be in that interaction context.

Dr. Hora: Yes. If we think nice thoughts about someone, or if we think nasty thoughts about someone, or if we reject someone, we are still in the interaction context. Some people would say that this is impossible; there is nothing else but interaction in life. Everything is interaction. This would seem to be true. If we don't have the blessing of a Metapsychiatric education, there is no way we can expand our mental horizon and get out of this trap of interaction thinking—that is the world. Jesus said that we have to "overcome the world." What did he mean? What is this "world" that Jesus overcame? The world is made of, and is the product of, interaction thinking. What happens to the world when we overcome it?

Student: We transcend our erroneous thoughts, and it disappears.

Dr. Hora: Interestingly enough, the world is redeemed. What does that mean? The world is redeemed—from a miserable conflict-filled world, it turns into a harmonious, peaceful, intelligent divinely governed situation.

Student: What about wars and such?

Dr. Hora: That is someone else's world. If we are involved with the thoughts about a war, then it is our world. But our world, the world of our experience, is redeemed—everyone in this world of ours will become a spiritual child of God.

Student: Does that include those sufferers who are still living in the world?

Dr. Hora: There is the world at large, and then there is "our world." For instance, at this moment, this group is our world. When we are in a family situation or on the job, whatever is immediately around us, it is our world, and we can redeem it by expanding our mental horizon. Instead of seeing interpersonal relationships, we see the Presence of God. When we see the situation in the context of God, immediately there is peace, assurance, gratitude, and love—no conflicts, no hatreds, no jealousies, no rivalries, no deceptions, no evil—everything is pacified and harmonized and intelligent. That is what a beneficial presence in the world is: the way he sees reality redeems the world around him. He is a focal point of harmony and healing by virtue of his ability to see the situation in the context of God.

What Is Thinking?

Student: I seem to be critical when I try to judge "righteous judgment."

Dr. Hora: We must understand that judgmentalism is ignorance. We do not say, "You are wrong." We say, "This is not valid." What happens when we make a personal remark? Whenever we make a personal remark about ourselves or others, even if it is good, it is interactional. We avoid interaction like the plague. There is just one thing that we avoid even more than interaction—-what is that?

Student: Influencing.

Dr. Hora: Influencing is interactional. Self-confirmation is even worse because it is self-destructive. "Righteous judgment" distinguishes between what is valid and what is not valid. It is not an accusation, if we say this reasoning is not valid. We are not accusing and judging someone; we are evaluating the behavior, as such, entirely apart from the individual who is displaying the invalid behavior. We say that this behavior is invalid because it is based on a mistake, if they are interested in hearing. If they are not interested in hearing, then we keep quiet. We have to be tactful—tactfulness means that we are alert in seeing whether someone is interested.

Student: Sometimes critical thoughts seem to flow automatically.

Dr. Hora: If we do not understand that it is ignorance, then it is easy to slip into critical thinking. If we understand, it is not difficult to avoid judging.

Student: Being human is tough.

Student: What is life all about? It seems so confusing. Life just doesn't make sense on a human level, but it seems so real. I go to work; work seems real, but it is such a hassle. There are so many personalities, and I can't find peace in my life.

Dr. Hora: Life is a dream, a dream of personal existence.

Student: How do we lose interest in the concerns of personal existence?

Dr. Hora: The Zen Master has a simple prescription: "Erase yourself utterly." I have recommended certain steps: "Never talk about yourself; never talk about others; be here for God."

Student: What is the difference between that and just being withdrawn? I don't really talk that much at work; I am actually very quiet unless I have an issue to deal with. I can't tell if I am quiet because I am self-conscious about how I am performing on the job, or if I am really being issue-oriented. It is not clear to me.

Dr. Hora: We have to be silent in a nonpersonal way.

Student: If one is concerned about one's performance, then work is on a personal level, and it wipes out the whole idea of being nonpersonal.

Dr. Hora: Yes.

Student: Metapsychiatry says not to speak about ourselves or others. We would have to eliminate our thoughts about ourselves and others, to quiet our thoughts besides quieting our conversation.

Student: That is what I have been struggling with, and it seems that we cannot "do" it because it is operational. So we have to know something. What is it that we must know so that self-confirmation wouldn't be what we are most interested in?

Student: Does it have to do with personal mind? What do we need to do to stop thinking about ourselves? Isn't the belief in a personal mind at the core of that problem?

Dr. Hora: What is thinking?

Student: It is an illusion.

Dr. Hora: So?

Student: The way that we can start to see that it is an illusion is by understanding that ideas "obtain" in consciousness—that is really the healing.

Dr. Hora: It is true that ideas obtain, but this information is not appropriate to this question. The question was, What is thinking? Thinking is paying attention. Isn't that simple?

Student: No, because in order to pay attention, we lose sight of ourselves, and that is the payment—right paying attention to the issue. When one is thinking, it seems as if the self is doing it.

Dr. Hora: Yes, but that is not valid. We have the illusion that we are thinking. When we have the illusion that we are thinking, we are not really thinking—we are paying attention to certain thoughts.

Student: That is confusing because I read in one of our books that love is "paying attention."

Dr. Hora: Yes, love pays attention—

Student: And that is the opposite of calculative thinking.

Dr. Hora: Yes, but again this information is not appropriate to the question. Don't lean on the written word—let some original ideas occur.

Student: Are we distinguishing between thoughts and ideas? In this dialogue, is thought the same as an idea?

Dr. Hora: We asked the question, What is thinking? There is no such thing as thinking. We are not thinking—we are paying attention to thoughts. There is the famous conundrum where people are asked to try not to think of pink elephants. What does this question mean? Don't pay attention to thoughts about pink elephants—pay attention to thoughts about yellow kangaroos? Thinking is paying attention. If we understand that, then there is no problem. We can always shift our attention from one issue to another issue. If our attention is focused in one direction of the room, we will have different thoughts than if we are looking in another direction. So we are not really thinking—we are paying attention to certain thoughts. Therefore we cannot be victims of thoughts. There are people who suffer greatly from obsessive thinking. They claim that they cannot stop thinking about a certain issue. They suffer greatly because they try to stop thinking. We cannot do that because we are not really thinking— our attention is simply focused on a particular issue. But we can shift our attention to another issue.

Student: What about certain thoughts that seem to have a strong, attractive pull on the mind, like worry, for example? It seems as if something very powerful in the thought keeps drawing the attention back.

Dr. Hora: There is not only the illusion that we are thinking, but there is also an illusion that we can control events with our thoughts. When we worry about something, we fall prey to an illusion that by thinking about what should not happen, we can in a magical way assure that it will not happen. We are ensnared by our own ignorant illusions, and it is all based on the idea that we are thinking; but it is not really thinking—we are paying attention to something that should not happen or to something that should happen.

Student: But there seems to be another side to that—and it is kind of perverse. We have the illusion from personal mind power that if we worry obsessively about something, we can make it not happen. However, if we take the principle that "Nothing comes into experience uninvited" [Seventh Principle of Metapsychiatry], it seems as if the mind does have that power in the opposite direction, that if we keep thinking that something should not happen, we will invite it.

Dr. Hora: Yes, of course that is the double-edged sword of ignorance. If we understand that we are not really thinking, but that we are just attending to thoughts, then we can attend to something that is really helpful, like love or generosity or gratitude or freedom.

Student: So the illusion that we are thinking is based on a belief that we can change events with our thoughts?

Dr. Hora: Yes, on personal mind power—there are religions based on this illusion. Now the question is, How many people would be willing to admit that they cannot think? Someone could ask, "Am I mindless or stupid?" It could be a great insult to try to explain to someone that he cannot really think.

Student: It is hard for us to admit that we cannot think?

Dr. Hora: Of course, it hurts our mental vanity. All our lives, we are being educated to think and to be proud of our thinking ability. And now, here comes Metapsychiatry, which throws a monkey wrench into the whole idea by saying that no one can think—there is no such thing as thinking!

Student: It lifts a big burden.

Student: Where does repression fit into all of this?

Dr. Hora: In repression we say, "I will think of something else."

Student: So it is still thinking.

Student: It seems that this realization is the way to understand that thoughts and experiences are actually illusions. But what about a problem or a condition? We can realize this and not pay attention to it for awhile, but then we find that the condition still persists.

Dr. Hora: It was just self-deception.

Student: Do we deceive ourselves unconsciously?

Dr. Hora: Unconsciously, peripherally, any way we choose.

Student: So there are some thoughts that we pay constant attention to without even realizing it?

Dr. Hora: Yes.

Student: How could we lose our connection to these thoughts that we carry around with us all the time?

Dr. Hora: That is where prayer, study, and meditation come in.

We must be interested in being aware of divine Reality to such an extent that we lose interest in those invalid thoughts. When the thoughts are gone, the symptom disappears—symptoms are just thoughts in visible form—that is the dynamic of healing.

Student: How does that work?

Dr. Hora: If we have a symptom, and the symptom is annoying or frightening or hurting or troublesome in any way, attention gets riveted on that symptom. If we are not a student of Metapsychiatry, then we run for help and draw the attention of the helper to the experience, and the helper reinforces our rivetedness to the symptom. Soon the symptom becomes the problem, and it grows by being reinforced from many sides. This is what happens to people who go to hospitals. Recently someone went to the hospital with phlebitis, a very minor condition. Within a week or two, they released him from the hospital with terminal cancer—to die. What happened? It is not understood that attention has to be shifted from the physical symptom to the thought which is in consciousness and which is manifesting itself as the symptom. When we understand the meaning, we can see that we have gotten involved with a thought; and then we ask the Second Intelligent Question, which shifts our attention away from the invalid thought to something valid, and that thought then has a chance to disappear from our consciousness and with it, the symptom.

Student: It seems sometimes that the way we can become aware of the thought that is behind the symptom is to turn our attention to something valid.

Dr. Hora: You said, "The thought that is behind the symptom." The thought is not behind the symptom—the symptom is the thought. There is not a symptom and a thought. No, the symptom is the thought; the symptom is talking.

Student: The way symptoms get worse, then, is by our paying increasing amounts of attention to them. Is that the only way symptoms get worse?

Dr. Hora: Yes, we get more and more riveted to the symptom; then we expand on it, and it spreads and completely engulfs us.

Student: It is like a vicious cycle. First we see a mole, and then we start to worry, and then it becomes cancerous. It is just a vicious cycle of paying increasing attention to it.

Dr. Hora: That is what is happening to thousands and thousands of people.

Student: Even if there is no devil in the world, it certainly seems a devilish way of tricking us. It is really perverse.

Dr. Hora: That's right.

Student: The way to break that is to understand what thoughts are and what thinking is?

Dr. Hora: Yes, we have to understand the language of the body.

Student: What are we doing when we are thinking about the condition in the first place?

Dr. Hora: We are paying attention to certain invalid thoughts.

Student: In order to realize what that means, we would have to break the illusion of having personal mind power?

Dr. Hora: That is already gone, long ago. Today we are talking about "what is thinking." There is no such thing as thinking— there is just paying attention. And if our attention is riveted to some invalid thoughts, we are going to have experiences corresponding to those invalid thoughts. However, if our attention is oriented toward God, toward Christ-consciousness, we are going to lose sight of those invalid thoughts.

Student: Is it a good idea to think spiritual thoughts and affirm God's presence?

Dr. Hora: There is no such thing as thinking a spiritual thought, even if we are affirming it. We can affirm spiritual thoughts without even being aware of it. There is no thinking— there is just paying attention, and our attention can be focused on valid thoughts or on invalid thoughts. That is the whole story.

Student: What is an affirmation?

Dr. Hora: An affirmation is a lie. It says, "I am really thinking good thoughts." But this is not true because we are not really interested.

Student: So we are not admitting what we are really paying attention to?

Dr. Hora: Yes, we are just lying to ourselves on a religious basis—it is self-deception.

Student: Is that also mental vanity, not wanting to be embarrassed by seeing those thoughts?

Dr. Hora: Probably. Sometimes our attention is so captivated by certain positive or negative stimuli that it is very difficult to shift attention.

Student: Is it intelligent to avoid stimuli?

Dr. Hora: Suppose you are watching television, and there is a gorgeous blonde there, half-undressed.

Student: We turn the television set off?

Dr. Hora: But you can still think of it. We have to recognize that this is sensualism, and then we don't have to turn off the television—we can just turn our attention to something really beautiful, like joy, or to some spiritual value, and then it disappears from consciousness.

Student: What about invalid thoughts that we have been riveted to for a long time?

Dr. Hora: The longer we have been riveted to an invalid thought, the harder it is to turn our attention away from it. There are these long-standing preoccupations with invalid thoughts we are too embarrassed to admit to, and then unfortunately we have chronic conditions.

Student: Is the shifting away from that usually a gradual process?

Dr. Hora: It depends on how clearly the meaning is discerned. If it is a powerful, shocking, embarrassing situation, it rips us away from the invalid thoughts.

Student: Does disengaging our interest from the symptom itself enhance our ability to receive the meaning spontaneously in consciousness?

Dr. Hora: The most important thing is the willingness to be embarrassed. The second important thing is to keep asking, "What is this symptom saying to me?" Remind yourself that Dr. Hora said, "Every physical symptom is a message about some interaction."

Student: Just by asking the question, What is this symptom saying? we are already taking our attention away from the symptom itself?

Dr. Hora: Yes, we are moving into the meaning. There is an unwillingness to admit that we are preoccupied with certain illness-inducing thoughts. It is interesting how symptoms change in the world. When I was a medical student, we very frequently observed that certain people had compulsive hand-washing symptoms. These individuals could not stop washing their hands. A thousand times a day, they would run to the washroom and scrub their hands with soap and brushes—this was a very frequent symptom in those days. Now we don't hear about it anymore. Of course, it was a mystery to psychiatry then; no one could understand it until, through Freudian analysis, it was discovered that many of these individuals were very religious, and they felt terribly dirty for using their hands to masturbate. It was unconscious; they were mentally preoccupied with this terrible "sin," which they had learned about in the church, and they developed this hand-washing compulsion.

No one could relieve them, and they couldn't admit that they were trying to wash away their sins. In Shakespeare's play Macbeth, Lady Macbeth tries to wash away the blood. So the meaning is not admitted because of the tremendous guilt. People feared being cast into utter darkness and being punished by God. Nowadays people are not so much afraid of God.

Student: Do you have to have a willingness to feel guilty as well as a willingness to be embarrassed?

Dr. Hora: No, just embarrassment is required. Guilt is self-confirmatory. These were examples of an unwillingness to admit to thoughts.

Student: Dr. Hora, if we would like to understand the meaning of an experience or the meaning of a symptom, how can we avoid falling into the trap of trying to figure it out? We can ask ourselves, "What is this symptom saying to me?" But then it would be very easy to try to figure it out.

Dr. Hora: Yes, you could.

Student: But it is not helpful.

Dr. Hora: It won't work—that is all. We don't have to feel guilty about trying to figure it out—it just won't work.

Student: Is it a question of receptivity and humility?

Dr. Hora: If we are trying to figure it out, then we are saying, "I believe that I can think." And there we are back to thinking again—you think that you are thinking, but there is no such thing as thinking.

Student: Is it self-confirmatory that we think that we are thinking?

Dr. Hora: Yes.

Student: Meditation really teaches us that we are paying attention to thoughts instead of thinking that we are thinking.

Dr. Hora: That is the value of meditation among other things— if we lose the illusion that we can think, we become intelligent.

Student: Is that how we can be healed of just repeating words that we have read and become receptive to having an original idea?

Dr. Hora: Of course. ". . . The serpent said . . . 'In the day ye eat thereof [of the tree of knowledge of good and evil], then your eyes shall be opened, and ye shall be as gods, knowing good and evil'" (Genesis 3:3; see also Genesis 2:16-17). You will be able to "think for yourself," as the saying goes. The moment that we begin thinking that we are thinking, we are in trouble. Human beings are the only life form on this planet who have the illusion that they are thinkers. Animals don't think that they are thinking. They are much happier than we are. This illusion that we are thinkers makes for much suffering.

Student: It prevents us from being spontaneous.

Dr. Hora: And from being intelligent. We are not receptive to Intelligence if we are involved in the illusion of thinking.

Dialogue No. 21

Freedom

Student: We have said that it is better to be a freedom-realizer than a freedom-fighter. I seem to be fighting for some degree of freedom, so it probably means that I don't understand what real spiritual freedom is. Would you please clarify what spiritual freedom is?

Dr. Hora: You would like to be free?

Student: Yes.

Dr. Hora: A freedom-fighter will never be free—he is always fighting for freedom. What is the difference between a freedom-fighter and a freedom-realizer?

Student: A freedom-fighter is always fighting the duality of the human condition.

Dr. Hora: Exactly. Now what are the signs of spiritual freedom?

Student: PAGL [PAGL is an acronym for Peace, Assurance, Gratitude, Love, and Its Presence in consciousness informs us that we are in tune with the One Mind].

Dr. Hora: Yes, and more specifically, it is the possibility of expressing all the talents, gifts, intelligence, and love with which we are endowed by our Creator. This is freedom. We are not talking about political freedom or economic freedom or other kinds of freedom—although they are by-products of spiritual freedom. We define true freedom as having the ability to express all our God-given potential, and there is plenty of that in everyone. If we are a pianist and cannot play the piano freely enough, then we are not free. We haven't realized our spiritual freedom. No matter how talented a musician may be, he will not be able to play the piano adequately, to do justice to his potential, without spiritual freedom. How many musicians there are in the world who could be a hundred times better, if they would only have the freedom to express what is within—and that goes for communicating, writing, or participating in a group situation. Last week the whole group was hamstrung by fear—there was no freedom to participate.

Student: It is helpful to think of freedom as the freedom to manifest—which is different from the freedom from mental enslavement.

Dr. Hora: That is the freedom-fighter's point of view—the focus is on the blocks, the obstacles to freedom and beating one's head against a wall. A freedom-fighter will just fight all the time and never be free.

Student: So we have to turn away from that. We realize it is there, but we turn away?

Dr. Hora: Yes, that is the secret of becoming a freedom-realizer. How does one become a freedom-realizer? Who has the freedom to say?

Student: Knowing who we really are.

Dr. Hora: Could you say something more?

Student: That each of us is a divine Consciousness, made in the "image and likeness of God." If we really knew this, and not just the words, it would make us free.

Dr. Hora: Yes, good point. The right sense of self-identity, as a spiritual manifestation of God, is an essential aspect of realized freedom—knowing who we are, what we are, where we are, and what our purpose is [the Four Ws of Metapsychiatry]. How does that do away with all the mental forces that are always working to rob us of this freedom? Those of you who were here last week know that there was a complete mental enslavement in this group: no one was able to express himself.

Student: I notice that I am sometimes intimidated by filling out forms because I think I am a stupid person. My thoughts immediately tell me I am going to make a mistake when I fill out a form, and since I don't know "who" I really am, I make a mistake.

Dr. Hora: You don't have the freedom to utilize your God-given intelligence, to function in an effortless, efficient, and effective way.

Student: We always think someone is going to give us that freedom—our parents will finally set us free, for example. But if this freedom is spiritual, no one can give it to us.

Dr. Hora: That's right, and no one can take it away. "Whatsoever God doeth, it shall be forever"—it is perfect. "Nothing can be put to it nor any thing taken away from it . . ." (Ecclesiastes 3:13).

Student: This morning I couldn't get started into my day, and I wasn't feeling well. I meditated and realized that I was frightened. This fear was preventing me from doing whatever it was I had to do. I didn't know exactly what the fear was, but I realized that

I must be intimidated. Right after that, slowly but surely things started rolling. But it seems as if there are so many things that need to be done, and I think I have to "perform." Then, of course, I can't do it, and the fear sets in, and it is a vicious cycle. How can we realize spiritual Reality first, when, in fact, it seems as if all these other things need to be done? The more we think about it, the less we do—and then there is more to do!

Dr. Hora: That is a very good question. The first requirement for freedom realization is to see the difference—we have to be really aware. Are we free, or are we enslaved? Most people don't realize that they are enslaved. It is so widespread that they think it is just natural to be paralyzed with fear. So the first thing is to know the difference between being enslaved and being free. Once we know that we can be enslaved when we could be free, then the question is, What is the next step? We spoke about it last week. Suppose you are here and find that you are so scared that you don't dare to participate—you don't even dare to admit to yourself that you are scared. You sit there and pretend that everything is okay, and you think it is okay. You don't even fight for your freedom, let alone realize your freedom. You are just a scared spectator, and you don't know it. So the first thing is, we have to cultivate the ability to be aware of what we are experiencing in every situation. Once we are aware that we are experiencing some kind of restrictive sense of being or some kind of rigidity or passivity, then we have to ask ourselves, "What is the meaning of my experience?" Then, if we sincerely want to know, it will be revealed that we are a victim of some kind of interaction process that is occurring on a subliminal level. There are certain mental forces around us that want us to be immobilized, fearful, or embarrassed, that want us to shut up and not have the freedom to participate. So once we become aware of the meaning of our experience, then there is a possibility of liberation. How does that happen?

Student: The invalid idea is exposed, and there is no place for it to hide—we recognize it.

Dr. Hora: Right, exactly, and then we can remember that God wants us to be free: it is the will of God that we express all our potentialities to their full extent—without worrying if someone will approve or not.

Student: That is the crucial moment, right there. We have this choice, but sometimes we fight it and think to ourselves, "They shouldn't be thinking that."

Dr. Hora: We do not blame—we just remind ourselves that it is the will of God that we have complete freedom of expression under all circumstances. At that moment, we go free!

Student: I have noticed that in making some demos, my heart starts to beat, and I become tongue-tied. But as soon as I realized that I was intimidated, there was a calming down because I recognized it.

Student: I have a question about the pianist whom we were talking about earlier. I assume that the lack of freedom has nothing to do with his technical ability or with his ability to perform the music. He may even be a virtuoso and yet still not be playing freely?

Dr. Hora: Yes.

Student: So then, exactly what does freedom mean in the case of musical expression?

Dr. Hora: The same thing.

Student: You talked about the freedom to express . . .

Dr. Hora: The freedom to express our God-given talents whether they are musical, artistic, writing, or speaking. This kind of realized freedom is graceful; there is no conflict about it. If one is a freedom-fighter, he may violently claim his right for self-expression, but it will not really be freedom if he has to fight for it. A realized freedom is completely effortless and conflict-free.

Student: But the pianist is expressing more than just his talent; there is a specific content to it, that of spiritual ideas.

Dr. Hora: Whatever he is capable of expressing, he will be able to express as a pianist. If it is "Chopsticks," he will play "Chopsticks" with total abandon! Whatever level of proficiency he is able to realize, he will give expression to that without inhibition, hesitation, or violent protest. There are pianists who are banging away because they are freedom-fighters, not freedom-realizers.

Student: Would you define creativity? Is it the same thing as spiritual freedom?

Dr. Hora: Yes. God is the only creative Principle in the universe, and we are His instruments. God expresses Himself through us, if we are receptive. If we are hampered by all sorts of inhibitions, we are not free, and that is a miserable condition to be in. Freedom-realization is very precious, and we are all entitled to it.

Student: The freedom of choice, whether to be on the spiritual path or to be continuously in the "sea of mental garbage," is the same thing.

Dr. Hora: It is the will of God that we be free; but, we have to receive this idea, and we have to develop the faculty of awareness in order to know the difference. Many people are unaware.

Student: If we are not free, we could not know what our potential is because it is covered over with all this other garbage.

Dr. Hora: We don't know until we have realized freedom, and, then, we are in for surprises every step of the way.

Student: I didn't play the piano for months; I wouldn't go near it. I just started again, and I noticed that when I was practicing, I was physically tired; I realized that it was a strain. I was wondering why I even play. I love the music, and I love the idea— there is a sense of appreciation, but there is no freedom. So do I continue?

Dr. Hora: No. Stop, and turn to spiritual books, and pray until you realize that you are free; then you can return to the piano.

Student: Is all the suffering of the freedom-fighter about fighting interaction thoughts?

Dr. Hora: I was watching someone write with the left hand, and I said, "Isn't that interesting—you are writing with the left hand. Isn't that clumsy?" And she answered, "I can write with my right hand too, but I never do because I got used to writing with the left hand." Have you ever heard such a thing? She was told that she is a lefty, and she believed it; but actually she was ambidextrous—she could write with the left and the right hand. She had this freedom, right? But writing with the left hand met with the approval of the family—there was no freedom of choice.

Student: Will the blacks in South Africa ever be free? They are all fighting so hard for freedom.

Dr. Hora: Not only the blacks but the whites also. No one can be free, whether in Africa or Russia or the United States, unless blessed with the understanding of the whole process of liberation on the basis of realization; otherwise there is no freedom. There is no other kind of freedom than spiritually realized freedom— peaceful, assured, grateful, gracious, effortless, loving, and supremely intelligent. A "person" can never be free because a person is locked into pretending. If we have a pretending mode of being-in-the-world, our energies are exploited in the effort required to maintain a fiction about ourselves. We are not free; we are always thinking, "What kind of impression am I making now?" There is no freedom there.

Student: It seems that when I am around different people, like grandparents or friends, I don't act the same, but do I remain free?

Dr. Hora: As you said, you don't "act" the same, which means that in every situation you have to put on a certain act appropriate to that particular situation. This is called being a well-adjusted faker. But an individual who has spiritually realized freedom does not act: he is constantly manifesting the qualities of God without ulterior motives. He is simply loving and intelligent, graceful, free, assured, and joyous—the most attractive mode of being possible. It is called the beauty of holiness, which is not synonymous with piousness.

Student: Holiness is a religious-sounding word. What does it mean—when understood spiritually?

Dr. Hora: Holiness is wholeness, which means conscious union with God.

Student: Dr. Hora, is it possible to introduce the idea of freedom when there is anger and pain, when the pain is lasting and does not seem to go away? Do we say that pain is anger?

Dr. Hora: Pain is an angry interaction thought.

Student: I have had a pain in the shoulder for weeks now.

Dr. Hora: It is still angry.

Student: Maybe I am focusing more on the physical, on the idea that perhaps a muscle was pulled, so somehow I don't seem to meditate on the idea of anger. I seem to think it is really muscles that were pulled—it seems so logical. I do know clearly that there were angry thoughts on the weekend that this took place, but there was still a physical pull. So what is preventing a healing?

Dr. Hora: An unwillingness to forgive and an unwillingness to be embarrassed—those are the two things which prevent a healing. When there is a willingness to forgive and to be embarrassed, there is an instantaneous healing—the thought is gone. As long as the thought is present in consciousness, the symptom is present—it cannot leave because the symptom is a thought.

Student: How do we know that the pain is an angry thought?

Dr. Hora: It is very simple. How do we know that? Has anyone ever discovered that it is true?

Student: Yes. A few years ago, I had a sore throat for a very long time and found that the meaning of it was anger—I was angry at my boss and about my job. But, when I faced this, it still didn't go away because I realized that I didn't want to forgive. Then I had to work on forgiveness, and when I was finally ready to let go of the whole issue, the sore throat went away, and it never came back. The truth was validated in my experience.

Student: Would you please explain the process of becoming spiritually free?

Dr. Hora: First we have to become aware that we are not free. Then we have to ask, "What is the meaning of my experience?" Once we can see the meaning, we have to become embarrassed— "How could I be so unaware as to allow myself to be enslaved like that!" Then we ask, "What does God want?" God wants us to be absolutely free, completely free.

Student: Maybe I am more interested in being free from the pain in my shoulder than the anger.

Dr. Hora: If we have a pain, we think that the problem is where the pain is. The problem is not there—the problem is in consciousness. Everything must be healed in consciousness, not in the body. The body is just thought in visible form.

Student: There seems to be a problem recognizing this truth, because the self is angry and the pain is located in the shoulder; there seems to be a separation there.

Dr. Hora: The self is just a thought, and the pain is just a thought—the body is just a thought. The place to find liberation and healing is in consciousness. The physical is mental. This statement seems like a preposterous claim, but nevertheless it is true.

Student: When we are saying what should not be, we are freedom-fighters.

Student: That gives it a reality; that makes it more real.

Student: Is yielding what we are talking about?

Dr. Hora: She would have to yield her resentment, her anger against a certain someone who shall remain anonymous.

Student: We don't have to take responsibility for our thoughts when we are in pain. It is easier to say, "I have a pain; it could not have anything to do with my thinking."

Dr. Hora: We would rather say, "I'm not crazy; it's physical."

Student: So we don't really take responsibility for our own thoughts. It is easier to blame something else, like our bodies or someone else. It is very important for us to be willing to be embarrassed, because in the embarrassment we are taking responsibility for the thought.

Dr. Hora: Exactly. It is a revolutionary discovery that to be embarrassed is salutary—it is good for you.

Student: Doesn't that mean freedom?

Dr. Hora: No, that is salvation.

Student: I know that guilt is bragging, but does guilt have to do with embarrassment?

Dr. Hora: If we feel guilty, we are not embarrassed—we are proud. It goes like this: "I am such a wonderful person. I have such a wonderful sense of conscience, and I am so righteous. I know what is right, and I know that I shouldn't have done what I did; and now I feel guilty; now I am a bad person. Before I was a good person, but now I am a bad person." That is guilt. There is no embarrassment with guilt—there is pride in guilt. "Am I not wonderful that I can feel so guilty?"

Student: The human condition is so perverse, yet we are part of it as long as we are human.

Dr. Hora: Who said we are human?

Student: I am glad you keep reminding me.

Dr. Hora: We are not really human—we just seem to be—we have an erroneous impression that we are human. God never made a human person. He doesn't know us that way.

Student: Would we rather see ourselves as victims of physical problems than as "crazy"?

Dr. Hora: People don't like to be told that they are crazy; it is embarrassing.

Student: Is some part of embarrassment the willingness to admit that we really are crazy?

Dr. Hora: No. What embarrasses us is admitting that we are ignorant—especially those of us who love to be known as knowing. It is very embarrassing to admit that we are ignorant and that we made a mistake.

Student: If we recognize that we are unwilling to forgive, can we still meditate on the idea of forgiveness, or are we kidding ourselves? What do we do in the interim? If we have a difficult problem, and we are very angry and we know it is ridiculous, is just meditating on the idea enough?

Dr. Hora: Some psychiatrists recommend punching a bag.

Student: Then I would hurt the other shoulder. I don't know if I could take it!

Dr. Hora: And some psychiatrists recommend punching somebody.

Student: That's better.

Dr. Hora: But in Metapsychiatry we just yield—yield up our anger.

Dialogue No. 22

The Millennial Vision

Student: Recently, I was with someone who seemed to be very angry with me. What is the right way to respond in a situation like that? I am interested in seeing this individual happy, and I wish she would let go of the anger and forgive.

Dr. Hora: We have no right to be interested in someone being happy because that is a verbal smoke-screen, covering up a want.

Student: Is it valid to be interested in seeing that individual healed of anger? What is a valid interest?

Dr. Hora: You use the word "interest" to cover up a want.

Student: So what I am really saying is that I want her to be happy and that I don't want her to be mad and that I want her to come around?

Dr. Hora: Right, "come around" to liking me again.

Student: We have said before that individuals have the right to be angry.

Dr. Hora: Yes, everyone has the right to be angry.

Student: Instead of wishing that the anger would go away and that she would be happy, what is a valid way to see this?

Dr. Hora: Here is an angry person—we do not have a right to want her not to be angry, and we do not have a right to be interested in her being happy or loving or healed. We cannot want anything, even if it is referred to as "interest."

Student: Is the word "interest" being used here instead of saying that she "should" be happy?

Dr. Hora: Something like that, of course.

Student: We can be interested in not reacting, and, instead, be interested in responding, because we are going to be affected by this situation one way or another.

Dr. Hora: Not necessarily.

Student: There was some degree of transcendence in my viewpoint, because I did not run away.

Student: The highest form of love is compassion, but it requires a high degree of understanding.

Dr. Hora: All right, compassion is always valid—if we really understand what it is. What is compassion?

Student: Giving the other individual the right not to understand the situation.

Dr. Hora: No, that is "letting be."

Student: Compassion is "understanding the lack of understanding." When we say we understand the lack of understanding, are we understanding the error that is happening?

Dr. Hora: How would you describe the error that was happening?

Student: She got mad because I seemed to fail to live up to certain family expectations—she wanted something from me.

Dr. Hora: So when we are confronted with someone who is angry at us, what is happening? Here is an individual who thinks in terms of "self and other." Right? If someone is angry at us, this individual is a victim of a certain, limited perspective. Now if this individual is angry at another person, then the other person will either let her be angry or try to defend herself and fight back, and things will go from bad to worse. So, if we are confronted with someone whose perspective on life is so constricted that he can only see "self and other," then it behooves the compassionate one to refuse to participate in this narrow-minded perspective and to say, "There is no interaction anywhere; there is only Omniaction everywhere" [Third Principle of Metapsychiatry]. There are no two persons here in a hostile relationship— God is the only reality. There are no relationships—there is only the "good of God" here, the harmonizing Principle of the universe, where all of God's creations coexist harmoniously, intelligently, and in Love. So we destroy the narrow-minded perspective without saying a word, but refuse to see the situation the way the other sees it. The Third Principle solves the problem, and the whole thing fizzles out because, if there is no "self and other," there is no one to change or to heal, nor can we be interested in another self being happy. Nothing is going on—no one has to interfere with the situation—only the Reality has to be discerned. And the discernment of Reality abolishes all that seems to be: "The right seeing of what really is abolishes all that seems to be" [Tenth Principle of Metapsychiatry]. So if there is no one to be angry at, how can there be anger? The whole thing just fizzles out, and that is what the Third Principle can do if practiced with understanding. Now the question is, suppose we had such an experience a few days ago and we failed to apply the Third Principle—is there still a chance to correct our mistake? Of course there is, because omniactive Love-Intelligence is not time-bound. In the realm of Love-Intelligence, there is neither space nor time, and whatever happened two days ago is still happening now. And if we see that what happened two days ago never really happened, then it isn't happening now, and there is nothing—no problem. There is only the "good of God" going on right now, here and everywhere.

Student: Amen.

Dr. Hora: So all we have to do is to abolish the phenomenal world.

Student: Did you say what was happening two days ago is happening now?

Dr. Hora: Yes.

Student: That means that all it is is the thought that we have about it?

Dr. Hora: What else is there besides thoughts? Time is thought, and space is thought. So what we failed to respond to appropriately two days ago, we can respond to now, and the whole situation is healed.

Student: That is another way of saying that it didn't really happen.

Dr. Hora: Of course it never really happened. Have you ever heard of a book entitled Beyond the Dream? That is what it is all about.

Student: That is beautiful, because formerly those interaction thoughts were still present, and now they are absolutely gone.

Dr. Hora: Of course, they never were anything. If "there is no interaction anywhere, only Omniaction everywhere," then there was no interaction two days ago either. Even two days ago, there was only Omniaction, and Omniaction is now also, because Omniaction is not time-bound, and it is not spatial. The temporal-spatial illusion of life is suspended when we understand Omnipresence.

Student: Please say more about the process when this understanding of Omniaction is occurring during a dialogue and not a word is spoken.

Dr. Hora: If someone is being assaulted angrily and not a word is spoken back, that can be a provocation—it infuriates the other. That would not be desirable—we cannot say anything, neither can we say nothing. We cannot speak nor not speak. We cannot want, neither can we be interested, right? If we are a "goody two shoes," that is a provocation. If we are the silent one, it is a provocation. So what can be? Only seeing "what really is"— and when we are maintaining a consciousness of Omnipresence, the Omniaction of infinite Love-Intelligence—then we are neither talking nor not talking, we are a beneficial presence, a consciousness that is manifesting Reality. This Reality does not recognize any kind of interpersonal conflict, so it is healed; it is abolished. "The right understanding of what really is abolishes all that seems to be" [Tenth Principle of Metapsychiatry]. And even though it was two days ago, we can still abolish it right now by understanding that it never really was.

Student: Would that be a healthy process to undertake when an embarrassing thought surfaces about something that happened a long time ago? Sometimes a thought will come up about the way that I behaved or about an interpersonal conflict that I had years ago, and I am embarrassed when the thought comes up.

Dr. Hora: We would have to understand what it means when we are embarrassed years later.

Student: It could be a good thought, couldn't it, showing that we have come along in consciousness?

Dr. Hora: It is good and bad. It is good because we are recognizing our ignorance, but it is "bad" because it indicates that we still think that others should not have seen us like this or that they should not think "this way" about us. We want to change people. We want something, and that is not going to work. We cannot want, and we cannot be interested; but we can sincerely behold Reality, which is the same today as it was two years ago. Two days ago or two years ago, it makes no difference, because in Reality there is neither time nor space. We just have to abolish this "unreality" by beholding and by really understanding what we mean by Omniaction. All the interactions since the beginning of time can be abolished in the moment that someone understands Omniaction.

Student: That certainly is freeing. What about forgiveness in interaction? I have avoided being in the presence of someone whom I feel I harmed; I have tried to make some amends. But it is very painful, and the person keeps bringing it up again; so I avoid the situation. I know it is not good to avoid it, but it seems to be about all that I can do.

Dr. Hora: It is not good to avoid it, and it is not good to not avoid it.

Student: What would be healthier?

Dr. Hora: The healthier way would be to abolish the past. There never was a time in the history of the universe when there was such a thing as interaction between people.

Student: So none of the bad things that have happened to us have really happened?

Dr. Hora: Absolutely.

Student: That's a great relief.

Dr. Hora: Whenever we succeed in beholding Reality in this fashion, there are very beneficial consequences. When we pray the Prayer of Beholding, something good always follows. It is one of the most powerful, effective prayers that we can learn to pray "beholding the Reality which abolishes all problems."

Student: I also had an instance where someone was angry and critical; and it occurred to me that she had a right to be angry, but I didn't really mean it. I didn't like it, and in those kinds of situations, it is hard to turn to Omniaction in the midst of what seems like an interaction—to have it be not just an affirmation but really to be a realization at that moment. I just want to ask what to do—I feel that operational question coming up—what do I do if someone yells at me?

Student: We could juxtapose existentialism with operationalism—what we really understand is already part of our being, meaning that we don't have to "do" anything.

Dr. Hora: It is also important to stop ruminating about it because, in rumination, we revert to interaction thinking and a desire to smooth it out—to make a negative form of interaction into a positive form of interaction. Just as there is no negative interaction, there is also no such thing as positive interaction. All there is is divine Love, which is not personal. "For the earth shall be full of the knowledge of the Lord, as the waters cover the sea" (Isaiah 11:9). But if we are ruminating, then we say, "All right, there is this Reality, but there is also she and I." So, drop it! There is no such thing, and there never was such a thing as interaction— it is a dream, an illusion. Now the question is, after having abolished interaction, what is left? Is there life after interaction?

Student: Without interaction there must just be PAGL [PAGL is an acronym for Peace, Assurance, Gratitude, Love, and Its Presence in consciousness informs us that we are in tune with the One Mind], because it is the interaction that robs us of PAGL.

Dr. Hora: After we realize that there is no more interaction in the whole universe, there must be something left. What is left?

Student: Spiritual blessedness, where all things are working together for good, and we are grateful and peaceful.

Dr. Hora: So are we the only ones left in the universe?

Student: What about harmonious coexistence?

Dr. Hora: Yes, harmonious coexistence. We don't abolish life— life is discerned as a harmonious coexistence of all of God's creation in the universe of Mind, the creative Mind. So there is no more interaction, which is like this [two hands, horizontally intertwined]. There is only everything everywhere coexisting harmoniously—like this [two hands in a prayerful position, vertical and parallel but not touching. These concepts were demonstrated with hand positions].

Student: Would it take a form? Would we see it, like people getting on the train one after the other and not pushing each other?

Dr. Hora: That's about it.

Student: Is that what is meant by "the lion lying down with the lamb"?

Dr. Hora: All creations of God, instead of interacting in any way, coexist harmoniously.

Student: If we were to realize that, would we be in surroundings where that would actually occur? Like on the subway? Would we see that?

Dr. Hora: In Metapsychiatry, we say, "As thou seest, so thou beest." We would experience life in terms of harmony and peace, and as effortless, efficient, and effective [The three Es]. When we observe a symphony orchestra playing beautiful music, we see a model of harmonious coexistence: everyone is attentive to the conductor and is issue-oriented, and the musicians do not fight or compete with each other. Everyone participates wholeheartedly in manifesting some aspect of the music, and this is a good way to remember the ideal condition of enlightenment, where there is harmonious coexistence.

Student: What makes people want to take drugs? What is this craving for drugs?

Student: Do they want excitement or want to feel good?

Dr. Hora: Most people would say this, but that is a very simple explanation. There is this tremendous craving in people to see the world in a different light, because what we see is usually very ugly and very painful. All unenlightened people see life in terms of interpersonal conflict—that is all we see when we go out and

observe life, especially in cities. Here and there we see a couple
in love, but the prevalent view is one of interpersonal conflict,
and one can get awfully tired of that. These drugs come along and
promise a different view of life; one gets hooked on that, and this
is called a "high." But what we really need is the "millennial vision." It is a "high" for everyone. It is not chemical—it is spiritual
and everlasting.

Student: What did you call it?

Dr. Hora: The millennial vision. What does that mean? What is
a millennium?

Student: A thousand years.

Dr. Hora: Right. It takes thousands of years to understand this,
but we have explained it here tonight.

Student: Drugs alter perception by chemical means, but we are
contrasting that approach with a spiritual shift in perspective.
Everyone would really like to see that.

Dr. Hora: Yes—a different reality. The one that meets the eyes
of unenlightened vision is a very ugly and troublesome life— especially if we walk in slum neighborhoods with all the graffiti,
the poverty, the stench, and the perversions. We can get very
discouraged if that is all we see day after day. And here comes
someone who says, "Snort this white powder, and you will see
something much better, more beautiful." And in no time at all you
get hooked. In contrast to that is the "millennial vision"— harmonious coexistence. We can be very grateful for being able to see
something that millions of people would like to see, but go about
"seeing" in the wrong way.

Pain

Student: Dr. Hora, I would like to understand the dynamics in being a victim and in being a victimizer and the meaning of being tempted to victimize one who wants to be a victim. I realize that I am surrounded by quite a few people who see themselves as victims. There is a woman at work who reports to me and who is always looking to be victimized, and people victimize her all the time. Usually I don't join in, but I have to admit that today I found myself greatly tempted to attack her. She was asking for it! But that is not being loving, so I worked myself out of it. The woman had invited an attack from someone who immediately came to me and told me about it. I fixed it up, and everything was fine. She desired to be a victim, and it was a disturbing temptation not to fulfill her fantasy. I see this all the time: people set themselves up to be victimized—they are asking for it— and they wonder what happened. I need to understand the dynamic, so that I am not even tempted. I would like not to be involved.

Dr. Hora: Is anyone else interested in this subject? It is a very important subject. What is the difference between the victimizer and the victim?

Student: They are the same.

Dr. Hora: In what way are they the same?

Student: The victim ultimately becomes the victimizer.

Dr. Hora: How is that?

Student: I am not exactly sure, but I see it happening both ways.

Student: The victimizer is a victim of assault; in other words, he becomes an assaulter, which is destructive to his being, to his serenity.

Dr. Hora: To his serenity, yes, but he gets a great deal of pleasure out of it, doesn't he? There is a sexual condition called "SM," sadomasochistic coupling, where the sadist is hurting the masochist. What do they get out of it?

Student: It is self-confirmatory, whether it is negative or positive; it confirms them each as a specific kind of person.

Dr. Hora: Yes, so the victimizer is confirming himself as being an aggressor, or a "boss," or superior. What does the victim get out of it?

Student: Self-confirmation.

Dr. Hora: How is that?

Student: "Oh, poor me!"

Student: He feels sorry for himself.

Student: He gets negative attention.

Dr. Hora: Could you explain that?

Student: The victimizer is giving his attention to the victim, even if it is a negative kind of attention.

Dr. Hora: In other words, a masochist wants attention. Well, can't he get attention in some other way? If the issue is attention, then what does the sadist, the victimizer, get out of it?

Student: A false sense of power, that he can rule over someone else.

Dr. Hora: Yes, that could be a self-confirmatory experience of having power over someone else. What kind of a self-confirmatory experience does the victim have?

Student: He sees himself as a poor, abused person.

Dr. Hora: There was a television program about a man who was arrested because he kept a woman blindfolded and handcuffed day after day. He was torturing and abusing this woman in many other ways, but primarily he kept her blindfolded and handcuffed. The program showed pictures of that situation. He also took this woman out for walks and for a drive, but always blindfolded. They even went shopping to the supermarket together—she was wearing this blindfold, and he was leading her. It was a situation where this man was a sadistic abuser, and this woman was a victim—a victimizer and a victim. This went on for some time. It seemed that he also had other women going through this kind of abuse and conditioning. One day, one of his victims tore off her blindfold, ran away from him on the street to the police and told them about the situation. The man was arrested, and when he was questioned, he said, "I didn't do anything; she volunteered." He said that she was free to leave at any time. For a few years, she did not run away, but she could have run away. She not only accepted that kind of life, but apparently she enjoyed it. What is happening here? In such a situation, there is a coupling—the man enjoyed abusing her, and she enjoyed being abused. Now this sounds very unusual because it is so dramatic. But in certain subtle ways, this goes on all the time—between husbands and wives, between friends and among associates, all kinds of variations on the same theme. Some people enjoy being victimizers, and others enjoy being victims. How in the world is this possible? This story is an observation of an aspect of that kind of mode of being-in-the-world. There are people who do not have partners, but they go to the hospital and insist on being operated on, getting injections, or being patients. The doctors oblige and give them what they are asking for. One can conceive of an infinite variety of combinations that people go through where they are being either victimizers or victims. What in the world is this? Psychoanalysis attempts to explain it on a sexual basis. There is a form of sexual intercourse where a victimizer is victimizing another male or female. But it is about more than sex—there is much erotic stimulation in these situations. However, there does not have to be. A hypochondriac asks the doctor to give him injections and all kinds of treatments. There was a middle-aged man, working in a factory, who developed a little cough. He went to the doctors and convinced them that he had lung cancer! The doctors then subjected him to all kinds of tests, sticking a big tube down into his throat under anesthesia, and taking all kinds of X-rays. Finally after many tests and invasive procedures, they concluded that he had bronchitis! This is not just sexual: it is existential. This is a mode of being in-the-world where there is a desire to be abused or to abuse. Now you could ask, "Isn't that very rare?" It is not rare at all. It cannot be explained purely on the grounds of eroticism or sex; there is much more to it than that. What does Metapsychiatry have to contribute to the understanding of this mystery of human perversity?

Student: I have an idea what Metapsychiatry has to offer, but I cannot say that I fully understand it. In order to be a victim or a victimizer, one has to be thoroughly convinced that one is a person. And Metapsychiatry's answer to personhood is that we are nondimensional transparencies, "here for God." So there cannot be any attack, and there cannot be any attacker—if one knows the truth.

Dr. Hora: How does that illuminate the human condition?

Student: Metapsychiatry says that one basic element of the human condition is the "dread of nonbeing," or existential anxiety. Metapsychiatry also says that there are certain parental fantasies by which we are influenced, so that we have some notion that we exist—like being a victim, for example. When growing up, some of us learn to be victimizers and others learn to be victims, and that identity relieves our fear of nonbeing, so that the pain or suffering associated with those invalid modes of being is less important than the satisfaction of knowing that we exist.

Dr. Hora: Yes, okay. If we consider this carefully with a broad view of the human condition, we arrive at a very interesting insight, namely, that human beings desire pain.

Student: That is so incredible!

Dr. Hora: Human beings have a desire to experience pain—physical pain, mental pain, social pain—any kind of pain is welcome.

Student: So that there is a sense of self-being?

Dr. Hora: Exactly. This pain can become eroticized, so that some people can get an orgasm by being subjected to painful abuse or by subjecting themselves to pain. There is a desire for pain and suffering. Therefore, when we are being bombarded with images of sickness, we feel very uneasy about it. What is this uneasiness?

Student: We are afraid of being mesmerized.

Dr. Hora: We are afraid of yielding to the temptation to experience that pain—any pain! It is like a window in a bakery store with many delicious cookies in it! If one goes to a hospital to visit someone, there is a tremendous selection and variety of painful experiences which you could inflict on yourself. Disease and suffering are very contagious and very seductive—and at the same time abhorrent. You see how crazy we all are! The real issue is that pain is a self-confirmatory experience that says, "I have a pain; therefore I am sure I am a physical person, and that makes me feel temporarily okay." It relieves the fear of nonbeing. If anyone would tell us, "Look here, you just want to suffer because you are afraid that you are really nothing," we would say, "Oh, that's nonsense!" This is the dread of nonbeing. So we have a compulsion to suffer continually and have pain and have problems—people go from one pain to another all the time.

Student: But on a conscious level, aren't we interested in pleasure?

Dr. Hora: We all say that we want pleasure, but it is a lie—we want experiences, and the more painful the experiences, the more sure we are that we are really here and that we are persons and that we are what we seem to be. We want the confirmation of our egos, and so there is comfort in suffering. Now this can get out of hand, and there can be all kinds of complications; but this is the way it is. Now is there any advantage in understanding this? Does it help, or does it hurt, to understand that there is no involuntary sickness and that there is no involuntary suffering and that we are always "asking for it." It is embarrassing to admit it, but it helps.

Student: It would help us to ask the First Intelligent Question ["What is the meaning of what seems to be?"] a lot more quickly. No more excuses—we would take responsibility.

Dr. Hora: Yes.

Student: Do we want the suffering so that we can get attention, or do we want the suffering whether we get the attention or not?

Dr. Hora: It is not the attention that we really want—we want to convince ourselves that we are really here as physical persons. That is the issue. Even people who always seek attention are really seeking the confirmation of their physical reality here and now. They are afraid it is not so, that maybe the Texas philosopher was right when he said, "You ain't never was nothin'." This is a universal human dilemma. How can anyone be at peace if he has a constant urge to experience pain of some kind—be it just a girdle, the pinching of shoes, an itch or a conflict? We are always looking to experience physicality in some way. Now suppose someone is a pleasure-seeker instead of a pain-seeker. What is the difference?

Student: Pleasure doesn't seem to last as long!

Dr. Hora: The sad fact is that there is no pleasure without pain, and the more we seek pleasure, the more pain we find—it is one and the same thing. It is like saying that the good of life can be found in suffering.

Student: Dr. Hora, in this process does the suffering have the potential of leading us to seek something better?

Dr. Hora: Of course, but if you are not a student of Metapsychiatry, you rationalize your suffering and you blame this and you blame that, or you deny this and you deny that. And you bludgeon your consciousness with drugs or alcohol or go out and buy yourself a hat! There are a million ways to cope with this human condition. Of course it doesn't work: there is "no exit," as Sartre says, from this human condition. Whether you are married or not married, whether you are gay or sad or Jewish or Greek—it is always the same. As St. Paul said, the whole world "groaneth and travaileth in pain" (Romans 8:22), and there seems to be no solution to this human condition.

Student: Does the fear of nonbeing come with the human condition?

Dr. Hora: Of course, it is inevitable.

Student: And if we don't study Metapsychiatry, we never hear about it.

Dr. Hora: Yes, and that is a great tragedy. There are a few mystery schools that dare to deal with this question, but here we have an escape. Metapsychiatry is a unique teaching that offers people an escape from this trap of suffering. What is the exit door? Sartre said there was "no exit," but he was an atheist. Unless you are given the great blessing of the First Principle of Metapsychiatry, there is "no exit"—you are stuck in the human condition, and it goes on and on and on. I suppose that is what the Catholics call "eternal damnation." How is the First Principle an "exit door" from this ridiculous human condition? How can the First Principle open the door to freedom and salvation? It is interesting that Jesus at one point said: "I am the door; by me, if any man enter in, he shall be saved, and shall go in and out and find pasture" (John 10:9). Jesus speaks of the "door," and we are speaking of the First Principle as the "door." Who can explain how the First Principle can be a door that helps us to escape from this human condition which is so miserable and so hopeless?

Student: The First Principle changes our focus from self-confirmatory ideation to a God-confirmatory way of life. So it changes our mode of being—

Dr. Hora: From self-confirmation to God-realization, to a discovery of bliss consciousness. We are not looking anymore to be victimizers or to be victims. We are not looking for pleasure or pain—we are looking for bliss consciousness.

Student: So, on a very elemental level, our attention is shifted from concern about our own being to the source of all being.

Dr. Hora: To "what really is." One very embarrassing point must be realized, that we crave pain.

Student: Is that the meaning of struggling with wanting to be the victimizer?

Dr. Hora: We are fascinated with the issue of interaction between victim and victimizer. All interaction is the coupling of victim and victimizer. The victimizer is fascinated by inflicting pain and identifies with the victim—he enters into the experience of the victim and shares the illusion of self-confirmation. The victimizer is called a sadist, but he really wants to experience what his victim is experiencing. So actually everyone craves pain; as human beings we are "thriving" on pain. Whenever you develop some painful condition, just remember, "Nothing comes into experience uninvited" [Seventh Principle of Metapsychiatry]. When you have enough integrity to face up to this embarrassing insight, in what way will it be helpful for you to deal with your pain if you acknowledge that you desire it? How will that help?

Student: Maybe at that point it becomes intolerable because, existentially, it really is unbearable.

Dr. Hora: Well, most people are tolerating it.

Student: Yes, but it destroys peace in consciousness, and, if we see this, wouldn't we want to turn away from it?

Dr. Hora: The point is that if we have the integrity to admit that our pain is invited, that we have a desire to suffer, then we become sufficiently embarrassed to reach out for the First Principle and seek to enter into that "door" which leads to freedom and salvation. It is easy to recite the First Principle, but to enter into the First Principle means to abandon personhood and become a spiritual consciousness—incorporeal. What does that mean?

Student: Without body.

Dr. Hora: Without body. We lose interest in physical existence, and we become wholeheartedly and gratefully interested in being individual, spiritual consciousnesses—nondimensional transparencies for God. We become an aspect of God, consciously. We are always an aspect of God, but this way we will be consciously aware of the truth-of-being—that is the "door" that Jesus was talking about. The First Principle is the "door" to freedom and bliss consciousness, where the human condition, the human mockeries, are transcended—we also speak of self-transcendence. So, we rejoice in discovering our true "nothingness" which is the glorious freedom of the spiritual understanding of Reality in God, which is infinite Mind.

Student: If a child is being abused by an adult, is there already a desire there for pain? It seems that the child is dependent on the adult.

Dr. Hora: The child is being educated to appreciate pain; we have to be educated to that. This human condition is all perverted, but no one can be blamed for it. It is just "the way the cookie crumbles."

Student: Dr. Hora, today I picked up the newspaper, and on the front page there were about three gruesome stories. I got to a certain point in one article and stopped reading—I could not continue to read it. Painful experiences are around us all the time, and we hear about these horrible things. Do we stop reading the paper?

Dr. Hora: If you did not understand what we were talking about today, you have no other choice but to stop reading it. But if you do understand what we were talking about today, you will read the paper with a transcendent perspective. There was a story about a young man who murdered as many as seventeen people. He invited every one of them into his apartment where they allowed themselves to be handcuffed, drugged, sexually abused, and gradually murdered and dismembered. How do you explain that someone is willing to accept an invitation from a stranger, allow himself to be handcuffed, rendered helpless, endure sexual abuse, and then become a victim of murder and dismemberment? How in the world can we explain this? Are they all stupid? What is it? It is not so rare. This young man was just very clever in the way that he went about gradually murdering seventeen people who cooperated with their victimizer. Always there is the issue of co-operation—without cooperation, he could never have handcuffed anyone. Anyone who is free of the desire to be victimized would never allow himself to be handcuffed. But this desire is very great and very widespread, and most people think that it is fascinating and perhaps even sexually pleasurable, erotic. These things are happening in certain variations all the time. The fact is that the victim cooperates willingly with the victimizer. There is some-thing within him—an inner urge to experience pain and abuse.

Student: Dr. Hora, what about the Holocaust?

Dr. Hora: Let us not speculate about the Holocaust—it is too painful and too gruesome to consider. The issue here is not his-tory, not politics, and not psychology—the issue is liberation of the individual. How can an individual student of Metapsychiatry attain such a broad understanding of the human condition that he can enter the "door?" As Jesus put it: "I am the door." We see the door as the First Principle—we enter that "door" and we are saved. What are we saved from? We are saved from the human tendency toward and the human fascination with pain. So there is an exit, but it is a well-kept secret. Not many people understand it, even though it is explained in the Bible. Millions of people read the Bible, but few understand what it says.

Student: Dr. Hora, I don't know if this applies or not, but would that be why many times in the Christian religion, Jesus is pictured as a victim?

Dr. Hora: Well, that is a terrible mistake because Jesus demonstrated how to overcome the desire to be a victim.

Student: I brought it up because throughout history people have thought that suffering not only can make you feel alive but that it is good.

Dr. Hora: Yes, everyone wants to suffer. It "feels good" to suffer, not too much, just enough to relieve the existential dread of nonbeing.

Student: Because the pain feels so real that it has to be that I am a person, or I wouldn't have this pain?

Dr. Hora: We could even speculate about the meaning of the crucifixion—that Jesus allowed himself to be crucified, to demonstrate to the world that it was no "big deal" and that he could overcome it in three days! And he did. Jesus said: "Destroy this temple and in three days I will raise it up" (John 2:19). He was not a masochist or a sadist; he wasn't interested in human suffering—he was interested in the relief of suffering and in liberation from suffering. Today if we study his teachings carefully, we see many important lessons which he was teaching the world. "And the light shineth in darkness; and the darkness comprehended it not" (John 1:5). The Bible also says: "And this is the condemnation, that light is come into the world, and men loved darkness . . ." (John 3:19).

Student: We have all been used to understanding that "pain is an angry interaction thought." Sometimes if you have a pain in a particular part of the body, you can find an invalid thought that is manifesting itself in consciousness. That was the only framework that I ever had in which to put pain; I never knew anything beyond that. Now here is something more—how do we put all of those things together? We still have to understand the angry thought that the pain is expressing. I do not understand how to work in consciousness with the idea that we desire pain.

Dr. Hora: Recently someone called in the middle of the night and complained of severe pain in his stomach and back. It occurred to me to tell him to pay attention and find out at whom he was angry in order to forgive him right away. This individual is an advanced student, and as he was making an effort to forgive, suddenly the pain stopped; and he had the impression that a kidney stone was passing through his organism, disappearing, and suddenly he was well. Now here is a situation in which we say that "pain is an angry interaction thought." By forgiving, we cut the interaction, and we can turn to God. When we forgive someone, we stop blaming the individual; we let go of the hatred and turn our thoughts to God—perchance, to the First Principle—and suddenly there is a healing. How does that tie in with what we are talking about today, wanting to experience pain? Later when I spoke with this individual, he explained that he had had an interaction experience with a woman who was behaving in an unethical way. As he listened to her, he became judgmental. As long as he was condemning this woman, he experienced a very severe pain. What makes us so violently judgmental? It is a desire to think about something that hurts. When we are judgmental about another, we are entertaining sadistic, aggressive, hurtful thoughts about that individual. It is characteristic of that condition that there is great resistance to letting go of judgmental thoughts. It is like when a sadist has a whip and keeps beating his victim and doesn't want to stop. It is hard for him to stop, no matter how much the other screams. The urge to condemn and to judge and to criticize and to curse is difficult to let go of. But then comes the pain. So forgiveness stops the sadistic, condemnatory thoughts, and we no longer enjoy hurting another—we are no longer involved with the pain—and, if we can forgive and let go and become compassionate, the healing is at hand. This is a direct continuation of what we already said, that "pain is an angry interaction thought." What is anger? "Anger is a desire to punish." When we are judgmental of someone, we have a desire to punish that individual; so that is how it is connected. But if we let go of it, then we are relieved.

Student: Dr. Hora, maybe we could also say that until we really know that the angry thought and the pain are one, not just intellectually, the angry thought and the pain are going to seem unconnected. But they really are not. It seems that there is an angry thought and a pain, but it really is one; it happens simultaneously, not separately. The angry thought is there, and the pain is also there—they are the same thing and arise at the same time.

Dr. Hora: Yes, that is the way it works. The Bible says: "Judge not, that ye be not judged. For with what judgment ye judge, ye shall be judged" (Matthew 7:1-2). "For wherein thou judgest another, thou condemnest thyself; for thou that judgest doest the same things" (Romans 2:1). If we are hurting someone, we are participating in his pain. So it all comes back to man's fascination with and secret desire for pain.

Student: Dr. Hora, you said that we need to have a lot of integrity to admit to ourselves that we have the desire to participate in pain. What does that mean? Is it that we reach the point where we cannot take these types of experiences anymore?

Dr. Hora: Or that we have reached a certain point in our studies of Metapsychiatry where we cannot lie anymore.

Student: No more pretending.

Dr. Hora: We are "afflicted" with a large dose of honesty! That is what we call integrity.

Dialogue No. 24

The Serpent and the Dove

Student: Dr. Hora, in the Bible there is a passage that says: "Be ye wise as serpents and harmless as doves" (Matthew 10:16). Harmlessness seems like a very beautiful quality. I was wondering what it is that makes one harmful or cruel, and what it is that makes one harmless? What is the spiritual value that leads to harmlessness?

Dr. Hora: If we are loving, if we are grateful, if we are godly, if we are imbued with spiritual values, we are not interested in hurting anyone. Recently we spoke about the medical principle *Nil nocere*, which means, "Above all, do not cause harm to anyone."

Student: That is what brought it to mind.

Dr. Hora: Certainly, if we are spiritually minded individuals, we do not enjoy causing harm to anyone. Jesus taught this principle to his disciples when he said: "Behold, I send you forth as sheep in the midst of wolves: be ye therefore wise as serpents, and harmless as doves" (Matthew 10:16). It is an interesting combination because most people think of serpents as out to harm, but a snake will never attack unprovoked. No matter how poisonous a snake is, if it is not provoked it will do no harm. Metapsychiatry adds to this interpretation another element: Wherein lies the wisdom of the serpent?

Student: I seem to recall that you said that it moves quickly away from any danger coming toward it—it has the wisdom not to interact.

Dr. Hora: The wisdom of the serpent is not to draw attention to itself, whereas human beings—what do they want? Primarily to draw attention to themselves. So Jesus recommended to have the "wisdom of the serpent" and the "harmlessness of the dove." These are beautiful qualities of an enlightened man. An enlightened man has lost interest in self-confirmatory ideation. Serpents know that: they do not draw attention to themselves—they slither away; they are not itching to be seen or noticed, and certainly

206

they do not harm anyone who does not threaten them. It is an interesting combination that helps us to develop an enlightened character. This is the Christly character—there is no desire for self-confirmation, no desire for admiration; we do not ask to be loved or hated or persecuted, and we are not interested in the suffering of people—so we would not harm anyone.

Student: If we were not drawing attention to ourselves, then, would that also keep us from inviting harmfulness or cruelty?

Dr. Hora: Of course.

Student: Because it seems to be part of human nature to be cruel?

Dr. Hora: Yes, and it is very often connected with the desire to be paid attention to. There are people who get very frustrated and angry if they are being ignored. Actually the worst thing you can do to an unenlightened individual is to ignore him. It is said that a masochist will get furious if you refuse to hurt him. The basic problem that man has is the desire to confirm himself—out of that essential element, all kinds of complications can arise in life—the desire to draw attention to himself and to be recognized and confirmed as a person. If it doesn't work, one can get very upset and vindictive. What is vindictiveness? It is a desire to hurt. Jesus was a magnificent teacher of character: "Be ye wise as serpents and harmless as doves." Now the question is, If we are not going to attract attention to ourselves, no one will notice us, so how will we survive? In Metapsychiatry, we say it is existentially invalid to want anything. Isn't that strange? All people would say, "This is nonsense; you would have nothing!" Everyone wants to be famous; everyone wants to be admired, respected, noticed, and get promoted; and here and there someone wants to get kicked in the pants!

Student: A kick is as good as a boost!

Dr. Hora: You will go down in history with this comment.

Student: Better that way than not at all!

Dr. Hora: If we do not want to be recognized and confirmed, no one will notice us; if we do not go after what we want, we will never have anything. Right? Isn't this logical? Now what is the answer?

Student: What God wants. If we are delivered from the bondage of the self, by not asking for what we want or what we do not want, which always causes trouble, then we can ask, "What does God want?" in terms of being a transparency for God. What God wants is never troublesome.

Dr. Hora: The Bible tells us that "all things work together for good to them that love God" (Romans 8:28). If we are interested in the good of God, if we love being loving in the right way, then whatever we are interested in sincerely, if it is a valid interest, comes to us like a magnet attracting the good of God. It is not necessary to want it. As a matter of fact, if we get what we want, it will not work out—there is no blessing in it. But if we are sincerely interested in whatever is good in life, it will unfold in our experience. If we understand these principles of intelligent living, we will have the "wisdom of the serpent" and the "harmlessness of the dove." You will not be a namby-pamby or a wimp, not a passive individual. No one goes around kicking a snake. A snake doesn't ask to be kicked—it is not interested in attracting attention. There are certain values to live by, and Jesus was teaching them. Was there anything else you had in mind, when you asked this question?

Student: That was perfect and very helpful. The other aspect I was trying to understand is what it means when someone is cruel, so if we see it coming toward us, we can somehow rise above it and understand it. But if we have invited it—

Dr. Hora: Yes. There is nothing worse than someone who is eager to be paid attention to or is pleading for acceptance verbally or nonverbally, trying to get people to appreciate him. This either seduces the cruel one to be cruel, or it provokes the other, the one who is interested in drawing attention to himself. If two people who want to draw attention to themselves come together, they are enemies at first sight. Then there are the intimidators— a serpent can appear to be very menacing and intimidating if you keep looking at it; but if you leave him alone, he will slither away, and there will be no interaction. We can learn a lot from this.

Student: It seems to boil down to wanting something; that is what provokes cruelty.

Dr. Hora: Yes. If we want to be confirmed, to be accepted, to be right—this is also something that is very often troublesome— if we want to influence people—all kinds of things just ask for trouble. If we are not interested in self-confirmation, we will not be lost. If we are not interested in hurting anyone, no one will be interested in hurting us. "Nothing comes into experience uninvited" [Seventh Principle of Metapsychiatry].

Student: So even what seems to be a good deed, if we are doing it from a personal perspective, could invite malice.

Dr. Hora: We see that all the time. The United States is hated throughout the world because we are doing so much "good" everywhere—throwing money at everything—and people have contempt for us. We seek acceptance.

Student: The other day I went to visit my mother-in-law—it seems like a perfect example of what we are talking about—it was seven o'clock, and my sister-in-law was in the kitchen, helping to get dinner. She snapped at me and said, "Why do you always come at dinner time, just when I am trying to feed my mother!" Whereupon I turned around and left. But I can see that this was invited. I certainly thought it was cruel for her to say that, but I can see that I was going there for acceptance and probably self-confirmation.

Dr. Hora: Right, so you got what was coming to you.

Student: And I haven't been back since!

Dr. Hora: It works every time!

Student: Next time, you will wait for an invitation.

Student: It is tricky, because I do many things throughout the day that seem to be right from the perspective of being a "good person," but they need to be transcended; otherwise they could elicit anger.

Dr. Hora: It is dangerous to be a "good person." It is bad to be a bad person too. We have to be nonpersons; then we are safe. How can we be a "nonperson"?

Student: By knowing who we are—we are each an expression of God, a nondimensional entity [of awareness].

Dr. Hora: The best way to be a "nonperson" is by understanding and practicing perfect love. How is that?

Student: Within the definition of perfect love, there is the non-personal aspect and the nonconditional motivation.

Dr. Hora: What does it mean, "nonconditional"?

Student: No strings attached.

Dr. Hora: We do not ask for anything—we are only interested in being benevolent because God is benevolence. Divine Love is not sexual love or interpersonal love; it is just benevolence. The goodness of God is expressing itself throughout the universe—with no strings attached. All that is required of us is to understand it, and if we do not understand it, we cannot practice perfect love.

Student: What can help us to understand it?

Dr. Hora: The study of Metapsychiatry. Perfect love is "non-personal, nonconditional benevolence." We are transparencies of divine Benevolence.

Student: So is it a way of seeing? If it is not something that we are doing, and it has no object, then it must be a way of seeing.

Dr. Hora: It is a way of being and a way of understanding Reality. Reality is nonpersonal, nonconditional goodness—the goodness of God. Consciousness is filled with a sense of gratitude, which means that there is an open channel between the divine Mind and individual consciousness. When this channel is open, whatever ideas are needed, in whatever situation, come through— God is reaching us through the open channel of gratitude. Communication is from God to individual consciousness. And there are no problems; there are no decisions to be made; everything is clear, and the right ideas come from moment to moment. Many people have problems "hearing" God. They have decisions to make; they pray and meditate and spend a lot of time studying and cannot "hear" what God is saying. We cannot hear what God is saying unless our consciousness is an open channel—only a grateful consciousness is an open channel. We constantly need intelligent, creative ideas, and we can only get them from the divine Mind. The secret is the cultivation of gratitude in consciousness. There are people who are in the habit of complaining—they are lifelong complainers, and they see everything as a difficult problem. "As thou seest, so thou beest." It is very important to guard ourselves against the temptation to complain. If we are in the habit of complaining, we are going to have reasons to complain—we attract them.

Student: What is the meaning of complaining?

Dr. Hora: It is a statement: There is no God; there is no love; life is difficult; everything stinks! There is even a book entitled, *Life Is a Lousy Drag.* We can develop such a fantasy about life, and we hurt ourselves. It is very widespread—people just like to complain. What is it that is so good about complaining?

Student: It makes you feel important.

Dr. Hora: For instance, I just noticed here that someone was scratching himself. What is that? It is a complaint, "I'm itching." It is easy to become a complainer. But then we are saying, "I am interested in problems." It is very self-confirmatory to talk about our problems. Traditional psychology says we have to express or ventilate our problems; otherwise we will get sick, implying that it is good to complain and tell everyone our problems. What do we say to this? It feels good, but it is not good. Because the more we complain, the more reasons we will find to complain; and every time we feel better for having complained, we get a little bit more addicted to this habit of complaining. But if we are in the habit of preserving a grateful outlook on life under all circumstances, then we shall find healing and spontaneous solutions to whatever we need; and the wisdom of God, infinite Mind, will reach us, and the right ideas will be available to lead us into a better life. So if we find ourselves troubled with a problem—be it financial, social, marital, physical, or emotional—we do not have to burden others by telling them about it. We have to sit down in a quiet place and confront ourselves with a question, Is my consciousness filled with crap, or is it filled with a sense of gratitude? In other words, Is the glass half-empty, or is the glass half-full? The pessimist says the glass is half-empty, and the optimist says the glass is half-full. What do we say?

Student: "My cup runneth over?"

Dr. Hora: Metapsychiatry recommends that we say, "I am grateful that there is water"—just be grateful. There will always be everything that we need; we will never suffer any lack. A skeptic hearing this would say, "How can I be grateful when I don't feel grateful? Do you, Dr. Hora, want me to be a liar and a hypocrite and to fool myself into being grateful when I am not grateful?" Will that work? No, of course not. Someone called today who had come across one of our books in the library. She was amazed and asked, "Can you really live as you describe in your book?" I said, "Are you calling me a hypocrite?" When we say we have to be grateful to God all the time and under all circumstances, we do not say we have to be a hypocrite—we must understand what we are grateful for. We have to be grateful for life, for the good of life, for whatever good we are able to see. We must reach a point where we really understand that God is a Cosmic Principle of Love-Intelligence. When we acknowledge this, we are filled with gratitude that this is really so, and everything else is just ignorance. We do not have to be hypocrites; we just have to understand Reality. Certainly, if we do not understand Reality and we force ourselves to say, "I'm grateful, I'm grateful, I'm grateful," this is not what we are talking about. No one is teaching rote learning here. We are focusing attention on Reality; we seek to understand Reality, not just to pay lip service to it. One of the younger students of Metapsychiatry said once, "I was praying last week." I asked, "How were you praying?" And he said, "I was saying the Four Ws." Is that prayer, when we "say" the Four Ws? It is not prayer.

It is just magical thinking, that God will be flattered to know that we are saying the right words. We have to be careful. Prayer is not "saying words." If we think that prayer is saying words, then we do not understand prayer. Now what is prayer? And what are we praying for anyway?

Student: There is only one thing that we can pray for—understanding. If we have a problem, we look at the problem from the perspective of our mode of being and seek to see the meaning of it, to be still and listen if that is possible.

Dr. Hora: We said today that when we sit down to meditate, contemplate, or pray, we have to ask ourselves, "What is in my consciousness? Is my consciousness full of crap, or is my consciousness getting filled with genuine gratitude for the good of God, which is spiritual blessedness?" Now we could just say these words, but that would not be prayer. When we are really interested in understanding what these words mean in terms of our mode of being-in-the-world, then our prayer is sincere. Even if we do not understand right away, we are not just saying the words. The words are just helping to focus attention on something that is important to realize. We repeat and contemplate these words until we reach a point of PAGL [PAGL is an acronym for Peace, Assurance, Gratitude, Love, and Its Presence in consciousness informs us that we are in tune with the One Mind]. When we reach a point of PAGL, this indicates that we have understood something. And when that happens, we can get up and go out and conquer the world, because we have conquered our own resistance to the truth. There is always something good that flows out of that effort. And the Bible says: "To him that overcometh will I give to eat of the tree of life, which is in the midst of the paradise of God" (Revelation 2:7). What does that mean? What kind of a tree is the "tree of life"?

Student: Maybe that is symbolic of gratitude.

Dr. Hora: The "tree of life" is a symbol of being in conscious contact with Reality. Life becomes real at the point of PAGL—the "good of God" is a reality to us at that point. We do not have to kid ourselves or lie to ourselves or pretend or congratulate ourselves because we have touched Reality. That is the purpose of prayer and meditation—to touch Reality. We have to live this way all our lives—it is a lifelong project, to be in contact with Reality.

Student: When we sit down to pray, is the resistance we experience just that we are so much more conditioned to the human way of thinking? Switching over, being quiet or being still, seems difficult.

Dr. Hora: It is a discipline; it requires great, sincere discipline to be still and to understand what prayer is and what the purpose of prayer is, and how to reach that point. Jesus said: "When thou prayest, use not vain repetitions, as the heathen do: for they think that they shall be heard for their much speaking" (Matthew 6:7).

Student: When one is suffering, it is not that difficult to turn to prayer, because it seems to be the only way out.

Dr. Hora: No, there are other ways—you can go to a bar; you can take a pill or beat up on your friends. There are many ways.

Student: Well, prayer is the only healthy way—it seems easier to turn to prayer when there is suffering. When things are going well and there is a sense of blessedness, the need does not seem as great. Am I just to be grateful throughout the day? Is this a good idea?

Dr. Hora: Sure, if you can sustain it. Unfortunately the blissful moments are very short. Things become easier after we have practiced and understood. We can pray while we are doing work and even at night, in our dreams. Once we reach a point of true appreciation of the good of God, we never want to stop praying—even all night we are praying. This is not a religious prayer—it is an existential prayer, and our very life depends upon it.

Student: Dr. Hora, you said to contemplate words in the context of life?

Dr. Hora: The meaning of the words.

Student: In terms of values?

Dr. Hora: What is the meaning of "meaning"?

Student: Understanding.

Dr. Hora: Yes, if we understand the meaning of "meaning," we are praying that our lives may not be meaningless. What is a meaningless life? When we are "deadheads" and do not understand anything and are even unable to consider the possibility of a meaningful existence, we are just some kind of automaton or "trendy" guy. What makes us follow trends? We are hoping to find meaning through conformity.

Student: Is that because we think that meaning is in the experience?

Dr. Hora: Yes. Everyone is looking to experience life. What is the Ninth Principle of Metapsychiatry?

Student: "Reality cannot be experienced or imagined; it can, however, be realized."

Dr. Hora: That's right. Most people think that life is what we experience, but, no, it is what we realize. When Reality becomes real to us, then we have a realization. When we have experiences, or try to experience what others are experiencing, we are just dreaming. We want to have the same dream as other people.

Student: Dr. Hora, once a mode of being-in-the-world is established, does it stay with us until we become enlightened?

Dr. Hora: The mode of being-in-the-world is determined by the prevailing values we cherish at any particular time. It is not set in concrete. It is set in the culture that we imitate and in the values that prevail in certain cultural subgroups. The values that we espouse at a particular time determine our mode of being-in-the-world.

Student: Is the way that we can know that an invalid idea is a dream, by seeing it dissolve when it is replaced by a valid idea? Is that how we can really know that?

Dr. Hora: A student of Metapsychiatry is learning, studying, and reading about all the valid values that have been mediated to our understanding by Jesus Christ and the prophets and also by the Oriental sages—there is considerable "coincidence" and dove-tailing. We know what spiritual values are; we do not need any more proof. If we replace an invalid value—for instance, self-confirmation is an invalid value—if we replace a self-confirmatory value in our lives with gratitude, we see the self-confirmatory tendencies disappear, and with their disappearance comes a sense of liberation. There is no mystery about it. When $2 + 2 = 5$ is replaced by 4, the 5 disappears, and no one misses it. We do not ask anyone, "Did it really go away?" No, we just know that it was nothing—it turns into nothing because it always was nothing. The Tenth Principle of Metapsychiatry says, "The right understanding of what really is abolishes all that seems to be."

Noah's Ark

Student: Dr. Hora, I know this is a frivolous question, but what is the meaning of all of us sitting in pairs?

Dr. Hora: Maybe this is Noah's ark—"two by two."

Student: Dr. Hora, during the last three weeks or so, our building has had seven or eight break-ins, and the conversation in the building between the tenants is constantly about this subject—people are extremely fearful. There have also been some muggings outside of the building, and some muggings in the elevator. It seems to be heightened at this time because there is a real rash of them. The person who is breaking into the apartments is using the fire escape, so he is getting the ones that have fire escapes adjoining their apartments. Two days ago, the woman that sublets one of our apartments downstairs heard a noise in the living room, came out, and there was a fellow who was halfway through her window. She wanted to talk to me about security in the building, and other tenants had also heard about the break-in that day. The conversations that come up around this issue are extremely fearful, and we happen to have a fire escape that adjoins our kitchen window. The two questions that I would like to ask are: first, how can we not be hypnotized into becoming fearful? I notice that when I go to the door those thoughts are present, and they never were before. Second, is there a way that we could have a beneficial effect in the building?

Dr. Hora: That is a serious problem—the more one talks about it, the more one invites it. It is a real conundrum. You are damned if you do and damned if you don't. What do you recommend that we do?

Student: Is it important for us to understand the meaning?

Dr. Hora: It is always important to understand the meaning

Student: Is there a specific meaning for each of the individuals in the building, or is there a general meaning?

Dr. Hora: The general meaning is mental contagion; it is hard not to invite these things if everyone is mentally preoccupied by them.

Student: In the hallway downstairs, everyone who has been robbed has posted an account of the robbery and what has been stolen; other people are writing notes about what security measures they think should be taken. There are physical representations of the fear everywhere in the building, and one is reminded of the robberies constantly.

Dr. Hora: So there are human attempts at solving these problems, which usually prove to be unsuccessful. There must be a spiritual way to be safe. We can say that the only way one could get burglarized is by wanting it or by not wanting it. How can we become immune to this mental contagion? We are always suffering from mental contagion. The more effective our communications in the mass media are, the more we are suffering from contagion. It is interesting to consider the failures of the space rockets, one after another. For a long time, everything was working very nicely; then suddenly after the first failure, there was one after another. Even in Europe it has failed. How is that possible? What happened? Are we suddenly inept? Have all these brilliant engineers suddenly become drug addicts? Irresponsible jerks? What happened? There is also a belief that problems come in series. How do we explain that? Is it bad luck? We are victims of mental contagion. What is the spiritual solution to the problem of victimization—mugging or theft, burglary, violence, rape, or fraud? The Bible gives us a very clear answer to the issue of safety, and it is better than guns, the police, bars on the windows, locks, or alarms.

Student: In the past when we spoke about this, the incident that we spoke about occurred when Jesus was able to walk unharmed through a crowd that had at that moment an extremely hostile intent.

Dr. Hora: How did he do that?

Student: He knew something.

Student: Does it have something to do with personhood? If you think of yourself as a person you are liable to be robbed.

Dr. Hora: Certainly to think of oneself as a person makes us vulnerable, but it is more than that.

Student: There are two ideas that we need to know, and we have spoken about them here—that our lives are "hid with Christ in God" and that we are dwelling in "the secret place of the Most High."

Dr. Hora: The Ninety-first Psalm, when it is really understood, can protect us from all forms of victimization. Now there are many religious preachers who make nothing out of it—they are even preaching about it—but to most people, one Psalm is like another Psalm, just religious words. But if you read the Ninety-first Psalm with a sincere desire to fill your consciousness with the message and remain with it all the time, that is the best possible protection you can get. You have to read it as if your safety depended on it, rather than just as an interesting religious treatise. "Because thou hast made the Lord thy habitation, there shall no evil befall thee, neither shall any 'burglar' come nigh thy dwelling." What is a dwelling place? Is an apartment a dwelling place? The dwelling place is that which we dwell on. If you dwell on your apartment, then you are in danger. But if you dwell on the presence of omniactive Love-Intelligence in your consciousness, to the exclusion of other interests, then you are safe. There is really no other safety than spiritual safety. "He that dwelleth in the secret place of the Most High shall abide under the protection of the Almighty." Real security is a well-kept secret—no one thinks of it. Instead of spiritual solutions, there are all kinds of human solutions to the problem of crime; but the spiritual solution is the only one that is really effective. If we allow ourselves to be distracted, we will lose it; it is very easy to lose. We need constant, conscious mindfulness that our dwelling place is God. Can this protection extend to the rest of the building? It may or it may not. We cannot control other people's thoughts. We are now today in this group, in "Noah's ark," since we have positioned ourselves "two by two." What is the meaning of the story of Noah's ark? Noah was a spiritually minded man in the midst of a terribly degenerated community—all kinds of sinful and criminal and perverse sexuality dominated that particular community. Noah was a patriarch who upheld spiritual values; he was a godly man, and his influence extended to his immediate family, including the animals around him. The whole story of Noah is about safety and survival. We can be safe even if we are surrounded by dangerous mental climates. In spite of the mental climate, Noah preserved the purity of his consciousness, and all those individuals who were around him and who respected these values were also saved. The rest of the community was totally destroyed. That is the meaning of Noah's ark—it stands symbolically for protection from the mental contagion of the community. That is the way to be safe. How did you know before we started this session that you were going to be in Noah's ark today?

Student: We all sat this way.

Dr. Hora: How is that possible?

Student: Divine Intelligence.

Dr. Hora: The Bible says: "The father knoweth what ye have need of before ye ask" (Matthew 6:8).

Student: What is the meaning of "two by two"?

Dr. Hora: Noah was given a command by God to save two representatives of all life forms.

Student: Dr. Hora, I was wondering, How is one to benefit more from each of these sessions?

Dr. Hora: That's a good question that no one ever asks. How could we make these sessions more profitable? How could we really learn something?

Student: Is it our lack of interest?

Dr. Hora: No. There are "knowers," there are "thinkers," there are "thieves," there are "dreamers," and there are "hitchhikers." None of these people ever learn anything until they become sincere "seekers"; then they begin to learn, and it can take years and years. It cannot be controlled; it can only be clarified. Nobody can twist your arm to become a "seeker."

Student: But is not a seeker someone who is really interested in learning?

Dr. Hora: That is what it is.

Student: Is the interest lacking?

Dr. Hora: The interest is misdirected. A "knower" wants to know that he knows, and he wants to be known as knowing. A "thinker" wants to think about it till doomsday. A "thief" wants to accumulate information; a "dreamer" is just dreaming, fantasizing; and a "hitchhiker" is having fun. Maybe conferences are full of "hitchhikers"—everyone is having lots of fun, but not many people are really learning.

Student: What disposition, or mode of being, do you have to be in to learn? I have read about it, and when it happens we really are not controlling it. What happened to me over the weekend was interesting: I had a dream, and as a result of the dream I saw that a hang-up that I have had for years was gone— the hang-up was that I was being used by people. I was always complaining that somehow I would get myself trapped into being used or allow myself to be used. In the dream, there was a choice given for an occupation. Someone was chosen to go out into the field, and somehow I wanted to go out into the field. Then gently I was asked to come to the office—everything was very gentle. Ordinarily I would have been envious or jealous of the other going to the field and of not being given a choice of what I wanted to do. And then I awakened, and I tried to think of the meaning. It came afterwards that maybe I am letting go— maybe I am allowing, maybe I am not trying to cling or possess and am really trying to allow whatever will happen to happen. I thought that was good.

Dr. Hora: What was the dream?

Student: We were at something like a Quaker Community. The individuals there were enlightened and intelligent and living harmoniously. Someone was chosen to go off with an older person to the field, and that was my yearning; and then they brought me gently in and wanted me to do the work that I usually do. But when I went in, it didn't matter what I did. I saw that it didn't matter where I was or what I did—I just wanted to be part of this harmony—and it was good, and I was happy.

Dr. Hora: Sounds good.

Student: The very next morning, though, something interfered with the harmony. I was wondering how I could be immune to interferences in order to stay in a harmonious state. It seems, for instance, with the space program that we were all in such awe of it—we always want something beyond us—and that we were grateful for the success of the space program. But, then, maybe we became too smug.

Dr. Hora: Yes, gratitude has a tendency to elude us after a while, and then self-congratulations and pride and arrogance and rivalry take over—all kinds of things, instead of being grateful. It is so easy to forsake God; we do it every day. Jesus was on the cross, and he cried out: "My God, my God, why hast thou forsaken me?" (Matthew 27:46). These are very important words. He was really saying, "Why are we forsaking God all the time?" Everyone keeps forsaking God, and then we blame God for doing it.

Student: We say that we have to be mindful all the time, but if we work hard at being mindful, if we try really hard, it's the same as forsaking.

Dr. Hora: Trying too hard is not good.

Student: There needs to be a genuine interest and mindfulness all the time, but we can't force it.

Dr. Hora: We have to be mindful of being mindful.

Student: It is gentle and non-willful.

Dr. Hora: Of course. If you become a fanatic, what are you? Are you enlightened?

Student: You're obnoxious.

Dr. Hora: No, you are just self-confirmatory. Fanaticism is just self-confirmation gone haywire.

Student: What is a valid process of learning?

Dr. Hora: We start out by learning how to "be here for God"—constantly identifying ourselves as instruments of God and seeing that we are under the control of divine Wisdom and Love. Our focus is always on wisdom and love and the presence of God. The presence of God within us manifests itself as wisdom and love. It is not willfulness—it is effortless, efficient effectiveness, which is conflict-free. Our mental horizon transcends the interaction context and is maintained in the divine context. We have a broader perspective on life; we are mindful of that divine context without willfulness, without banging on the door of God. We seek to be aware of God's presence in the form of wisdom and love and PAGL and gentleness and letting be—all these spiritual qualities. And then we are safe and things go well. But we lose it—and it is easy to lose it—because we are impressed by the world, and again we suffer. We have forsaken God the moment that we slip down into the interaction context of the world. We have turned our back on God; we have offended God. That is what is meant by the words, "Why has thou forsaken me?" We have the impression that God has turned his back on us when we are suffering and in trouble, and we say this. We have this clear impression that God has forsaken us, but the truth is that we are forsaking God. We assume, with all good religious people, that God is here for us. And if we have this assumption, then naturally it seems that God has forsaken us. But if we really understand that God is not here for us but that we are "here for God," then God cannot forsake us. It is we who forsake God.

Student: When we talk about "being here for God," I've always thought we meant the person, being a good person for God.

Dr. Hora: God knows nothing about persons. It says in the Bible that God has no respect for persons. A person is just a psychological pretense. But we are not persons—we are "living souls," nondimensional aspects of divine Consciousness.

Student: So that which is "not appearance" is "here for God?" We are each a nondimensional aspect of God, and if we are not persons, then is it only the spiritual part of us which is "here for God?"

Dr. Hora: How many parts are you?

Student: Two. I am trying to understand what is "here for God."

Dr. Hora: The whole universe is "here for God."

Student: We think that if we are a "good person," then we are "here for God."

Dr. Hora: If you are a good person, then you are a psychologist!

Student: A white witch.

Student: What is "here for God?"

Dr. Hora: The whole universe is "here for God." The universe of divine Reality is nondimensional; we cannot draw a picture of the universe.

Student: When we ask about infinity, we are always told that it takes so many light years to get to a certain star; we were taught in terms of spatial concepts. So all that is limited thought. Is there no such thing as light years? Is there an outer edge to God? Does the universe have a place in space?

Dr. Hora: These ideas are just human ways of coping with the unbearable truth of infinity.

Student: What makes it so unbearable?

Dr. Hora: It annihilates us.

Student: There is a fear of not knowing what infinity is.

Dr. Hora: Anyone who realizes infinity disappears. How can there be anything finite if Reality is infinite?

Student: How would we even know to be afraid of something that isn't real? What is real is God, so how do we know to be afraid?

Dr. Hora: We have the impression that we are dimensional. We are attached to dimensions, and losing this impression of dimensionality is frightening. If you have a teddy bear and love this teddy bear very much and like to hug it and go to sleep with it, if someone would take it away or say that next week your teddy bear will disappear, wouldn't you be frightened?

Student: If I thought the teddy bear was the source of my security.

Dr. Hora: Yes. Children always cling to their teddy bears or a blanket or something because it is something they can hold—it is dimensional, furry, cuddly—and it gives them the impression that bodies, or matter, are real. And we each have a certain idea of ourselves as a dimensional, physical entity, as a finite, circumscribed structure. Now if someone says that you have to realize that Reality is infinite—that it has no dimensions, it has no structure, it is not tangible, it is not circumscribed, you cannot cuddle with it—everything disappears. Now that is frightening.

Student: What do we need to know not to be afraid?

Dr. Hora: Will you take my word for it? We gradually evolve—our consciousness evolves over the years of sincere seeking to the point where we are at peace with it. And at that point, the fear of dying disappears; the fear of sickness disappears; the fear of losing loved ones disappears—there is complete PAGL. That is enlightenment—peace with the truth of infinity. When Jesus realized his infinity, he disappeared, and so did Elijah and a few other interesting fellows.

Student: There is a classic book about the evolution of the human mind written by Richard Bucke entitled Cosmic Consciousness. It seems that all these fellows, like Walt Whitman and Bacon, who had attained a moment of this realization, lost their fear of death. But what happens when I read that book is that I want that too. I think, "How can I have that experience?"

Dr. Hora: Yes, but it is not really an experience. They talk about it as if it were an experience, but it is a realization.

Student: When one has that realization, is it forever?

Dr. Hora: There is no returning from infinity—no more reincarnations, no more making mistakes. We are liberated from the cycle. The Buddhists call it the "karma of cause-and-effect."

Student: It seems that what we are talking about is learning to see in a completely new context—to see as God sees. It seems that this is what our work is in Metapsychiatry and on the path.

Student: I keep wondering if one could be too afraid to learn. But this just may be the problem of being a "knower" and trying to skirt the issue.

Dr. Hora: Yes. "Knowers" cannot ask questions, and they are not learning because they cherish a fantasy that they already know everything—it is just a self-delusion: "I already know."

Dialogue No. 26

"Take My Yoke . . ."

Student: Dr. Hora, in the passage where Jesus says, "Come unto me, all ye who labor and are heavy laden, and I will give you rest . . . . Take my yoke upon you . . . . My yoke is easy, and my burden is light" (Matthew 11:28-30), what is this "yoke" he is asking us to take upon ourselves?

Dr. Hora: "Being here for God" is the yoke.

Student: And he says, "My yoke is easy, and my burden is light."

Dr. Hora: Yes, everything becomes more intelligent, efficient, effective, and effortless, if we are here for God. To an unenlightened individual, it seems like a yoke—a burden—because we must give up whatever we want or whatever we do not want. It seems like a great sacrifice.

Student: So if we are here for God, then we don't have to run our business all by ourselves?

Dr. Hora: Yes, everything becomes effortless, efficient, effective, and clear—no confusion, no shenanigans. Jesus' words are a paradoxical statement—we think of a yoke as a burden—but a yoke makes it easy: "My yoke is easy, and my burden is light."

Student: But the yoke that we carry in the human world is heavy and like a burden around our necks.

Dr. Hora: Yes, but you get a lot of ego gratification in the world—you can become rich and famous, even get on TV!

Student: And you lose your soul.

Dr. Hora: Yes.

Student: I wonder what it is about the right motivation that makes things easier?

Dr. Hora: Right motivation is the right yoke; it does make it easier.

Student: How is that?

Dr. Hora: You don't understand?

Student: Well, I can see that if we are not here for God, then it is a heavy burden.

Dr. Hora: How do we know that it is a heavy burden?

Student: Because we see the suffering that results from false motivations.

Dr. Hora: Well, we also see people happy, excited, prosperous, riding in limousines and living in penthouses, right?

Student: Right, and we look at that, and it is almost contagious.

Dr. Hora: It is almost very contagious. But we can tell that that yoke is not "easy," because it creates anxieties, affects health, makes for high blood pressure and fear and rivalry and various symptoms like headaches, disingenuousness, and seriousness.

Student: If the motivation is right, then the priorities automatically fall into place. One's priorities are automatically set when the motivation is in place.

Dr. Hora: Yes, and then life is lived more intelligently: there is no pressure, no anxiety, no heart palpitations, no grinding of the teeth—no teeth!

Student: Dr. Hora, I would like to ask a question, but I would like to ask it without complaining; I need help in formulating the right question so that it will not be a complaint.

Dr. Hora: Well, sing it!

Student: When I talk to my parents, their goodness is so sickening, I just want to scream. When I know I have to see them, it makes me sick, and I just can't stand it. Then I ask myself, "How could I be so unloving, when they are so good?" It is disgusting, so I am stuck.

Dr. Hora: Well, what exactly is disgusting?

Student: Their goodness, because it is so unreal—it is a cover-up for such bullshit that I just can't stand it. Whenever I say no, that I can't see them, and I haven't seen them for months, it just comes back to me, over and over, "How could you be such a lousy kid, when we are so good to you? Look at what we try to do for you." On and on and on, and I am just disgusted. I would like very much not to spend any time with them, but I realize that is not the answer either. All I am doing is avoiding them, but the real truth is that it is sickening. I realize what the payment is, and I cannot participate in it.

Dr. Hora: What is the payment?

Student: Fulfilling their fantasy, which is disgusting.

Dr. Hora: Marrying a Jewish doctor? That's not so bad.

Student: That is the pretty side of it. There is more to it than just that—more disgusting in my mind's eye and, in a lot of ways, being with them only makes it harder.

Dr. Hora: Yes. Well, how could you find immunity to disingenuous, conditional love? Is that what you are describing?

Student: Yes, by not wanting anything, but the only difficulty with that is . . .

Dr. Hora: "Not wanting" is wanting.

Student: Okay, what I am really angry about is, if they are so good . . . then I am just frustrated. I feel like I am trapped; I just can't get out of it.

Dr. Hora: How is "not wanting" wanting?

Student: It is the other side of the coin.

Dr. Hora: Which side of the coin? "Not wanting" is wanting them to "not be" the way they seem to be.

Student: I am so sick of them telling me that I am a horrible person.

Dr. Hora: Well, what is wrong with that?

Student: If we want our parents to love us, or even like us, that is what is wrong with it.

Dr. Hora: So the problem is not in telling you that you are a horrible person; the problem is that you do not want them telling you this.

Student: So then, what is the sense of going to see them if that is all I am going to hear? I can't seem to get over this idea of wanting them to like me.

Dr. Hora: Oh, so then the problem is not with your parents but with you—with what you want and what you do not want. Isn't that wonderful? You see, you cannot change your parents, but you can be healed of wanting and not wanting—get it?

Student: I get it; it is just difficult.

Dr. Hora: What's difficult? It is so simple.

Student: The other day in group, you put it beautifully when you spoke about Love-Intelligence. It helped me to understand what it means when we say that God loves us, that Love-Intelligence manifests itself and that we are part of that manifestation, and suddenly it clicked! You said that we are all participating in that Love-Intelligence.

Dr. Hora: It is the "swimming pool" story, yes. We were in the swimming pool yesterday frolicking, and now we are high and dry.

Student: So wouldn't it be helpful if we could understand what that meant, to be loved in a nonpersonal way? No? Is it the wanting and the not wanting?

Dr. Hora: Right. What is the remedy to the problem?

Student: I asked you this question a couple of weeks ago, and it seemed that the answer was "coming to understand God's love." If we could understand that God loves us, then it wouldn't matter so much if we got the human love from our parents.

Dr. Hora: Well, of course that is true. But there are people who are swimming in a swimming pool and still asking for water from the other swimmers! Really, the remedy is "being here for God"— that is the universal remedy to all problems—taking the yoke of Christ upon us and suddenly finding that it is freedom. You see, if you are not "here for God," you are seeing every situation in terms of interaction, and that is troublesome—that is a heavy yoke to carry. But the Christly yoke is no interaction, only Omniaction. If you are "here for God," what your parents think and say and do has no effect on you because your outlook on life has been expanded into infinity. So you can be a transcendent observer, and you will neither judge nor not judge.

Student: It is hard.

Dr. Hora: It is hard? Not really.

Student: Judging and not judging have come up quite a bit lately; it seems almost as though it is built in; it is automatic. If you see a particular thing, for instance, that chair, there will be a judgment.

Dr. Hora: What does that chair do to you?

Student: It was just an example.

Student: Maybe it has to do with opinions; somehow, we think that we need to have an opinion about everything or a thought about everything.

Dr. Hora: Yes, most people do like to spout opinions; that's true. But, the problem we were speaking of indicates that we want to change our parents—they shouldn't be the way they seem to be; they shouldn't talk; they shouldn't think that way, right? She has to change them, and they want to change her—the result is mutual despair. It is amazing how tenacious these thoughts of wanting can be. Now people try to give it up, or they try to replace it by not wanting; and that is a trap. There is no way of being set free from wanting and not wanting—except by turning to what God wants, and then suddenly we are free.

Student: Then the desperation is just being stuck between the two things—wanting and not wanting?

Dr. Hora: Right. You have to admit to yourself that you really want to change your parents.

Student: I can't believe that my parents are so ignorant and oblivious. . . . To me, it is amazing. . . . I just can't believe that what they want for me is good.

Dr. Hora: They have a right to be ignorant and oblivious.

S*tudent:* Their fantasy is so disgusting.

Dr. Hora: They have a right to have fantasies. What's it to you? If you did not have this desire to change them, you would have no problems. Do you see? We do not suffer from other people; we suffer from our thoughts about them.

Student: But to some extent my parents have convinced me that their fantasy is my reality, and all those thoughts that I grew up with are thoughts that I have to confront and see that they are not my reality. They are very painful.

Dr. Hora: That would not be a problem if you would just let them be.

Student: Is forgiveness an issue here? Do we release ourselves from our parents' fantasies by forgiving them?

Dr. Hora: I don't think so. If you forgive them, you are saying that they really did something.

Student: I didn't mean it in that sense.

Dr. Hora: They didn't do anything. We have to forgive ourselves for what we want from them. We can see that we have no business wanting anything.

Student: Is it helpful to understand what the meaning of wanting to change somebody is?

Dr. Hora: Yes, it is stupidity. What would you say if you saw someone beating his head against a wall?

Student: That he was stupid.

Student: See, that's a judgment; it is built in.

Dr. Hora: That is not a judgment; that is "righteous judgment," which says it is not valid to beat your head against a wall— it doesn't make any sense to want people to change. "Righteous judgment" is an existential evaluation of a phenomenon. Is it valid, or is it not valid? If we pursue an invalid objective, this is not intelligent—another word for it is stupidity. It is not valid for us to want to change other people, even if they pay you for it. I get paid for this, and I gave up trying to change people years ago.

Student: Will some of it rub off?

Dr. Hora: Do you know the story about the two psychiatrists in the elevator? One was very exhausted, and the other was fresh and dapper. The tired one had not yet learned that you cannot change people. What can we do?

Student: Shed light.

Dr. Hora: Right.

Student: Nonverbally. It is true, isn't it?

Dr. Hora: Yes.

Student: So regarding judgment, to help us break the habit of judging, we must quickly turn to the question, Is it valid or not? because that is the only real judgment there is.

Dr. Hora: Yes. Suppose we find out that our parents' behavior is existentially invalid. All right, but they are not asking us to explain whether it is valid or not—that would be unsolicited solicitude, right? So we establish in our thoughts that their behavior and values are existentially invalid, but it is not for us to change them—that is God's job, and we will never get anywhere trying to do God's job. We are too small to "box with God," this was the title of a Broadway show, I think—we do not try to change anyone. We seek to know the truth which sets us free, that's all. All the various fights that go on between people are always about people wanting to change one another—"You shouldn't be like that; you shouldn't say this; you should do that . . ."

Student: What do we do with the thoughts that we identify with our parents? On the one hand, I can sit here and say that their value system is not healthy or valid, but, on the other hand, some of those values are ones that I have to struggle to outgrow in order to become spiritually mature. Whenever I come into contact with an invalid idea, it is very disturbing, and I get very angry at myself for still being a part of that value system.

Dr. Hora: Well, who is to blame for that?

Student: Well, at that point, I am not blaming them. I recognize that I have to give it up, or I have to understand something better.

Dr. Hora: What makes it difficult for you to be set free of their value system? What do you think?

Student: It's because I believe a lot of the things that they have taught me.

Dr. Hora: Blaming is making it difficult.

Student: I am blaming them for teaching me?

Dr. Hora: Yes, and as long as you blame them, you cannot be free.

Student: So forgiveness ultimately becomes the issue.

Dr. Hora: Of course, when we forgive, we set ourselves free.

You cannot blame them, neither can you not blame them. Do we understand this?

Student: I don't think I really understand the "not blaming" side. I can speculate that it means we just refuse to look at it—we bury it—and then it comes out in funny kinds of ways.

Dr. Hora: Yes, that is what it is. I once talked to a group of Episcopalian clergymen, and the atmosphere was so thick with blame, you could cut it with a knife. And what were they doing? They were trying to "not blame."

Student: What was being blamed?

Dr. Hora: They were thinking, "How dare you have different theological opinions from ours!"

Student: Oh, and they were trying to be liberal about it?

Dr. Hora: Right, and the result was that they were "not blaming," and the room was filled with this tension of blame.

Student: Is that why the atmosphere is often so sickening at liberal ecumenical theological conferences?

Dr. Hora: Absolutely. They are trying so hard to "not blame" and not criticize—"not blaming" is worse than blaming.

Student: Because it is the same thing, under cover.

Dr. Hora: Yes, exactly.

Student: Is that a form of repression, "not blaming?"

Dr. Hora: It is suppression.

Student: What is the difference?

Dr. Hora: Repression is when you relegate something into the unconscious; it happens unconsciously. But suppression is a conscious effort at hiding something. There is repression, and there is suppression.

Student: I see. You wouldn't want someone to know that you were judging, so you suppress it.

Dr. Hora: If someone is sitting on you and he doesn't know it, that is repression; if someone is sitting on you knowingly, that is suppression. See how simple it is.

Student: When you address an audience like the one with the atmosphere of blame, do you respond to that in any particular way, or do you just make your statements without regard for those vibes?

Dr. Hora: It is very unpleasant. We just do our best. One of my tapes is called "Casting Pearls," and it addresses this problem.

Student: I had the opportunity to see Dr. Hora speak before a group like that one time, and what I saw was forthrightness, humor, and absolutely no judgment. Those three qualities really softened something that could have been very destructive.

Dr. Hora: Yes, that was in San Francisco.

Student: Are we talking about dualities when we say neither judge nor not judge, want nor not want, repress nor suppress? What do we need to understand to get out of that duality?

Dr. Hora: When we say you must neither judge nor not judge, this is not a duality—this is just uncovering a falsehood. Because if you are not judging, you are just saying that you are not judging, but you are really judging. So all that is going on is judging. That is not a duality. Black and white is a duality; yes and no is a duality; but judging and not judging is just saying that not judging is a disguised way of judging.

Student: Is it the same thing, the same issue?

Dr. Hora: It is the same thing. Now if you would juxtapose judging with permissiveness or being liberal, that would be a duality—they do the opposite. There is a liberal viewpoint and a judgmental viewpoint—these are dualities because they are two sides of the same coin—we call them "flip sides." Repression and suppression are not dualities—they are two different phenomena of human thinking. Consciously suppressing something or unconsciously repressing something is not a duality.

Student: What is the flip side of repression?

Dr. Hora: Expression.

Student: How do we get out of that duality?

Dr. Hora: We don't get out of dualities. We are hopelessly trapped in them until we have learned transcendence.

Student: God.

Dr. Hora: Who else?

Student: So there is no way out of that thinking until . . .

Dr. Hora: Until transcendence. We have to transcend the problem with the parents, which means that we have to take a view from a higher standpoint, from the standpoint of God. In the context of God, all these dualities and problems disappear because the context of God is nondual—there is only Love-Intelligence and the perfect peace which passeth all dualities, beyond good and evil. Good and evil is the original duality of the serpent. It said that if you eat of this fruit, "your eyes will be opened and you will be like gods, knowing good and evil." That is what it said, and ever since then, we have had a problem with our parents. If we could lose interest in changing our parents, we would be immediately set free. Would you believe that?

Student: If I could do it, I certainly would.

Dr. Hora: It is just that we want to change them—that is the problem. We always complain about them, but we are only suffering from what we want.

Student: What makes it so desirable?

Dr. Hora: To change them? Well, then they would like us; they would approve of us.

Student: I always skip that part.

Dr. Hora: And we would feel good, right?

Student: Does that mean that wanting them to like us is really the deeper issue of want?

Dr. Hora: Yes, of course.

Student: So it is that particular thought that invites the interactions that we unfortunate offspring find so unpleasant?

Dr. Hora: Of course.

Student: Would the interactions cease when that thought is healed?

Dr. Hora: Absolutely—no more problems.

Student: Once the issue of being liked or loved is healed, then the interaction stops.

Dr. Hora: Yes, right. Sometimes instead of wanting to be liked, we can have a desire to punish, which is the flip side of that. Vindictiveness can be very powerful, very strong. And essentially it makes no difference whether we want to be liked or whether we want to hurt someone—we still want.

Student: With vindictiveness is the idea that if someone does not like us in the way that we want them to, then we might become vindictive toward that individual?

Dr. Hora: You might, yes; or maybe you were abused as a child and feel very bitter about it, and you would like to get back at your parents and punish and hurt them. Again the problem is the wanting, always the wanting. To give up wanting is difficult because it feels like dying. Jesus said that whoever would lose his desire to want will have an experience of dying for his sake, and then he shall be resurrected to a new life, a spiritual life. "He that findeth his life shall lose it: and he that loseth his life for my sake shall find it" (Matthew 10:39).

Student: What helps us go through this "dying" experience without being so afraid of it that we just fall back?

Dr. Hora: Metapsychiatry can do it, nothing else, because

Metapsychiatry can reveal to us the "life after death"—it is called PAGL. When we know what good is awaiting us after we are willing to "die," we are willing to "die"—it is not as difficult.

Student: What is the meaning when one is willing to "die," and one sees all the error in one's consciousness, and there is tremendous depression and remorse about it? Is that just the recognition phase?

Dr. Hora: It is not even the recognition phase. If there is depression, it means that there is repressed rage and vindictiveness, and we want to punish. But we haven't begun to "die."

Student: I see—we haven't even begun to recognize it.

Dr. Hora: Right. It is repressed. We are boiling with rage inside, and we are afraid to express it; we are "stuck" with it, so to speak. So first we have to recognize it, then regret it and let go of it, and finally reorient ourselves toward the transcendent view where there is nothing to want or to not want.

Student: So the depression is just the suffering that is driving one? If you get tired of suffering enough . . .

Dr. Hora: Yes, depression is very painful. We don't dare express our rage, because we are afraid that we would get so angry that it could kill us. Anger is very painful and dangerous, and repression is very painful—also dangerous to some extent— but explosive anger is really dangerous.

Student: If it is so dangerous and we realize it is so dangerous, how would we ever look at it?

Dr. Hora: You consult a Metapsychiatrist.

Student: You go to see Dr. Hora year after year after year.

Dr. Hora: Little by little, we open the floodgates of rage and bitterness and anger and release the pressure by talking about it and dreaming about it, by facing up to it, until it is dissipated and until you can see that it is not necessary to punish anybody, or to avenge oneself—that the whole thing was a dream. And then we go "beyond the dream" and the wanting stops, and we become interested in "being here for God"—and then we really are resurrected. That is resurrection: being resurrected to a life in the land of PAGL [PAGL is an acronym for Peace, Assurance, Gratitude, Love, and Its Presence in consciousness informs us that we are in tune with the One Mind].

Student: Dr. Hora, when something becomes very clear and gratitude comes, I find myself remembering the way it was and then seeing the way it is. What is it that makes the past experience, which made me suffer, keep coming back when I am grateful? Suddenly things are very clear and wonderful and there is so much gratitude.

Dr. Hora: Well, that is good.

Student: And then, I remember the past that caused the suffering—I recognize it. Is that just recognition?

Dr. Hora: Right, and you don't have any emotions about it anymore, right? The healthier we are, the easier it is to remember the past without feeling threatened or provoked by it—and we can forgive. There is an automatic process of forgiveness and giving up blame.

Student: Gratitude washes it away.

Dr. Hora: Right. We give up blaming, and we go free. But as long as we are blaming, we are suffering. There is no interaction anywhere, and there never was any—we must realize that there never was any interaction—it just seemed that way. So if we realize that there never was any interaction, even in childhood, then we have no more problems—then there is nothing but God, and you are in God and God is in you, and your life is spiritual blessedness. Do you know what that is? It is when "all things work together for good"—when life becomes effortless, efficient, and effective—no sweat. It is when there is a pleasant wind on the sea, and the jib and the mainsail are flying with full sail. What do they call the big sail in the front?

Student: The spinnaker.

Dr. Hora: The spinnaker is billowing in the sun; it is beautiful.

Student: So when we say, "There is no interaction anywhere," then what seems to be interaction really is just thoughts acting themselves out in our experience, like a movie?

Dr. Hora: Yes, or a dream—it is just a dream, an illusion. God is All-in-all. And in the context of God, there is no interaction, and there never was—there is only harmonious coexistence of all God's creation. When "the wolf shall dwell with the lamb, and the leopard shall lie down with the kid" is Isaiah's blissful image of this millennium where there is no more interaction (Isaiah 11:6). There is harmonious coexistence of God's creation—there is no rivalry, no hostility, no trespassing, no envy, no jealousy— everyone is happy and peaceful.

Dialogue No. 27

Existentially Engaged

Student: Dr. Hora, I was wondering if self-transcendence is the same thing as self-understanding.

Dr. Hora: What relevance does your question have to your life?

Student: I thought about that; it occurred to me that my question doesn't seem important.

Dr. Hora: It could be important if it has some meaning to your life.

Student: I was wondering if transcendence is the same thing as understanding.

Dr. Hora: I heard you say that. What prompts your question?

Student: I don't know. Maybe it would be easier to grasp, more accessible to me, because understanding is a more common term than transcendence . . .

Dr. Hora: What relevance does this question have to your life? One of our group here just asked me a question about erudite, intellectual people, talking for hours, seemingly very intelligently, but nothing had any existential impact that you could sink your teeth into. Here is a very good illustration of this: we have a seemingly intelligent question, but it is "out of thin air"—we could not find any relevance to the price of butter either. We could talk about transcendence; we could talk about understanding; but how do these relate to your life? Are you trying to engage in an intellectual conversation? This is called the fraudulence of the intellect: intellectuals can talk and talk and have long discussions with each other, never touching any base. They pretend to engage in some kind of a communication, and they are just throwing words around. People who listen to them can't get anywhere with it. What possible benefit is there to asking whether understanding is the same as transcendence? Where does it get you? It is a pretense of asking a question. You are not saying, "I have a bellyache, and I don't know what to do about it." You are asking an intellectual question which has no contact with anything. You might as well come here with the Encyclopedia Britannica, open it at random, pick a place, and say, "I want to know what is written here." So what? This is going on in universities and colleges, where people talk to each other on levels totally devoid of existential relevance. One of our students reported today that she listened to some very famous intellectuals on television who seemed to be talking very intelligently, but she could not find anything of value in it.

Student: Yes, I was trying to find a pearl there, just one perhaps, on which I could meditate or contemplate that would be, in some way, beneficial to lifting my consciousness. There was not one sentence.

Student: They were certainly intellectuals of the highest order on this program; I turned to my wife and said, "Do you have any idea what they are talking about?" We felt so stupid, and they were speaking English! But we just had no idea what they were talking about.

Student: Some people devote their lives to such pursuits, but it seems fruitless; and yet they are so highly regarded and well-respected.

Dr. Hora: People are very much impressed by intellectualism, and it is nothing but a devious, hidden way of confirming oneself.

Student: You have said that intellectuals believe in the power of the personal mind.

Dr. Hora: Yes, you might as well read a dictionary. What will you get out of that? A dictionary is not a book for reading—it is a book for research. Similarly, the Bible is not a book for reading. Jesus never said, "Read the Bible;" he said, "Search the scriptures." What are we searching for? A useful idea. And if we ask a question here, we have to have some relevant need to gain clarity on an idea or issue that is important to us in terms of our mode of being-in-the-world.

Student: I have made that same mistake, too. You think that you are studying the book, and maybe you even underline it; you can then get up from reading and feel as if you have done something for an hour or two, think that it was an accomplishment. We have to remind ourselves constantly what the purpose of study is, because it can easily turn into intellectualism.

Dr. Hora: What are intellectuals interested in?

Student: Showing how much they know.

Dr. Hora: This is the basic fraudulence of intellectualism. Intellectuals talk and lecture and debate and say words, and these things have absolutely nothing to do with life. They are only saying, "I am a highly educated person; I have read this book, and I have read that book; I have heard that lecture; I know this person who is a Nobel Laureate; I know, and I want you to know that I know." That is all there is to it—it is empty, totally empty because of the motivation. In Metapsychiatry we must talk in such a way as to really say something. If we ask a question, it must have something to do with our lives. What benefit will we get out of explaining the difference between understanding and transcendence? We will get nothing out of it, and we will have the illusion that we have engaged in a dialogue of some kind—but we haven't. It is nonsense, plain and simple.

Student: Dr. Hora, it gets more and more difficult to have a conversation outside of here with "normal" people. I find more and more that I would rather be by myself. It is so difficult. No matter how it starts, I have been unable to transcend what others say and to understand that it is just ignorant or invalid thoughts operating and not to take it personally. I walk away and keep repeating in my mind what I heard. I don't want to be a hermit. I don't know how to . . .

Dr. Hora: How to avoid nonsense? People have somehow gotten stuck and don't know how to avoid it—there is a lot of nonsense in the world. I remember a student of Metapsychiatry, a middle-aged lady, who was always concerned with being nice. Whenever you talked to her, she would make sure that you thought of her as nice. When she would attend our group talks, she would pick up certain things and next time regurgitate these ideas to show that she was nice, hoping that people would be impressed not only with how much she knew but also with how nice she was. One day she was told in a private session, "Look here, nice is not nice. It is actually very ugly because it is just nonsense." This upset her very much. Some people are stuck in their ways about "how to win friends and influence people."

Student: Most of my life, I have been trying to please someone so that she would like me, and I would have conversations that were surely full of nonsense. But now I am finding that it is difficult to have a conversation with that individual.

Dr. Hora: You cannot stop the nonsense.

Student: Probably.

Dr. Hora: What is the alternative?

Student: Keeping quiet.

Dr. Hora: That is no remedy; it still goes on in thought.

Student: Clarification of issues?

Dr. Hora: Could you elaborate on that?

Student: It seems that if one is discussing an issue, and if one's motivation is clarification, then there is no nonsense involved in the conversation, and it is a useful dialogue.

Dr. Hora: Well, the earlier question here was asking for clarification. What was the issue?

Student: I don't know what his issue was.

Dr. Hora: His issue was wanting us to think that he was participating in the group. The question was just a means of pulling the wool over the eyes, like saying, "Look here. I am here, and I am a regular student of Metapsychiatry. I am even asking questions." It looked as if it was a clarification of issues, but it was not really. It was just a way of trying to make us think that this was an issue. He was just trying to create a favorable impression.

Student: Is the alternative to nonsense authenticity?

Dr. Hora: Of course. Forthrightness, truthfulness, and being existentially engaged—we have to be "engaged" in life. If we are speaking nonsense, then we are just pretending to be engaged in life. Actually, we are not really here—we are just fantasizing about something else—but we want people to think that we are here.

Student: When you say "engaged," are you saying that it has to be relevant to something? Is relevance the issue?

Dr. Hora: Surely. Intellectual questions are relevant to nothing: they are a pretense to relevance; therefore, they are a lie; they are fraudulent. Everyone knows, especially in academic circles, that intellectuals are frauds. They are not only lying; they are constantly pretending, and they are constantly arguing with each other. This is called contentiousness—intellectuals have a tendency to be contentious.

Student: Dr. Hora, you said "existentially engaged." I am not sure I understand that.

Dr. Hora: Whatever you are interested in, you have to be interested in the quality of life. What is the quality of my life, and how could this quality of my life be improved? Everyone has a need to improve his quality of life. We do not have a need to collect intellectual concepts which have no relevancy to our lives. We come here so that our lives could be improved.

Student: I can understand that this applies here; does it also apply when we are not here? Can we say that in order to be authentic, we have to be existentially engaged all the time?

Dr. Hora: Well, of course. If you are not engaged, you are just up in the clouds. There are many people like that—they will not communicate—they make conversation. What does it mean to make conversation? It means to pretend that we are engaged in living. But, if we are truly existentially engaged, then we are interested in finding ways of elevating and improving the quality of our existence—this is existential involvement. When we talk to such an individual, we are never bored—everything is very interesting and awakening. You never fall asleep with such an individual. With a nice person, you fall asleep! There are people with whom we fall asleep, and there are people with whom we wake up. I am sure you have found such situations. We wake up! Such an individual doesn't have to talk a lot or shout; the quality of his presence is such that you wake up.

Student: Is that a broader way of seeing a beneficial presence, or are we talking about something different?

Dr. Hora: It is the same thing. A beneficial presence is present. An intellectual is not really present—he pretends to be present.

Student: Is communication about a quality of consciousness? Probably 99 percent of what goes on outside is just conversation. Communicating has to be more than words, because most people do just want to make conversation. So how do you communicate, when most of the time what's happening is just conversation.

Dr. Hora: Yes, if someone is making conversation with you, you tell them it is nonsense.

Student: That will cut it short!

Student: I don't understand because we say, "Do not show your pearls to unreceptive minds" [Eleventh Principle of Metapsychiatry]. So we cannot talk about the things we talk about here; and if we cannot make conversation, what do we talk about? I don't know what is left . . . I can't see it in practical terms.

Dr. Hora: It is what we don't talk about that we have to know. We don't talk about things that are not relevant. A beneficial presence is, first of all, "present"—he is not somewhere else. Second of all, he deals with whatever is relevant: if the weather is relevant, he talks about the weather. Whatever is relevant to the moment and the situation, he deals with it, but in a forthright and authentic way—not just pretending.

Student: How is talking about the weather relevant to the issue of life?

Dr. Hora: Very much so. The weather colors our life experiences very much, and one can talk about that. One can talk about anything—as long as one is sincere. You see, the nice lady was a phony; she was never sincere. She was talking about Metapsychiatry, but it was never relevant to anything. She was just using sentences and words that she read and heard, and it was absolutely empty. We have to become genuine, authentic individuals who respond moment to moment.

Student: An individual whom I meet with talks primarily about her health, or she gossips; this is what is relevant to her, and I am finding it a problem.

Dr. Hora: Health is very important; it is relevant to everyone.

Student: But she talks about symptoms.

Dr. Hora: If someone is talking about symptoms, he is not talking about health. What is he talking about? "Poor me." He is complaining.

Student: Right, but that is what seems important to her.

Dr. Hora: So, either you have compassion and you let her complain—you patiently let her talk—or you don't have compassion, and you say this is just complaining, and I am not going to listen.

Student: That will cut it short!

Student: But you say it silently.

Student: You want to be nice!

Dr. Hora: There is an awful lot of nonsense going on in the world, but we have to know that we must be alert. We must be aware; we are letting people talk for a while, until we cannot stand it anymore, and then we say goodbye. We are nice—we are tolerant and compassionate and let them be—but we do not pretend to be interested. You can have compassion for people who are forever complaining about something.

Student: For a long time I was gossiping and engaged in making conversation. Then, after coming here, I went in the opposite direction and decided that I wasn't going to talk at all. Then I came out of that a little bit, but I still remained very quiet and just tried not to gossip and not to be "nice"—I tried not to do all the things that I knew were invalid. It seems that I was living like that for a very long time, and then suddenly, just this year, something changed. A couple of times you spoke about the idea that "we are friendly because God is Love." It started to really make an impression on my consciousness, and I was thinking about it all the time. I found myself going out into whatever situation I was in, and that idea was the record that was playing. I started to live that way. I became aware that when I was talking to people, I was no longer thinking about talking to them or not talking to them, or anything on a human level, I was just aware that we are "friendly" because God is Love. It is as if you become an "ambassador" of this concept—everything becomes joyful. You are talking to people, and you seem to be very friendly; but you are friendly because God is Love, and you are always in contact with God. The people are there, and they are talking; but they are not really the issue. I would like to know if this is just making conversation, which is invalid, or is this another wrong solution?

Dr. Hora: No, this is being a beneficial presence.

Student: I also found that I was always very happy after these encounters because it was an opportunity to express something of God.

Dr. Hora: Of course. Here, the spiritual teacher cannot afford to be "friendly," because no one would learn anything if he was.

Student: It is different here, but it is valid to respond in that way when we leave these group sessions.

Dr. Hora: Of course it is. People you meet are not paying you [for spiritual guidance or to be educated about what is existentially valid].

Student: When this beautiful process was just being described, it seemed that never for a moment was she not in contact with God. Is that what being "existentially engaged" means?

Dr. Hora: Certainly, because God is Life and if we live that way, we are representing God as Love and as Life, and we are participating as a beneficial presence. Sometimes it can be a very healing experience when someone is just friendly and asking nothing in return, but usually people forget it very fast. And friendliness, of course, can be suspect; sometimes friendliness is misinterpreted for niceness, and we have to be careful never to be nice. We can be friendly because God is Love—this is not the same as being nice.

Student: Because being nice is insincere?

Dr. Hora: Yes. Being friendly, because God is Love, is a non judgmental, compassionate attitude, and that is very helpful and very good.

Student: The content of the conversation could be about the weather, but does that mean that you are not existentially engaged, if you are just talking about things like that?

Dr. Hora: You are not just talking; you are listening. When we are friendly, we usually just listen. There is nothing we can say, and no one is interested in what we would say anyway. So we can just be friendly and attentive, and we cannot really participate in what they are talking about. That is compassion, an authentic way of being compassionate. We do it for God.

Student: I just realized that when you are being nice, you are expecting something in return; you are expecting to be liked because you are being nice. That is what is wrong with it.

Dr. Hora: It is a way of influencing people, of "pulling the wool over their eyes." There are many ways that one can be inauthentic. Only humans have the talent for nonsense; animals do not.

Student: Dr. Hora, sometimes I have a personal issue that I would like to ask about, but it seems that it would be more appropriate for a private session. I am never sure when a question is appropriate for class dialogues.

Dr. Hora: Any question is appropriate if it sincerely relates to your experience. We are not squeamish here—it is all right. There are some people who are very squeamish in general; we call them vain. Vanity will make us squeamish and fearful: "What will they think of me if I ask such a question?" Just ask a straightforward question. Suppose you are traveling on a train and you would like to read Beyond the Dream, and you are afraid to read it. You may think, "What will people think of me if they see that I am reading this kind of a book?" This I call squeamish! If you were to read a "porno" book, you wouldn't be squeamish because that is the "manly" thing to do. But to read a book on Metapsychiatry when other people might see you . . . there are some people who are afraid to read it. Or you are traveling on a train and you would like to read a booklet, but you are afraid that people will notice that it's titled A Hierarchy of Values, and they might think, "What kind of a guy would read such a book!" You see how that is?

Student: Dr. Hora, what is the thought that I had when we were sitting here at the beginning of this group session? It was quiet, and no one was asking a question, but when someone finally asked a question, I was very grateful that he had.

Dr. Hora: Right, and he got what was coming to him!

Student: If I had asked a question at that point, it would have been even more out of the blue!

Dr. Hora: Aren't you happy you didn't?

Student: What is that uneasiness when everything is quiet, and no one is asking a question?

Dr. Hora: What is it?

Student: It must be self-concern.

Dr. Hora: Well, maybe you are afraid to ask a question because people might think that you are a dummy!

Student: Yes.

Dr. Hora: There is a saying that if you keep your mouth shut, people will think that you are very smart. There is another saying about this, that before you spoke, we were thinking that you were a dummy, but now that you have spoken, we are sure! You see, when you sit here, you have a thought, "Somebody should say something." You are thinking about what "should" be. And after somebody says something, you are thinking this "shouldn't" be. Unenlightened life is lived on the horns of this dilemma— "what should be" and "what should not be"—we are always thinking this. Most of the time, people think about what should not be— the weather shouldn't be bad; sicknesses shouldn't be; the political situation shouldn't be like that. Unenlightened man is forever preoccupied with what shouldn't be, and occasionally with what should be. As long as we think that way, we are always having anxieties and conflicts and suffering of all kinds. How can we not think that way? After all, this is life, and we said we have to be engaged in life! That is not life—that is ignorance and error—it is unenlightened life. Enlightened man doesn't think about what should be or what should not be. What does he think about?

Student: What is.

Dr. Hora: "What really is"—that is what enlightened people think about. How does that help? It depends on whether you know "what really is." You think that today is Wednesday; is it really so? According to conventional thinking and the calendar, it is really Wednesday. But what does the calendar know? What do conventional thinkers know? Enlightened man knows that even though it is stated that today is Wednesday, it is not necessarily so.

Student: But "neither is it otherwise!"

Dr. Hora: That's right. "Nothing is as it seems to be, and neither is it otherwise" (Zen koan). So what is it? It is neither Wednesday nor not Wednesday. What is it?

Student: It is an opportunity to be aware of Reality or to be engaged in fantasy.

Dr. Hora: Okay, so what is this Reality? Is it on Wednesday or not?

Student: It has nothing to do with time.

Dr. Hora: Right. Reality has nothing to do with the calendar; it has nothing to do with the time of day—it has to do with eternity. "What really is" is eternity. What's that, and how is that helpful? What calendars do they use in eternity? No calendars. "Spiritual blessedness" is "what really is." Apart from that, nothing is real. Imagine, the only reality that "really is" is spiritual blessedness. How could that be?

Student: Dr. Hora, it seems to me that you have to be grounded, as we said in an earlier session; otherwise it is a flight into this other realm without being grounded.

Dr. Hora: What did we talk about before?

Student: About being "existentially grounded." When we start this kind of talk, if someone is not existentially grounded, it could then be a flight into spiritual truths; but that individual will be disconnected, unable to contact Reality.

Dr. Hora: Yes, that is a very good point. But let's assume that we are all "grounded." Of course, if someone here is interested in "picking up pointers" with which he can then impress people outside with what he knows, what he heard, then he makes use of that. It is a free country; you can do whatever you like. But we are trying to understand "what really is" because all unenlightened people live by what "should" be or what "should not" be. As long as we live this way, we are suffering all the time because we say, "Pain shouldn't be, and pleasure should be; sickness shouldn't be, and health should be." Everything is either what should be or what shouldn't be. As long as we think that way, we will never know "what really is." Only if we know "what really is," only then can we be healthy and free and alive—then we are in touch with Reality. When Jesus said, "I am the door: by me if any man enter in, he shall be saved," what did he mean? What happens when we enter this door? He also said that if you enter this "door," you will "go in and out, and will find pasture" (John 10:9). What does that mean? Do you become a goat?

Student: Does it mean a state of consciousness?

Dr. Hora: When you become conscious of Reality, you attain a state of the Christ-consciousness, and then you can function effectively in the world without any difficulties: all things will work together for good because you went through that "door." This is the First Principle of Metapsychiatry: "Thou shalt have no other interests before the good of God which is spiritual blessedness."

We discover that the only real thing in life is "spiritual blessed-ness"—bliss consciousness

Dialogue No. 28

Humility

Student: There is a passage in the Bible that describes Jesus washing the feet of his disciples (John 13:5), and it was clearly a spiritually symbolic event. Paraphrased, what he said is that unless I do this, you cannot be redeemed, and you must do it for one another as well. "Know ye what I have done to you? . . . If I then, your Lord and Master, have washed your feet, ye also ought to wash one another's feet. . . . Verily, verily I say unto you, the servant is not greater than his Lord; neither he that is sent greater than he that sent him" (John 13:11-16). What did that mean? What was he teaching?

Dr. Hora: He said that to Peter.

Student: Peter wanted him to wash his head and everything else too.

Dr. Hora: Well, he was a little squeamish at first, but then he yielded—he accepted. What is squeamishness?

Student: It is an uncomfortable feeling.

Student: Reluctancy to undergo certain things.

Dr. Hora: The Master was washing Peter's feet, and Peter was reluctant to let him and didn't understand right away. What could be the meaning and purpose of such an act? Maybe he thought Jesus went temporarily off his rocker.

Student: What was the meaning?

Dr. Hora: Well, Jesus explained it—to be humble. He was saying, I am your Lord and Master, and yet, I am doing this to show you an example in humility; and you ought also to wash each other's feet, which means you have to be humble, as I am demonstrating this humility to you. He was just trying to teach them; he was always teaching how to express spiritual values—humility is a spiritual value.

Student: Does that mean that he was really showing them he wasn't better than they were?

Dr. Hora: No, he was showing them how to be humble. He was

245

better; he was greater; he was smarter, more enlightened—he was, in every way, superior to anyone who was alive in the world at that time, and yet he was humble. So he was teaching that humility is greatness; it is dignified. Genuine humility is not inferiority; it is not subservience; it is not self- effacement—it is a quality of God, and it is a great freedom. If we could be truly humble, we would never know anxiety.

Student: What does humility mean?

Dr. Hora: Humility means being what we really are and what God wants us to be.

Student: What is it that promotes anxiety?

Dr. Hora: Anxiety indicates that we want something. We want to be admired; we want to show off; we want to control, to possess, to have and to hold. We want sex; we want hamburgers. . . . You see, if we are truly humble, we are completely at peace with what God wants us to be. It is ultimate freedom, and it is very rare. Anyone who is truly humble is completely free of anxiety. It is anxiety that grinds us up and is responsible for aging and sickness and strife and deterioration of physical, mental, and emotional processes. Anxiety is inner friction—it is burning us up and wearing us down. So a truly humble individual could probably live 150 years without ever being sick. No one is born with the gift of humility; it is something we have to learn, and that is why Jesus taught it.

Student: But was Jesus born with it?

Dr. Hora: No, I don't think so, not according to the Bible. The Bible says that he had to solve all the problems, just like anybody else. It says that he was tempted at all points, just as we are. ["For we have not a high priest which cannot be touched with the feeling of our infirmities; but was in all points tempted like as we are, yet without sin" (Hebrews 4:15).] He attained that great humility.

Student: Is pretending part of anxiety?

Dr. Hora: Yes. What is pretending? It is wanting to appear in the eyes of others as being more or less or something other than what we really are. That is pretending. Pretending means to put something forward. In German, it is *vorstellen,* "to put another face in front of your face." The Chinese say "to put another head on top of your head."

Student: I notice that when I meet people, I never really get to "meet" the individual because everyone has this something . . .

Dr. Hora: It is called personality. Everyone pretends to be someone whom he would consider better than someone else. Yes, you are right—we can rarely see each other for what we really are. Actually, it is impossible with the eyes. The eyes can only take notice of appearances, never of the Reality. Just as we have never seen God with our eyes, we have never seen each other with our eyes—we see illusions.

Student: What aspect of us recognizes a value or a spiritual faculty?

Dr. Hora: We have a faculty called spiritual discernment. In Metapsychiatry, we are helped to awaken within us this faculty of spiritual discernment, and then we can see spiritual values manifested in everyone.

Student: Where is that spiritual discernment?

Dr. Hora: It is not in your left pocket. Where is it? Where is spiritual discernment?

Student: In consciousness?

Dr. Hora: In an awakened consciousness. Anyone who has an awakened consciousness, which is unfolding as we study, pray, and meditate, has this spiritual faculty of discernment. Such an individual can tell what is valid and what is not valid, what is real and what is phony or "put on." He or she can "see"—but it is not the eyes that can see it. So there is this unfathomable something in all of us that makes it possible to see spiritual Reality in everyone.

Student: But when someone dies, there is no more consciousness in that individual, right?

Dr. Hora: Well, Jesus explained it this way: "It is the spirit that quickeneth, the flesh profiteth nothing" (John 6:63). Individuals who are blind can have spiritual discernment. Some blind individuals have beautiful, awakened consciousnesses and can know spiritual qualities—we don't need eyes for that.

Student: Sometimes it seems that being blind with your human eyes would make it easier.

Dr. Hora: Well, it looks that way; perhaps there is something to it.

Student: Because we don't get distracted.

Dr. Hora: Yes, there is no distraction.

Student: Even with your eyes closed, you can tell a loving presence?

Dr. Hora: Yes, this presence is not dimensional. The eyes are always focusing on dimensionality: color, form, formlessness, behavior, gender, and appearance. The eyes are forever distracted this way.

Student: Would a beholding consciousness see past the pretense, past the appearance? Is that what beholding is?

Dr. Hora: Yes. Anyone who has progressed in his studies always keeps a transcendent perspective on everyone and everything all the time without consciously endeavoring to do so—it becomes part of our way of seeing. Someone said, "Well, I am coming to study Metapsychiatry, so that I might become a nicer person." What do you think of that? This individual has no idea of what Metapsychiatry is all about. It is not a charm school. We are studying here to see better—to "see the unseen"—and that is what St. Paul says in the Bible: "We look not upon the things which are seen, but upon the things which are not seen, for the things which are seen are temporal, and the things which are not seen are eternal" (2 Corinthians 4:18). So we are learning to "see the unseen."

Student: It is not so hard to become aware of the unreality of a personality, but I don't really see beyond that, to who the individual really is.

Dr. Hora: Yes. Well, can you see love?

Student: Sometimes.

Dr. Hora: Can you see good will? Can you see kindness? Can you see honesty? Can you see joy? Of course. We can see God in individuals, but we cannot see these divine aspects with our eyes.

Student: I attend business meetings where people are very diagnostic, very critical, and showing off what they know. I don't see spiritual qualities; I can't kid myself. What could you see when you don't see them?

Dr. Hora: You see that they are hidden. They are repressed—that's all—that belongs to the psychology department.

Student: These people aren't even psychologists!

Dr. Hora: Everybody is a psychologist—it is "normal" to be a psychologist, more or less.

Student: If we see these other human characteristics and not the spiritual qualities—are we being tempted to see another in that way?

Dr. Hora: Tempted or forced or even intimidated or pressured. Some people pressure others to see whatever they want them to see.

Student: Don't we also see through the lens of our own mode of being-in-the-world?

Dr. Hora: Yes.

Student: Sometimes my wife and I look at something, and I am very aware that she will see something very differently from the way I see it.

Dr. Hora: That's right. "As thou beest so thou seest," and vice versa!

Student: Dr. Hora, you were talking before about being anxious—and that people put on a facade to cover it up—but, if we are in a state of being anxious, what benefit would there be to appear anxious in front of other people? I mean, isn't it more intelligent to . . .

Dr. Hora: To cover it up?

Student: Yes, it seems so.

Dr. Hora: Well, it seems so, but if we cover it up, when is it going to get healed?

Student: When you come here, you can at least let it down.

Dr. Hora: Yes, that's true, but you see, we don't speak about what "should" be or what "should not" be—we speak about how to know "what really is." So to be anxious is not the will of God and to cover up anxiety is also not the will of God.

Student: But if you are at work, I can't see the benefit of appearing anxious.

Dr. Hora: No one is recommending that you show people how anxious you are, and no one is recommending that you cover it up and pretend that you are not anxious.

Student: So what is left?

Dr. Hora: What is left?

Student: It is not the anxious behavior or the suppressing it that matters—it is the realization of what is really going on.

Dr. Hora: That's right.

Student: So it is not whether you show that you are anxious or you show that you are not anxious—the realization of what's occurring must be acknowledged within yourself. At work, I would very often pretend that I knew something, and then I would say to myself, "Stop pretending; you don't know it"; or "You are learning it," or "You are getting better, but stop acting like a big shot when you don't know."

Dr. Hora: Yes, but now you are telling us how to behave. You see, ordinarily people think in terms of behavior. The problem is that we think we have to know how to behave—we cannot show that we are anxious, so we have to show that we are not anxious.

But to be anxious or not to be anxious is the same. The issue is how to understand what humility is.

Student: In the example where Jesus was washing the feet of his disciples, how could they accept the fact that Jesus was doing this to them? Was that demonstrating their humility?

Dr. Hora: You see, Jesus apparently made a mistake. His intention was to teach the meaning behind the operation, but the people only saw an activity, an operational technique, which was supposed then to make the disciples humble. But did it? I don't think so. Nothing operational or behavioral will ever accomplish what is needed.

Student: Dr. Hora, in the Catholic Church they do that too, with rituals.

Dr. Hora: In many religions, there are rituals and symbolic actions—like swallowing a wafer. What is this? It is a symbolic act, all right, but what happens after you leave the church? Have you become Christlike? The point is to become Christlike. How do you become Christlike? By learning how to pretend that you are Christlike or by going through ritualistic, symbolic ceremonies? None of these things will help you to realize your Christhood. On the contrary, it will all be counterproductive because it sets your thoughts on an operational approach. Ritualism is an operational system of reminding people of something, but it does not lead to healing and enlightenment—nothing behavioral and nothing operational will do the job.

Student: But in communicating ideas Jesus used symbols much of the time, for example, when he said that we must eat his flesh.

Dr. Hora: He tried in every possible way, and people were always misunderstanding. Even today, if people read in the Bible, "This is my flesh, this is my blood," some will, immediately, say that this guy is recommending cannibalism. I knew a psychiatrist who wrote a book about Jesus and tried to prove that he was a schizophrenic—there are many misinterpretations. The history of Christianity is full of misunderstandings of Jesus' words.

Student: What is the actual meaning of that passage? ["I am the bread of life . . . He that eateth my flesh and drinketh my blood dwelleth in me and I in him" (John 6:48, 56)].

Dr. Hora: Some of his disciples said we cannot even listen to this, it is so shocking—and they walked away. He was hoping that by shocking them, he would elicit some realization. He was talking about his teaching—the "flesh and blood" of his teaching was the attainment of Christhood and of the qualities of God that he manifested. If you take in his teachings in the right way and "drink in" the spirit of his teachings, it will transform you and you will become a Christ yourself. You will become just like he is. He was talking about his teaching.

Student: He also said: "I have meat to eat that ye know not of" (John 4:32).

Dr. Hora: That's right: "My meat is to do the will of him that sent me" (John 4:34). Again, is he talking about nourishment of some kind, or is he talking about a new recipe? Is he talking about eating? No, he is using symbolic language, like a koan. When the Zen Master presents a koan, it is a nonsensical statement—there is no way with rational reasoning that one can understand what he is saying. It has a specific purpose: to shock you into awareness of a truth which cannot be communicated in simple terms. But, unfortunately, how many people are able to understand? It is difficult because we "judge by appearances"— we think in terms of behavior and operationalism.

Student: For instance, if you appear anxious in front of people, they are bound to say, "What's wrong?" and we have discussed how unbeneficial it is for someone to ask, "What's wrong? You look like you don't feel well." It focuses attention on the nonreality of whatever problem seems to be.

Dr. Hora: Yes, so?

Student: So it seems to me that it would be intelligent to try not to appear anxious.

Dr. Hora: We are back to that?

Student: I am trying to understand it.

Dr. Hora: But that is not the issue—how you appear in front of people. What it is that you understand about life—that is the issue. This is not a charm school; we are not learning how to make favorable impressions on other people.

Student: I am not talking about here in group, but when we are functioning outside.

Dr. Hora: We are not concerned with functioning—you can function any way you like. Metapsychiatry is not concerned about functioning. What is Metapsychiatry concerned about? Being. Do you know the difference between functioning and being? Who can explain that?

Student: Functioning is what you "do," and being is what you are.

Dr. Hora: Right.

Student: It just seems to me that at the office when we "put a head on top of our head," it is just a means of coping with the anxiety.

Dr. Hora: Yes, but we are not interested in that.

Student: If someone has a problem and doesn't yet understand a particular issue, it seems to me that it is okay to recognize that we are coping at the office, because we are involved in what other people think about us. So if we are involved in what other people think about us, we cope by using the "head on top of our head."

Dr. Hora: We don't say you shouldn't cope.

Student: But I think it just has to be clarified what the issue is—this pretending, this covering up the anxiety . . .

Dr. Hora: Still, you are talking about an irrelevant issue as far as Metapsychiatry is concerned.

Student: But we have to understand the "meaning" of the problem we are having, with the anxiety and the pretending. We need to ask, "What is the meaning?" If we are having a problem and we don't understand a certain issue, we have to ask what the "meaning" is first, before we can go on.

Dr. Hora: The meaning is that you don't know what Metapsychiatry is all about—that is the meaning!

Student: But perhaps that idea is preventing me from knowing what Metapsychiatry is teaching us.

Dr. Hora: What idea?

Student: The behavioral idea.

Dr. Hora: Well, of course it does. You are sitting here and not hearing what we are talking about because you are thinking, "How am I going to function in the office?"

Student: Well, if you take away my mask, then I see that I am going to have anxiety.

Dr. Hora: Nobody takes away anything from you—you can keep it. It is none of our business. How you function—that is none of our concern. Who you are—that is our concern. Yes? You have heard that Metapsychiatry is an existential teaching. Have you heard this word, existential? What does it mean? It means that we are focused on the issue of being—not on functioning. You can function any way you like—you can walk on your head in the office, in the kitchen, or in the living room—but this is none of our concern. And if you come here in the hope that it will improve your functioning, you are missing the point. This is not a school for behavior—this is a study of being. Jesus did not teach how to be a well-behaved Christian, a nice person, or how to be a beneficent person, doing good deeds. That is okay; it is an aspect of human civilization; but that is not what he was teaching. He wasn't teaching us to have clean feet—he was teaching us to discover who we really are, and what we really are, and where we really are, and what our purpose in life is. That is what he was teaching.

Student: I guess we think that if we can really learn Metapsychiatry the right way, we can improve all the things in the world.

Student: If I am anxious at work, one of the only things that ever helps me is to be issue oriented.

Dr. Hora: The worst part of unenlightened life is the interaction context in which we have a tendency to drown in concern for self and other. If enlightenment is not yet at hand, we have recognized that one escape valve is to be issue oriented. In this way, we can shift attention away from the interaction context. We worry about what people will think of us if they see that we are anxious. How can we cover up anxiety so that people will see that we are not anxious? This is living in an interaction context. One can escape from this context by being issue oriented. It is very helpful, and it is very good; but it is not the bottom line. The bottom line is being what we are and what God has created us to be. And humility is the supreme truth-of-being—it relieves all anxiety and gives us intelligence and poise and an ability to respond effectively to situations from moment to moment. The whole business of emphasizing functioning is absolutely hopeless. The harder you try to improve your functioning, the further away you will get from Reality—until you become a complete phony that people can smell a mile away—and you cannot function in life because nothing will really work. No matter how nice you are and no matter what a good actor you are, "You can fool some of the people some of the time," but you cannot fool everybody.

Student: How is it that unenlightened man can recognize that somebody is a phony or is pretentious?

Student: You don't have to be enlightened to "see" it.

Dr. Hora: No, anyone can be aware of that. Some people create a tremendous amount of anxiety in other people by the very fact that they are anxious. Have you noticed that? Anxiety is contagious. It is contagious because it is self-confirmatory, and no matter how you cover it up with behavior or coping or functioning, it creates discomfort in other people.

Student: Is that because others are also suggestible to self-confirmatory ideas?

Dr. Hora: It is contagious, right? So covering it up or coping is not a solution.

Student: So if you "catch" anxiety, if someone is anxious and you become anxious, it is just a desire to confirm yourself?

Dr. Hora: Of course. Metapsychiatry has made a tremendous discovery when it explains contagion on the basis of the universal inclination toward self-confirmatory ideation. All kinds of contagions are based on it. We also explain the mysterious fact that doctors do not get sick in a contagious ward—it is not because they took injections—it is because they become insensitive to the human condition through diverting their attention into scientific inquiry. If you are a good doctor, a scientist, then you are so much involved and interested in the scientific elements of a particular illness that you do not even notice anything else. And that interest and involvement are a protection from being contaminated by what the patients have.

Student: That is a perfect analogy to what often happens at work. Co-workers will come into my office so hysterical, so worried, because they need a certain answer. And if you don't get involved with their emotions, but just ask them questions regarding what it is they are really looking for, then you find an inspired answer. But if you become involved and think, "This person is so worried; I have to help her not to be worried," then you are spending all that time . . .

Dr. Hora: Sympathizing, empathizing, and antipathizing—

Student: And not getting the answer.

Dr. Hora: Yes, that is the human mockery.

Student: But it is interesting in that analogy about contagion, concerning the doctors, the context is so clear—the doctors see from a scientific point of view. That means that our context has to be from a God-centered point of view.

Dr. Hora: Right, exactly.

Student: And that's our immunity.

Dr. Hora: That's our immunity, right.

Student: Would you please explain how contagion works?

Dr. Hora: As long as we have the slightest inclination toward self-confirmatory ideation, we are in danger of catching colds from other people, catching AIDS from other people, catching whatever other people have—we are a magnet to it. The only protection is to lose interest, somehow, in self-confirmatory ideation.

Dialogue No. 29

Real Communication: God to Man

Student: My question has to do with the learning process. I would like to learn the Third Principle so that it is automatic, like walking or talking. It seems that we learn how to read and write through repetition and memorization. Can existential truths, like the Principles of Metapsychiatry, be learned in the same way, or is there an entirely different process? I have memorized the Principles, but when I am in a situation where interaction is going on, the Third Principle doesn't seem to come automatically. How does the right Principle eventually get to be part of us?

Dr. Hora: The word "automatically" doesn't apply. When something is "automatic," it means that an individual can regurgitate it without having the slightest understanding. This very frequently happens with newcomers to Metapsychiatry—they have a great urge to "spill the beans"—and, of course, they get hurt this way because they are violating the Eleventh Principle. The question is a good one: "What does it mean to understand a Principle?" Certainly, reciting it is not difficult, and conditioning ourselves to recite it at right moments is not difficult. Forgetting it is also very easy. So how could we describe that condition when a Principle or an insight has become existentially integrated to the degree that it becomes part of us?

Student: It has to do with knowing. It seems that if you really understand any one Principle, then you couldn't know it without knowing the others because they are related—they are part of the same truth. It almost seems as if really knowing any one Principle is equivalent to being enlightened.

Dr. Hora: Yes. Now, of course, if we are just normal students who came out of high school and college, we believe in the power of reciting words. This is actually an obstacle. There are very sincere students who are ambitious about learning Metapsychiatry; they keep reading and underlining the books and memorizing concepts—but in the end this doesn't work. We must be radically

sincere about the following questions: Do I really understand
this? Do I know what this Principle is saying? And, does it make
a difference to my outlook on life, now that I know about this
Principle? It is a struggle—it takes time. One must be radically
sincere with oneself. It is no tragedy if you can face the fact that
you don't yet really understand; it doesn't come right away. And
it is good to know whether you really know—when we begin to
know, we lose the urge to let other people know that we know.
As long as there is the urge to let people know that we know,
we do not know anything. Isn't that an interesting paradox? In
Zen Buddhism, the Zen Master clearly said, "He who knows does
not know, and he who does not know will come to know." It is
a struggle. Everyone has to wrestle with himself. But when we
finally understand, it is a great blessing—we are at peace with that
understanding, and it transforms our way of seeing and responding
to daily life situations. Now the most difficult of Metapsychiatry's
Principles is: "God helps those who let Him." What is so difficult
about that?

Student: Letting.

Dr. Hora: Yes. If we "let," it means that we are willing to be
"nothing"—we are willing to face the fact that we don't have
personal power and personal willfulness. We could have diplo-
mas, but we are still "nothing" and don't really "know" anything.
We could be highly educated, but as spiritual students we do not
have opinions, and we do not try to win arguments. Gradually
we become aware that intelligent ideas just flow through us, like
light shining through glass, and, whatever the situation, there is
always an appropriate response which flows effortlessly into our
awareness; and when that happens, things begin to work together
for good. Then all the Principles make sense. In Zen, there is the
koan system: a candidate receives a koan [riddle] from the Master,
a seemingly idiotic intellectual statement that he has to struggle
with, sometimes for years, in order to understand it; but once the
meaning of this koan comes to him, he can understand every koan
thereafter. If we really understand one koan, we understand all
koans. There are no more riddles in our lives. "There is a goose
in a bottle. How does the goose get out of the bottle?" This is a
koan. Now there are many people who will immediately blurt out
the solution to this koan—" There is no bottle, and there is no
goose." The answer is known, but that means nothing. When the
time comes that we really understand, we do not talk about it—we

have no desire to talk about it because we know how ridiculous it would sound. The issue is not about having the answer; the issue is about being transformed by the answer. Once we are transformed, why talk about it? It speaks from us— the whole body, and everything about us, is a communication. When we look at a statue or at a painting, we can think of it as a communication—the artist is trying to communicate an idea. The whole body is also a communication—we can just look at someone, and we can get a message, even if he or she doesn't say anything. Everything in the world and in the universe communicates. A tree is a communication; an animal is a communication—they are all saying something. We have spoken about the statue of the Buddha. We see that the Buddha is not just a piece of metal or clay. Buddha statues communicate the idea that man is a perfect creation of God—flawless. He is peaceful; he is loving; he is happy; he is serene; he is beautiful, and he is joyous— the statue gives us these messages. Some Buddha statues also communicate the idea "I receive and I give." The Bible says: "Freely ye have received, freely give" (Matthew 10:8). The Buddha statue communicates everything about man as a perfect "image and likeness of God" who is "here for God," as one who hears the divine message. What is the divine message? The message from God to man is: "I am Love; I am Wisdom; I am Joy; I am Power; I am Perfection." Compare this message, which comes from God to man, to all the other messages that the world is communicating to us: "I am lousy; I am afraid; I am jealous; I am angry; I am envious; I am rivalrous; I am sick; I am miserable; I like pleasure." All those messages which come from the world into human consciousness are lies. They are not true—they are slanderous messages about God. You have an itch; you have a pain; you have a sickness; you have a problem—these are messages that are lies about God, because God never created them. Therefore, they are not realities—they are lies, and lies can be abolished with the Truth. The way to abolish all the millions of false messages that are constantly being communicated to us is by acknowledging and contemplating the one right message [Tenth Principle]. God is communicating to his creation the truth-of-being, which is perfection. So now there is a collision of communications— those from man to man with those from God to man—and we are the target. The first communication from man to man is called "interaction thinking"—all the difficulties and miseries and sicknesses and troubles and wars come from this communication between man and his fellow man. The Third Principle of Metapsychiatry states: "There is no interaction anywhere; there is only Omniaction everywhere," which means communication is from God to man. Blessed is the man who understands this truth. Simply by understanding the message from God to man, we can abolish all the lies the world is constantly feeding us. When we succeed in abolishing the false communication by replacing it with the right communication, there is a healing— the world's messages get abolished. What does the Tenth Principle of Metapsychiatry say?

Student: "The understanding of what really is abolishes all that seems to be."

Dr. Hora: Correct. Therefore, the most important thing is to be aware of what God is communicating to us. We can think of life as a problem in communication.

Student: You used to tell me that I had to outgrow "life" in the family context. Really what you were saying was that I needed to outgrow the communication that is taking place in the family context. We identify ourselves in that context, so there is a constant nonverbal communication going on there.

Dr. Hora: That is very important. The Buddha doesn't talk, but he is sending out the right message for anyone to see and understand. One sees the Buddhists rushing to these big Buddha statues and bringing flowers and praying. What could they expect from a statue? What can the Buddha statue do? It seems like a strange superstition. Of course, religions call it idolatry— they are idolizing a piece of marble or clay or a picture or a memory of the dead Buddha. Then we come home, and we go to church, and we pray to a dead man hanging from the cross— he is bleeding—it is a gruesome picture of violence. Little children would get nightmares if you took them to church. Here again, what sense does it make to pray to a dead man hanging from a cross? It doesn't make any sense unless you understand the communication. I have already explained what the "dead" Buddha is communicating, and it is a beautiful message. Now what is Jesus communicating when he is hanging on the cross?

Student: That we can transcend the body in spite of the appearance?

Dr. Hora: Yes, the crucifixion means man is immortal: no matter what you do to his body, he is still a "living soul." Life is indestructible, even though it seems to be very fragile. Always

it helps to ask ourselves, "What is the message?" If you understand the message of the Christ, you are on the same plane as the
Buddhists who understand the message of the Buddha. They are
communicating a truth about life and about what is valid and what
is not valid. In order to understand this message, we also have to
understand the communication from God to man. There are three
[progressive] steps here: "God to man," "God through man," and
"God as man." Who understands this?

Student: Isn't it the same as the Buddha example? First we are
receiving from God; then we are giving forth, demonstrating God,
which blesses the world.

Dr. Hora: Yes, and "God as man"?

Student: We have become what we really are: an "image and
likeness of God."

Dr. Hora: Right. Some people worship Jesus and claim that
Jesus was God. Jesus was a transparency for God, so perfect that
he could say: "He that hath seen me hath seen the father" (John
14:9). This means that we are here for the same purpose.

Student: What is the difference between "God through man"
and "God as man"?

Dr. Hora: When "God through man" is allowed perfect expression, this man will then be manifesting the fullness of God. So first
we have "God to man," where we contemplate God communicating the truth-of-being to man, and this understanding helps us to
heal all our problems. When we go a little further, and we understand that God is expressing Itself through us, increasingly we become transparent. When this transparency attains the fullness of
realization, then we are the God-man, or "God as man," and then
we walk "two inches above the ground"; and wherever we go,
"even the dead trees come to life," and dogs cease to bark at us. St.
Francis was so imbued with God that wild animals were tame in
his presence. And there is the story of Daniel who was thrown into
the lion's den and remained unhurt. There is something significant
to be learned from such a state of consciousness. Suppose you are
working—you are out in the world, walking around and suddenly
you are seized by a pain of some kind. You could become frightened and think, "Something is happening to me; I have to go to a
doctor right away or call an ambulance or some help." You can accept this as a fact, as the truth, because you can feel it. You could
think, "If I can feel it, it must be something real." This is a normal
way of reacting—we react with fear when something seems to be

wrong—but we could have another approach. Let's say you are aware of hemorrhoids, and the condition is painful and bleeding. You can run to the doctor or to the pharmacy and buy something, or you can sit down and ask yourself, "What is the nature of this communication, what is this message? This is a message from the world to me." And then you can counter this message by asking yourself, "What message is God giving me at this moment?" Then you contemplate the communication from God to man. And God says: "You are perfect. There is nothing wrong with you. You are a transparency, and you are here for Me. I made you for Myself, perfect and flawless." You can reach a point where you realize that this message is the truth, and the other message is a lie. When you reach the point where you can understand the divine communication, it will abolish the message from the world.

Student: That is the great mystery—how does that happen?

Dr. Hora: You look at it as a message. For instance, there was a famous psychologist whose name was Werner Erhardt. When Erhardt had a big audience, he would start his meetings not by saying, "Good evening," but by saying, "You are all assholes!" No wonder people got symptoms. We receive many kinds of communications, all day and all night long. The other day a student of Metapsychiatry reported to me that she was getting cramps in her womb. "They come and they go"—she could not explain it. So I said to her, "How is it that you don't know? It is very simple—your mother is in Florida, and what is she thinking about?"

Student: She wants her to have a baby?

Dr. Hora: Exactly. Space is no problem. There is a message, a communication—the mother is desperate because her daughter isn't getting pregnant. She has been married for a few years and still no baby. Every time they talk, the mother says, "Still nothing?"

Student: Dr. Hora, when you talk about the problems of communication coming from the world to us, do they also go from us to the world, I mean our own erroneous thoughts?

Dr. Hora: As long as we think we are part of the world, we are also making people sick.

Student: And making ourselves sick?

Dr. Hora: Yes. That is true; it is a sick world.

Student: Dr. Hora, in relation to that question, we are talking about working with the three steps of communication—"God to man," "God through man," and "God as man." When we are with someone and we know that garbage is coming, maybe both ways, is it good to see the other as in the process of "God to man," "God through man," and "God as man"?

Dr. Hora: Yes, when your understanding is very clear, the simple thought that someone is a "transparency for God" can mysteriously heal him or her. This is how Jesus healed. He touched a leper or a blind man, and that person was instantly healed. Jesus knew and was able to "see" in his consciousness that the individual who appeared to be terribly sick was a transparency for perfect God—and the individual was healed. Now, to the extent that we understand what we are talking about here tonight, people could be greatly blessed when they come into contact with us.

Student: Will that kind of healing enhance another individual's understanding of God?

Dr. Hora: Not necessarily—maybe in one out of ten. There is the famous "experiment" in the Bible where Jesus healed ten lepers, and only one came back and was interested in learning something. The other day a student informed me, "There are so many psychics nowadays on television, so I decided to call one up. It was very interesting. She told me all kinds of things about myself. I wondered why I should study Metapsychiatry if, in a simple telephone call, I can talk to this psychic." What is the difference between Metapsychiatry and these impressive psychics on television? I said to her, "The psychics tell you what you want to hear, and Metapsychiatry tells what you don't want to hear." There is a great difference. Astrologers are always much appreciated because they say things like, "You are going to take a trip; you will get a promotion; your mother-in-law will die!" What you want to hear, they tell you.

Student: There are so-called out-of-body experiences, and there are people who can predict the future with some accuracy, even tarot card readers . . .

Dr. Hora: And there is psychoanalysis, which is more respectable than psychic mind-reading, and there is also psychotherapy. It is a very fascinating world.

Student: Is psychic "power" limited to discerning only where we are functioning as persons in the realm of the phenomenal world?

Dr. Hora: Yes.

Student: In other words, the psychics hit a responsive chord, and we say, "Oh, yes, that's me; I can see that." It is just about reinforcing the human picture—they may, in fact, have unusual powers to discern an individual's "mental garbage."

Dr. Hora: Jesus said: "Many shall come in my name . . . Ravening wolves . . . in sheep's clothing" (Matthew 24:5; 7:15). What did he mean?

Student: The psychics.

Dr. Hora: They have always been fashionable—people have always wanted to know the mysteries. Jesus went to a mystery school called the Essene group, not unlike this group. He learned everything in that group, and then he went out into the world and put it into practice. I have read that since time immemorial there have existed these groups where seekers were learning the mysteries of life—like G. I. Gurdjieff, for example. There were always such schools. But we are demystifying the mysteries. It is just a simple matter of communication: What is the message, and what is the countermessage? That is all we need to know.

Student: There does seem to be a tendency to get very interested in complexity. I remember reading in the Bible where Paul said to his brethren: "I fear, lest by any means . . . your minds should be corrupted from the simplicity which is in Christ" (2 Corinthians 11:3). There seems to be a fascination with complexity. I don't know whether or not it is intellectualism, but we like to figure everything out, and we tend to go off on tangents.

Dr. Hora: We would like to feel that we are extremely intelligent with a "good head on our shoulders," that we are smart and very knowledgeable. There is a self-confirmatory element pervading life everywhere, all the time. We have concluded that the world is made of two elements: self-confirmatory ideation and interaction thinking—that is what makes up the world. Jesus said: "In the world ye shall have tribulation, but be of good cheer, I have" found a way to "overcome the world" (John 16:33).

Student: What did Jesus mean when he said, "Going in and out" and "finding good pasture"?

Dr. Hora: He said: "I am the door: by me if any man enter in, he shall be saved, and shall go in and out and find pasture" (John 10:9), which means that he will be able to go out into the world and come in from the world and that he will be able to function effectively. If you understand what Jesus taught, it will make you more effective in life.

Student: What did Jesus think about the world around him?

Dr. Hora: Jesus clearly expressed what he thought: "Ye are of your father the devil, and the lusts of your father ye will do. He was a murderer from the beginning, and abode not in the truth, because there is no truth in him. When he speaketh a lie, he speaketh of his own: for he is a liar, and the father of it" (John 8:44).

Student: What did he mean?

Dr. Hora: This is just what we are talking about: everything that the world is saying to us is a lie. The message—the communication—on the horizontal plane, from person to person and man to man, is called interaction thinking, and it is a lie—there is no truth in it. "He was a murderer from the beginning." What was the first murder described in the Bible? It was Cain and Abel, two brothers, and Cain murdered his brother Abel. They were jealous of each other—that is how it went, and it is still going on all the time. If we do not understand the truth-of being, we are immersed in the "sea of mental garbage" where we are communicating lies with one another—lies over lies over lies.

Student: But even though they are lies, do we still have to discern the meanings?

Dr. Hora: Yes, of course. The more clearly we see through a lie, the more powerful the truth is which we then apply to it. The spiritual counterfact abolishes the lie of personal communication.

Student: So the Two Intelligent Questions permit us the opportunity to grow. There can be a healing flow through a spiritual healer, but one does not necessarily learn anything as a result of that healing.

Dr. Hora: One in ten—ten percent maybe.

Student: There are individuals, such as Mary Baker Eddy, who had a remarkable healing consciousness. Many benefited from her on an individual level, but they may not have grown spiritually.

Dr. Hora: Many are called, but few choose to come. ["The harvest is plentiful, but the laborers are few" (Matthew 9:37).] That is the way it is with people who find out about Metapsychiatry too—they come, and then they leave.

Student: They get healed, and then they leave.

Student: But if we really understand, we are free.

Dr. Hora: When we understand, we are free.

Student: Understanding gives us complete freedom.

Dr. Hora: Be careful with the word "understanding," because understanding is the most misunderstood word in the world.

Student: Next to love.

Dr. Hora: Right.

Student: Dr. Hora, if we have a pain, and we see that we had an interaction . . .

Dr. Hora: Thought, an interaction thought . . .

Student: As if there was something going on between two people . . .

Dr. Hora: Interaction thoughts, yes. It is important to say "thought," because if we speak about interaction per se, we are implying that it is real. But if we say it is an "interaction thought," we are clarifying that these pains or symptoms are just thoughts; it is a very important semantic point.

Student: A thought can manifest as a pain.

Dr. Hora: Yes.

Student: Is it just an ignorance of "what really is," or is it perhaps that a message was sent from another? If pain is manifesting, is it best to avoid the situation that seems to be the source, or is it just my perspective that is invalid? What is the pain? Is it my invalid perspective, or is it possible that it is real?

Dr. Hora: That what is real?

Student: If someone speaks to someone else.

Dr. Hora: They are both lying.

Student: And one gets a pain—the pain is a message. So then what?

Dr. Hora: In principle we have said, "Every physical symptom is an interaction thought"—it is a thought. "Every pain is an angry interaction thought."

Student: Is it just that I am not getting what I want?

Dr. Hora: Not necessarily.

Student: Is it anger? For me, anger means that I am not getting what I want. Therefore, it is not necessarily that the other individual is communicating negatively; it could be my perspective on the situation.

Dr. Hora: Not necessarily. You could become angry because someone is parting his hair on the left side instead of on the right side.

Student: So let's say I want him to part it on the right side. I guess that I am just trying to understand if it means that I shouldn't get involved with the other—or if it has nothing to do with the other. Since everybody communicates, it seems that it is from the other.

Dr. Hora: What is the difference? It is a lie anyway.

Student: What is a lie?

Dr. Hora: Every communication between man and man, person

to person, is a lie—it is not real, and it is not valid.

Student: But if I have a pain, is it coming from my perspective on reality?

Dr. Hora: No, it is a thought [an angry interaction thought]. Is it about interpersonal relationships or about a dysfunctional family?—these are fashionable clichés these days. People are flocking to these psychological ideas, hoping that something good will come out of these questions.

Student: But all of that is painful.

Dr. Hora: Yes, some people would say pain is good for you. The Bible says: "Let God be true, though every man be a liar ..." Therefore, "Enter ye into the joy of the Lord"—and stay there! (Romans 3:4; Matthew 25:2 1).

Dialogue No. 30

Immunity

Student: What does it mean when a pain doesn't go away?

Dr. Hora: Good question. I suppose many of you have experienced this. What does it mean when a pain does not go away?

Student: We are holding on to an invalid idea?

Dr. Hora: What is pain?

Student: Anger.

Dr. Hora: Is it anger, or is it a thought?

Student: An angry thought.

Dr. Hora: It is an angry interaction thought. If we have a pain, and if we want the pain to go away, how can it go away? Pain doesn't know that it is a pain. How can the pain go away, if our thought is on the pain going away?

Student: Isn't it understandable, in normal terms, to want a pain to go away?

Dr. Hora: Yes, but we are not "normal" people—we are spiritual beings—so it is a fallacy to reason in "normal" terms. A pain cannot go away, because it isn't there.

Student: It seems to be there.

Dr. Hora: It "seems to be," yes—but "what seems to be" is not. The pain cannot "go away," but an invalid thought can be replaced by a valid thought. If we have a pain, we make the mistake of thinking about the pain, rather than seeking to understand the invalid thought, which needs to be corrected and replaced by a valid thought. So if we are seeking a healing, we must transcend the pain and become more interested in the thought than in the pain.

Student: Interested in the valid thought?

Dr. Hora: No, first we must be interested in the angry thought that we are involved with. That is, we must disregard the pain and be more interested in a thought. When the thought becomes clearer and clearer, then we can replace it with a healthy thought. An angry thought is always a sick thought—it is "normal," but it is sick. You will find that everything "normal" is really very sick, whereas everything spiritual is very healthy. A "normal" thought has to be replaced by a spiritual truth, and then we discover that the pain was never really there. I remember someone who was healed of a cold and was happy that the cold had gone away; and then we told her, "Now, at least, you know what you never had!" If we had it, it would never "go away." The trouble is, we can get stuck on the pain and want the pain to go away, but the more we want it to go away, the less it will go away. We have to become more interested in the "meaning" [mental equivalent] than in the symptom. Now, if someone is a "pain in the neck," this is an angry, invalid thought, and it has to be replaced with a valid thought. What would be a valid thought? A valid thought is the truth-of-being about another individual. We are all aspects of divine Consciousness, made of Love-Intelligence, and that is the only truth about us. We cannot afford to have any other thought about another. Remember also that every physical symptom is a thought about a relationship: "A man's foes will be those of his own household" (Matthew 10:36).

Student: Jesus said, "Get thee behind me, Satan" (Matthew 16:23; Mark 8:33). Is that saying not to think about wanting to get rid of the pain, but to get the pain behind you?

Dr. Hora: Well, what does "Satan" stand for? Satan is a distraction—anything that distracts us from being conscious of God. All interactions are the activities of Satan.

Student: Pain is certainly a distraction from God.

Dr. Hora: Exactly.

Student: It is hard to think of anything else but that pain.

Dr. Hora: It is not so much the pain—the interaction is the distraction from God—the pain is just a sign that we are involved in interaction thoughts. We have to understand this process and then quickly heal our thoughts about another.

Student: Even welcome the opportunity? This could be a wonderful way to learn something. So rather than being involved in wanting to get rid of it, we could almost welcome it as a "teacher."

Dr. Hora: Yes. "Problems are lessons designed for our edification" [Eighth Principle of Metapsychiatry]. Some people run to chiropractors, acupuncturists, midwives, and doctors—we will try almost anything to get rid of the pain—which just means that we are thinking that this pain should go away. If we think about the pain, we are not facing up to the interaction thought, and then there can be no healing.

Student: Dr. Hora, it can be difficult if the pain is so bad that you cannot function. Sometimes, I wake up from a dream, and I feel so oppressed that I can't breathe—it is as though I am immobile. So right away I go to take the medicine—that is the only way I can breathe—because the pain is so great. I know that this is not a solution.

Dr. Hora: It is a relief.

Student: That's it. But I can't breathe, so I go to the medicine, even though I understand the meaning.

Dr. Hora: Tonight you are relieving yourself, and tomorrow you have it back.

Student: Right. I go to sleep, and I am very happy and peaceful. When I wake up, I am in pain. So . . .

Dr. Hora: So what happened?

Student: I don't know. The meaning of that sense of oppression is becoming clearer. There is one thing that I am very fearful of—I am very susceptible to being influenced by mental despotism, and I am aware of it.

Dr. Hora: Even if it is a loving kind.

Student: I grew up with a mental despot, and I can see how vulnerable I am to that type of individual.

Dr. Hora: There is hostile mental despotism, and there is loving mental despotism—and the essence of both is "being influenced." Now how can we become immune to being influenced?

Student: By not wanting anything.

Dr. Hora: Not wanting is the same as wanting.

Student: Knowing who and what we really are.

Dr. Hora: When you are in the midst of an asthmatic attack and you are struggling for air, it doesn't help to say, "If I knew you were coming, I would have baked a cake!" And neither does it help to think, "I don't want to be influenced by my mother and father."

Student: Dr. Hora, I am a little confused by that. Is there a pain or asthmatic attack because we haven't faced the meaning and it has to manifest itself some way?

Dr. Hora: "Because" indicates you are reasoning from the standpoint of cause and effect.

Student: But if we are sidetracked by a physical symptom, doesn't that imply that we haven't seen what the thought, the "meaning," is? Or could we have seen it even though it is still manifesting itself?

Dr. Hora: If we have seen it and it is still manifesting itself, we have a certain weakness that makes us vulnerable to this kind of mental despotism.

Student: Wanting to be liked?

Dr. Hora: That's right. Did you all hear that?

Student: Very loud and clear.

Dr. Hora: You see, there can be no immunity as long as we want something from the oppressors. Do you realize that some people want to be beaten with whips and tortured and subjected to all kinds of abuse and humiliation and debasement? As long as there is this secret desire, there is no immunity—it is impossible. We have to attain immunity to mental despotism, to oppression, to abuse, to pressure, to seduction, to provocation, to intimidation—we have to find a way to become immune. Today we hear a lot about acquired immune deficiency syndrome (AIDS). We all have certain weak spots in our character that make us vulnerable to certain types of interaction. Suppose our weakness is a desire to be liked—I once knew a woman who suffered from cystic mastitis. Do you know what that is? Cysts in the breasts. It is a very painful condition where one must go regularly to a surgeon to aspirate the contents—it is a very miserable condition. Anyway, the "meaning" was uncovered that she had lesbian desires. But her desire was so great that she kept returning to the woman with whom she was having the lesbian relationship, and after every one of these encounters, she would blow up with a new cyst—extremely painful. Here was a situation where this woman had no immunity against lesbianism—it was hard for her to give up the desire for this kind of sexual interaction. Then one day she went to the surgeon for another treatment, and he said that there was cancer and that they would have to operate. Imagine the despair. At that point of desperation, she forsook the whole idea of lesbianism—at that very moment— and decided never again to be interested in it. Then came the date for the operation, and she went to the hospital. The surgeon opened her up and found nothing; so he sewed her up again, and from that time on, she was healed. You see, we must recognize what thought is preventing us from having immunity to our problems. We complain about symptoms, but we are not willing to give up certain desires—to be liked, for example. Until we lose interest in invalid desires and commit ourselves to being "here for God"—rather than for self-gratification—there will be no immunity. We must understand how to become immune.

Student: Dr. Hora, this woman was scared to death, and that is what forced her to commit herself to being "here for God." How did the actual interest die? She could have said, "I will never have another encounter," but that is not losing interest. How does it happen that the interest dies?

Dr. Hora: When you commit yourself to being "here for God," you become "established." The Bible says: "Commit thy works unto the Lord, and thy thoughts shall be established" (Proverbs 16:3). You shall be "established" when you commit your ways to God.

Student: When we are committed to being "here for God," do we see that the invalid interest was just a dream? Is this what happens?

Dr. Hora: Man's adversity is God's opportunity. At the point of panic and tragedy, she understood that holding on to the invalid interest had too high a price, that it was ridiculous and that she didn't need it. Then she could commit herself.

Student: Do intelligent ideas come to one then?

Dr. Hora: One becomes immune to the temptation. This lady was suffering from interaction—lesbianism or heterosexual relationships or oppressive and despotic relationships are just interaction. And the way to escape from interaction is to commit oneself to "being here for God"—that is what gives us immunity.

Student: When something of that magnitude occurs, one is willing to do anything.

Dr. Hora: Yes.

Student: And stay with it.

Dr. Hora: We come to God either through suffering or through wisdom. At that point of desperation, she woke up.

Student: And stayed with it.

Dr. Hora: Well, certainly. She woke up so much that by the time the operation took place, there was nothing there—it just disappeared. Whatever the surgeon saw a week before, it was gone.

Student: What is it about an interest in lesbianism that makes it a problem?

Dr. Hora: Homosexuality and lesbianism are particularly troublesome forms of interaction because they are based on very severe forms of envy, jealousy, and rivalry. There is no such thing as an harmonious homosexual relationship.

Student: Is it possible that there could be exceptions? I know of one lesbian couple who seem to be very happy.

Dr. Hora: You cannot judge by appearances.

Student: Sometimes there seems to be a judgment on homosexuality. I too have encountered what I thought were very satisfactory relationships.

Dr. Hora: Judgment means condemnation. There is no condemnation in Metapsychiatry, but there is "righteous judgment," which means asking if it is existentially valid or invalid. There is no valid "relationship" at all.

Student: Hetero- or homosexual?

Dr. Hora: Any kind. All relationships are inherently troublesome.

Student: So that is really the issue—the relationship itself.

Dr. Hora: Of course. In such situations as we mentioned, there is a powerful emotional involvement, and the participants worry about social embarrassments—it is clandestine and loaded with guilt. It is very dangerous to have relationships. .

Student: What is the difference between being selfish and "being here for God"?

Dr. Hora: When you are selfish, you are here for yourself. When you are here for God, you are here for God.

Student: Sometimes I experience judgments—people tell me that I am selfish.

Dr. Hora: Yes? Well, you are experiencing judgments. But if it upsets you, it has a meaning—it means that you don't want it. Whenever we want something or don't want something, we suffer.

Student: We don't want to be seen as selfish?

Dr. Hora: There is no immunity as long as we want something.

Student: How can we observe whether we are in a relationship or in harmonious coexistence? What do we need to know to coexist harmoniously in the good of God, as opposed to interacting?

Student: We would all be beholders of one another.

Dr. Hora: Not necessarily. To be a beholder is a very advanced state, but we don't have to be completely enlightened to live harmoniously. We can learn to focus attention on issues, and that way we will avoid getting involved in interaction and be able to live a nonpersonal life.

Student: Is that a step toward becoming a beholder?

Dr. Hora: That is a way of being protected from interaction thinking.

Student: When a young man is first experiencing love and girls, how can he avoid interaction?

Dr. Hora: Well, he'll just have to sweat it out.

Student: We don't have "shoulds" about it, right?

Dr. Hora: Right. We have no "shoulds."

Student: In fact, the interaction could be a teacher. It seems as if most of us have to go through it in order to learn.

Dr. Hora: Yes, but most of us drown in it.

Student: Most of us suffer from it; so we hope that if we have this education, we will learn something.

Dr. Hora: Yes. There is a whole scientific system designed to make interaction tolerable. What is it?

Student: Psychology.

Dr. Hora: Right. We can die from interaction involvements; there can be so much suffering, so many complications. What is murder, and what is suicide? What are illnesses?

Student: What is the meaning of being possessive?

Dr. Hora: It is not enough to have—you also have to hold, to have and to hold. It is not enough to have children—we also have to hold onto them, right? And this is called possessiveness. It's all right to hold a baby, but a seventeen-year-old?

Student: I don't understand nonpersonal love—without any emotions—it seems to be very sterile, joyless.

Dr. Hora: Do you hear psychology talking? What are emotions? Emotions are thoughts. If there is no emotionalism, no feelings, are we joyless?

Student: The joy that we seem to get from human love—or interaction—is very precarious, and there will always be a flip side to it. The only real joy is from perfect Love.

Dr. Hora: There is no joy in interaction. When two people love each other, hug each other, have sex together, and have these emotions, they are just having pleasure. That is not joy— that is pleasure. So what is wrong with pleasure?

Student: It has a flip side of pain.

Dr. Hora: That's right, and it comes from using each other to get pleasure. Every little pleasure has to have the corresponding amount of pain. With joy, there is no unpleasant "aftertaste." Whenever there is a high, there will be a low—it is not possible to have a high without a low. The vast majority of people live this way. But that doesn't make it valid.

Student: But we are attached to it.

Dr. Hora: Yes, attached, but can you really deal with the pain? Of course, some people take a pill, and it relieves the pain a little.

Student: What I mean is, why isn't there a strong attachment to the nonpersonal kind of existence?

Dr. Hora: "Why" is a futile question. But we could ask, "What is the meaning of being attached to the pleasure/pain principle of life?" It is Freud's fault. Freud legitimized the idea of pleasure/pain and wrote very erudite books about it, saying that it is all right because that is how the "cookie crumbles"—and all human beings crumble eventually. He didn't know about joy. He was an utterly joyless and humorless man, although intelligent and very gifted.

Student: The Bible speaks of joy in terms of strength, that "the joy of the Lord is thy strength."

Student: I would like to understand commitment better. I would like to be able to commit myself to that life of understanding and freedom without having to suffer as greatly as that woman we mentioned before.

Dr. Hora: What is preventing you?

Student: Commitment . . . the willingness to forgo all the self-confirmatory things. Is it just in thought that we commit ourselves?

Dr. Hora: Does anyone have a constructive idea of how we could become committed without waiting for some crisis? Is it possible to become committed to being "here for God" without reaching a point of desperation?

Student: Isn't that why we are here?

Dr. Hora: We cannot assume things—that is not necessarily why we are here. Everyone has his or her own secret motivations.

Student: Some people just come along for the ride.

Dr. Hora: Yes, some people are just "hitchhikers."

Student: Or "thieves."

Dr. Hora: Yes, Metapsychiatry has seven categories of students. Do we know them?

Student: The dreamer, the hitchhiker, the knower, the thief, the thinker, the seeker, and the finder.

Dr. Hora: There are seven types of motivations in Metapsychiatry.

Student: What does it mean to "come along for the ride" only?

Dr. Hora: These students are just curious and find it entertaining.

Student: We don't seem to realize that pain has to do with pleasure. Could we become aware of the relationship between them, reach a point of desperation and then become committed to "being here for God?"

Dr. Hora: That is the same question as in the beginning. We are thinking of how to get rid of the pain; we are wondering when the pain will go away. But the more we want the pain to go away, the more it will be there, because we are focusing on the pain.

Student: Well, in this case, would it be possible just to focus on commitment—how we could be committed to God and not think about the pain?

Dr. Hora: It couldn't hurt!

Student: I am wondering if it is invalid just to think about commitment.

Dr. Hora: Thinking about it is not enough.

Student: It is the same issue we have discussed many times before—it is about interest.

Dr. Hora: If you have a piano at home and you keep thinking about playing this piano and you buy sheet music and pass by this piano every day and say, "I want to commit myself to becoming a musician and making music on this piano," as long as you are just thinking about it nothing will happen. We must dig in and become involved with the idea until the idea takes over our lives.

Student: I have been trying to be "here for God" with a particular problem I experience. I get really bad headaches that sometimes prevent me from working or functioning well. An aspirin does relieve the pain, but I realized that if I take an aspirin, I will learn nothing because I am taking it just to feel better. So the past few times, I haven't taken an aspirin. I didn't function very well, and I don't necessarily know that I even fully understood the "meaning." But I was committed to "being here for God" in spite of the pain, and I gained some strength from that—the strength of knowing that I came through it. And now the headaches come less frequently.

Dr. Hora: "Problems are lessons designed for our edification" [Eighth Principle of Metapsychiatry].

Student: But we don't indulge ourselves while learning the lesson.

Student: There came a point in this example about the headaches when this student realized that there was no point in taking any more pills. We have to get to a point where we realize that it is a "no-win" situation, that it is just never going to work out that way for the long term.

Dr. Hora: Yes, but this was an example of being a "tough student," of "toughing it out" with her headache. But there is a more effective way, and that is the way of the Two Intelligent Questions.

Student: In the midst of the headache pain, for me at least, I am so overwhelmed by it that I can't ask them.

Dr. Hora: The way to proceed is to ask the First Intelligent Question: "What is the meaning of what seems to be my present experience?" Be still and quiet, and then a thought like this will occur: "Someone was demeaning my mind; someone implied that my mind is inferior to his mind, and this infuriates me." When we understand the "meaning," then it is much easier to turn to God and to ask the Second Intelligent Question: "What is what really is?" We don't have to be stoical about it—there is a better way. This two-step method is the great contribution that Metapsychiatry has made to individuals who are interested in understanding life in the context of God.

Dialogue No. 31

The Universe Speaks

Dr. Hora: Jesus said: "Blessed are ye, when men shall revile you, and persecute you, and shall say all manner of evil against you falsely, for my sake. Rejoice, and be exceeding glad: for great is your reward in heaven; for so persecuted they the prophets which were before you" (Matthew 5:11). Jesus was talking about the "Herodian thoughts" which are in the world. Essentially, the "personal mind" is threatened by spiritual progress. God is the only Mind, and the "personal mind," which seems to be our life, will have to "die" as we evolve spiritually.

Student: Yielding or giving up all these personal things seems very difficult; there must be a way of making it easier.

Dr. Hora: Suffering makes it easier.

Student: Nevertheless we survive it and invite it again.

Dr. Hora: Now Jesus made one great mistake. He said: "Go ye into all the world, and preach the gospel to every creature" (Mark 16:15).

Student: Do we know that he really said that?

Dr. Hora: He must have said it because the history of Christianity shows that indeed all of his disciples and followers became gung ho about it and went around trying to push his teachings on people who were not interested. This approach gave the whole movement a tragic flavor—preaching is always a mistake. In Metapsychiatry we admonish people to preach without words. We can preach in writing for the wider public, or we can study in small groups with people who are already receptive—otherwise it is impossible. If there were one or two people here who were not receptive, we could not go on. They would disrupt the whole situation, and no one would learn anything.

Student: Is that what happens in the presence of someone with a very strong sense of "personal mind"? It is very disruptive.

Dr. Hora: Yes, it is not possible. So it is good for us to be aware of the Herodian problem which besets all spiritual teachings. We don't preach. An interesting thing is that Jesus knew this—he advised us not to throw "pearls before swine": "Give not that which is holy unto the dogs, neither cast ye your pearls before swine, lest they trample them under their feet, and turn again and rend you" (Matthew 7:6). And yet he sent his disciples out to convert the world—that was a tragic mistake.

Student: But didn't his disciples heal people?

Dr. Hora: Yes, they did heal, but people were more interested in the healing than in the teaching. The vast majority of mankind is not interested in being preached at or in being taught anything. The Zen Masters understood this very early, long before Jesus, and they made it very hard for people to become their students. Anyone who came to a monastery and asked to be accepted as a monk was immediately thrown out. It has become a tradition with the Zen Masters to throw people out and let them wait—to prove their sincerity before they are admitted into the teaching system. That approach is very wise. As the saying goes, "Never try to teach a pig to sing; it wastes your time, and it annoys the pig!" So we don't do that. Metapsychiatry says, "Let us learn to preach nonverbally."

Student: I understand that this is not correct, but it seems to me that the "personal mind" has an existence of its own and the power to go forth into the world and be destructive.

Dr. Hora: Yes, and create mischief and suffering. But what is an illusion?

Student: It is nothing, but if it causes so much suffering, how can it be nothing?

Dr. Hora: So what is an illusion?

Student: It is something that "seems to be."

Dr. Hora: Yes, the "personal mind" seems to be—it "seems to be" powerful, and it "seems to be" ruling the whole world and creating catastrophic conditions and suffering.

Student: Where does it get its seeming existence from? What is the source?

Dr. Hora: What is the source of ignorance? "Judging by appearances." If we "judge by appearances," we arrive at invalid conclusions about life, and if ignorance compounds itself more and more, we begin to drown in the "sea of mental garbage."

Student: What appearances are we judging by? What appearances manifest ignorance?

Dr. Hora: Suppose someone develops an illness, a physical illness. What happens? We look at it—let's say it is a rash—we look at it, and we can see that there is a rash, a skin condition. So we go to a dermatologist, and he looks at it with his eyes and says, "Yes, this is a skin condition." And then he will make tests, and the tests could prove that it is leprosy. There was a television program about a lovely young girl who had something on her skin, and the doctor diagnosed it as leprosy. A sequence followed, showing what would have happened to this girl if she had developed leprosy in the old days. The possible tragedy of her life was outlined on television—she would have been isolated and sent to a leper colony. Then gradually she would have deteriorated completely, and all kinds of horrible suffering would have dragged on for years, until she would finally have died there. If we "judge by appearances," we arrive at conclusions and compound the original, naïve ignorance into ever-greater evils and complications—and this is going on all the time. But if we judge "righteous judgment," we ask, "What is the meaning of this?" Here is something that seems to be, but it is not what it seems to be—it is something else. In Metapsychiatry we say that every physical symptom is not what it seems to be. It is not a physical symptom—it is a statement about some interaction thoughts. If we judge by appearances, we can drown in illusion. If we understand that we cannot judge by appearances because that is not Reality, then the interaction thoughts can be healed, and the appearance disappears—no matter what name it has been given.

Student: Dr. Hora, regarding this point, it seems easier to understand illness as an appearance than it does to see a healthy body as an appearance. But that is also just as much an illusion, is it not?

Dr. Hora: Of course. A sick body talks about interaction thoughts—disturbed interaction thoughts. What does a healthy body talk about?

Student: Good interaction thoughts?

Dr. Hora: A healthy body talks about the glory of God—the vigor, the vitality, the life, the joy, and the harmony of divine Reality. We have to "speak" the language: the body is a language, and it speaks. It is a great blessing to be able to understand what the body is saying. The Bible says that the body is "the temple of God"—a beautiful healthy body is the temple of God. What is it saying? "God is glorious; life is beautiful—it is joy; it is power; it is vigor; it is harmony and freedom; and it is happiness." The body is worshiping God. We must not worship the body—the moment we start worshiping the body, we get sick. It is like going to church and worshiping the stained-glass windows. So a healthy body is a statement about God—a sick body is a statement about disturbed interaction.

Student: But one isn't always sick, even though there are interaction thoughts; interaction doesn't always show in the body, does it?

Dr. Hora: One is more or less sick all the time.

Student: One is?

Dr. Hora: Unless one is healthy.

Student: But it seems to me, one is healthy.

Dr. Hora: No, we must understand health as spiritual. Again we speak about a healthy body, a beautiful, flawless body, but it is just "speaking" about health. There is no such thing as a "healthy body"—it is a body which is "speaking" about health. And then there are also bodies that are speaking about disturbed interactions. Everything in this world is a symbolic statement about the condition of divine Reality, and that statement can be true or false or slanderous or counterfeit.

Student: Let's say that there is health . . . what happens if we think we have a healthy body, instead of recognizing that the body is a statement about the presence of health?

Dr. Hora: Then it would get sick because we are worshiping a false God. It happens to athletes and beauty queens—they start worshiping their own bodies. They keep looking in the mirror, and pretty soon the body begins to deteriorate.

Student: What if they had a spiritual perspective?

Dr. Hora: They would see that the body is "speaking" about God.

Student: Can the body speak about God, even when we don't understand?

Dr. Hora: Certainly the body can speak about God, even when the consciousness does not understand. God is Omniaction—in divine Reality, there is no interaction. The point is that when we admire a piece of art or a beautiful individual—a beautiful, healthy, physical specimen or anything beautiful in the world— that is not God; it is a statement about God. Whatever is good and beautiful and true is a statement about God- whatever is decrepit and rotten and troubled is a statement about ignorance.

Student: God is not to blame for that.

Dr. Hora: It "speaks" about ignorance; it "speaks" about the world. The world is made of interaction thinking and self-confirmatory ideation.

Student: When I was driving here today, I saw a beautiful sunset. How can we say that the sky wasn't glorious, that it is only pointing towards God's glory?

Dr. Hora: What is the sky made of?

Student: What was glorious about it were the colors and light and form.

Dr. Hora: Okay, those were statements about God. When we say the sky is glorious, we are not using precise language—the sky is "speaking" about the glory of God.

Student: How can the sky speak?

Dr. Hora: The sky speaks English!

Student: For a specialist in physics, the sunset would have something to do with particles.

Dr. Hora: Dust particles—without dust particles there would not be a fantastic sunset—it is the dust particles that help it along and water vapor and electrodes. However, if we subject beauty to a scientific, materialistic analysis, we will become very disappointed. Suffice it to say, everything in the material world is a symbolic statement—either about God, which is Truth and Reality, or about unreality, illusion, and falsehood. In Metapsychiatry, we have discovered that the world is not made of rocks and grass—it is made of interaction thoughts. The substance of the world is interaction thoughts.

Student: Is that what our bodies are made of?

Dr. Hora: Our sick bodies, yes.

Student: Dr. Hora, you said that there were true statements, false statements, and counterfeit statements. What is a counterfeit statement?

Dr. Hora: A counterfeit is a counterfeit. Have you ever seen a wooden nickel?

Student: Is the sky a counterfeit statement?

Dr. Hora: No, the sky is a statement about beauty and the glory of God. But if we subject this phenomenon to scientific analysis, we will come out with a very different viewpoint. Science doesn't see God—science sees only matter. Scientific materialism is much respected in the world.

Student: There was a program on television about how babies are made. It showed a cell and how this one cell can become either a human or a sea horse or a fish. I was watching this phenomenon, and it was just wonderful to see the intelligence taking place.

Some DNA was discovered that has a master gene that seems to be in every phenomenon, whether it is human or otherwise. But what occurred to me was how incredible and highly intelligent this phenomenon was, and I hoped I would remember it because then perhaps I would be able to see how divine everyone is. But what seems to happen is that we don't see this amazing creative Intelligence in all things, and we take it for granted. What is the "meaning" of taking things for granted? We seem to take life and everything for granted, so it is difficult to appreciate one another or life or God.

Dr. Hora: When we look at these beautiful, microscopic photographs of cell division and the fantastic configurations, the tendency is to believe or accept that we have scientific evidence of how things are happening.

Student: In this program, they said that they cannot answer how these things are happening.

Dr. Hora: If we formulate it from a Metapsychiatric standpoint, we ask, "What is this saying?" It is fascinating. "What is the DNA saying? What are the cells saying?" There is macro speech and micro speech and subatomic speech. No matter how we slice it, no matter how many tiny details we uncover, they are always saying the same thing: "God is great—infinite Intelligence and creative Mind at work."

Student: At one point they took some kind of bug and mushed up the cells and did everything they could do to make things crazy, and what happened? The thing developed into exactly what it was supposed to be, even with all this mushing up! They were trying to destroy the intelligence of the cell, but the cell knows that it has to be a finger—or a whatever—and it manifests that intelligence, no matter what.

Dr. Hora: Right.

Student: So is that a true statement?

Dr. Hora: Of course it is. It says, "God is unfathomably great." Everything "speaks" about God—whether it is a glorious sky or the fascinating minutiae of cells, or of subatomic particles, or the celestial phenomena of stars and planets—everything speaks about God. God is great, creative Mind.

Student: I don't quite understand something. We say that the power of God is the only power. But it doesn't seem to work that way with the "personal mind." There ought to be a spiritual counterfact which, when we go astray, would redirect us and say,

"No, you must be what you were intended to be—you must be authentic and spiritually minded." But it doesn't work that way.

Dr. Hora: It doesn't work with Herodian thinkers. A Herodian thinker will say, "See, there is no God—matter is doing it by itself. The DNA molecule, by virtue of its very complex structure, makes it work; this structure does the job. Therefore, there is no God. The material configurations are the source of life and of the diversification of the phenomena of life." So the "Herod" says, "You have to see that there is no God, that matter itself is producing everything that seems to be." If we give credit to the structure of the molecules, what is that? It is like seeing a beautiful body and worshiping the body—we always make this mistake. In the old days, people worshiped the sun and rocks and the golden calf. This is idolatry, and it reveals a tendency in ignorant, unenlightened minds always to give the credit to something material—that is what the "Herod" does. It is antispiritual, and it is also called the anti-Christ. But when we give credit to phenomena, then there is a lot of trouble in the world. If we understand that everything and everyone is here to speak about the glory of God, in its own language, then it makes a lot of sense, and there is hope for the world. We cannot produce life; neither can we govern life.

Student: If we understand what everything is "saying," then it seems that we will learn how to "see" in the right way.

Dr. Hora: That's right.

Student: And we will move away from material worshiping.

Dr. Hora: It is very helpful to say that everything is talking all the time—the stars are talking, the molecules are talking, and the atomic particles are talking. Everything in the whole universe is talking, and it is good to hear what is being said.

Student: It is easy to see that the universe is manifesting the glory of God when there is harmony. Going back to that program about birth, is there something to the actual time of birth? In this order and harmony, is there significance to when events occur?

Dr. Hora: Everything is talking about the glory of God. Timing and events and phenomena, whenever they are harmonious, beautiful, and good, are talking about the glory of God. If they are sick and troubled, they talk about the misery of interaction thinking.

Student: What is the meaning of the conundrum that, on the one hand, this divine Intelligence creates beauty, but, on the other hand, that beauty, which it creates, seems to think it is powerful on its own? "Personal mind" is really saying that there is no

God—there is only me—and that is where the trouble begins. So what "meaning" does that have, that "what we seem to be" thinks that it has a "personal mind" that can create and govern life?

Dr. Hora: The "personal mind" is "a liar, and the father of it" (John 8:44).

Student: Is it only experienced for dialectic purposes?

Dr. Hora: We could speculate that it is like darkness. What is the value of darkness? It helps us appreciate light.

Student: Is it the only way that we can learn about God?

Dr. Hora: It seems that it is the only way we can become conscious of God.

Student: By having a contrast?

Dr. Hora: Right. That is "cognitive dialectics."

Student: Is that a conundrum?

Dr. Hora: No, a conundrum is a condition or a human experience that defies explanation; it is a puzzling problem.

Student: What is a koan?

Dr. Hora: A koan is a riddle that defies rational reasoning; one cannot reason or figure it out.

Student: There is a koan that you once told us. "The Ocean is not in the pollution, and the pollution is not in the Ocean." You were describing God's creation and the absolute perfection of it and of God, and the garbage thoughts that seem to manifest but do not touch that perfection.

Student: That's what they showed when they tried to mush up the cell; they tried everything to change it, and it came back perfect. It knew what it was intended to be.

Student: That's what reminded me of the koan.

Student: Does the "personal mind" also speak?

Dr. Hora: Sure, everything "speaks"—Reality speaks, and unreality also speaks.

Student: What is the language of the "personal mind"?

Dr. Hora: The "personal mind" is always promoting itself. The personal mind is constantly saying, "I am real. I really am."

Student: What about the "personal mind's" God, or is it just worshiping itself?

Dr. Hora: When did the "personal mind" get born?

Student: When the first interaction thought occurred?

Dr. Hora: When Eve was created from Adam's rib. Adam was lonely, so God gave him someone to interact with, and then the whole world developed.

Student: He needed someone to blame.

Dr. Hora: Who, Adam?

Student: Sure.

Student: It seems that evil becomes something created by God, so that we will know the good; but that is not what Metapsychiatry says about it.

Dr. Hora: Evil was created by the talking serpent, not by God. Do you remember the talking serpent? What does the talking serpent stand for? The serpent appears when there are already two people, so there is already interaction. And what is characteristic of interaction thoughts? It is deviousness—serpentine reasoning. The serpent is a symbol of calculative thinking and influencing. "For as in Adam, all die, even so in Christ shall all be made alive" (1 Corinthians 15:22).

Student: Adam represents the "personal mind."

Dr. Hora: Yes, and it is not viable.

Student: But the Christ is viable and immortal.

Dr. Hora: In divine Mind there is no calculative thinking, only forthrightness.

Student: So the "mushed up" bug does die? But we speak of immortality . . . so what is death? We understand life now, I think.

Dr. Hora: That is not life. When you see a "mushed up" bug, that is not life.

Student: But it is speaking about life, about God.

Dr. Hora: Yes, it is telling a lie about life—everything in the material world is telling a lie about life. What is the lie?

Student: The appearance?

Dr. Hora: No, the lie is that life is finite—finite life is a symbolic counterfeit of divine Reality. Divine Reality—Life—never dies. There is no death. On the symbolic level, everything is finite, and so it dies—that is a counterfeit statement. It is a symbolic counterfeit which says, "There is life; God is life, but life dies." Again we see the talking serpent telling a lie.

Student: Do phenomena have to perish?

Dr. Hora: Everything in the phenomenal world is Herodian, and its aim is to bear false witness to God. Herod said, "Go and search diligently for the young [Christ] child . . . that I may come and worship him" (Matthew 2:8). We can see the falseness, the deception, the lie. Everything in the phenomenal world is both symbolic of life and a counterfeit at the same time—both yes and no—material life is a binary system.

Student: So the mistake is that when we look at this marvelous, intelligent process taking place on television, we think that life is finite—this is it—this is what it is.

Dr. Hora: It says two things: life is material—it is beautiful, fascinating, frightening—and it is all "mushed up."

Student: It is the "personal mind" which is looking at that, but we talk about the "transcendent observer" which is present, making decisions or judging . . .

Dr. Hora: The "transcendent observer" does not judge.

Student: No, I meant that the "personal mind" is interacting with it.

Dr. Hora: Well, Jesus said that it is "a liar, and the father of it" (John 8:44). Counterfeit structures die.

Student: But why is it that life dies?

Dr. Hora: Everything material is finite, and it dies. But in spiritual Reality, there is no death.

Student: Suppose we look at matter or phenomena, then, just as the glorification of the wonders of God?

Dr. Hora: Then we are misled into believing that life is finite.

Dialogue No. 32

Infinite Structure

Student: Dr. Hora, would you please define the difference between "mind-fasting" and discipline? It occurred to me today that I need to become more committed, and this could probably occur through "mind-fasting." But I seem to be a little tyrannical about what I need to do. I do not really understand what is needed, and I am not really clear how discipline applies to spiritual studies. Somehow, it seems easier to study accounting—I know what I need to do; I know how much time is required, and I can sit down and do it. But with spiritual studies, how much time is required? There is no real structure, whereas in accounting, there is a structure. But maybe that is a different type of discipline.

Dr. Hora: It sounds like the man who was hanging over a cliff, and God told him to "let go." What did he need? Did he need mind-fasting or accounting or discipline or what? What did he need?

Student: I don't know the story about the man who was hanging over the cliff.

Dr. Hora: There was a man who fell over the edge of a cliff. As he was falling down, he grabbed hold of a branch, and he was just hanging there—he couldn't climb back, and below there was a deep ravine—and he cried out to God, "Oh, God save me. Help me!" And God said, "Yes, I will help you—now let go."

Student: Is that trust in God?

Dr. Hora: Yes, that is what is needed—trust in God and learning to lean on God for our survival. Is that a discipline or is that accounting? It is a counting on God to save us!

Student: Is that also helpful in making decisions?

Dr. Hora: We never make decisions. Did you know that?

Student: I have heard that, but it seems as though decisions are made.

Dr. Hora: No, we make choices—intelligent choices.

Student: Choosing between what?

Dr. Hora: "Choose you this day," says the Bible, "whom ye will serve" (Joshua 24:15). So you can keep hanging there—or let go.

Student: But the problem would eventually resolve in some way. Is that right?

Dr. Hora: Yes. We have to learn to rely on God.

Student: When I get up in the morning, I start to plan my day—I will spend an hour doing this and an hour doing that and find time to be with God.

Dr. Hora: Do you enter it into the ledger?

Student: I guess what I am looking for is some kind of structure in order to find the right amount of time for my spiritual studies. In prior years I was going to school at night and also to work. I was in such a rigid structure. Now, I don't have that structure, and I keep looking for it.

Dr. Hora: God is infinite structure. How is that?

Student: God is our guide, and that is more important than thinking about what "should" be or what "should not" be or what to do.

Dr. Hora: Could you explain that?

Student: We don't have to manufacture a structure, I guess, if we see the value of our studies.

Student: Does it mean that God is always with us?

Dr. Hora: In the computer, is there something like that—infinity?

Student: Where I work, there is infinite chaos.

Student: It seems to me that although we say that the material is nothing, if you look at the structure . . .

Dr. Hora: We did not say that material is nothing.

Student: Is it symbolic?

Dr. Hora: It is thought.

Student: It just seems to me that this "thought" that we walk around in, this body, seems so beautifully and intelligently constructed. There is such an intelligence operating, and everything seems to be working together.

Dr. Hora: "The knee bone's connected to the thigh bone . . ."

Student: Right, and there's a song about it.

Dr. Hora: Infinite structure simply means: if we live in the context of God, all things work together harmoniously and intelligently, and we don't have to put into the daily ledgers—one hour for makeup, one hour for choosing a dress . . .

Student: Five minutes for makeup and three hours for choosing a dress—we have to get the priorities right!

Dr. Hora: Imagine if someone tried to explain to a centipede how to walk—scientifically, mind you—he'd need a computer to figure it out. In the context of God, Intelligence is always available, and things work together for good. Everything is harmonious, effortless, efficient, effective—you don't come too early to an appointment, and you cannot come too late—you are always on time. In this divine context, our actions and responses are divinely impelled—we don't have to figure things out—we just respond to ideas from divine Mind.

Student: With "should" thinking, it is so difficult to be spontaneous because we are so busy thinking of what "should" be.

Dr. Hora: Yes, of course.

Student: But don't we need to schedule things?

Dr. Hora: If you schedule things, then you get caught up into a "should" system.

Student: I have an example of that regarding meditation that really surprised me. When I plan to take time to meditate, I never get around to it in the morning, and I find that I am also late for work.

Dr. Hora: Yes.

Student: And when I am in a frame of mind where meditation is a priority, it seems natural to do it first; then I am ready on time, and everything works out.

Dr. Hora: Yes. So we don't use our heads—life would become very difficult if we did, and we are liable to get migraine headaches or sinus trouble. In the context of God, Intelligence governs our choices, and things are harmonious and effortless. That is called spontaneity and is not to be confused with haphazard living or mindlessness.

Student: The basic idea here seems to be living in the context of God. I would like to understand, a little more specifically, what that means.

Dr. Hora: What is meant by "living in the context of God"?

Student: Living by spiritual laws as opposed to human laws. Human laws say that if you get cold, you will catch a cold, which is cause-and-effect thinking. Spiritual laws are above that and override human laws. Spiritual laws operate from a higher perspective. If anyone understands spiritual laws, then he can transcend human laws.

Dr. Hora: Indeed, the Bible says: "The law of the Spirit of life in Christ Jesus" makes us "free from the law of sin and death" (Romans 8:2). Now the question is, "What is meant by living in the context of God?" This is a marvelous, miraculous condition where "all things work together for good." If you shoot an arrow you will hit the bull's-eye without even looking. The book Zen in the Art of Archery describes it so very beautifully in minute detail.

Student: That book offers a description of an individual who became an instrument of God—that individual was able to allow perfection to happen, and there wasn't anything standing in the way of it. Is that an aspect of "living in the context of God?"

Dr. Hora: That is the subjective aspect of living in the context of God. We are aware of ourselves as being governed by God—we never get tired; we do everything effortlessly, effectively, and efficiently, with no strain. There is a lot of stress involved in living in our culture, and everyone expects to suffer from these various stressful ways. But in the context of God there is no stress; there are no bellyaches and no headaches. What exactly is this mysterious thing?

Student: Perhaps it is the way we view life.

Dr. Hora: Exactly—it is a way of seeing. Unenlightened man sees life in the context of human relationships. In the context of God, there are no human relationships, and there is no interaction: there is only the harmonious coexistence of divine ideas in the universe of Mind. It is a way of seeing Reality. Does anyone know our "Principle of Safe Driving?" It is an example of driving with the perspective of the divine context. It says, "There are no drivers anywhere; there is only the harmonious flow of traffic under divine Mind's control." This principle offers an entirely different viewpoint on the situation. And when Jesus said, "If therefore thine eye be single, thy whole body shall be full of light" (Matthew 6:22), he was talking about the context of God. It is the same idea we find in the Third Principle of Metapsychiatry: "There is no interaction anywhere; there is only Omniaction everywhere."

Student: We have to acquire this way of seeing. So would it be true that the only way to acquire it is to look for evidence of it?

Dr. Hora: Yes, and practice, practice, practice. It's the same when we ask, "How do you get to Carnegie Hall?" By practicing! We learn to live in the context of God through conscious mindfulness of this possibility.

Student: I can see that in driving a lot more clearly, but the Third Principle is not so easy to see.

Dr. Hora: You could expand this realization to other areas of your functioning. As the Bible says: "Whither shall I go from thy spirit? Or whither shall I flee from thy presence? If I ascend up into heaven, thou art there: if I make my bed in hell, behold, thou art there. If I take the wings of the morning, and dwell in the uttermost parts of the sea, even there shall thy hand lead me, and thy right hand shall hold me" (Psalm 139:7-10). We cannot get out of the context of God—we must see it—but, if we are psychologically sophisticated, we cannot see it. We are blinded by miseducation, and all we see is people everywhere—that is all. Our mental horizon is restricted to human relationships—this kind of people and that kind of people, black people, yellow people, Hispanic people. We are always fascinated by people, and we don't see the [Omniactive] context; and, that is how we are suffering—from a kind of spiritual blindness. It is interesting to contemplate, when Jesus performed the miraculous healings of blind people, what was he healing? Their spiritual perspective. He opened the individuals up to the spiritual perspective on Reality. In that perspective there are no limitations—healings can occur spontaneously. We could postulate that to the extent that we learn to see life in the context of God, of infinite Mind, it would be reasonable to expect spontaneous healing to occur in whatever area is troubling us.

Student: Is there any difference between seeing in the context of God and beholding?

Dr. Hora: It is the same thing.

Student: It seems that there can be a trap regarding relationships because we may wish to avoid them. So the issue is not to have relationships nor to avoid relationships.

Dr. Hora: Avoidance is a form of relationship.

Student: What is the alternative? Seeing in the context of God?

Dr. Hora: See how simple it is?

Student: Yes, but it has to be clarified that we are not here to be impersonal.

Dr. Hora: Or detached.

Student: We have to recognize if we are being detached or impersonal. Sometimes we are kidding ourselves that we are spiritual when we are not.

Dr. Hora: We must understand what we are talking about, and if there are those who enjoy adulterating this teaching, then we say that we respect their right to do so.

Student: Maybe it isn't always about adulterating the teaching but about not really understanding it.

Dr. Hora: Misunderstanding it. If we misunderstand, we can always make an appointment for a clarification.

Student: Metapsychiatry teaches that relationships are existentially invalid. Does having a friend constitute a relationship?

Dr. Hora: Yes.

Student: But being friendly is valid.

Dr. Hora: That's right.

Student: How can we see the difference?

Dr. Hora: Well, you just explained it.

Student: Being friendly is being loving.

Dr. Hora: Yes, of course.

Student: So the difference between having a friend and being friendly is just a way of seeing. "Being friendly" is right seeing, and "having a friend" is having a relationship.

Dr. Hora: That's right, exactly.

Student: Is being friendly impersonal?

Dr. Hora: It is nonpersonal. An impersonal student of Metapsychiatry is a "stuffed shirt," but a nonpersonal student is an enlightened student—there is a radical difference. I read a description in the paper of a man who went to a department store to buy a necktie, and he asked the saleswoman, "Would you show me a necktie?" And she didn't say a word—she just pointed with her finger. That is impersonal.

Student: It is also poor salesmanship.

Dr. Hora: Yes, but she could say, "I do not get paid for talking." Life in a city like New York is too impersonal—one has the sense of being nothing, of being ignored—and in small cities, it is too personal. Suppose there is a mother and a daughter, and they love each other very much and always want to be together. Mother–daughter relationships are very personal. They just love each other and hug each other and kiss each other and buy each other gifts and make each other feel good. Is this love?

Student: It's oppression.

Dr. Hora: "It's oppression"—that's an interesting idea. Would you explain it?

Student: Neither the mother nor the daughter lets be.

Dr. Hora: Yes, but they have a belief that this is love.

Student: It is the same as what we discussed before—it is about seeing.

Dr. Hora: Yes, right. If individuals are too close, that is not love—it is mutual exploitation and interaction. If they are impersonal and ignore each other, that is not love either—it is rejection, perchance even hate. So what else is there? How is one to live with mother?

Student: In the context of God.

Dr. Hora: What would happen if you would see your mother in the context of God?

Student: We would no longer rely on one another for the comfort of being together; the love between us would be "nonpersonal, nonconditional benevolence," and there would be "letting be" and freedom. I would see that she is here for God and that I am here for God.

Dr. Hora: That's right!

Student: Does that also work if only one individual is aware of living in the context of God?

Dr. Hora: It is possible, yes.

Student: There is a situation with someone in my family who likes to be touched and hugged and comforted and doesn't know about anything higher. Would my awareness alone of living in the context of God be enough?

Dr. Hora: Yes, that awareness is called the "sound of one hand."

Student: I do understand, but if another feels that he needs something more, do we respond?

Dr. Hora: Sure.

Student: But knowing that we are not "giving" the love personally is what keeps us in the context of God?

Dr. Hora: Yes, if we are compassionate.

Student: And a beneficial presence.

Dr. Hora: Yes—and comfort them, but we don't overdo it.

Student: What about people who want to be touched and like a lot of affection? Can one be a "beneficial presence" and not give affection?

Dr. Hora: Do you have someone in mind?

Student: Yes, and she thinks that affection is the most important kind of love. So how can we refrain and still be loving?

Dr. Hora: This is a very complicated question. Once I had a patient who wanted to get me to talk to her—she enjoyed being spoken to—it was, for her, an experience of being fed. After the session, she didn't understand anything that she had heard; she never learned anything. She came to these sessions to be nurtured with words from Hora—from Dr. Hora's mouth—and that is not a happy situation. See how complicated it can become? And if I tried to explain to her the dynamics of her illness, she did not hear it. Many times, I said, "You are only coming here to be fed with words. You are not listening." And she would say, "Yeah, yeah, yeah," and nothing changed. Then one day she got up and said, "Doctor, can I kiss you?" She really wanted to bite off my head! You see, it is not easy being a psychiatrist!

Student: That sounds like a case in which a transference is trying to develop. What eventually happens in a situation like this? Does she just get frustrated?

Dr. Hora: Yes, she gets very frustrated and goes to various other doctors and gets pills, medications, and gets herself through life this way. In the old days, doctors got very frustrated with such patients; so they gave them electric shock treatments. Now if someone is very hungry for affection, be careful. You can become completely swallowed up by a hunger for affection.

Student: Isn't it also helpful to know that it is not our responsibility?

Dr. Hora: Of course.

Student: It is very easy to feel needed in a situation like that—you feel that someone has this need that you must fill.

Dr. Hora: That is not a need; it is just a crazy want.

Student: If you don't want to continue in a relationship, can God come into it and just dissolve it?

Dr. Hora: Yes.

Student: But, under the circumstances, it is not beneficial for both parties.

Dr. Hora: Do you know someone like this?

Student: Yes.

Dr. Hora: Is she insatiable for affection?

Student: Yes.

Dr. Hora: It is not your responsibility. You can never satisfy such an individual, and it is very painful to withdraw. It is like a fly trap, and you can get stuck; but usually it becomes increasingly unsatisfactory. Unenlightened life is a constant search for gratification. Sometimes it can be very troublesome, but it is not your responsibility.

Student: Sometimes there are elderly people who send you on a guilt trip in that area.

Dr. Hora: They may try.

Student: That is also not our responsibility.

Dr. Hora: It is our responsibility to refuse to feel guilty.

Student: But the constant trying and eliciting goodwill and spending time and this and the other, it is not our responsibility?

Dr. Hora: Of course not. Besides you, there is also God.

Student: It is hard to find God in a situation where you don't know how to turn to God because of the guilt in the situation. But it is not our responsibility?

Dr. Hora: No. As a matter of fact, if you accept the guilt, that makes them worse; then they can control you.

Student: They do.

Dr. Hora: So if we refuse to feel guilty, we are benefiting them.

Student: And ourselves.

Dr. Hora: Yes.

Student: Isn't it also an example of the "sound of one hand," because we are not feeding into that illusion?

Dr. Hora: That's right.

Student: We don't feel guilty because we understand that God is there?

Dr. Hora: We understand what guilt is.

Student: It is boasting.

Dr. Hora: Right—it is a devious way of feeling important. If you feel guilty, you are saying, "I am bad"; and if you regret, then you are saying, "Ignorance is bad."

Student: How does discipline fit into the infinite structure? What is discipline in that context?

Student: It seems to me we started this way.

Dr. Hora: Then we will wind up where we began.

Student: We never defined discipline, and I don't really know what it means.

Dr. Hora: It means discipleship. If you love the teaching, then you are a good disciple.

Possessiveness

Student: Dr. Hora, what are impure thoughts? As I asked myself this question, the first thing that came to mind was what we think of in terms of sexually impure thoughts. Are there other kinds of impure thoughts?

Dr. Hora: Sure. Does anyone know any nonsexual impure thoughts?

Student: You could write a book about it—there are millions of them.

Dr. Hora: Tell us some. What can you think of?

Student: The "Four Horsemen," for starters.

Dr. Hora: Right. Envy, jealousy, rivalry, and malice—evil of any kind—hatred, hostility, resentment. We can be preoccupied with an endless variety of impure thoughts, if we are interested in them.

Student: Would entertaining interaction thoughts be in the same category?

Dr. Hora: Mostly, yes. Are there pure interaction thoughts?

Student: That is what I was wondering.

Dr. Hora: Yes, there are. If we appreciate an individual and are happy about him or her, those are human interaction thoughts. The purest thought we can have is the Truth about someone. If we behold an individual in the context of God as a "living soul" or as a manifestation of divine qualities, and if we can rejoice in this, those are pure thoughts—they are very healthy, beneficial, healing thoughts. It is good to learn that. What happens if we see someone as a "living soul," a pure expression of Love-Intelligence, and we rejoice in seeing that individual in that light?

Student: It is a real blessing for both individuals.

Dr. Hora: Yes.

Student: And it opens the door to allow the good to flow, even if there is no problem; it opens the door to allow what is good in life to enter into the situation.

Dr. Hora: Yes. A "beneficial presence" is constantly seeing everything and everyone around him in the context of divine Reality, and that is what makes him a "beneficial presence." He doesn't have to say anything.

Student: Can he see any individual that way?

Dr. Hora: Yes, with a little effort.

Student: When you say "with a little effort," what do you mean? It has nothing to do with willing.

Dr. Hora: What is the "effort" involved in seeing people in the context of God?

Student: I think to be interested in God would be the motivation to want to see the world with God's eyes.

Dr. Hora: Wherein lies the effort?

Student: In overcoming "judging by appearances."

Dr. Hora: That's right. The tendency is to judge, to agree, to disagree, to criticize, to compare, and it takes a little effort to rise above it. Transcendence requires an investment of attention, but it is well worth it.

Student: It does seem to require willingness.

Dr. Hora: Yes. If you know what is good for you, you will be willing.

Student: What does it mean when you have heard something for years and years . . .

Dr. Hora: Thirty-five years?

Student: Yes, and suddenly you hear it?

Student: You see it or hear it as though for the first time. I am sitting here with my heart pounding. Dr. Hora was talking about seeing life and everything in the context of God, and I feel as if I was hearing it for the very first time. How many times have we heard that expressed? It seems to me that only now I really heard it and know it. I am overwhelmed by it, absolutely overwhelmed.

Dr. Hora: That's good.

Student: I can't get over it.

Dr. Hora: The word is "bowled over." That's wonderful. Let's hope it will stay with you.

Student: What happened?

Dr. Hora: As the Bible says, we are "hard of hearing." "For the heart of this people is waxed gross, and their ears are dull of hearing, and their eyes have they closed" (Acts 28:27). So it takes time until we begin to "see" and to "hear" and to "understand" with our hearts. Your heart is pounding because your heart understands. It is amazing that the heart can understand.

Student: You said, "seeing life in the context of God." I am aware of having heard that so many times and of having heard it differently all those times.

Dr. Hora: Yes.

Student: What does the heart symbolize?

Dr. Hora: It is an existential center of life. We touch the heart, and the heart responds by pounding.

Student: Dr. Hora, I have a question left over from last week's group in which you spoke about the fact that God loves us. I have difficulty understanding what that means. I see that God is a Principle, so what does it mean if a Principle loves an individual? Is it that we are part of and cannot be separated from this Principle which is God and which is always operating?

Dr. Hora: Yes. Love loves everyone that it is in touch with, and Love is infinite; therefore Love is in touch with everyone throughout the universe. An interesting thing happened last week. In the middle of the night, I received a call from Europe, where there was someone who was having an attack of severe heart palpitations and was panicky about it. It came to me to tell her that God loves her and that she is living in an Ocean of Love-Intelligence. In a few minutes, the heart palpitations stopped, and she became calm and afterwards had a good night's sleep. Suddenly, it clicked that in the context of Love-Intelligence, there is nothing to fear—we are safe, and we are loved. It is such an overwhelmingly important thing to understand that we are loved—not by a person, but by Love Itself. There is a universal benevolence enveloping all of us, but if we don't understand this, we can frequently fall into the belief that we are unloved— and that is very frightening, and we can get panicky: "Nobody loves me; I am all alone; and as a matter of fact, I am disliked." Once we get this idea, we can get scared, and then all kinds of symptoms can come up. But if our attention is turned to the Truth—that we live and move and have our being in infinite Love and that we are individually and collectively loved—then we can relax.

Student: I asked you last week about this, and you said that wonderful things show up every day if we think God loves us. But what is it that makes it so important for us to know that we are loved?

Dr. Hora: I just explained it.

Student: Because we can get panicky, if we don't know it?

Dr. Hora: If you think that you are not loved, you think that there is no God. If there is no God, then we would really be in trouble.

Student: I see.

Student: Dr. Hora, I watched a film the other night about a con-centration camp. How can you know, in a situation like that, that you are loved?

Dr. Hora: Well, I don't know about this movie.

Student: It is based on a true story about six hundred people in a camp who were survivors; they were strong and healthy and able to perform. They had useful tasks that they could do, making shoes or sewing, and therefore they were not annihilated in the gas chambers. They worked for the Nazis in the camp. The point of the story was that they planned an escape for the whole camp, but only three hundred people survived. It was a true story because they tell who the different people are and what they are doing today. My question is, in such a horrible situation, is it possible to know that we are loved when facing such hatred?

Dr. Hora: Yes. Well, of course, hate can destroy people. But you don't have to go to a concentration camp to feel hatred—you can just get married or have "friends" or get into a certain kind of hos-tile situation. Sometimes when we are confronted with intensive hate and criticism, we may get an attack of being unloved. So, in Metapsychiatry, we are learning to transcend personal reactions and to see ourselves in the context of God. In the context of God, we are aware of being loved, regardless of what anyone is saying to us or doing to us. We have this strength of understanding that we are loved, and that is a protection.

Student: And if we don't know that we are loved, we cannot possibly be loving.

Dr. Hora: Of course not, surely. We start out from the premise that God is infinite, omniactive, omnipresent Love-Intelligence. This is a very solid foundation from which to view life and all sit-uations in life, and, as we are solidly grounded in this basic truth, then we can withstand the assaults of hostility, jealousy, criticism, and malice. Then we can say, "Nevertheless, God is here; and God is Love, and we are loved." That is a very solid strength—it is the rock of Christ—a solid conviction that all is really well. It enables us to withstand the fiery darts of the devil and his three-pronged pitchfork—seduction, provocation, and intimidation.

Student: What is the meaning of despair? It seems that evil is everywhere. So I try to make a willful effort to get out of it, but I wonder if I really believe in the "good of God," and then I just get more despairing.

Dr. Hora: Well, you are a student of Metapsychiatry, and you are learning not only to believe in it but to really understand that the "good of God" is the Reality, and that everything else is just interaction. We know there is no such thing as interaction, even though it seems to drive us to despair.

Student: Not just to despair, but sometimes this malice can be almost frightening.

Dr. Hora: It is frightening in proportion to our lack of understanding of the omnipresence and the power of God. So it is important to be constantly mindful of the fact that "in Him, we live and move and have our being." We are learning to see life in the context of God, rather than in the context of interaction. The vast majority of the world sees life in the context of interaction relationships. This is what the world is made of—relationships. But Reality is not made of relationships—It is made of God. In the context of God, we are all aware of being loved—that is the Comforter. The Bible speaks about the Comforter—the Comforter is the understanding that God loves us. "Perfect love casteth out fear" (1 John 4:18).

Student: Dr. Hora, if one is in a situation where there seems to be an inordinate amount of malice or criticism or danger coming one's way, would being loved by God include being receptive to intelligent ideas that might take one out of this particular situation, or would one simply stay in the situation?

Dr. Hora: And be passive, right? Don't forget that we say, "God is omniactive Love-Intelligence." When we are aware of being loved, we are also aware that intelligent ideas are constantly available to us, to help us respond to situations in an appropriate way and to be protected—we make the right moves spontaneously, without premeditation. "Let not your heart be troubled, neither let it be afraid," says the Bible (John 14:27). "Because thou hast made the Lord . . . thy habitation, there shall no evil befall thee, neither shall any plague come nigh thy dwelling" (Psalm 91:9-10). There are many, many quotations relevant to this issue.

Student: Would we also be free of wondering what people think of us?

Dr. Hora: Of course. That is elementary, Mrs. Watson!

Student: It may be elementary, but I have become aware that I am always wondering what people think of me.

Dr. Hora: Yes, that is somewhat self-confirmatory.

Student: Somewhat? It certainly is, but if we are aware that that is the case, it must be something that can be healed.

Dr. Hora: Well, there is a very simple statement that helps to remind us of the Omnipresence: "Besides me, there is also God."

Student: Right.

Student: What does it mean to have a cough for over two weeks?

Dr. Hora: A cough? Well, there are all kinds of coughs. In your case, it is probably a cigarette cough.

Student: I haven't been smoking. I smoke very little these days.

Dr. Hora: Perhaps you are suffering from "existential dread," the fear of being ignored—that is the worst pain that you can inflict on another, to ignore him. If you want to learn how to be nasty to people, that is all you have to do—ignore them. And what is this self-confirmatory ideation that all of us are inclined to? What is it? It is a fear of being ignored. "If I don't toot my own horn, who will toot it?"

Student: Is the fear of being ignored related to the thought of being unloved?

Dr. Hora: Certainly, of course.

Student: If we understand that God loves us, all of these things are supposedly irrelevant.

Dr. Hora: Yes. See how simple it is?

Student: I guess we have to be aware of the context of our thoughts because they are clearly interactional, and there is no way out of that context when we feel ignored. We can try other things, somehow, to get people to notice us or love us . . .

Dr. Hora: Yes. We say, "Love me or hate me, but don't ignore me. I can't cope. I can't stand it."

Student: So if we really understood that God loves us, we would never crave any kind of attention.

Dr. Hora: Of course not.

Student: Does that mean, if we crave attention or recognition, that this is actually denying the presence of God? If we understood that God loves us, we wouldn't want those things, would we?

Dr. Hora: If we are aware of being loved, then we are loving, and we are aware of everything and everyone around us; and it is very pleasant. Otherwise, there are anxious thoughts: What does he think? What do they think? What am I thinking? How do I feel? How do they make me feel? et cetera, et cetera. There are all kinds of fearful thoughts. Most of the time, we are thinking interaction thoughts, fearfully.

Student: Being unloving seems as bad as feeling unloved.

Dr. Hora: Yes, but you cannot be loving unless you really know that you are loved. Nowadays we hear a lot of talk about stress. What is this stress? There are all kinds of stress-reducing exercises to help people to reduce stress in life. When you perspire under the arms or in the body or have itchy feet or something like that, it indicates that you are experiencing stress, right? What is it?

Student: Is it the effort to be somebody? To confirm yourself?

Dr. Hora: It is fear.

Student: Fear that you aren't anybody?

Dr. Hora: Right. It is simply trying to function in spite of the fear, and that is stressful.

Student: The fear of what?

Dr. Hora: What others are thinking about what you are thinking. In the land of PAGL [PAGL is an acronym for Peace, Assurance, Gratitude, Love, and Its Presence in consciousness informs us that we are in tune with the One Mind], there is no stress—there is "stresslessness."

Student: Is that what underlies ambition?

Dr. Hora: No, ambition generates stress. Ambition is a way of coping with fear in a future-oriented way. It is an effort at securing our future—that is ambition. We could define it as "an effort at securing our future," and that is stressful.

Student: Yes.

Dr. Hora: Ambitious people are always living under stress. What are futurists? Have you ever heard of the futurist movement?

Student: In painting?

Dr. Hora: Well, that is different; that is just a style. Perhaps when people don't understand your painting, you are a futurist. It may take the next one hundred years for the world to appreciate Metapsychiatry, so we are also in a sense "futurists," except that we don't sweat about it. No sweat! Futurists are people who try to figure out what will be, but we are concerned with developing the capacity to see what "IS." That's all.

Student: Dr. Hora, about the issue of love, it has occurred to me that one of the problems I seem to be suffering from is the idea that what I love can be taken away. It has occurred to me that this anxiety, which I always have about my sons, may have to do with my own childhood. When I was very young, my father left and my mother got divorced; everything changed very quickly. Whatever I had loved was gone. So it occurred to me that I am always wanting to be in control, so that what I love won't be taken away.

Dr. Hora: Yes.

Student: Therefore, if you suffer from this kind of idea, it is very. . .

Dr. Hora: Stressful.

Student: It is, and it seems very deep. I don't know if that is the right way to say it, but it seems very deep.

Dr. Hora: Deep-seated.

Student: Yes, the anxiety is deep-seated.

Dr. Hora: It is like psychoanalysis—you go deeper and you come up dirtier.

Student: So if something took place at an early age that was traumatic and it seems to have an effect throughout your life . . .

Dr. Hora: It is hopeless.

Student: Really?

Dr. Hora: It is hopeless because we cannot change the past.

Student: Well, I don't think that it is hopeless because I recognized that there was a belief that something that you love can be taken away. At least, I recognized the thought. We have to recognize what is not as well as what is.

Dr. Hora: This is cause-and-effect reasoning, and we can see the futility of it because if you have a cause, then you are lost. There is no remedy because no one will ever be able to change the past—there is no way to change the past. Now you have an excuse to be possessive, you see, because of what happened in the past.

Student: But the possessiveness causes pain.

Dr. Hora: Of course it does, but that is not cause and effect. Possessiveness is a problem now, but not because of the past.

Student: Where did it come from?

Dr. Hora: Possessiveness? It came from the "sea of mental garbage" which says, "Having is nice, but holding on to it is even nicer."

Student: I see.

Student: Is part of the futility of psychoanalysis that the more we see, the more there is no solution on that level? It leads us to think, "Now I know! That must be the reason."

Dr. Hora: Now, I know why.

Student: Is there any value in knowing why?

Dr. Hora: The value is that, if you find a cause, you have an excuse, and if you have an excuse, then you don't have to change. You are justified, you see? You are justified in being possessive or in being anxious or controlling, all because of what happened in the past.

Student: But I thought you have also said, "You have to remember in order to forget."

Dr. Hora: Yes, but you don't use it [to justify existentially invalid thinking and behavior].

Student: But I am bringing it up to understand it.

Dr. Hora: Remember, Metapsychiatry says that cause-and-effect reasoning is invalid, that there is no such thing. As long as you are justifying your present problem with events from the past, you will never be healed of the present problem.

Student: But the idea occurred to me that maybe this was the meaning of the fear. What does it mean, "You have to remember in order to forget"?

Dr. Hora: He who seeks reasons only finds excuses.

Student: I understand that.

Dr. Hora: No, you don't. You are using it to justify possessiveness. What is possessiveness?

Student: You have just said that "having is good, but holding onto is even better."

Dr. Hora: Yes. It is an erroneous idea, and that is all there is to it. It doesn't matter how it came about or why. It is important to know that it is an erroneous, existentially invalid idea—having and holding.

Student: Dr. Hora, regarding the topic of stress, there are certain environments which I find more stressful than others. One of them is in situations where people are being very nice to me. I can't handle it, and I am mistrustful of it. Sometimes people are very nice, gushing and wanting to say really nice things and do really nice things and be solicitous of everything that I am saying, and I find myself feeling terribly stressed.

Dr. Hora: Yes, you feel threatened.

Student: What could the meaning of that be?

Dr. Hora: Well, you are aware of the fact that they want something. What do they want? They want to possess you and own you and use you. Doesn't that sound familiar?

Student: But we can see that and be completely immune to it, can't we?

Dr. Hora: Absolutely, of course.

Student: Striving to be liked by people and noticed is such a fantasy—the whole thing is such a dream.

Dr. Hora: Yes.

Student: Could it also be a survival issue? Does our reluctance to let go of that idea have to do with "existential dread"?

Dr. Hora: Well, once you are possessive, you think that your survival depends on holding on to what you have; that reluctance to let go comes out of an existential dread. But we don't have to delude ourselves that our lives depend on being able to hold on to what we have, because we don't have anything. Everything belongs to God, and we don't have the power to hold on to anything. So if we don't have anything, what is there to hold on to, right? The issue in life is Being—not having and holding— but being free in God. Freedom, assurance—not certainty, but assurance—gratitude, love, being, these are the issues.

Student: Therefore, we must recognize the error and become issue oriented about it. I say this because I know this possessiveness. My mother had to go to the doctor recently, and while I was waiting for the results, I was scared; there was a lot of anger. My reasoning was going like this: I felt possessive of her, and I had to take care of her; but there was also an anger, as if she instilled this in me. She made me like this, and now I am worried about her. Why am I worried about her? And it was back and forth, and I couldn't elevate it to a nonpersonal issue between us and see that she is in God and I am in God. It was very difficult.

Dr. Hora: Well, you slipped there into cause-and-effect reasoning: "She made me like this; therefore I am the result of what she caused me to be." See? The moment you slip into cause-and-effect reasoning, you lose all logic and you are lost. Remember that the issue in life is Being—your being and her being in God—it is not having and holding. If we make the mistake of seeing life issues in terms of having and holding, we are going to suffer tremendously, and there will be a lot of stress and anxiety in our lives. It is a miserable thing, this possessiveness.

Student: While I was waiting for the test result, there was tremendous stress. And then afterwards I thought, "The results came back good this time, but what will happen in the future?" Can I learn anything from this?

Dr. Hora: Yes. You are looking forward to more stress in the future. It is important to have an existential viewpoint on life, on the issue of Being—the basic, philosophical position which we call existentialism. The emphasis is on Being.

Student: Besides having and holding, what about the issue of thinking you are responsible?

Dr. Hora: That is a self-confirmatory idea, connected with the delusional belief of having and holding.

Student: Does that mean "having and holding" in relationships too?

Dr. Hora: Of course. There is no such thing as relationships—there is only Being. In the context of God, there is Being—there is safety; there is peace, and there is freedom.

Student: You can't ever lose your being because you never "had" it.

Dr. Hora: Right. God owns your being, including your wardrobe and everything else.

Student: Like parents and children?

Dr. Hora: Right.

Student: Does God own all the things that we think we own?

Dr. Hora: Everything belongs to God—nothing belongs to you. You belong to God, too—you are God's property.

Student: Dr. Hora, a few minutes ago I asked if we could be immune to those who want to be possessive of us or use us, but I don't know how to attain that immunity.

Dr. Hora: It is a good thing to recognize that there is such a problem. Many people are afflicted with the idea that they own their loved ones and that they have a right to hold onto them and to use them. Let's say you have horses—they are your property, and you use them to ride—but if you are very possessive, you expand this "horse manure" idea to people, and you want to have them, to hold them, and to use them too. If you are clear about this widespread problem, which is essentially called materialism, then you will be alert and aware if someone is trying to do this to you, and you will say, "Ah-ha!"

Student: That's the way to do it?

Dr. Hora: That solves it.

Student: So you are just amused by it.

Dr. Hora: Of course.

Student: We can even understand the feeling of resistance that we get from another, if we have the idea of having and holding them.

Dr. Hora: Yes, they want to run away from you to Peru or India or wherever—they want to run, yes?

Student: Yes, that is very helpful.

Student: I understand cause and effect, but you have said that we need to remember in order to forget. What are we talking about in that respect?

Dr. Hora: It is good to remember everything that we ever experienced, but those experiences do not justify our present ignorance. We do not use them to justify our present problems. We assume responsibility for our own ignorance, and then we can be healed. Otherwise there is no healing possible—there is just rationalization for our ignorance.

Student: When we notice that we are remembering something that we haven't remembered in years, is it coming back to be forgiven and to be looked at from a different, a higher perspective?

Dr. Hora: That's right. We forgive the past, but we assume responsibility for our problems today, and we do not justify them by what other people have done to us in the past.

Dialogue No. 34

Collective Right-Knowing

Student: Dr. Hora, the Bible says that God knows what we need before we ask ["Your Father knoweth what things ye have need of, before ye ask Him" (Matthew 6:8)]. I guess that means that, in divine Reality, there is a recognition of what we need. Are our needs all different, or is there one need? How does it work? It seems a very necessary idea to understand, in order to transcend wanting.

Dr. Hora: Does anyone know the answer to this interesting question?

Student: Aren't each of our needs individual and also very specific to our uniqueness as spiritual emanations of God?

Dr. Hora: There is one common need: in the whole universe, every creature that is endowed with consciousness has the need and the responsibility to come to know the Truth. "And this is life eternal, that they might know thee the only true God, and Jesus Christ whom thou hast sent" (John 17:3). Humanity has a great need to know the Truth. There was a Jewish rabbi by the name of Joshua, and God instructed him to go among the people and help them to come to know the Truth. This is our common need.

Student: And the only "need?"

Dr. Hora: This is the only need. If an individual reaches the point where he really knows the Truth, what more could he ask? If we have the knowledge of the Truth, we are enlightened. What do we do then? We just sit down cross-legged and smile, and everything comes to us! That is all.

Student: It is wonderful to hear it described, but it is so hard to see it.

Dr. Hora: Yes, it is hard to see it, but at least we have the great blessing of hearing about it.

Student: So every time we see that we want something, we can use this idea as a spiritual counterfact?

Dr. Hora: Of course. What does the First Principle of

Metapsychiatry say? "Thou shalt have no other interests before the good of God, which is spiritual blessedness." Now what is so great about this "spiritual blessedness?" If someone is in a state of spiritual blessedness, what else could he or she want or need? They are absolutely free, absolutely perfect, absolutely intelligent, absolutely gloriously loving and joyous, and they live forever! They will never die, and they know it. They do not have to go anywhere, because God is everywhere present. So why run around the world looking for happiness if it is right under your nose! We are constantly hearing about the Truth; Truth is a very fantastic idea. The Bible says: "Ye shall know the truth, and the truth shall make you free" (John 8:32). It shall make you happy and infinitely wealthy; it shall make you satisfied—there is nothing else left to crave or to want. We are fearless; we have no worries; we know that not even an atomic explosion could destroy us.

Student: Dr. Hora, that seems to indicate that our needs will be met, if we are enlightened. Is there any alternative?

Dr. Hora: If our need is met, then all needs are met—our need is to come to know the Truth.

Student: So as life unfolds and we endeavor to keep this primary interest in the Truth, does the Truth take over because the interest is so focused? I mean, does that interest keep us out of the struggle between wanting and not wanting?

Dr. Hora: Yes. You could ask, "If this is so simple, so wonderful, and so universal, what is it that interferes with achieving it?" Wanting and should-thinking are what interfere. There was an alcoholic who was studying Metapsychiatry, and he said that the reason he drank was because there are so many liquor stores in the city. So I said, "If there were no liquor stores at all in New York, you would not have an alcohol problem? Then all you have to do is destroy the liquor stores, and you won't have any more problems." Is that so? Certainly not, because then he would be thinking about what "should" be and what "should not" be, and what he wants and what he does not want. What makes us so stupid? Everyone is constantly thinking about what they want and what they don't want and about what "should" be and what "should not" be. I remember a husband whose favorite saying to his wife was, "If only you would change, then I would be all right." We arrive at these ideas by "judging by appearances." That is the basic problem. Jesus said: "Judge not according to the appearance, but judge righteous judgment" (John 7:24). If we "judge by appearances," all kinds of invalid ideas occur, and then we are cut off from what we really need, and everyone has this one need.

Student: It is beautiful.

Dr. Hora: Whether you are an Arab or a Russian or a this or a that, we only have one need, and it is the same need for everyone. That is why racism doesn't make any sense: the blacks and the whites have the same need—there is one universal and unique need.

Student: Someone could ask, "What about the need to eat or the need to sleep or to perpetuate the species?"

Dr. Hora: Jesus had an answer for every "what about." What did he say to this "what about"?

Student: "Therefore, take no thought, saying, 'What shall we eat?' or 'What shall we drink?' or 'Wherewithal shall we be clothed?'" (Matthew 6:31).

Dr. Hora: Seek ye first the consciousness of divine Reality, "and all these things shall be added unto you" (Matthew 6:33).

Student: So it does seem that God takes care of all our needs—we have our shelter and our food—we just have to be aware that it comes from God.

Dr. Hora: Once the disciples of Jesus brought him some food because he hadn't eaten all day. And what did he say? He said: "I have meat to eat ye know not of . . . My meat is to do the will of him that sent me, and to finish his work" (John 4:32, 34). He knew the Truth—he had no need to drink water or eat food. None of these things was important to him, and whenever something was needed, it appeared.

Student: What about concern for the homeless?

Dr. Hora: Oh, yes. What did he say about the homeless?

Student: The poor shall always be with us (Matthew 26:11).

Dr. Hora: No, that is about the poor. About the homeless, he said: "The foxes have holes, and the birds of the air have nests; but the Son of man has no place to lay his head" (Matthew 8:20). Was he complaining? No, he was intimating the fact that he was not one of these creatures. He was of a higher order—he didn't really need a bed or a home. He could walk on water; he could transport himself over distances instantaneously, and he could walk into a room through a closed door.

Student: By the "Son of man," he meant himself?

Dr. Hora: Yes. Interchangeably he called himself the "Son of God" and the "Son of man," indicating that he was both at the same time. He didn't need to have a place to lay his head.

Student: What does Metapsychiatry say about the homeless and about social-justice issues, about the idea that we ought to be doing something for other people?

Dr. Hora: Metapsychiatry has a wonderful solution for every problem. Metapsychiatry never "does" anything. If there is a problem, we don't fix the problem. What do we do when we are confronted with a problem? We pray. "Normal" people say, "This shouldn't be, and we have to fix it." But Metapsychiatry says, "This is not [what really is]; a perfect, flawless universe is [what really is]." Prayer is the acknowledgment of the perfection of divine Reality. Whenever disquieting phenomena appear, people suffer and are anxious and fearful and try to fix them; but problems are never fixed absolutely. The only remedy to the ills of the world is the conscious awareness of the perfection of the universe which already is and always was and always will be. Now our knowledge is not sufficient to see immediately the disappearance of New York City's problems, but on individual levels we see marvelous changes taking place in people's lives when they stop thinking about what "should not" be and focus their attention on what "already is." To this effect, the Second Principle of Metapsychiatry was written: "Take no thought for what should be or what should not be; seek ye first to know the good of God, which already is." Whenever we are confronted with something troublesome, we pray with the help of the Second Principle, and we see changes happening, not on a large scale, because we do not have that amount of knowledge, but on an individual scale we can see that this is so.

Student: If it is the Truth, and we can see it at work on an individual level, what knowledge is necessary to see it on a larger scale? Is it the same knowledge?

Dr. Hora: This is a very good question, and Jesus somehow hinted at it when he said that the works that I do, you shall do also, and "greater works than these shall you do; for I go unto my Father" (John 14:12). How could anyone do greater works? And what did he mean? The answer offers itself that he may have hinted at the idea of a collective knowledge of the Truth: if one individual can know the Truth and see remarkable healings and changes and improvements occurring, then a collective of a large number of individuals who can join in knowing the Truth might result in tremendous blessings in the world. To this effect, people in various parts of the world formed groups, schools, and religions and tried to know the Truth collectively, for greater power. Unfortunately they have not succeeded in synchronizing their knowledge of the Truth. What happens when large numbers of sincere seekers of the Truth come together in order to pray? We see that many churches and denominations and all kinds of religious groups, small and large, come together to pray for the world, but we do not see any spectacular results. The only explanation is that, although they do pray, they do not pray with sufficient understanding because there are not too many enlightened individuals in the world yet—throughout history there have been only a few, scattered here and there. When people come together to try to pray, their prayers are not effective. There was a television program showing a Southern Baptist minister who has thirteen million adherents to his religion, and he got up and said, "God doesn't listen to Jewish prayer. Why? Because the Jews rejected Jesus." He made prayer a personal affair. Here is a man who is religious, but he does not really understand that the Truth is not denominational or personal. So there may be a sufficient, collective desire to pray for the world, but if the people praying do not understand, then even if one hundred thousand prayed, it would have no effect whatsoever.

Student: Because their prayers are asking for things?

Dr. Hora: Yes. They are asking; they are telling; and everyone has his own personal misconceptions. There are collective and individual misconceptions. Prayer is not effective unless it is according to the way Jesus specified. He said: "God is a spirit: and they that worship him must worship him in spirit and in truth" (John 4:24). But who has already advanced on this path sufficiently to worship God "in spirit?" Most of the world worships God in ceremonies and in pretty words. Relatively speaking, there are very few people who can worship God "in spirit and in truth," as Jesus specified. What did he mean by "in spirit and in truth?" He must have had some reason for saying it this way.

Student: It is the third step that you have been describing recently in the three levels of valid communication: God to man, God through man, and God as man. If you have reached the level of God as man, you would be worshiping "in spirit and in truth."

Dr. Hora: If we do not understand that we are spiritual beings, made of the same "stuff" as God, then we do not have the Truth, and we cannot pray effectively. In order to pray effectively, we must understand that God and His creation are made of the same "stuff," which is spirit. To the extent that this is understood, the Truth is known. If every one of us knew this in this group, who knows what would happen? Maybe all the homeless people would suddenly find palaces! Individually, we manage occasionally to see Truth—more and more as we progress—but, collectively, we do not know how to pray, and that is the problem. The more people learn how to pray and reach that level of enlightenment where prayer becomes knowledge of the spiritual truth, the better the world will be. For the time being, things seem to be going from bad to worse. There is so much ignorance in the world, so many tragedies, so many frightening things; the human race must become enlightened in order to pray effectively. But, of course, as we approach that level of enlightenment, the word "prayer" is not enough anymore. Instead of prayer, we can say "right-knowing"— "right-knowing" is the ultimate prayer. If we know the truth, there is nothing to pray for. Prayer has been imbued with the idea of begging, with the idea that man has to beg for everything and that God is the richest man—so we can beg Him to give us what we want. In Metapsychiatry, we learn to abandon the idea of pe- titionary prayer. In all religions there is petitionary prayer—man begging God—but we do not beg anymore because we wish to have self-respect, even in the face of God. Our prayer is called "Right-knowing." "This is life eternal that they may know thee the only true God, and Jesus Christ whom thou hast sent" (John 17:3). If we understand that prayer is "right-knowing," then it will be easier to stop thinking about what should be and what should not be or about what we want and what we do not want.

Student: Can the subconscious subvert the conscious? For in- stance, just when I think I am understanding Metapsychiatry, I may wake up with a dream that is not a happy one, or I think of something that I did before which I regret—the state of peace isn't constant. Is there any point in thinking in terms of the subconscious?

Dr. Hora: Subconscious is a psychoanalytic invention. We say we have to struggle against certain thoughts which we are not fully aware of, and these thoughts sometimes come to torment us, either during the day or at night when we are trying to sleep. They torment us because they are pressing for conscious acknowledg- ment. So we look eagerly at our dreams and ask, "What is this dream trying to tell me about my secret thoughts?" Very often we develop certain unacceptable thoughts during the day, or even from the past, and they can torment us and come up in the form of physical symptoms or disturbances in our social life or as economic problems. So the great value of Metapsychiatry's Two Intelligent Questions is that we can confront these mental phenomena with the question, "What is the meaning of what seems to be?" Then we may be inspired and suddenly realize the answer to this question, and we can see that what the so-called unconscious or subconscious was harboring invariably turns out to be some thought that we would rather not be aware of. Inquiring about the "meaning" is extremely helpful. The Freudian method aimed at the same thing in a way. Freud devised the method of "free association": at random, the therapist throws out thoughts in the hope that "the blind chicken will find the kernel." We have a method that is very effective if it is approached with a sense of radical sincerity and a willingness to be embarrassed.

Student: Do we just have to keep going on and on with it? It is not a quick fix, is it?

Dr. Hora: Sometimes we become quickly aware of the "meaning," and sometimes we have to wait; it depends on how squeamish we are.

Student: Recently there were two articles in the paper that dealt with the physiology of the brain. One article described taking an X-ray photograph of the brain in the process of remembering the meaning of a word. The other article was a review of a book in which a doctor has apparently very elaborately laid out what parts of the brain do what, and he has gone to some extreme effort to describe how these parts work. This doctor also said that all the other scientists have fallen back on the existence of a soul, or a consciousness, because it points toward some sort of organizing principle. But this book says that this is not so. I was wondering if you could address what seems to be a concern that has arisen in me that perhaps scientists are going to dissect things to the point where there is no room for God.

Dr. Hora: There was a very wise old doctor who said, "They know more and more about less and less, until they find out that they know everything about nothing." This is called reductionism. It has been a trend in scientific research for years. The scientists attempt to reduce everything to the molecular and subatomic level and to explain life in terms of this *reductio ad absurdum!* Of course, it doesn't explain anything—it just observes certain phenomena, which are only appearances. It has absolutely no real value. It is interesting, of course, but it cannot really ever explain life because it leaves God out of his own Creation.

Student: It all seems like a 1990s version of Darwin, and how, when Darwin's theories evolved, they seemed so threatening.

Dr. Hora: These are not threatening anymore; they are ridiculous. They do not explain anything—they just describe phenomena. Describing is not explaining.

Student: I guess what is disturbing is the determination of these people to say that there is no God.

Dr. Hora: Well, it is almost as bad as saying that God is Jewish or Arabic. Whether we deny the existence of God or misinterpret the existence of God, it is the same, because we deprive ourselves of the possibility of salvation through enlightenment. What good is a reductionistic explanation when we have a bellyache? We don't know where to go!

Student: Dr. Hora, maybe it has to do with the problem of understanding the idea of nondimensionality and being a transparency. You have told us that no one has ever really "seen" someone else. I can understand the doctor who wrote that book because we are so much in a certain mode of thought that looks for some "thing," so we can say, "This is it!"

Dr. Hora: Something dimensional, be it ever so tiny! As long as it has dimensions, it is respectable because it is material— except in atomic research. Here they reached a point where they would see subatomic particles as corpuscular, as material, little balls, and, as they were watching these little balls, suddenly they disappeared, and, in place of them, waves appeared. They lost their dimensionality, and they were just phenomena. So when we go far enough, we will know everything about nothing or nothing about everything. There was a lady in Los Angeles, at a church meeting where they were discussing bilingual religious services. This lady got up and said, "Why do we need bilingual services? If English was good enough for Jesus Christ, it is good enough for everybody!" This is folk wisdom.

Student: The idea of collective knowing, which we were discussing earlier, is such an interesting concept.

Dr. Hora: Collective knowing of the Truth.

Student: Yes, collective knowing of the Truth. Does that mean that the knowledge of the Truth could be potentiated?

Dr. Hora: Yes, potentiation is a good word. I have observed the

Tibetan monks' prayer on a television program. The more serious students of the Truth were humming collectively in very deep
voices, a continuous humming, until they were synchronized on
a certain wavelength. What kind of prayer could this be? There
is a collective humming, and every participant is tuned in, literally, on the same wavelength. I imagine it is an attempt at collective prayer where concepts are eliminated, and consciousness is
actually immersed into a collective kind of wavelength. Maybe
this approximates our Prayer of Right Knowing. I haven't seen
what they have accomplished. There is a beautiful exhibit here
currently of Tibetan art, which is mind-boggling. Hundreds of
years ago, moved by religious fervor, these people were able to
produce beautiful art. There is much we do not understand about
these cultures—there is a power of the Truth and the Spirit which,
throughout the history of mankind, has manifested itself through
individuals, either by miraculous healings or through artistic
expression.

Student: Dr. Hora, would that humming create an emptiness?

Dr. Hora: I really do not know.

Student: At this exhibit, there is a film of the monks making a
huge sand painting. Three monks were just working quietly, and
when they were all through, they just scraped it together, put it
into bottles and threw it into the sea. I thought it must mean that
life is meaningless. The monks seemed very cheerful, and they
said that their mission is wisdom and compassion.

Student: Someone explained to me that destroying the painting
and throwing the sand into the sea was to get across the Buddhists'
idea of impermanence. They are not saying that life is meaningless—they go to great lengths to build this beautiful mandala, and
in the end they sweep it up to teach the idea of impermanence.

Student: How would you evaluate what happens in this group as
a collective knowing? It seems that, at the end of these sessions, a
lot of error has been replaced in everyone's consciousness by the
Truth.

Dr. Hora: If you leave here enriched with love, with a loving
outlook on life, then it was a useful session.

Student: I have observed that this happens.

Dr. Hora: The quality of love is a very good indicator as to
whether we are responding to the Truth or not. It is highly desirable to be uplifted and to see life in the context of divine Love,
of nonconditional benevolence. When the Buddhists speak about

wisdom and compassion, their idea of compassion is benevolence. In Metapsychiatry we have a different definition of compassion—it is "understanding the lack of understanding." We speak of Love-Intelligence, and the Buddhists speak of wisdom and compassion. It is very similar, very close. Our definition of perfect love is "nonpersonal, nonconditional benevolence." It helps to know this. Human love is a whore. Throughout the world, we see love destroying people. It is very strange. How does human love destroy people?

Student: It is conditional.

Dr. Hora: If you love conditionally, you can drive someone crazy. Everyone is very eager to be loved. If this love, which you crave, has strings attached to it—and it always has—then you become entrapped in a certain way of behaving and thinking, and it can become very destructive. Human love is dangerous and outright harmful, believe it or not. But the understanding of perfect love is liberating. As the Bible puts it: "Perfect love casteth out fear" (1 John 4:18). If we ask what the Bible means by "perfect love," most people would say that it means unselfish love. Is there such a thing as unselfish love?

Student: Well, if you transcend the idea that you are a person, would that allow for being unselfish?

Dr. Hora: No, that would demonstrate selflessness, which is very close to perfect love.

Student: Unselfish love is being here for others.

Dr. Hora: Yes. Selfish love is being here for yourself, and unselfish love is being here for others, so that you can benefit from thinking of yourself as unselfish. This is the human condition.

Student: At first glance, it is difficult to understand love impersonally.

Dr. Hora: To understand love nonpersonally. We have arrived at this realization about "Perfect Love": it must be "nonpersonal" because it is divine and "nonconditional" because there are no strings attached, and it is synonymous with "benevolence" because it is goodwill.

Dialogue No. 35

Attachments

Student: Dr. Hora, I regret to some extent the ignorance that I participate in. I can see that my loyalties are quite often in the wrong place. I recognize it, and it is really embarrassing.

Dr. Hora: Where are your loyalties located?

Student: I am so very childish.

Dr. Hora: You are just suffering from an attachment.

Student: It is so unhealthy.

Dr. Hora: Many people suffer from attachments. What is the trouble with attachments?

Student: They seem to be the most important things in the world. I am possessed by all kinds of attachments, and I can't function adequately because of them.

Dr. Hora: Yes. Possessiveness is possessed by attachment.

Student: It limits freedom; it is restrictive.

Dr. Hora: Yes.

Student: The attachment becomes our god.

Dr. Hora: Exactly. An attachment can be to a person, a place, a thing or even to an idea. It can become so important to us that we are gripped with fear of dying if someone suggests that we must let go of this attachment. God is the only "lifeline" compatible with freedom. All other lifelines—every attachment is an illusory lifeline—fill us with the fear that we could not survive without them. This forming of attachments happens very often to people. Actually, this is the most fundamental idea in Buddhism. In Buddhism, they teach that all problems in life come from man's inclination to form attachments, and as long as we are attached to someone or something, we are going to suffer. So the Zen Master says, "Above all, cherish nothing." If we have an attachment, we cherish that person, place, thing, or idea, and we are afraid to let go. This is the real dilemma of attachment. We must trust God as our "lifeline" and then live that way. It is not enough just to talk about it; we must actually live as though our life is in God and as though our life does not depend on any person, place, thing, or idea. God will sustain us beautifully when we trust God to sustain us. Regarding this issue, there are two kinds of people: there are those who do not have any attachments to anyone—they are called "self-reliant"—and this is a troublesome condition; and then there are people who are "other-reliant." But to be healthy and free, we must be "God-reliant." When we are "self-reliant," we trust in our own abilities to survive; when we are "other-reliant," we trust in the attachment. How do we trust God whom we cannot see, hear, smell, taste, or touch? How can we rely on such a God which is nondimensional? This is the dilemma of the human condition. Religious people think that they rely on God, but really they rely on the church. In order to rely on God, we must have had some demonstrations, some awareness of the reality of God's sustaining power. Little by little, we can have conscious contact with God. God is not a theory or a belief system or a superstitious symbol of some kind. Metapsychiatry is "an epistemological method of God realization." In proportion to God's becoming more tangibly real to us, we can let go of attachments and move toward God-reliance.

Student: What is the "meaning" of fear in attachments?

Dr. Hora: Survival, existential dread.

Student: What about mother and daughter attachments?

Dr. Hora: It is interesting that an attachment can be a two-way street—you are attached to your mother, and she is attached to you at the same time. Here we have a double attachment, and this is a tough situation.

Student: Yes, we are both attached to each other. I am aware of her thoughts all the time.

Student: In the world, attachment is seen as love.

Dr. Hora: Yes, the world calls it "love"—we call it a problem.

Student: We must understand who our real mother is.

Dr. Hora: Yes, our heavenly Mother—God is our Mother.

Student: But it seems disloyal not to be with my mother.

Dr. Hora: This is called a rationalization. Loyalty belongs to God; we are part of God. If someone says, "I am part of my mother, and my mother is a part of me," then that individual is worshiping a false god and a false reality. Call no man your mother, for He is your mother, who is in heaven. This is an updated version of Christ's words: "Call no man your father upon the earth: for one is your Father, which is in heaven" (Matthew 23:9).

Student: The Bible also says, "Honor your father and mother."

Dr. Hora: If we honor someone, we do not cling to that individual. If we cling to another, we worship him or her. It is not valid to have "two masters" to worship; it leads to existential anxiety.

Student: When there is existential anxiety, it seems at that point we are willing to consider the idea that God is our Mother. But it seems easier to cling to the old than to go through the experience of that anxiety.

Dr. Hora: Yes, but look at all the problems and symptoms, year in and year out, that you are suffering. What is an asthma attack? What is it saying? It says, "I can't stand living with my mother—she suffocates me—but I cannot live without mother because then I would die." So one has a choice between suffocating or dying.

Student: Am I suffocating because I haven't been able to die yet?

Dr. Hora: Very close relationships are suffocating. We cannot let go because then we would perhaps die and be alone in this big universe!

Student: But we are alone anyway.

Dr. Hora: We are never alone.

Student: But there is the fear of being alone.

Dr. Hora: Of being alone or suffocating. What is asthma? Asthma is the body's statement about an oppressive, suffocating relationship with another. Every symptom is a statement about a relationship—the more intense the relationship, the more symptoms.

Student: For many years, I blamed my mother. I can now see how ridiculous the whole thing is.

Dr. Hora: You and your mother are "in this together."

Student: Yes.

Dr. Hora: I understand that you even know each other's thoughts—that is real closeness, a telepathic connection.

Student: What is the valid way to see a situation like that?

Dr. Hora: To understand that "only God's thoughts constitute our true being." Remind yourself of this: mother is not God— God is Mother and Father. What is the healing remedy to attachments? The healing remedy to attachments is forming a better attachment. What is a better attachment?

Student: Being attached to God.

Dr. Hora: Exactly. How can we become attached to a nondimensional Entity?

Student: Maybe through understanding the idea of "dwelling in the secret place of the Most High"(Psalm 91)—in consciousness, in thought.

Dr. Hora: Yes. It is interesting that the Buddhists talk a great deal about this problem with attachments. Zen training is particularly oriented toward helping its students to realize non-attachment. But if we try to live without attachments, then we become self-reliant, and that has its problems too. God cannot be ignored. If we try to ignore God, then we make ourselves into God, and that is not existentially valid. But if we are attached to God cognitively, rather than religiously, then this is ultimate freedom.

Student: How is this accomplished? You said that each demonstration of God's sustaining power strengthens our understanding and that, little by little, we see more and more that we can rely on God. But is this the answer to the question of how we become attached to something nondimensional?

Dr. Hora: The Bible puts it this way: "Acquaint now thyself with him, and be at peace: thereby good shall come unto thee" (Job 22:2 1). Every little bit of good that comes unto us helps us to let go of invalid attachments. When we let go, the everlasting arms of Love will catch us. Then we are free, and it is all effortless—we are constantly being inspired with intelligent ideas, spiritual energy, love, and joy.

Student: You said, "if we are attached to God cognitively, rather than religiously." Does "cognitively" refer to having ideas about God?

Dr. Hora: No, it refers to knowing—we must come to know God—it is not enough to know about God. If we are religious, then we know about God. But existential knowing means that we must actually realize the reality of God, so that we have a cognitive awareness of God, rather than just a belief in God.

Student: Will knowing God really lead us to attachment?

Dr. Hora: Knowing God will give you more than attachment—it is at-one-ment. Where there is an attachment between a mother and daughter, what are they trying to do? They are trying to realize at-one-ment. And when people are sexually drawn to one another, they are trying to realize an at-one-ment. This is just a symbolic representation of the real at-one-ment. It is not the real thing, and if you take it for the real thing, you will be left with an attachment and a lot of trouble. Now if a man and a woman get attached to each other and are one in the sexual act, does that make them whole? Hardly. No, it is just a symbolic act indicating a yearning in all of us for at-one-ment with God.

Student: Is that the "meaning" of the seeming power in sexual attraction?

Dr. Hora: Sexual attraction has a tremendous power when there are other motivations working; this kind of sex is compulsive sex. Some people are driven to sex because it has another meaning for them—it is a way of coping. There are many, many kinds of distortions entering into the sexual act. Sex is not a physical act—it is a mental problem. But real fusion is spiritual and occurs when we realize that we are individual aspects of divine Consciousness. Jesus said: "I and my Father are one" (John 10:30). The Bible also says: "Thy Maker is thy husband [wife]" (Isaiah 54:5). This is the "mystical union." When someone is sufficiently enlightened to realize his at-one-ment with God, it is called the mystical marriage.

Student: Jesus also said: "In the resurrection, they neither marry nor are given in marriage, but are as the angels which are in heaven" (Mark 12:25). What did he mean?

Dr. Hora: He was just saying that in this human scene, marriage and being "given in marriage" are symbolic expressions of the "real thing," where we are at-one with God. We just do not know it yet, but we must realize it. The realization of at-one-ment is the meaning of what is called the "mystical union." If we are enlightened, we do not need to get married, unless we want to. We are completely God-sustained, and we are conscious of it. We are all God-sustained—without God there is no life—but we are not aware of it. We are all divine consciousnesses, individualized aspects of infinite Mind, but we do not know this. So we make all kinds of foolish arrangements and cling to things, and we have interactions resulting from this—and you know what interaction does.

Student: How do we lose sight of our bodies?

Dr. Hora: "How" is an operational question. The Sixth Principle of Metapsychiatry says, "If you know what, you know how." If you know what the body is, then you will know that it is not what it "seems to be." What is the body made of? Flesh and bones? No, the body is made of thoughts. It is not made of material substance—the body is "thought appearing as form."

Student: What is the purpose of the body?

Dr. Hora: It has a purpose. What is the purpose of darkness?

Student: To help us to see the light.

Dr. Hora: To help us to see that we are not what we "seem to be"—we are something else.

Student: What does it mean when Jesus referred to his body as a "temple"?

Dr. Hora: A temple is a structure where God is worshiped. The body is a seeming structure where God can be worshiped by becoming aware of God.

Student: Do thoughts automatically take on form?

Dr. Hora: Thoughts have a tendency to take on form.

Student: Does the body represent a fantasy that our parents had about us? Do we continue to have a body because we also continue to think these thoughts?

Dr. Hora: There are thoughts that come to us from God, and there are thoughts that come to us from the "sea of mental garbage."

Student: You have explained that the purpose of the body is to establish a contrast through which we can see the nonmaterial. Just as darkness enables us to see the light, the experience of the body enables us to see spirit.

Dr. Hora: Yes.

Student: Is the purpose of the body to help us see?

Dr. Hora: Yes, to see nondimensional Reality.

Student: For me, the reverse is true. The body makes it almost impossible to see anything else. In other words, if we didn't exist in this material form, it seems that it would be easier to come to know God. But because I can see and touch and feel the body, it makes it impossible to say that the body is not real.

Dr. Hora: It is all in how we "slice" it. If we are attached to materialism, then we cherish the material "feel" and appearance of the body. As long as we have this attachment to the tangible and to the dimensional, it is a stumbling block on our way to enlightenment. But when we begin to realize that the body is going to torture us as long as we cherish it—it will give us pleasure, but it will also give us pain—then we will begin to change our viewpoint on physical existence, and healings will come. That is why Jesus healed people—he wasn't trying to set up a medical practice or be a physician through healing people. He was showing them that the body is not what it "seems to be." Any time we have a physical healing, through understanding the "meaning" of a symptom, we understand that the body is thought. Then the body will help us to go beyond it. If we are stuck and attached to the body, then it will be a stumbling block to our spiritual progress. The interesting thing is that the more we cherish the body, the more susceptible we will be to all kinds of illnesses.

Student: If we can see our bodies as "temples," or as "God's opportunity," as a "place" which reveals where our ignorance lies, will that help us lose sight of the importance of the body?

Dr. Hora: Yes, and then we learn to transcend the body and come to appreciate nondimensional Reality.

Student: If we have a pain, and we ask the First Intelligent Question, "What is the meaning of what seems to be?" does that start the transcendence process?

Dr. Hora: Yes. Medical science is enamored with the body; it researches and studies the body in microscopic detail. If you call a doctor during an asthmatic attack, he will examine you and will make a diagnosis that the problem is with the lungs. The symptom says that it is located in the lungs, so the assumption is that something is wrong with the lungs. But, if we study the condition with the help of the Two Intelligent Questions, then we see that it is not the lungs that are sick—the lungs are only telling us something about the thoughts of being suffocated by mother and about the attachment between yourself and your mother. Therefore, we do not have to give these lungs injections or operate on them—we just need to lose interest in the attachment between mother and daughter. And, indeed, the symptom disappears, and this reveals that there was nothing wrong with the lungs. This is how we discover that the lungs are just thoughts. What a glorious liberation it is to realize that we don't have to be victimized by the body—we just have to replace the invalid thought.

Student: Is the body helpful because it gets our attention?

Dr. Hora: The body is a language. It is the way a problem can speak to us, and if we can understand this language, we are greatly blessed. When we study phenomenology, we are learning to understand the language of the body—it always speaks about the same thing. What does the body say? It says, "I am involved in an interaction with someone." That is what the body says; it has a one-track mind!

Student: What are emotions?

Dr. Hora: Emotions are thoughts expressed organismically. They are also part of the language of the body.

Student: Science says that matter is energy, and Metapsychiatry says that thought is energy.

Dr. Hora: Yes, and Metapsychiatry goes a little further. It says that matter is thought, and thought is energy.

Dialogue No. 36

The Mystery of Evil

Student: Dr. Hora, I have difficulty in understanding what omniactive, divine Mind means. I know the words, but I cannot understand what they really mean.

Dr. Hora: The question is, Is there any dynamism in God, or is God just a dead lake? Is God dynamic or static?

Student: Both. I can imagine It is everything, but I cannot really understand it.

Dr. Hora: Well, it is difficult to understand. Does anyone understand what is meant by Omniactive, Infinite Mind—Love–Intelligence, All-Power, All-Presence—filling the whole universe? How can we make such statements? Isn't that just fancy talk? If God were not omniactive, then his creation would be made of stationary ideas, never changing, never having any impact on anything that is alive. Life itself is characterized by constant activity and dynamism. Think of the blood circulation, the heart, the breathing, the manifestations of life in individual humans and animals, even in plants and rocks; and think of the sea—consider the seas and the constant dynamic force of the movement of the seas—and the clouds and the celestial bodies— everything in the universe is in constant movement and activity. Everything is in perpetual motion, and this perpetual motion is a symbolic expression of the Omniactive Nature of the divine Mind.

Student: Why do you use the word "Mind"?

Dr. Hora: Mind is the source of ideas. We get our intelligence, wisdom, power and responsiveness from the divine Mind. We do not put it out ourselves. Everything is moving all the time; there is no stagnation. So God fills the universe and creates the universe and is the Source of Infinite Intelligence and creative ideas. That is why our understanding of God has evolved from a tribal Jehovah, a king, a judge, an animal, and a person into a broad understanding of a dynamism of Love-Intelligence. Metapsychiatry speaks of God as infinite Mind, as Love-Intelligence. What is the practical value of having this kind of concept of God?

Student: We would know that anything that is discordant is illusion.

Dr. Hora: Could you explain that?

Student: If divine Mind, which is infinite Love and infinite Intelligence, fills the universe, there is in fact no room for anything else but It; and if anything else appears to be, it can't be anything but illusion.

Dr. Hora: How do we account for discord in the universe, in our experiences, in our lives? How do we account for that?

Student: It is the consequence of our inability to be at One with the divine Mind.

Student: And our ignorance that Omniaction is so. If we do not know that God is everywhere present, we do not experience it, and we do not see it anywhere.

Dr. Hora: Yes, but someone could say, "Look at the world, and what a mess it is in—wars, murders, crime, divorces, fights, suffering, the AIDS epidemic, tuberculosis—so much evil everywhere." How can we reconcile the discordant experiences that everyone has with our magnificent concept of God as infinite Mind, as perfect Love and Intelligence?

Student: We can see these experiences as being like dreams. We all have the experience of dreaming and creating imaginary universes and imaginary relationship situations, and we can all readily see that this is imaginary, once we are awake.

Dr. Hora: But who in his right mind would want to dream discordant dreams? How can we account for that? There are people who commit suicide, murder, beat up their wives, or get beaten up by their wives! It is a challenge to account for these experiences.

Student: We can see that if we are having invalid thoughts, these thoughts can result in certain difficult experiences or problems, so we can understand how all of the discordant things that you mentioned before can seem to exist.

Dr. Hora: Discordant experiences reveal that there is a great mystery in the universe—the mystery of evil. Here we are glorifying God with lofty concepts like infinite Love-Intelligence and speaking of creative wisdom, beauty, harmony, and joy. But someone could say, "Look at all the evil that is everywhere. Where do you see this wonderful universe?" All over, wherever we look—we read it in the papers, we watch it on television—we have rape, murder, crime, corruption, "wars and rumors of wars."

This is all very startling. There is a passage in the Bible where the disciples of Jesus showed him the buildings of the temple, and Jesus said: "See ye not all these things? Verily, I say unto you, there shall not be left here one stone upon another, that shall not be thrown down" (Matthew 24:1-2). This great, divine, individual expression of the good of God suddenly poured water over the enthusiasm of his disciples! He becomes like a negative skeptic—he was making a negative, discouraging remark that was not so much in his usual style of talking. What was he trying to say?

Student: That human, or personal, achievement is rapidly fleeting.

Dr. Hora: Yes, it is dangerous to be proud of your material accomplishments because they cannot last. What is wrong with being proud of material accomplishments? Why would he put it down like that?

Student: It is like worshiping a false god.

Dr. Hora: Who is this false god that is being worshiped when human accomplishment is being appreciated?

Student: It is "personal mind." It is saying that the intelligence necessary to accomplish these things finds its source in the individual.

Dr. Hora: Yes. You are saying that all these things that we admire are signs of someone's self-confirmatory activities. Self-confirmation, even if it is architectural, is self-destruction; it carries within itself the seeds of defeat. We started out clarifying our concept of God, and we came up against the mystery of evil. In order to understand a little better the mystery of evil and suffering, it is not enough for us to talk about God; we must also talk about the nature of his very strange creation. Human personalities which claim to be the "image and likeness of God," which go to church and pray, and think that they are God-fearing men, are committing crimes and cheating and lying and are involved in evil, discordant experiences. The Bible speaks of the "talking serpent," the one who "whispers" to human individuals that they should be like gods themselves. "For God doth know that in the day ye eat thereof," from the tree which is in the midst of the garden, "then your eyes shall be opened, and ye shall be as gods, knowing good and evil" (Genesis 3:3-5). Humans, starting with Eve, start bragging and showing off and confirming themselves, left and right, openly and covertly. The whole human race is full of self-confirmatory ideation. People are blowing themselves up and then collapsing. This goes on and on. So we could ask, "Did God make a mess of His creation?" It would seem so. People say that this is the "human experience," but it is hard for us to remain committed to appreciating God if our experiences are constantly contradicting the goodness of God because we are constantly running into manifestations of evil.

Student: But if God created a perfect world, then where did the serpent come from?

Dr. Hora: God created a spiritual universe. He did not create a "perfect world." The "perfect world" that we observe with our senses is a misrepresentation of the real universe. Anyone who is interested in becoming enlightened has to struggle for years with getting beyond "what seems to be." Unenlightened man is always being caught up in "what seems to be." Metapsychiatry says that that which "seems to be" is not; only that which is, that IS. So we ask, "Is you 'IS,' or is you ain't?" If you translate these important questions, what do we mean? Are you really aware of your true identity, created by God? Do you really understand that you are not what you seem to be? As a matter of fact, you are mostly what you seem not to be! It is like a game of hide and seek—we are constantly seeking to behold what we really are and what others really are. But it is hard to stay with that because something is constantly pushing itself into our field of vision which is only "what seems to be." Now you see it; now you don't— this is the dilemma of life. If we are seekers, we work hard, for years and years, to reach a level of awareness where the truth-of-being, our own and that of others, becomes clearer and clearer to us. How can we tell if we are really seeing more of the real man, or if we are just being fascinated by the millions of disguises of the phony picture of man? In Christianity, we would ask, "Is your Christhood showing? Is it getting manifested?" In Zen Buddhism, we would ask, "Are you known by your Buddha nature? Are you manifesting your Buddha nature?" which is the same as manifesting your Christhood. How can we tell whether someone is manifesting his Buddha nature or his Christhood and whether or not we have reached a point where we are clearly an individual Christ-consciousness or just a person who seems to be made of flesh and bone?

Student: By the awareness of PAGL [PAGL is an acronym for Peace, Assurance, Gratitude, Love, and Its Presence in consciousness informs us that we are in tune with the One Mind].

Dr. Hora: Yes, that is a very important distinction or gauge, but there is more. There must be more to Christhood than PAGL.

Student: Being a "beneficial presence?"

Dr. Hora: The Zen student who becomes a Buddha says, "Wherever I walk, even the dead trees come to life!" Just simply by looking in the mirror, you cannot tell whether you are already a Buddha or a Christ-consciousness. There are many manifestations of the right understanding of the truth-of-our-being. We can see evidence of spiritual blessedness; and in the midst of oceans of evil and ignorance and misery, we can see shining through a reality that transcends everything material. Since time immemorial, there have been uniquely gifted individuals who have been able to attain that quality of consciousness where it was clear that they existed on a higher level than the average individual. In their lives, things are good—just good—the "good of God" is manifesting itself through such individual consciousnesses. So now we have a complete view because we can see God, and we can see man created by God. Where we can see God and man as infinite, inseparable One, with no separation, then we can understand Reality, and we can understand unreality. Reality consists of God-confirmatory living. When a consciousness is in constant touch with infinite Mind, that individual becomes an infinite mind, and his very being is God-confirmatory. The vast majority of people and animals on this planet are self-confirmatory, and therein lies the problem. Jesus put it this way: "And this is the condemnation, that light is come into the world, but men loved darkness rather than light, because their deeds were evil" (John 3:19). He clarified this whole problem in one single sentence. This is the brilliance of his utterances—they are simple; they are short; and they are very clear.

Student: The "darkness" refers to self-confirmation?

Dr. Hora: Exactly. Self-confirmation and interaction thinking are the building blocks of the world. Every problem can be brought down to these common denominators.

Student: Dr. Hora, is the Omniaction that we see in nature acting the same in individuals? Sometimes we look to nature because there seems to be an order and a harmony there—you know what time the sun is going to come up, for instance. But when it comes to us, it seems as if we have a choice not to enter into that harmony.

Dr. Hora: Nothing in the material universe is really harmonious. There is no perfection in an imperfect, material universe—not the planets, not the moon, not the stars—they are all manifesting imperfection because God did not create a material universe. The material universe is an "appearance world." God created a spiritual universe and "peopled" it with spiritual ideas of Himself. We admire and cherish nature, and we wish to preserve it because it is good. There is much beauty and goodness there, but there are the same problems of evil—animals feed on each other, and there are storms and earthquakes, which are erroneously called the "anger of the Lord." The "appearance world" claims to be a reality apart from God, but it is not really. In Metapsychiatry we speak of "symbolic structures." The material world is made up of symbolic structures pointing beyond themselves toward a spiritual, perfect creation. Anything material can never be perfect, but it can point toward perfection. So the way we seem to be—with our flesh and bones and our "personal minds"—we are not so perfect! But there is the potential to evolve into a conscious awareness of God's perfection within us as the Christ-consciousness. The whole process of enlightenment is a journey from a sense of personhood to a sense of Christhood.

Student: Dr. Hora, would you clarify the relationship between fear and peace? I have read where you have said that we cannot progress beyond our compulsions without being able to confront fear. We are "scared to be afraid" or something to that effect. I assume that I ought to be peaceful all the time, but I am not. Therefore, that passage was encouraging. It seemed to me at one point that it was perhaps a positive thing to be afraid, to face the fear. What is the relationship between peace and fear?

Dr. Hora: Before we answer that, we must bring to your attention that when we say we "ought" to be peaceful, we are talking about a "should." If we say to ourselves, "I should be peaceful; I should be enlightened; I should be Christlike; I should manifest the Buddha nature," therein lies the fear. Fear is the experience of wanting: it is irrational, unjustified, and self-confirmatory. You see how tricky it is—"I ought to be. . . ." People study and read the Bible and then develop the idea that they "should" be holy or "should" be able to accomplish walking on water—this is very popular! Our problem is that we do not understand the Second Principle of Metapsychiatry, which says: "Take no thought for what should be or what should not be; seek ye first to know the good of God, which already is." So we cannot say, "I want to be Christlike; I should be peaceful; I should be a realized man." Unfortunately, religions and the Ten Commandments are full of "shoulds" and create difficulties in well-meaning people by setting up certain strivings. This is not helpful. The Second Principle makes it clear that what is helpful is the "Prayer of Right Knowing": by acknowledging "what really is," we become that which really IS. But by thinking that we "should" become it, we won't, and we will get caught up in fearfulness. And then religion becomes very strenuous and difficult and frustrating.

Student: So a student of Metapsychiatry isn't necessarily more peaceful?

Dr. Hora: Well, he doesn't agitate himself by wanting—wanting is always a mistake—there is nothing to want. God has already created us perfect as spiritual ideas of Himself, so we are not talking about becoming something different from what we seem to be now; we are talking about knowing the truth of what "already is." That is what we mean when we are joking here and ask, "Is you IS, or is you ain't?" "Is you 'IS,' or is you just trying to become?" There is nothing to become: each of us already is. We say, "We are here for God." We do not say, "I want to be here for God," or "I will be here for God, after I finish my apple pie." We keep acknowledging, "I am here for God," and we do this until it becomes a reality. The Bible says it this way: "Commit thy way unto the Lord" (Psalm 37:5). Right now! This is the "Prayer of Right Knowing." We dwell in the timeless now; then there is no fear. If there is no time, then fear has no place to be.

Student: During the process of this realization, we might have to work through fear?

Dr. Hora: Work through fear? How do you do that?

Student: By being aware that maybe we have done something that raises in us a sense of abandonment, something that has made us sense our separation.

Dr. Hora: So we are sinners.

Student: Sometimes we think we are.

Dr. Hora: But God never made a sinner. We do not have to be individuals who are going to "be here for God," who have separated themselves from God and are now going to rejoin God. That is the meaning of the word "religion": religion means "to reestablish the tie" between God and man. If you are trying to achieve that, you will live in fear all the time, lest perhaps time might run out before you could succeed in this project. It is not something that can be done. We just have to become aware that there has never been existence apart from God—nobody has ever succeeded in separating himself from God. If you could do that, you would have more power than God!

Student: Sometimes I feel that I have let other people down, not necessarily God. What do we do with that sort of anxiety or fear?

Dr. Hora: We can fear that we have let other people down, which only means that we see ourselves as someone who is capable of letting somebody else down. God has never made such a man. You are just living in a dream that you are a bad person, and you have hurt some other person by letting him or her down. Now you are dreaming. When we pray the "Prayer of Right Knowing" with utmost sincerity, we discover that we have never been apart from God, that it is an impossibility. We are already, and are for all eternity, an inseparable aspect of infinite Mind. Where can you go from infinity? We have to come to know the Truth: "Ye shall know the truth, and the truth shall make you free" (John 8:32). It shall make you "free" of fear and of evil and of sickness and of suffering and of relationships—and of self-confirmation. Self-confirmation doesn't make any sense because "You ain't never was nothing!" That is the great value of praying and meditating on "right-knowing." Today we went into great detail about becoming acquainted with God and his creation and the millions of things that "seem to be" but aren't. The mystery of evil is an illusion. God never made evil. But religious teachings throughout the world in all denominations are very confusing, because mankind is confused. That is the function of the serpent—or whatever we call this illusory source of evil—to create confusions and divisions and fears and "wars and rumors of wars" and strife. It is just fantastic.

Student: What happens where it seems you have let someone down or haven't lived up to another's expectations? We have learned to turn to God, but how does the understanding we gain help them? They are still left with the hurt.

Dr. Hora: We do not help anyone. Jesus said: "Of mine own self I can do nothing. . . . The Father that dwelleth in me, He doeth the works" (John 5:30; 14:10). What does this mean? How can the Father dwell in a person like Jesus? How can that help other persons? It is very important to understand these very simple and brilliant utterances which he gave us. It is absolutely fantastic to consider. He just simply said: "I and my Father are one . . . I am in the Father, and the Father [is] in me" (John 10:30, 38). It is "the Father that dwelleth in me, He doeth the works" (John 14:10).

If you would want to become a "beneficial presence" because you recognize that this is God's requirement, then you have to ask yourself, "What is this individual who is able to manifest the quality of the 'beneficial presence' in the world?" When the Zen student walked around after his enlightenment and the "dead trees came to life," he wasn't becoming an arborist—he wasn't going out to fix the trees that were dead—and he had no intention of producing miracles. The individual who is imbued with the qualities of God is the miracle—the quality of his presence is such that good things can happen around him. So if you want someone to be healed, you make sure that you are imbued with the Father, that your consciousness is brimming over with Love-Intelligence. This will take care of everything. We cannot intend the works of God—we are the works of God. We just have to become conscious of it, and then good things happen. We do not say, "Tell ya what I'm gonna do!"

Student: Didn't Jesus have intentional desires when he was healing people?

Dr. Hora: When individuals appealed to him for a healing, he would sometimes touch them and remind them that God is present and can heal them. By virtue of his consciousness, the love of God communicated itself to any individual who reached out to him. There is a scene in the Bible where a hemorrhaging woman sneaked up behind Jesus and just touched the hem of his garment and was suddenly healed (Matthew 9:20-22). This is a symbolic story which says that when we come into contact with an individual whose consciousness is filled with divine Love-Intelligence, then something good will happen. You cannot prescribe what God should do to someone, but good things happen simply by virtue of the fact that God is a Cosmic Principle of perfection, goodness, wisdom, compassion, and love. There is nothing intentional here. You cannot be intentional in this area of thought—you are just a presence. You are not a person who wants something or does not want something or who wants to correct something or improve something. Nothing! There is just "IS-ness."IS-ness is our business!"

Dialogue No. 37

Work

Student: Dr. Hora, I have a question about being "in" the world but not "of" it, and it has specifically to do with work. It seems that whether one is an accountant, an engineer, or whatever, the more energy one spends in learning the trade or profession and in actually applying it, the better one is at that profession. Yet there seems to be a point where the profession becomes an end in itself, as opposed to a means of earning a living. My question is, How does one work and do a good job, so that the work is a means of earning a living and does not become an end in itself?

Dr. Hora: Yes. Does everyone understand this question?

Student: A very good question.

Student: Most of us use our jobs for self-confirmation, and without this we seem lost. The issue is, If work is not for self-confirmation, then what is it for?

Dr. Hora: Some people identify themselves with their work. They say, "I am a teacher." "I am a CPA." "I am a lawyer." "I am a doctor." "I am this," or "I am that." God never made such people. Our occupation is not our identity, but most people think that it is. Has Metapsychiatry answered this question before?

Student: "We work for money, and we live for God."

Dr. Hora: So you know the answer.

Student: I know the words!

Dr. Hora: Is this principle difficult to put into practice?

Student: If you are looking for self-confirmation from your job, and if you really do think the skill is who you are, then it is.

Dr. Hora: Yes, people who identify themselves with their work are in trouble at the time of retirement or unemployment. They are completely lost. It is as though they have been annihilated.

Student: That is why many people die when they stop working.

Dr. Hora: Yes. It is very important to know that we are "here for God"—that is our real "job." Everything else is just a means of earning enough money to have a certain standard of life, as good a one as possible. But are we just working for money? Now actors and actresses have a terrible problem because they get a lot of ego gratification from their work. Anyone who seeks to get ego gratification from work is living dangerously. It is like dancing on a tightrope: the moment we are not getting praise or medals, compliments or promotions, we are in trouble.

Student: There is a temptation to take credit for the work, and others certainly like to give us credit for our work. It is hard to pass the credit along to God.

Dr. Hora: Unless we have learned to "be here for God," we have no place to go. Most people have no idea what it means to "be here for God." They get stuck in their jobs, and then if there is no inflow of ego gratification from the job, where do they go? They go to the corner bar to get drunk, or they get into drugs or sexual excesses or adventures, seeking somehow to bolster their egos.

Student: Or they get depressed.

Dr. Hora: Yes.

Student: Is that just anger?

Dr. Hora: Repressed rage and hopelessness. It is extremely important to learn to be "here for God"—to live for God and to understand that we are emanations of God, and this is our reality. That knowledge is a great protection, and it gives us a solid grounding in life. Now what does it mean "to be here for God"? How do we "do" it? Is it practical?

Student: "Being" is the important word here, and it has something to do with the quality of consciousness with which we wake up and go through the day. I suppose it means trying to live life in a spiritual way, not "judging by appearances."

Dr. Hora: Isn't it boring?

Student: I find it boring at times, but that is because of a lack of understanding. I do have problems with it, where I think it is not fun.

Dr. Hora: That is a common experience. When we try to learn to be "here for God," we find our lives becoming boring.

Student: Is there a "meaning" to that, the thought that it isn't fun or that it is boring?

Dr. Hora: Life without ego gratification is boring.

Student: Even if it is the real thing? It would seem that if we really and truly are "here for God," it would not be boring.

Dr. Hora: How can you be sure?

Student: Can we define boring?

Dr. Hora: Yes, boredom is a desire for excitement and self-confirmatory experiences—a "hunger and thirst" after unrighteousness.

Student: I would think that if there is real understanding, one wouldn't experience boredom. There would be peace and harmony, and you couldn't ask for more than that.

Dr. Hora: How do you get it?

Student: By coming to know who and what you really are.

Student: By accident, sometimes.

Dr. Hora: By accident?

Student: Occasionally there are periods of such peace and tranquility that one can only appreciate them after they are over. I have known these, and I will take that kind of boredom anytime—it wasn't really boredom.

Student: Logically, we know that we have to come eventually to a right understanding. We have to come to an appreciation of "being here for God," and that seems to require work.

Student: Doesn't boredom imply wanting?

Dr. Hora: Yes, wanting ego gratification and excitement.

Student: Is being interested in doing a good job part of "being here for God"?

Dr. Hora: "Doing" a good job is an operational concept. But certainly, there is nothing wrong with being a "beneficial presence" at work.

Student: Doesn't being a "beneficial presence" ever look like "doing?" Does that mean one just sits and prays?

Dr. Hora: A "beneficial presence" is like an Airwick. Do you know what an Airwick is?

Student: It enhances the atmosphere.

Dr. Hora: There is a little bottle and inside it is a little wick. You pull out the wick and set down the bottle, and soon the whole atmosphere is cleared up. That is what a "beneficial presence" is—he doesn't "do" anything, but everything around him becomes placid and harmonious, loving and good. "In thy presence is fullness of joy" (Psalm 16:11). That is what a "beneficial presence" is.

Student: You raised the question of boredom. It seems that if one were a "beneficial presence," it would be impossible to be bored—the ideas seem to me to be mutually exclusive—because if one is bored, that is an indication that he or she is not "being here for God."

Dr. Hora: That's right. Now how do we get there? In everyday life, we have to "do" many things, but we must not think in terms of operationalism. We each have to become an Airwick. How can we become Airwicks and still do all the things that need to be done?

Student: How do we make the transition from doing to being?

Dr. Hora: That is a good question. Who can answer it?

Student: I read right before today's group, that all Love and Intelligence flow from the one source—the spiritual Consciousness. We could be interested in understanding that whatever we appear to be "doing" is, in Reality, Love and Intelligence flowing through us, and the rest, "what seems to be," is not. It may look as if nature is the source of the sunset, but the beauty is really God's. Work may look like something we are doing, but God is all that really is.

Dr. Hora: Sounds very good.

Student: But how do you get from "sounds very good" to seeing it?

Dr. Hora: What did Jesus mean when he said, "the Father that dwelleth in me, He doeth the works" (John 14:10)?

Student: When we say that it is "the Father that dwells in me who does the work," maybe it means that some aspect of spiritual Reality has been realized, like order. Order is a spiritual value that we can come to appreciate, and as we value order, it starts to do its work and becomes orderliness. You can actually see the spiritual value of order, which is an attribute of spiritual Reality "doing" the work of orderliness.

Student: But what if we think we need recognition for being orderly or doing a good job at work? What if I think that I need recognition to survive?

Dr. Hora: Do we need recognition to survive?

Student: I think so, probably.

Dr. Hora: What is recognition? It is ego gratification. It is important to call a spade a spade, because our society has accepted recognition as a positive value.

Student: That is the point—that is what we have grown up with—that you do what you do for recognition. There are some people who may do what they do just for money.

Dr. Hora: Some people make money for recognition. I once heard a psychiatrist say, "I'm a one-hundred-dollar-an-hour psychiatrist." He was making money for recognition.

Student: There are a lot of values that the world says are the right values to have, but they don't work. The world says it is the right value to want to be recognized in your work, to work for recognition, but it doesn't work ultimately.

Dr. Hora: We don't use that word "recognition," because it has become socially acceptable. It is a respectable word, according to our culture, and it is also socially acceptable to work for recognition. We think that we need recognition—psychology has elevated recognition to a level of respectability—but if we call a spade a spade, it is more effective. Ego gratification is not so respectable anymore. What is the trouble with ego gratification?

Student: You can't get enough of it.

Student: But how can we recognize that it is truly invalid to desire ego gratification? Do we have to suffer from it? It seems to be a very difficult issue to let go of.

Dr. Hora: It was just explained: there is never enough of it.

Student: So people keep trying and keep getting it.

Dr. Hora: Yes, and then they could get fat, or they could reach out for newer forms of ego gratification—from food they could graduate to drugs or to alcohol, to beer and champagne and to bragging—there are endless possibilities for self-confirmatory behavior. We could ask, "What is wrong with self-confirmation? It feels good, and if it feels good, it cannot be bad." This is the commonsense, rational reasoning that deludes us into believing that whatever feels good cannot be bad. We hear this all the time.

Student: But when it does feel bad, we don't necessarily connect it with a self-confirmatory mode of being-in-the-world.

Student: That seems to be the important point, that we are not really willing to isolate what the issue is. We blame it on the weather or anything else, but we don't really associate it with the self-confirmatory interest that is the problem. So what leads us to become willing? I guess it is calling a spade a spade—to see what the issue really is. But what allows that?

Dr. Hora: In Metapsychiatry, we have a saying: "Self-confirmation is self-destruction, and self-destruction is self-confirmation." It is just existentially invalid. It is all right to work for money, but it is not all right to earn money for self-confirmatory reasons. We can get ego gratification from earning a great deal of money. It is all right to earn as much money as we can, but do not make it into an ego trip—be grateful for it as a blessing. That is the way Metapsychiatry looks at life—"We work for money, and we live for God." A "beneficial presence" is "here for God." What is the value of being a "beneficial presence"?

Student: It is crucial—being a "beneficial presence" is the answer to everything we have been discussing. Sometimes with these ideas, it happens that we have heard them so much and read so much and said so much, and yet we need to ask a simple question, How is one to be a beneficial presence? It is almost as if we don't know the answer.

Dr. Hora: Yes, it is difficult to put it into words because the danger is that we will run into intellectualization or operationalism.

Student: Would there be a conscious recognition of being a "beneficial presence," or would that in itself be self-confirmatory?

Dr. Hora: Yes, exactly, it would be.

Student: So, we would not be aware of it?

Dr. Hora: We would be aware of it, but we would not dare to say it.

Student: Because we cannot "do" it—and yet you say we can be aware of it?

Student: Wouldn't it be that we would be aware that all things were "working together for good"? Not necessarily that we were doing anything, but just that everything seemed to be working harmoniously.

Dr. Hora: Yes, that is one of the signs.

Student: "The dead trees come to life."

Dr. Hora: Yes.

Student: Oh, so it is more of an observation of what is taking place?

Dr. Hora: Yes. The air is cleaner wherever we are. There is no pollution—there is harmony. If we are thinking of someone, the telephone rings, and the individual is calling us on the phone; we don't even have to dial. All kinds of interesting things happen. A "beneficial presence" must reach the point where he understands incorporeal life. What is that?

Student: Spiritual qualities, nondimensional life.

Dr. Hora: Right. Is it possible that there can be life apart from the body? This is a difficult question to answer sincerely, but it is crucial for a "beneficial presence" to understand it. Extra corporeal life or incorporeal life—how is that possible?

Student: We transcend the body, rise above it.

Dr. Hora: We are so anchored in a physical sense of personhood that it sounds inconceivable to claim that we really are not physical persons living in the body, and that we really are living in divine Consciousness as individual aspects of that Consciousness. It is like this: suppose you are standing at the beach and you look at this infinite ocean, but you see a lot of garbage in the ocean—you see the waves, but you also see pollution and dirt. Now the pollution is not part of the ocean—it is in the ocean, but it is not the ocean. It has nothing to do with the ocean; it is just garbage. It seems that the pollution is part of the ocean because it is in the ocean, but it is not the ocean—it is entirely separate from the ocean. The waves are part of the ocean; they are not separate from the ocean—the waves are the ocean, and the ocean is the waves. But the garbage floating in the ocean is in the ocean, but it is not the ocean—it is no part of the ocean. Is this clear?

Student: Yes.

Dr. Hora: So there you have it—there is something in the ocean, but it is not the ocean. There is the ocean, and there are the waves—and the waves and the ocean are one. God, infinite Mind, is the Ocean, and this infinite Ocean has an infinite number of wavelets in It. Some are bigger and some are smaller, but they are all individualized aspects of the Ocean. So the wave is the Ocean [and it is made of the same substance as the Ocean]. We could say waves are individualized aspects of the Ocean, emanating from the Ocean, but the garbage, the pollution and the debris, is no part of the Ocean. Enlightened man sees that he is not a material piece of flesh and bone—this is only what he "seems to be," and it is no part of God. We, as individual consciousness, are an aspect of God because God is infinite Mind, divine Consciousness. So if you are looking for the truth-of-your-being—and you would like to know who you really are and not just what you "seem to be"—then you may, by the grace of God, come to the realization that you are not this physical appearance, that you are an individualized wavelet on the infinite Ocean of Love-Intelligence. You are not a physical person—you are a consciousness dwelling in incorporeal Life, entirely apart from the body, even though the body seems to be floating around like debris on the Ocean.

Student: How is consciousness an aspect of divine Consciousness but not the rest of us?

Dr. Hora: Consciousness is not material—it is spiritual—and the physical appearance, man, is just a phenomenon. The phenomenon seems to have form, but it is just a thought. We are just "garbage" floating around on the Ocean, except that this garbage is a special kind of garbage—it can observe itself, and it can eventually come to know its own nothingness.

Student: What about evolution?

Dr. Hora: Well, if you reach the point of understanding what was just explained, that is evolution.

Student: It seems to me that the physical form is so busy coping with the garbage, that it has to evolve in order to cope in the physical world.

Dr. Hora: What is the physical world?

Student: There were the dinosaurs, at the beginning . . .

Dr. Hora: You are mixing the Darwinian theory of evolution with spiritual evolution. We are talking about spiritual evolution and about evolving into a realization of incorporeal life; in order to be a "beneficial presence" in the world, this must be realized. It is not something we can do overnight, but if we keep at it, by the grace of God, we can realize it. Then we see that we were never born; we never had any parents; we will never die, and we are "hid with Christ in God," which means that the Christ-truth of our self-identity as wavelets on the Ocean of God becomes clear. Now what happens when we really understand this? Something great must happen.

Student: One becomes "a focal point for harmony and spiritual blessedness."

Dr. Hora: Yes, we turn into Airwicks.

Student: Is a spiritualized consciousness a "beneficial presence"? Are they synonyms?

Dr. Hora: Yes.

Student: Is it correct, then, that if we reach a point of understanding what you just explained, we would no longer be identifying anymore with our work, and life would be fulfilling by virtue of this understanding? Or must we have some useful activity? Can life be fulfilling if we are not engaged in any material activity whatsoever?

Dr. Hora: Is the ocean engaged in any activity whatsoever? The ocean is Omniactive—it never stops moving. It is [a symbol for the divine] Omniactive Awareness. The "Ocean" is aware of Itself, and It is aware of the whole universe as an aspect of Itself. It is Omniactive Love-Intelligence. The Airwick doesn't seem to be doing anything, yet it is emanating some kind of substance into the environment that swallows up the impurities from the air. We don't see what it is doing; it is just there, but it is active as it is working. So it is with an enlightened individual—he does not seem to do much, but things are happening around him, good things in terms of qualities of life and healing and wisdom and love and peace and assurance and gratitude, and "dead trees coming to life."

Student: What about "symbolic structures"? Would they have more meaning at this stage of evolution?

Dr. Hora: By then this concept is obsolete. A symbolic structure is a helpful concept because it points beyond itself. For instance, it is consciousness that sees—it is not the eyes. The eyes are material structures, indicating the existence of the faculty of sight within this spiritual Consciousness which we call God. "The Eye of my eyes is open. . . ." We have a meditation on this which we call the Prayer of Glowing: "Now is the accepted time . . ." Now the Eye of my eyes is open; Now the Ear of my ears hears; Now the Mind of my mind knows; Now the Love of my love glows. "I and my Father are one . . ." A symbolic structure points beyond itself to the existence of incorporeal Life. It is "transcendent regard," which has the ability to see this Life beyond the physical, phenomenal world.

Student: Do we now have an answer to the original question about work? Can we be completely involved with our work as long as our motive is not self-confirmatory but God-confirmatory?

Dr. Hora: Motive, of course, is very important. But beyond motive, there are also levels of enlightenment, and we start on that journey toward enlightenment when we begin to learn how to "be here for God." The waves are here for the ocean, and the ocean is at One with the waves. So we must discover our Oneness with God, that we are aspects of God. As Jesus said: "Is it not written in your law, 'I said, ye are gods'?" (John 10:34). The Bible says that we are all gods. How is that possible? Have you introduced yourself lately, "I am God"?

Student: I am a godlet?

Dr. Hora: The answer was actually contained in the question regarding how to be "in" this world and not "of" it. We do our work as if we were human persons—we go on as in a charade or a dream, but we have also to go beyond the dream.

Dialogue No. 38

Progress

Student: It seems that whenever I realize I am making progress, I become frightened. I understand the "meaning," but I don't think I understand it well enough to be healed. Every time that I seem to make progress, I become frightened that I won't be loved, and I don't know where to go from there.

Dr. Hora: Don't tell anyone about it.

Student: I can see by the blessings occurring in my life that God loves me, but somehow it does not seem real. On the one hand, I can see God's blessings, but, on the other hand, there is also a fear.

Dr. Hora: Imagine that you get up early in the morning before sunrise. It is dark and you are sitting and looking out. Gradually, as the light dawns, more and more of the surroundings become visible. Would it be right to say, "I am making progress"?

Student: Is the error that I am taking credit for what I am able to see? Are you saying that becoming more aware is a natural unfolding?

Dr. Hora: It is unfolding, but it is not natural. In Metapsychiatry, we cannot really say, "I am making progress." It would be like taking credit for the "good of God," which is increasingly reaching our consciousness. So we are not "making progress." By the grace of God more and more of Reality is coming into view, and there is no fear connected with this expansion of vision.

Student: There can be fear only if we are taking personal credit for our progress.

Dr. Hora: It is always the personal perspective that creates our difficulties in life—the belief in personhood is the great stumbling block. Actually, the "person" is the devil that separates us from the right understanding of Reality. Jesus said: "For he is a liar, and the father of it" (John 8:44). Anyone who thinks he is a person is lying, and the lie keeps lying—"a liar and the father of it." Whenever we think, "I am a nice person," or "I am a progressing person," we are building a wall between ourselves and God. The concept of personhood is a wall, separating God. So we cannot say, "I am making progress." We can say, "It would seem that progress is happening"—things are getting clearer and better, blessings are in evidence—but we are not "making progress." We cannot take credit for anything; we can only be grateful for the progressive realization of Reality.

Student: What if someone wants to blame herself for everything? Is that simply a manifestation of self-confirmation?

Dr. Hora: Of course. Suppose you are sitting early in the morning and watching your environment, and it doesn't get lighter. Would you blame yourself? Of course not.

Student: The original question here today touched on the idea that we might not be loved if we make progress. What if progress is being made and you are still looking over your shoulder to see who is with you or not with you? We have discussed that when we enter into the land of PAGL, we go in one at a time, as individuals. But there is still the tendency to care about others, like your family or your spouse, hoping they will see your progress. This is a hard one to let go of.

Dr. Hora: What's the problem?

Student: Wanting to be liked, wanting people to agree with me and be encouraging, and they are not going to do that.

Dr. Hora: Now suppose you get up early, while it is still dark; and as you are sitting there, observing the dawn, while more and more light is appearing around you, will you think to yourself, "I wonder what people will think of me because of what is happening here? Will they stop loving me because the sun has risen?"

Student: I would probably think that.

Dr. Hora: This concern indicates that we are deeply rooted in seeing ourselves not in relation to God but surrounded by friends and enemies in a structure of interrelationships with other ignorant people, and that we are afraid that we may lose their affection because the sun has come up on the horizon—the light has increased around us. We think, "What will they think of me now that the darkness is gone?"

Student: They won't like me.

Dr. Hora: Isn't it amazing to think that? So don't ever get up early in the morning to watch the sun rise wondering what people will think of you if the sun actually comes up! In other words, we are constantly thinking about what others are thinking about what we are thinking. This is called being normal—it is absolutely insane to be "normal."

Student: It is filled with fear.

Dr. Hora: How can we explain that? What are we afraid of? What will happen if the sun actually rises?

Student: We are afraid that people might envy us or be jealous of us.

Dr. Hora: Because the sun has risen?

Student: Because of the thought processes—thinking about what others are thinking about what I am thinking. It is difficult to move from the dimension of interpersonalism to the metaphor of the sunrise, except when I am meditating. When I am meditating, it is wonderful—everything is gone; there are no people.

Dr. Hora: Where did they go?

Student: There is no attention focused on people. But then I get on the subway and go to work, and there are people everywhere.

Dr. Hora: And they are all thinking about the sunrise and how you are responsible for it!

Student: The way you have described the sun rising, you are talking about it as a metaphor for "what really is," aren't you?

Dr. Hora: What we are talking about is, "I am making progress." We are really saying, "I deserve credit for the rising of the sun."

Student: Is the intent of the metaphor to show us how ridiculous that idea is?

Dr. Hora: Yes.

Student: Then it is also ridiculous to be concerned about others. If we are seeing Reality and our loved ones are not seeing Reality, then it is ridiculous for us to be concerned because actually it is none of our business.

Dr. Hora: Of course. Everyone has the right to be wrong and the right to be ignorant and to live in darkness, and we have no right to interfere with it.

Student: So our concerns and worries—all those thoughts—are an interference.

Dr. Hora: Suppose you get up early in the morning while it is still dark and while most people are still sleeping—consider how many people might be up at the same time with you. This is an analogy of the way enlightenment occurs in some conscious-nesses, even while the vast majority of people live in darkness or dreams, not participating in that realization which you are undergoing. Are you responsible for the ones who don't get up in the morning to watch the sunrise? You are not responsible. Of course, you could wake them up, and then they would crucify you for it. How many times was I in danger of crucifixion while teaching Metapsychiatry! People who are sleeping do not want to wake up. Of course, I quickly stopped "teaching"—it is dangerous to be a teacher of Truth. It is all right to teach error. People like that, and you can become very popular; you could even wind up on television. It is interesting to observe that the more invalid some teachings are, the more popular they become, very quickly. Overnight you can become a very famous personality if you are sufficiently ignorant about whatever you are talking about. People like that because then they don't have to wake up—they can go on sleeping—it is very comfortable.

Student: It is clear that there are more blessings moving along this path; but then I tend to start looking around and wonder if I may be deceiving myself because there are times when it does make me seem different, and that can be disconcerting.

Dr. Hora: So you are afraid that if you get up early in the morning and actually participate in the great phenomenon of the dawning of the light and the sunrise, that people will notice that you have had this realization, and then they will attack you for it?

Student: That sounds so ridiculous!

Dr. Hora: Again it is personalizing the process of enlightenment. Of course, if you are a student of Metapsychiatry, making progress and becoming very wise, and are able to recite the Eleven Principles, people might say, "Look at her, what's happening to her? She's got something that we haven't got." But you know what was happening to her? Nothing. As long as you see yourself as a person who is undergoing some fabulous change, nothing is changing. If your consciousness has expanded and you are aware of the power of God and you can see the "good of God," spiritual blessedness, no one will notice it. Nothing will happen; there is no outward change—maybe you'll go to a better hairdresser! But no outward change will occur. People will notice if you have gone on a diet and lost weight—they may envy you and be jealous—that's a different story. But don't think of enlightenment as something external that will be immediately noticed by people around you— no one is interested, and no one will notice it—don't hope to be noticed. As a matter of fact, the more enlightened you are, the less interested you are in being noticed—you enjoy insignificance. The important thing is laughter.

Student: What is happening when it seems that the world is responding differently to us?

Dr. Hora: You are thinking about yourself—you are thinking about how other people are responding to you. It means that you didn't make any progress!

Student: The sun started to go up and then just stopped.

Student: Went back to bed!

Dr. Hora: Now you can see that it is really true, the story written about the monk who was studying Zen for thirty years. One day while on a walk in the garden, this monk kicked a pebble with his foot, and the pebble hit a bamboo tree. The bamboo tree gave out a sound of some kind, whereupon the monk had an attack of laughter. For two days he couldn't stop laughing—he almost died from it—and that was his enlightenment experience. If you look at it, it is really funny—the human condition is very funny.

Student: In the two days of laughing, he realized just how ridiculous everything is?

Dr. Hora: Right. It is very rare to laugh for two days nonstop.

Student: Did something change?

Dr. Hora: They thought he went crazy.

Student: What makes the ego so perverse? Every which way, this idea of wanting to take personal credit keeps coming up.

Dr. Hora: It comes from the collective belief of the human race that everyone is a person, autonomous and capable of functioning without God—this is the illusion of a selfhood apart from God.

Student: What if one tends to take his ignorance seriously?

Dr. Hora: What do you mean, assuming personal responsibility for it?

Student: Well, the illusion of selfhood apart from God seems to be the primal ignorance of all of us. The tendency for me is to see it as insurmountable, that the whole earth is covered with it, and to get serious about it. To be able to laugh would be great.

Dr. Hora: The second chapter of Genesis says: "There went up a mist from the earth . . ." and covered the whole territory "and watered the whole face of the ground" (Genesis 2:6). After that was when Adam discovered that he was a person. He didn't know it yet; he had not undergone the operation to get a woman out of his rib. He was still alone.

Student: What is the "mist" symbolic of?

Dr. Hora: Judging by appearances. It seems that we are autonomous units of intelligence and power and strength with personalities. There is a whole scientific system which studies man as a personality, and it is called psychoanalysis. It is like studying the structure of darkness. It is like fog, trying to rearrange the fog all the time, when it is nothing.

Student: Regarding the metaphor of waking up in the morning and watching the sunrise, my thought would probably be, "Oh, isn't it too bad I'm watching the sunrise all by myself." Sometimes that seems to be a problem, but it occurs to me that everything we learn about ourselves and our inseparability from God can be learned about everyone else at the same time.

Dr. Hora: So what's the point of your comment?

Student: Making progress on the spiritual path and doing away with the notion of personhood can actually be reflected by the people around you. Instead of excluding them or feeling sad that you are "separate," you might come to see that you are all part of divine Reality.

Dr. Hora: Yes. The Bible says that when we are sitting in the darkness and the sun comes up, the sun shineth on the enlightened and on the unenlightened equally. "For he maketh his sun to rise on the evil and on the good" (Matthew 5:45).

Student: What is the difference between the enlightened and the unenlightened individual?

Dr. Hora: Well, the unenlightened individual, who got up early in the morning and is watching the sunrise, says, "I wonder how I feel now? This makes me feel good—or makes me feel bad—the sun rising gives me a certain feeling about me and myself." That's the psychoanalytic way of watching the sunrise: "How does it make me feel?" The enlightened man says, "How glorious! God is great—here is beauty, harmony, light, freedom, joy, a wonder of wonders, divine Reality." That's the difference. The enlightened individual is looking to see God all the time, under all circumstances—his focus is on seeing God. The unenlightened individual says, "How do I feel, and how will others feel about me and what I am feeling? I wonder what they feel now about what I am feeling. It makes me feel so good." An advertisement in a psychiatric journal showed a teenager who was working on some carpentry, and the caption said, "It feels good to have good feelings about yourself." It was advertising some drug. Unenlightened man is looking for himself, and enlightened man is looking for God. That's the whole thing; that's all there is to it.

Student: But beauty makes you happy. It isn't possible to see something beautiful and not be happy. How can you really make sure that you are not making yourself feel good?

Dr. Hora: Happiness lets you see beauty—if you are not happy, you do not see beauty.

Student: But doesn't beauty also make you happy?

Dr. Hora: The truth is that happiness is and beauty, also, is, but we have to be able to appreciate them.

Student: But we can see beauty and be unenlightened.

Dr. Hora: For various people, beauty has a different meaning. There is a church in Barcelona whose architect was named Gaudí. It is the most hideous thing that an architect could possibly have conceived of—everything about the structure is so ugly that it almost makes your flesh creep. Gaudí became famous for this hideous church, and now people don't know whether it is beautiful or ugly because it was labeled as beautiful. If it is the official announcement by the church that this church is beautiful, then people are afraid to think it is ugly; but an enlightened individual can see that it is hideous. There are no redeeming qualities about any part of the structure, absolutely none. Coincidentally, Gaudí's architecture happens to be "gaudy." Beauty is that which is uplifting to the spirit; flowers are beautiful because they uplift the spirit.

Student: But you might not be enlightened and could still see that.

Dr. Hora: Yes, but most of the time you won't see it. It reminds me of the lady who came into this living room and went over to those flowers and smelled them and said, "You know, Dr. Hora, I always enjoy the flowers in this living room." So I said, "The flowers are not here for your enjoyment—the flowers are here to glorify God. They are not just an item of consumption to be inhaled by your nose." She assumed that they were "here for her" to enjoy, here to make her feel good. This is the basic approach of unenlightened life; it is a personal search for pleasurable experiences. But the enlightened way is always looking for God. If you look at the flowers in an enlightened way, you can see the smile of God—something uplifting, something reminding you that there is a God and that this God is glorious and gives meaning to life. Without God, life is just a continuous concern with self.

Student: How can we know that what we experience is not real?

Dr. Hora: Experiences are never real. Nothing that we experience speaks of Reality—Reality cannot be experienced. This is the Ninth Principle of Metapsychiatry: "Reality cannot be experienced or imagined; it can, however, be realized." Unenlightened man is forever looking for a better experience. This is called sense-existence, which is actually nonsense existence. The alternative to sense-existence is soul-existence. What is soul-existence?

Student: When we are living in the context of divine Consciousness and are concerned with what we are aware of and not how we "feel," that is soul-existence.

Dr. Hora: Right, exactly. As long as we are unenlightened we are always looking for a better experience, which means for a better dream. Experiences are thoughts perceptualized. What does that mean?

Student: That we know them through our senses.

Dr. Hora: Yes. We think something, and we begin to perceive it through our senses, and that we call an experience—we can "feel" it. What is drug addiction all about? It is a constant quest for experiences—everyone wants to experience good feelings, and we human beings are convinced that that is what happiness is, having good feelings.

Student: Coming back to fear, is that also an experience?

Dr. Hora: Yes.

Student: Is it a feeling?

Dr. Hora: It is organismic, and it is self-concern. We are involved with self, and then we suffer the feelings. Experiences can be pleasurable or painful or frightening.

Student: Dr. Hora, is life without feelings conceivable, or is it simply a question of not paying attention to them?

Dr. Hora: Is life without the body conceivable?

Student: It doesn't seem so.

Dr. Hora: It is the same way with feelings. We tend to say, "I feel; therefore, I am alive," but these are just experiences, and there will never be a time while we are seemingly in the body when we will not be aware of experiences. But we do not have to make a federal case out of them, because we understand that they are just dreams. An enlightened individual knows what is going on in the world, and he understands what people are looking for and yearning for and what they desire. But an enlightened individual will also be able to grasp St. Paul's words when he said that those things did not interest him anymore: "But none of these things move me, neither count I my life dear unto myself, so that I might finish my course with joy, and the ministry, which I have received of the Lord Jesus, to testify the gospel of the grace of God" (Acts 20:24). When he had reached a certain point of enlightenment he could say, "I can see these things, but that's not what really is." And we are interested in knowing "what really is." In order to know what really isn't, we have to know "what really is." Suppose we have a backache—we have to know that this really isn't, that it is only a thought. So if we really know "what really is," then we know what really isn't, and that helps.

Student: It heals what really isn't.

Dr. Hora: Exactly. God really is—nothing else. God's grace is all there is. Divine Love fills the universe, and if we would like to be enlightened and free of all the miseries of personhood, we have to learn to look constantly to see God everywhere. As an Indian philosopher said, "When you can see the Taj Mahal in a blade of grass, then you are enlightened." We do not worry anymore what our mothers and fathers will say. What does it mean to "see the Taj Mahal in a blade of grass"?

Student: It means that the most beautiful creation is everywhere, in the humblest of things.

Dr. Hora: When you can see beauty in a simple blade of grass, you are seeing the marvel of creation. You are seeing the Taj Mahal as an architectural masterpiece, as a jewel of beauty. The enlightened man does not see chlorophyll or brick and mortar— he sees the beauty and harmony, the marvel of divine Mind's creation everywhere. So when you get up early in the morning while it is still dark, make sure you don't miss the sunrise.

Student: It is so hard for us to understand that experiences are not real and to see that error is not real. I would like to share something with you. When I came here earlier today, I was in such pain that I could not lower myself into the chair to wait for my private session with Dr. Hora, so I stood. When I walked into Dr. Hora's office, I told him that I didn't think I was going to be able to sit down. Dr. Hora said, "There's nothing wrong with you." I told him that Monday I got a piercing pain in my back, and when I wasn't having piercing pain, it was a very hurtful ache. I knew it was an angry interaction thought, but I wasn't aware of the usual things that bother me. So I realized I must just be quiet and let the "meaning" reveal itself. In a little while, it occurred to me. I had taken my first piano lesson for the new term that day, and I had happened to run into the teacher from whom I had taken lessons a couple of years ago, and who had dismissed me the following year. I thought it was a friendly encounter, but it was the only thing that happened that day that seemed to have any significance.

I wondered if it was possible that I resented her dismissal and was not aware of it—perhaps I had just pushed the feelings down somewhere. I thought that maybe this was the meaning of the pain. I was praying the "Prayer of Correct Self-Identification" [offered at the conclusion of this dialogue] and I was trying to see myself correctly, but I was just miserable. I explained this to Dr. Hora, and he thought this discernment was on the right track. We discovered that I really had been very hurt when the teacher dismissed me, and I had pushed these feelings down. Dr. Hora said when I had related this little incident to him last year that I was strangely calm about it and showed no emotion or anything at the time. We discovered that the feeling of being hurt and rejected had been pushed down and repressed, and it had sort of lain there until now when I ran into the teacher. At my piano lesson, there was also something strange—my new teacher said that I was playing so much more freely than before—I felt so strange about playing at that lesson, and that is what made me think that seeing the other piano teacher, who had dismissed me, was the "meaning." Dr. Hora helped me to see that I am not a person who was rejected and cast aside. We discovered that this new teacher is a blessing to me, whereas the old teacher was really not a blessing and that I had also become very attached to her and was really hurt when she said goodbye to me. So I left our session and went outside and found that I was walking down the street without pain. Dr. Hora said that I had perceived being dismissed as a "bad" thing when, in fact, from the standpoint of Reality, it was really a blessing to be lifted away from an individual who wasn't good for me to someone who really loves music and is able to communicate that to me. What was occurring in divine Reality was a great blessing and something to be very grateful for. That is what healed me after the session while I was walking, that thought of being grateful for God's Omniactive Presence governing my life—it healed the angry interaction thought. So seeing "what really is" allowed the healing to take place.

Dr. Hora: Let us praise the Lord.

Metapsychiatry's "Prayer of Correct Self-Identification" endeavors to help us see ourselves correctly, beyond the appearance of flesh and blood, in order to realize Christ's words: "I and my Father are one." We are nondimensional transparencies through which God's presence is revealed—in all situations, under all circumstances—One with and inseparable from the divine Mind.

"I am what God is."
God is not a person—I am not a person.
God is Mind—I am intelligent.
God is Love—I am nonpersonally, nonconditionally benevolent.
God is Perfection—I am healthy.
God is infinite Mercy—I am compassionate.
God is Humor—I am laughter.
God is Peace—I am peaceful.
God is Life—I am vitality.
God is Goodness—I am generous (in thought as well as in deed).
God is Infinite—I am nondimensional spirit.
God is Joy—I am joyful.
God is the divine Parent—I am assured forever.
God is Eternity—I am "never born, never dying."
God is the only I AM—I am because God IS.

Regular devotion to understanding these ideas can lead individuals to realize enlightenment.

Overcoming Self-Confirmation

Student: Dr. Hora, it seems that everything we do could be interpreted as self-confirmatory—unless we really understand God. It is difficult because, just when I think I have understood something, another opportunity to confirm myself comes up! I am amazed at the intensity of this desire to want to confirm oneself—especially at work where there are so many people, and there is so much interaction. I would like to understand it better, so that it does not seem like such an arduous process. How do we get beyond the effort it seems to require of us?

Dr. Hora: Any commentaries on this problem?

Student: In the Metapsychiatric interpretation of the Lord's Prayer, the last line reads, "God-centered living is the only alternative to self-confirmatory ideation."

Dr. Hora: Yes. Now what is wrong with self-confirmatory living? Is there a law against it? This is a free country! Has this term been invented by Metapsychiatry to make your life miserable? Is it a cruel joke?

Student: It is just that if we are involved in self-confirmation it brings trouble.

Dr. Hora: Are you sure that this is really so?

Student: I am sure—that's the easy part.

Student: It seems as though we could even be involved in "good" self-confirmation. In Metapsychiatry we learn to express spiritual qualities. For instance, we are friendly because God is Love, which is a wonderful quality, but it seems that even those good, divine qualities get stuck in a sense of personhood. When it comes to manifesting these "good" qualities, there can be a problem because it can seem that we are "doing" it—or I see myself also as someone's son or as someone's friend and not as an expression of God. I don't know how to get beyond what seems to be "good" self-confirmation.

Dr. Hora: Well, whose son are you?

Student: I am God's son, but I cannot honestly say I have realized this truth. There is such a big difference between repeating the Principles we learn here, paying attention to them in prayer, and suddenly bursting through to that point of transition where we are living them. It is so easy to fool yourself into thinking, when you are praying and studying and meditating, that you are doing what is required by God. There must be something beyond this process where we can really become what we are learning, so that these ideas are not just something that we are praying about, but ideas that we really know and are.

Student: Dr. Hora, is that what you refer to as "actualizing the Principles"?

Dr. Hora: The Principles are actual. They reveal the nature of Reality, every one of them, but they do not need to be actualized—they need to be realized. Reality needs to be realized. When Reality becomes real to us, we have a "realization." Are we just playing with words here? There are "realized individuals," which is synonymous with enlightened individuals, and there are intellectually informed students of Metapsychiatry who know all about these things—they can even quote you verbatim— but they have not realized them yet; so they do not have the benefit of the knowledge. There are people who are skeptical about Metapsychiatry, and there are people who do not know anything about the ideas or Principles of Metapsychiatry, which constitutes the majority. In the realization process, we must first get the information; then we must study and seek realization, which appears as transformation. When we have realized the validity and the Truth that these Principles speak about, then we can be transformed. The Bible says: "If any man is in Christ Jesus, he is a new creature; old things are passed away, and behold, all things are become new" (2 Corinthians 5:17). How do we climb into Christ Jesus? What does it mean if anyone is "in Christ Jesus"? It means that he has undergone a transformation to the point that he is a new creature—he has new shoes, new clothes, a new hairdo! But this outer transformation is not what we're talking about—it is not enough. This transformation must be existential, and it will validate itself in a change in character, in style, in mode of being-in-the-world. And many of the vicissitudes of unenlightened life will disappear and not bother us anymore. "Get thee behind me, Satan," and don't bother me anymore! The inclination toward self-confirmatory ideation and behavior is the devil. It is always whispering to us, "A little bragging, a little bellyaching, a little gossip—it won't hurt you—almost everybody is doing it!" Like the teenager who says, "But, Mom, everyone is wearing these skirts!" People have an urge to conform and to go one better. If we just conform, we get lost in the shuffle; but if we conform and go one better, then we become outstanding—like a sore thumb! Now one thing is very mysterious: whenever someone yields to the temptation to think in self-confirmatory ways, be it any kind of issue, but essentially where there is a self-confirmatory element, very often somewhere in the body, a symptom will arise. There is no way of knowing where it is going to hit us, but invariably self-confirmatory ideation becomes manifest in the form of a symptom, a problem, a pain, an itch, a scratch, or an accident of some kind. Now how does the body know that the mind is involved in self-confirmatory ideation? I listened to a lecture on the radio this afternoon that featured a man who is an expert on consciousness. He said, "Consciousness is very mysterious, but I know that it is on a material basis. However, there is one thing that I don't know, how consciousness is connected with the body." He cannot figure this out, but he "knows" that consciousness is material— which means that he doesn't know anything. If we try to understand consciousness on a material basis, we don't get anywhere. Some of you have experienced healings of certain physical symptoms, but the connection between the symptom and the self-confirmatory ideation was not clear. You ask, "Why should I get a neck ache or an earache if I am thinking about how wonderful I am?" Most people don't understand how the body "selects" the symptom to go with the self-confirmatory thought. Jimmy Durante had the answer. He said, "The nose knows!" We can say that the body seems to know our innermost secret thoughts, and the body "speaks." A student of Metapsychiatry is learning to understand what the body is saying. It is always saying the same thing, "You are bragging; you are bellyaching; you are bullying; you are bullshitting; you are bickering"—that is what the body keeps saying—you're full of baloney! The body tells us what we need to know, and if we learn to listen to what the body says, we discover the remedy to the problem. The remedy is always to abandon self-confirmatory ideation and turn our attention to the truth-of-our-being. When we become more interested in the truth-of-our-being than in self-confirmatory ideation, we are released from the consequences of self-confirmatory ideation.

Student: How does the body know? I see that it knows the corresponding self-confirmatory thought, but how does it know?

Dr. Hora: How does the body know? The body is a language that can translate human thoughts into physical symptoms. It is like a computer when there is something on its screen—you can press a button, and the printer will know what is on the screen. If you have a migraine headache, how does the head know what the mind is thinking? If you get a charley-horse in your leg, how does the leg know what you were dreaming about, what your thoughts are? The answer is that the body and the human mind are just one phenomenon.

Student: Isn't there also something associated with the repression of thought? If you have an angry thought but you are fully aware of that thought, it doesn't express itself as quickly as a physical symptom because you are fully aware of the angry thought. It is the repression of it that seems to result in the appearance of the symptom, isn't it?

Dr. Hora: Yes, this dynamic is called somatization. If we have learned to be conscious of what we are thinking, day and night, then physical symptoms will be less likely—the thought does not hit us over the head, because we were already aware of it. It is very helpful, through the training of regular meditation, to develop the faculty of conscious awareness of our thoughts, day and night, whether asleep or awake. If we learn this, we will be spared many physical symptoms. Physical symptoms are very dangerous. What is the danger in physical symptoms?

Student: They lead us further and further away from God and closer and closer to material man, and then we are lost.

Dr. Hora: Yes, that is correct.

Student: I had a physical symptom for years that was finally healed. But I had a little backsliding toward certain thoughts that I had held all my life and that were invalid, and right in that spot where the symptom used to be—there is nothing there anymore—but right in that spot, I got a pain. I told Dr. Hora, and he said that the body remembered.

Dr. Hora: Yes, you have a very talented body!

Student: Asking how the body "knows" seems like a bit of a trick question, because it attributes a power to the body that really does not exist. We know that the body is simply a manifestation of thought; therefore, it is the thought that is the issue and not the body.

Dr. Hora: Yes, that is right, but this "trick" question is helpful. We are complaining, "Why can't I indulge myself a little bit in the office and show off and confirm myself as this wonderful person which I really am?" Isn't it cruel of Metapsychiatry to deprive us of the pleasure of self-confirmatory behavior? It seems like a great sacrifice, turning attention away from the self, but selfhood, which is apart from God, is an illusion. If we are confirming ourselves, we are nowhere—we are in an illusion, and we are an illusion—we are not in touch with Reality. It is dangerous to be out of touch with Reality. On the other hand, we think it would feel so good if we could just show off a little with a new dress, or hairdo, how beautiful we are! We are constantly being tempted. There is a universal inclination in humans to confirm themselves, to entertain self-confirmatory ideas. Now this is a "no-no," but if we cannot confirm ourselves, then what do we do? The Bible says that we have to commit ourselves to God: "Commit thy works unto the Lord, and thy thoughts shall be established" (Proverbs 16:3). Commit thy thoughts, thy motivations, thy interests—every thought, everything concerning yourself, has to be focused in on the "good of God." To that end, we have a gyroscope. The First Principle of Metapsychiatry is the "gyroscope" for us: "Thou shalt have no other interests before the good of God, which is spiritual blessedness." How is the First Principle moving us in the right direction? Self-confirmatory winds are blowing, and they keep dislodging our interest toward "self and others." Now the gyroscope keeps bringing the interest back to the "good of God, which is spiritual blessedness." The question is, What do you appreciate more, bragging or spiritual blessedness?

Student: Even after we see time and time again the fruits of spiritual blessedness, there is still a strong temptation toward self-confirmation.

Dr. Hora: Yes, on television and in the media, in society, at parties, these things are always shifting the direction of our interests toward the sphere of interaction thinking and self-confirmatory ideation—this is what the world consists of—and Jesus said we have to "overcome the world": "In this world ye shall have tribulation, but be of good cheer; I have overcome the world" (John 16:32). We have to overcome self-confirmatory ideation and interaction thinking. This is the value of a "spiritual gyroscope" in our lives.

Student: When we are trying to understand self-confirmatory ideation, do we need to look at the doubts that we have that this self, that seems so important, actually does exist?

Dr. Hora: If you have a doubt, you will agonize over it.

Student: It seems so natural to think that I am a self; if at some point I doubt it, then I might ask, "What am I if I am not a self?"

Dr. Hora: This kind of speculation comes later. The first thing to learn is: "Self-confirmation is self-destruction, and self-destruction is self-confirmation." Once you can see clearly that this is so, then you begin to lose interest in this kind of sense of self. Then your question becomes clearer. You cannot start out by saying, "There is no self—Hora says so. But I am not so sure; maybe there is." No, the best way to understand this problem is to experience the pain and the consequences of self-confirmatory ideation. When you have had several, painful experiences, and you can see the connection between them and your thoughts, then you are already understanding that here is something that appears to be completely human and normal, even desirable, but it is an enemy—it is dangerous and harmful and inevitably leads us to suffering. Once we can see that there is a direct connection between our problems and this type of self-confirmatory thinking, we can ask, "Where do I go from here?" You might ask, "Is it so bad to think that I am pretty or that I am smart or that I am better than the next guy?" There are a million ways that we can entertain self-confirmatory ideas, and invariably we will run into trouble with them. Once we understand this and have seen it and experienced it, seen that it is not theory or intellectual information, once we have tasted the bitter fruits of that kind of thinking, then we can say that entertaining self-confirmatory thoughts is not worth it. Many people, when they hit this dilemma, and realize that they are hurting, try to find another solution—through drugs or alcohol or sex or fighting, in millions of ways—avoiding the issue and getting deeper into trouble.

Student: If we were to examine our thoughts honestly from moment to moment, we would find ourselves all the time in self-confirmatory ideation, to the point where we couldn't stand ourselves!

Dr. Hora: So then you find a solution. Unfortunately, most people find the wrong solution. There is only one right solution: "Commit thy works unto the Lord, and thy thoughts shall be established" (Proverbs 16:3). We are here to manifest the perfection of God's Being—this is our purpose in the world, to manifest the perfection of God's Being. When we appreciate this truth, then self-confirmatory ideation fades away from our thoughts, and we find ourselves in the land of PAGL. Do you know where that is? Have you ever visited this land? In the land of PAGL, there is peace, assurance, gratitude, love, freedom, wisdom, joy—and healing, which is a fringe benefit!

Student: Dr. Hora, what if all we know about is just self-referential? I have just discovered that I see everything that is happening in terms of how it is affecting me. How can we go from that state to God-confirmatory or God-referential thinking, if we really don't know anything about God? I can see the mistake of self-referential thinking, that it is a problem; I can meditate on these ideas, but how can I possibly know God?

Dr. Hora: It is interesting that a word was changed. Did any of you notice? Self-"referential" thinking. It sounds as though we are talking about the same thing, but what happens if we accept this word, "self-referential"?

Student: The idea of self-confirmation loses its impact.

Dr. Hora: Of course, because the important word is "confirmation." "Self-referential" means that we are "referring to something" that is not immediately connected with "me." There are reference libraries, for instance, and we can refer to this one or that one, and we can refer to God. But when we speak about self-confirmation, we are speaking about something that is not a reference to a self—it is a confirmation of the reality of the self. So when you engage in self-confirmatory ideation, it is entirely different from self-referential thinking because it is saying something else. The self-confirmatory thought says, "I am a person in a body, a physical entity entirely apart from God." When you say "self-referential," you are talking about another thing, just referring to it, and this is not the same as confirming yourself. If you confirm yourself, and if this self which you have confirmed as real gets you into trouble, then it is immediately clear and offers a way to help you understand that you have hurt yourself. What is the "meaning," after forty-five minutes of talking about self-confirmatory ideation and after writing fifteen books about it, that a student changes the word into something that is less powerful than the original word? It is the urge to confirm the reality of the self. If we say "self-referential," it gives us the false impression that we are thinking about something that may not necessarily be something of importance. But every time someone entertains a self-confirmatory thought, he is saying, "I am a physical person." When you do that, you discover yourself as a liar. You are lying— you are confirming something that "seems to be" but is not. If someone alters this term, "self-confirmation," he is trying to avoid facing this lie. And he or she is saying, "I am not talking about this lie; I am referring to something that is not very intimately related to my existential reality." There is always this tendency in people to trivialize the technical terms that we use. For instance, every time I ask individuals if they remember the definition of perfect love— which is "nonpersonal, nonconditional benevolence"—what do they say? They immediately forget about the word "nonpersonal" and start with the word "non-conditional." What are they doing? They are trying to make it easier for themselves. But then what do we get out of it? If we make it easier for ourselves, why bother? Then we will just be satisfied with knowing intellectually about something that we have read or heard. We are not just nit-picking about the precision of our words. Words must be precisely used; otherwise, we deprive ourselves of the benefit of understanding.

Student: I wasn't throwing out the word "self-confirmation." What I have been struggling with is the issue of personalism. I have trouble understanding the word "personalism."

Dr. Hora: Can you tell us the definition of "personalism"?

Student: No, but "self-referential thinking" came to me to help me see how I am personalizing everything.

Dr. Hora: Send it back! It "came to you"—send it back! Who knows the definition of personalism?

Student: "Thinking about what others are thinking about what we are thinking."

Dr. Hora: Yes, this is personalism. Now what's wrong with it? Isn't it very sociable?

Student: The main thing that's wrong with it is that it leads to insanity!

Dr. Hora: Yes, of course. If you have ever spoken with someone who was deranged—everything this person says is about persons thinking about other persons, involving personal relationships— you would discover that "self and other" is the essence of their thinking, and they cannot see beyond it. How is it possible that there could be a Reality that is beyond the relationship between "self and other"? What else is there? We have to transcend this limited perspective on reality, and that is why Jesus told us: "In the world ye shall have tribulation: but be of good cheer; I have overcome the world" (John 16:33).

Student: Dr. Hora, I always assume that I understand the word "ideation," but I am not sure that I do understand it. What is the definition of "ideation"?

Dr. Hora: Ideation is "a preoccupation with ideas," any kind of ideas. If you are preoccupied with ideas about yourself, then you are engaged in self-confirmatory ideation. Actually ideation is just a fancy word for "thinking," and when we say "thinking," the implication is that we are "doing" the thoughts; but no one can "do" a thought. If we say "ideation," then we are saying that certain ideas have "obtained" in consciousness and that we are preoccupied with these ideas. So we cannot very well say that we are engaged in self-confirmatory thinking, because it would indicate that we make up thoughts. No one produces thoughts in his brain. When we say that we are involved in self-confirmatory ideation, it means that a certain idea about ourselves is present in consciousness, and we are messing around with it. And if we do this, there is a price to be paid. Ideation may be a very strange concept to some people. Recently I spoke to an individual who had just started reading some of the books on Metapsychiatry, and he said, "I told my wife that I have learned a big word— self-confirmatory ideation!" And his wife asked him, "What in the world is that?" Yes, it is a startling term, self-confirmatory ideation, but we can grow to appreciate working with the concept of self-confirmatory ideation when we carefully consider the implications and the consequences of being unknowingly involved in that kind of mind-practice.

Dialogue No. 40

Life, Love, Laughter, and Listening

Student: Dr. Hora, I am wondering how Metapsychiatry looks at creativity. Recently I was looking at a book called *The Courage to Create*, by Rollo May, and it seemed to be very operational.

Dr. Hora: And heroic!

Student: There is one passage where Picasso is quoted as having said, "Every act of creation begins with an act of destruction," referring to the process of transcending an old medium or form in order to go into a new realm of creativity.

Dr. Hora: So he is writing a book about how to "do" it. Suppose a mother has a baby, and she wants to become creative. What will she do, destroy the baby? No. These are attempts at explaining things without God. Anyone who tries to explain anything without God will find things extremely complicated and will certainly need courage. Does God need courage? God is the Creator of the universe. How does God create? The source of all creativity is God. How does he do it? God creates by proclamation. It is very simple, and you don't need courage for true creativity. God says, "Let there be light," and there is light. He creates everything by proclamation. Without God, we cannot explain anything. Whether we have courage or not does not matter: we must have ears to be creative. The Bible says: "The hearing ear, and the seeing eye, the Lord hath made even both of them" (Proverbs 20:12). That's what we need—not courage, but listening. If we can hear what God is saying, we are creative. It is no problem; it is very simple. Jesus said: "As I hear, I judge: and my judgment is just; because I seek not mine own will, but the will of the Father which hath sent me" (John 5:30). This is creation. So don't get confused by such books. We don't have to be heroic; we just have to be quiet, and then we will have creativity. Whenever Edison was engulfed in a creative experience, he would always hold his hand to his ear. He received many creative ideas.

Student: Dr. Hora, in the Bible there is a passage in Samuel that

363

says, "Speak Lord; for thy servant heareth" (1 Samuel 3:9).

Dr. Hora: It is a lovely story about Samuel. Samuel was a little boy, and he was with his father. It was night, and the father was sleeping when Samuel heard his name called. The little boy didn't know what to make of it. He just heard his name being called, and after a while he woke up his father and said, "Someone is calling my name." And his father answered, "Is that so? The next time you hear your name called, say out loud: 'Speak Lord; for thy servant heareth.'" From then on, Samuel became a hearing prophet who would always get his instructions acoustically! It is worthwhile reading these stories from the Bible. The Bible is about life; it is about love, and it is about laughter. Life, love, and laughter: what more can we ask?

Student: In the Bible everything seems to have another layer of meaning, though, beyond the story. What is the "meaning" of people thinking that God is telling them to go to war and to kill?

Dr. Hora: It is very simple. What is it?

Student: Interaction?

Dr. Hora: No, ignorance. If God tells someone to go to war, what is it? It is an ignorant thought—not from God—but from the "sea of mental garbage," which is full of interaction and which has nothing to do with God. God is getting credit for that which he doesn't deserve!

Student: All through the Bible, actually.

Dr. Hora: The nature of God as Life, Love, and Laughter is a well-kept secret. Who has ever heard about that? We have heard here and there that God is Love, but "He" never has sex! Now how can there be love without sex?

Student: Isn't the Bible just a record of man's interpretation of God's ideas?

Dr. Hora: The Bible is whatever we make of it. If we have a smattering of knowledge about the Bible, we will say that it is the word of God reaching human consciousness in many distorted ways.

Student: And those that heard the valid thoughts of God were on a higher level of understanding?

Dr. Hora: Yes.

Student: I remember that Moses told the people to go out of Egypt, but no one really wanted to go. They were sort of forced to go, but they really wanted to stay.

Dr. Hora: It is not that simple. The people were in slavery and bondage, very much abused and unhappy. Initially they were grateful to go, and Moses, who was a political leader, had to fight for their release. But, after trudging through the sands of Sinai for weeks and months, they began to complain, "Where are we going? How long will this take?" Moses did not tell them that it would take forty years. They were getting desperate. And when they came to the Red Sea and they couldn't move—and the Egyptians with their armies were right behind them, wanting to take them back— they said, "We were better off in Egypt anyway. There was food there, and we could eat. Here we are dying of starvation and from snake bites." There were fiery serpents, and they went through all kinds of miserable experiences. But eventually they passed through the Red Sea, and the Egyptians drowned—and they are still drowning; it is still going on. The Bible is not finished. Some people think that the Bible is a religious book, a prayer book, and some people think that it is a sex manual. [Metapsychiatry describes it as "a textbook for intelligent living."] You can read almost anything into the Bible. Anyone of you could ask, "Dr. Hora, you talk a lot about the Bible. How do we know that what you say is valid, if the whole world reads the Bible and everybody is confused about it?" This would be a legitimate question, es- pecially for some skeptical minds. All the teachings of the Bible and the *Qur'an* and other religious books can be validated. They are not offered to people as a fate. Metapsychiatry does not offer the Bible as a fate. It would be absolutely ridiculous for me to say to anyone, "You have to believe this," or "You have to believe what I say about this book." You would walk right out of here. In this respect, Metapsychiatry is really quite unique. It says, "Don't believe anything that anyone says. You don't have to believe." All you have to say is, "I am from Missouri. Show me!" We base our studies of the Bible on a principle. Which principle is that?

Student: The Principle of Existential Validation.

Dr. Hora: Exactly. The Principle of Existential Validation. What is that?

Student: If the principle or idea that we follow produces har- mony and good and well-being, then it is existentially valid; if it does not manifest in this way, then it is existentially invalid.

Dr. Hora: Yes. [Jesus formulated this principle with these words: "By their fruits, ye shall know them" (Matthew 7:20).] Existential validation has to do with the right understanding of the true nature of existence. If we understand the human experience correctly, then the wisdom in the Bible can be validated by the way in which it alters man's mode of being-in-the-world. The right understanding of the Bible can alter our mode of being-in-the-world and redeem us from our ignorance and its terrible consequences. All suffering indicates a universal tendency to be ignorant about the true nature of life.

Student: Without Metapsychiatry, I would not be able to understand correctly some of the statements in the Bible, for instance, "Love thy neighbor as thyself."

Dr. Hora: Yes, if you take it literally, it is a troublesome concept. There is another biblical statement which has been an endless source of suffering throughout the planet. Which is that one?

Student: "Be fruitful and multiply."

Dr. Hora: Yes. The Bible says: "Be fruitful, and multiply, and replenish the earth" (Genesis 1:28). The earth is getting so "replenished" that there is no space to live anymore and to produce enough food. Religious people keep propagating themselves and think that the more children they bring into this world, the better. So they are all being religiously pregnant, especially the Latin Americans. I saw on television a horrendous picture in Mexico, an area filled with garbage, trash, and pollution, and there were children, half-naked, running around in this area where the wind blows the toxic substances from the trash, and they breathe it, and then they die. This kind of misery happens when the Bible is misunderstood. How could anyone write such a stupid thing into the Bible? "Be fruitful, and multiply, and replenish the earth." It is attributed to God as if God commanded it. If God would give such stupid advice to mankind, he would not be God.

Student: What does it mean? Either it means that someone wrote it and it didn't come from God, or it has a different meaning from the one that it is generally given.

Dr. Hora: Somebody wrote it; it didn't come from God; and it has a different meaning—all these three possibilities. God is not interested in human birth; God knows better. Man was never born, and he never dies; he is "hid with Christ in God" (Hebrews 7:3; Colossians 3:3). How could God have said this, to go and "multiply?" He may have said it for rabbits, but not for man. God could not have said this. God is Spirit, and "they that worship him" and understand him "must worship him in Spirit and in Truth." What is the Truth? The truth is that we are not rabbits. Man is not a rabbit—man is a divine, incorporeal, nondimensional consciousness. Now if such a man "multiplies," there will be no space taken up anywhere—there will only be more and more intelligence and love and laughter coming into the world. Wouldn't that be a nice place to live? In life, love, laughter? And after? There is no after: it is all eternal, and that is Reality. If God imparted the idea to "be fruitful and multiply," it means that there must be more and more wisdom expressed in the universe, more and more love and intelligence and joy and harmony and beauty.

Student: There is nondimensional Reality, and then there is "what seems to be" dimensional. If the important thing is to multiply spiritually, how does that manifest in a dimensional way?

Dr. Hora: What are the dimensions of wisdom?

Student: There are no dimensions.

Student: They are limitless.

Dr. Hora: Yes. Wisdom is a nondimensional, infinite good. What are the dimensions of good? What are the dimensions of joy?

Student: But isn't there a purpose for "what seems to be" a physical manifestation, for dimensions?

Dr. Hora: Yes. What is it? It is just a trick to confuse us. Have you noticed that, when there is a beauty contest, areas of the body are measured with a tape, and that measurement is the evidence of beauty? If the right measurements are found on someone, they are proclaimed to be beautiful. It is really very silly. Everything human is very silly, if not tragic.

Student: What is the purpose of the human condition?

Dr. Hora: What is the purpose of $2 + 2 = 5$?

Student: To reveal the ignorance, the error?

Dr. Hora: If there were no $2 + 2 = 5$, no one would become a mathematician, and we wouldn't know what is right or what is true. What is the purpose of darkness?—this is a biblical point. And actually there is no darkness because the light is always somewhere in evidence on the surface of the earth. But the experience of darkness makes it possible for us to appreciate the light. If there were only darkness, then no one would know that there is light. At one time we had a sightless girl studying Metapsychiatry. I asked her, "What is the experience of your blindness? Are you seeing darkness, always and everywhere?" She answered, "I don't even know what darkness is. I have no concept of darkness." She was born blind, so she has never experienced darkness. She just knows that there is a way of moving about in this world without getting hurt. She is a whiz on computers and has a doctorate. God has given her the intelligence and ability to live in the sighted world, practically fully functioning. God looks after everyone according to his need.

Student: What is the "meaning" of the population explosion?

Dr. Hora: I just explained it to you. It is in misreading the Bible.

Student: Isn't every individual a unit of awareness?

Dr. Hora: Yes, but unfortunately we can also be aware of invalid ideas. If we were only aware of valid ideas, we would all be brilliant and loving and laughing and living.

Student: And listening.

Student: Do we hear God speaking to us in ideas?

Dr. Hora: God speaks to us through ideas "obtaining" in consciousness, which we then express in words.

Student: Edison was creative, and all of the ideas he received ended up in a certain language.

Dr. Hora: Yes, he translated what he received into the idea of electricity.

Student: And a composer hears God's ideas too, but in a different language.

Dr. Hora: Yes. It would drive God crazy to learn all the languages on the earth, but he doesn't have to know them, not even one. God imparts ideas into consciousness, and we translate these ideas into the words of our own language.

Student: How is it that Edison understood ideas that were necessary for his particular work, and a computer specialist hears ideas that are necessary for his particular work? They are not the same ideas after all.

Dr. Hora: God does not have a one-track mind or just one idea to impart. Suppose you hear a certain melody on the radio, and immediately you translate it into the words "Beethoven's Fifth." God does not say these words, but it is God which gives us our ability to identify ideas. Let us say that there is a musical idea that we can hear, a musical idea that helps us to appreciate Beethoven and also what the music is trying to tell us. With a little training we can hear what the music is saying—music is just a language. We can get a notion of what the composer was trying to express, and this makes the music most enjoyable, having the right appreciation of the composer's message, the message received through inspiration from God. It is said that whenever Gustav Mahler sat down to the piano to compose, he made a little prayer inviting the creative Spirit to come express Itself through him on the piano.

No courage was needed, just the love of music.

Student: In our daily life, can we do the same thing, invoke God?

Dr. Hora: You have my permission!

Student: If we are sitting quietly and listening for God, are we invoking God to speak to us?

Dr. Hora: You could say that, but Mahler, invoking God formally, apparently said, "Veni, Creator Spiritus"—"Come, creative Spirit."

Student: We say that we can't ask God for anything, and yet we really need to be listening all the time. I was wondering if there is a valid way to do this.

Dr. Hora: Yes. This is a perennial problem with prayer: we cannot tell God what God should do for us. I do not know whether Mahler believed that God really heard his invocation, but we can certainly say that he prepared himself to be receptive to inspiration—he was sincere. By offering these words and contemplating them, he became receptive to whatever inspiration might reach his consciousness.

Student: We have the ability to focus on being receptive to God's ideas, and then we can hear valid ideas; but we can also hear invalid ideas. The important thing is to be able to discern the difference. But what about those individuals who are able to hear another person's idea or need which you have called "being telepathic." Lately, the moment I get home from the office, whatever time it is, the phone rings, and it is my mother. She just seems to know my whereabouts. I don't have to tell her anything. Sometimes I'll be sitting at my desk, and I'll become aware of something I need, and in the mail it will come! My mother knew. I would like to understand this occurrence. More and more I am aware of certain thoughts, and I can't always tell whether or not they are her thoughts that I am receiving.

Dr. Hora: There is such a phenomenon of telepathic connectedness between two kindred spirits—many such incidents are described. It is rather puzzling. Communication is based on receptivity—it is like the telephone. If your telephone were out of order, your mother could not possibly reach you, but you might get the same idea she is entertaining and not know it—you might think that the idea just "occurred" to you. There is a mysterious "cordless telephone" between people when one becomes aware of certain thoughts that another is thinking. Your mother has perfect timing and perfect pitch!

Student: But I don't always understand it. What am I to make of it?

Dr. Hora: You just accept it, and be happy. Your mother wishes you well, and you can be grateful that this telepathic connection is not threatening. Now there is another kind of telepathic phenomenon, where people receive telepathic messages that are hostile, malicious, jealous, and therefore destructive, and we call this kind "mental malpractice." For instance, there are certain people to whom bad things are often happening. They don't understand it, and they may even think that it is because of the weather or something that they ate. They don't realize that they are receiving hostile, malicious thoughts from someone with whom they are deeply involved in interaction thinking. It doesn't come from strangers—it always comes from someone who is close to us—from family members most of the time. The closer we are to someone, meaning the more we are involved with someone interactionally, the more likely we are to be vulnerable. If the other one is entertaining hostile and malicious thoughts about us, we can be vulnerable to these thoughts. There are exceptionally perceptive people who get panicky over this phenomenon, and this is called paranoia. Some people are aware of "mental malpractice" and become frightened, panicky, or disorganized, and then they develop a full-blown, paranoid psychosis. Psychiatrists have known about this for ages, but they still do not understand the process. Under normal circumstances, you might have a friend with whom you are involved in an interaction relationship—he is not a murderer, but maybe he envies you a little or is jealous of you, and occasionally he may have a thought like, "I wish something would happen to him; he is too happy." And if you are receptive to this message—you'd be surprised—suddenly you wake up in the morning and find you have a backache or a headache or a runny nose or maybe an asthma attack in the middle of the night. "Malicious malpractice" can reach us quite often at night while we are asleep. We wake up with a symptom, and we think we just caught a cold; or we have a pain here or a pain there, and we don't know what happened unless we go to see someone who can read the messages of the body. The body will always tell you what hit you, and then you can dismiss it. This is a great help because you could be afraid about a symptom and go from one doctor to another, and the doctors don't know that these symptoms are thoughts. No doctor will dare to say this out loud; he might be accused of being crazy. Malicious "mental malpractice" takes advantage of the fact that it is possible to have an impact on someone else's thinking at a distance, if that individual is tuned in on you. In a way, that is "normal."

Student: But "tuning in" means that there is a relationship going on.

Dr. Hora: Right. A relationship is the most dangerous thing in the world—any kind of a relationship, good or bad.

Student: In the case of my mother, when I reach a point where I can see her in a different light and myself too, then there would no longer be a telepathic connection, right?

Dr. Hora: In what different light?

Student: If I can see myself and my mother as spiritual beings, then there would no longer be telepathy between us, would there?

Dr. Hora: Yes, there would be. As long as there is interaction between mother and daughter, there is telepathy. Fortunately, your mother is not malicious, except occasionally you wake up at night with a runny nose, or you can't breathe. Yes, these are some of the mysteries of communication between man and man. But it is important to know that real communication is in one direction only—from God to man.

Dialogue No. 41

Mental Arm-Wrestling

Student: Dr. Hora, what does it mean to be awake?

Dr. Hora: What does it mean to be awake?

Student: It means to go beyond the dream.

Dr. Hora: That's right.

Student: But to go "beyond the dream" means to transcend.

Dr. Hora: Yes. What does it mean to transcend? Suppose you think that $2 + 2 = 5$. How do you transcend it? By saying that two and two is three? Today it came to our attention that some people find it difficult to stop thinking bad thoughts. We are always admonishing ourselves to think good thoughts—it is very dangerous to think bad thoughts. I know of someone who was entertaining the thought that someone should "drop dead," and then this individual had a blackout in the street. It is dangerous to think bad thoughts. People who are in the habit of thinking bad thoughts find that their life is one crisis after another, one disaster after another—all kinds of unpleasant things can occur. When we explain to people that we must be careful to think good thoughts, what happens? They start fighting against the bad thoughts. But if we fight against bad thoughts, these bad thoughts will get worse, because to fight against a bad thought is a bad thought in itself, and you will get yourself into a funk. The harder you try to "not think" bad thoughts, the more you will become involved in bad thoughts, and your life will just get worse and worse. It is a tricky thing. Bad thoughts cannot be fought against. Suppose you try to wrestle with a rattlesnake, what will happen? It will kill you. You cannot fight against a rattlesnake. You have to replace the rattlesnake with a blacksnake, because it is harmless! Similarly we don't fight against bad thoughts. We replace the bad thoughts with good thoughts. We can only "think" one thought at a time. So if we have a bad thought, we quickly replace it with its spiritual counterfact. What is a spiritual counterfact? Suppose you think that someone is a rattlesnake? What would be the spiritual counterfact to such a bad thought?

Student: God never made an individual like a rattlesnake?

Dr. Hora: Okay, but you are still in the negative. What will you do to get out of the negative?

Student: Practice the Prayer of Right Seeing? "Everything and everyone is here for God, whether they know it or not."

Dr. Hora: That's a good way. You replace the bad thought with a good thought, a spiritual truth. Spiritual truths are always good. We replace a bad thought with a spiritually valid, good thought, and then we don't have to wrestle against the bad thought—it disappears.

Student: Isn't the wrestling an indication that we don't fully recognize the invalidity and troublesomeness of this thought?

Dr. Hora: No, it is possible to have fully recognized it. You may even have read the right books about it, but with the best of intentions, if you keep wrestling with the bad thoughts you may find you are getting nowhere, only getting worse. There was a period in the United States where all problems were solved by arm-wrestling. When two people had a problem, they sat down and leaned against each other and arm-wrestled—this was a way to deal with life and its problems! A man who tries to improve his thoughts this way, by fighting against them, is like an arm-wrestler. We could ask, "What is the meaning of getting stuck with the idea that we have to overcome the bad thoughts?" We don't have to overcome bad thoughts—we just have to replace them with the right thoughts. Suppose someone has AIDS—and AIDS is a bad thought—some might say, "Well, tuberculosis is better. We are not going to think AIDS thoughts, we are going to think tuberculosis thoughts." And it happens that many AIDS patients develop very virulent forms of tuberculosis. There was a time, when I was a medical student, that if someone had malaria, he was injected with typhus; the idea was that the typhus fever would kill the malaria. Imagine how much those poor patients suffered from the brilliant, scientific "wisdom" of research in those days. Syphilis was treated with malaria in a similar fashion. These were absurd remedies, and they were all based on the idea of arm-wrestling, that we have to conquer the evil. We go out and fight against the evil, but the more we fight against evil, the worse it gets until it engulfs us and destroys us. It happens on many levels. There is a fight in people who want to improve life by fighting against evil, especially intellectuals, who have a great tendency to go into battle against bad thoughts. The bad thoughts have to be conquered by other thoughts. Syphilis has to be conquered by malaria, and malaria has to be conquered by typhus, et cetera, et cetera. How stupid can we get? The solution will never be found until mankind understands that the source of all good and valid thoughts is the divine Mind. This does not mean to go fight against the bad thoughts with divine Mind thoughts—God does not have to fight. God says: "Let there be light"—and there is light, no matter how dark it was. It is very important not to be arrogant or belligerent or militant or to try to conquer the evils of the world with our minds. It is our minds that have conjured up the evils of the world. We just simply replace every bad thought with an appropriate spiritually valid, good thought. It is effortless; it is effective and efficient! [The three Es] How grateful we can be for this. If we don't understand this method, there is no way of being saved from negative thinking. What does it take to kill a negative thought? Is it firing bullets of positive thoughts? No, that doesn't work. All true communication is from God to man. [See Dialogue No. 29: "Real Communication: God to Man."] When we are facing a problem, we listen to God, which is infinite Mind—All-Knowing, All-Loving, All-Good—to provide us with the right idea, which will then replace the negative thought. It is not just a simple negative/positive. No. The negative thought is not replaced by a positive thought. A negative thought can only be effectively replaced by a right thought—the right thought is from the divine Mind, and in order to receive this right thought, we must be able to listen to God's thoughts.

Student: Dr. Hora, let's say we dislike someone a lot, and consequently our thoughts about that individual are negative. To have a good thought would be to see this individual as a child of God but that might only be words. We might not mean it.

Dr. Hora: You could see that individual as a rotten child of God, too!

Student: I am trying to understand what thought would effectively replace the negative one.

Dr. Hora: Well, we could prepare a vocabulary of right thoughts or an encyclopedia, and whenever you catch yourself with a negative thought, you could look it up.

Student: Or put it on the computer!

Dr. Hora: No, that is not the way it works. You have to listen to the good, valid thoughts which come constantly from the divine Mind. There are four things that we have to learn: life, love, laughter, and listening.

Student: The listening only works if it is sincere and if you really understand it.

Dr. Hora: So do it, and don't complain about it. Just be grateful that there is a God—unless you doubt it. What happens if we are skeptical about the existence of God? If we are skeptical about the existence of God, then the whole dynamic is not available to us, and we are deprived of this precious gift of healing.

Student: Yet individuals who claim to be atheistic seem, nonetheless, to have inspired ideas.

Dr. Hora: Yes, but they will "arm-wrestle" the rest of their lives. Most people do a lot of "arm-wrestling" with infinite contortions of logic and rationality; everything is always designed to conquer the evil through the "personal mind." When they hear us talking about replacing an evil thought, they think, "Let's see, let me figure it out. How can I figure out the right thought which I will then be able to apply to this problem, so that I can conquer it with the good thought which I figured out?"—and they do not get anywhere. There are Four Freedoms: life, love, laughter, and listening, and the Fourth Freedom is very important. Listening is the most important one: it is listening to God to give us the right thought that will replace the bad thought. Then we can be healed.

Student: Is sincerity a necessary aspect of the act of turning and listening? Do we have to say, "I need help"?

Dr. Hora: We need to learn to listen to what God is constantly saying. We learn this in meditation. It is not something that we can "conjure up" in our heads or apply in a mechanical way.

Student: It is easy to get discouraged about the issue of sincerity if I am having a problem with a person or with a situation in which I am constantly turning to God for help. I wonder if I am sincere, and I often feel like giving up.

Dr. Hora: First of all, you must have the integrity to admit that you are entertaining bad thoughts—you like to criticize; you like to judge; you like to envy; you like to be jealous; and you wish people ill. You have to be aware that you are engaged in bad thoughts all the time and that these bad thoughts are expressing themselves in personal tragedies. All right, so you have reached a point, by studying Metapsychiatry, that you already know that you are bringing disaster into your life by entertaining bad thoughts. Now you say, "We are supposed to replace these bad thoughts

with valid thoughts, spiritually valid thoughts. How do I do that?"
It is not a mechanical process; it is not an intellectual process, and
you cannot fool God, not even once. You have to really listen as
God is supplying you with what we call the spiritual counterfact.
The bad thoughts are material lies—human, personal, mental, material lies. You cannot "arm-wrestle" against the evil. You cannot
use your head to overcome a thought that was conjured up in your
head. You cannot bang your head against your own head! If you
listen to God, then God will always provide you with the right
thought, which will replace the bad thought, and which will heal
you.

Student: Sometimes in the beginning of this work, when we sit
in meditation, it seems as if all we hear is our thoughts. How can
we know that we will eventually be able to hear divine Mind's
thoughts, when, in fact, maybe all we are hearing is static?

Dr. Hora: We hear what we are listening to, and we listen to
what we are interested in. If we are interested in mental arm-
wrestling, then that is what we are going to hear, and we will get
nowhere. The Bible says, "Be still," which is the biblical way
of saying, "Shut up!" "Be still and know that I am God" (Psalm
46:10). But there are many people who are skeptical about the existence of God. As long as you doubt the reality of God, it is very
difficult—you cannot hear God. You have at least to acknowledge
that there must be a God because nothing makes sense without It.
Let's not arm-wrestle with evil. Let us know that God gives us the
valid ideas which replace the evil thoughts so that they disappear,
and we are saved.

Student: One time last week when I was meditating, I was thinking the kind of thoughts that you just described, and I thought I
would put a stop to them and just try to listen. It was very clear
that I wasn't hearing anything. I was trying not to think, and it was
like a stalemate. Then I got distracted and restless . . .

Dr. Hora: Trying not to think! Isn't that "arm-wrestling"? You
have a thought, but you don't want to have that thought. You are
fighting with that thought, and it doesn't get you anywhere. Now,
for the benefit of learning how to replace bad thoughts with right
thoughts, we have the Eleven Principles of Metapsychiatry. Every
one of these Principles directs our attention to some spiritually
valid idea. For instance, let's start with the First Principle. Suppose
you are involved with some fear or with a physical, mental, or
emotional pain. Suppose you are thinking about a colleague—

how much you hate him—and you are getting aches and pains in your body. You might be thinking that he is a lousy character, and he has this fault and that fault, and you cannot stop thinking about it. You can get very tired of "arm-wrestling" with these bad thoughts. Just remember that in Metapsychiatry there are the Eleven Principles, and start with the first one. Focus attention on the First Principle. What does it say? It says, "Thou shalt have no other interests before the good of God, which is spiritual blessedness." It can immediately replace the thought of how much you hate that "lousy guy." We cannot think of two things at the same time. So if you catch yourself thinking about a colleague who has many negative qualities, and you ruminate about it and think about how to get back at him and get even, you can remember that the First Principle says, "I am interested in the Good of God, not the evil of this guy." If you turn your attention to the First Principle, the torment, the pain, the headaches, the cramps in the legs, the stomachaches will suddenly disappear, and you will be entertaining spiritually valid thoughts of "spiritual blessedness," and the previous negative thoughts will fade out of your awareness. Right then and there, you can be healed. But if you doubt the possibility of spiritual blessedness, then you are without hope. As the Bible says: "Acquaint now thyself with Him, and be at peace: thereby good shall come unto thee" (Job 22:21). We can replace the bad thoughts with valid thoughts. Bad thoughts are not valid, no matter how real they seem to be—they are not valid because God has never produced a bad thought. If the First Principle doesn't do the trick, then you can go to the Second Principle. Metapsychiatry offers a wide choice of Eleven Principles. This is the great value of the Eleven Principles.

Student: As far as listening is concerned, it seems that there are no rules or mechanics to follow.

Dr. Hora: Once we give up "arm-wrestling," it is easy. There is a national obsession with this historical phenomenon of arm-wrestling. It is so funny: somehow we all have it in ourselves to wrestle against evil and against people whom we consider evil. Criminality is widespread—we are wrestling against guns and against crime—and the more we wrestle against it, the more there is of it.

Student: That's because of the ego. But if we have humility, we don't have to "arm-wrestle."

Dr. Hora: Where do we get humility?

Student: Is humility a spiritual value?

Dr. Hora: Yes.

Student: What makes humility spiritual? It seems that it is about acquiescing or surrendering . . .

Dr. Hora: And becoming a wimp!

Student: If I could understand what makes humility spiritual, maybe I could understand spiritual values better.

Dr. Hora: Unfortunately, humility is very often faked. There are many people who learn how to fake it, and they believe they are humble, and sometimes others even believe it. It is like the man who said, "In business the principal thing is honesty, and when you learn how to fake that, you've got it made." So it is with humility and all spiritual qualities—they are of God. It is not man-made, and that's what makes it spiritual. You can fake it, but you cannot make it.

Student: How do we know that it is of God?

Dr. Hora: Because it is—it is not something that is made, even though you can fake it.

Student: You have to recognize it, realize it.

Student: Can you sort of sense it?

Dr. Hora: We need to use the word "awareness": when we are truly humble, we are aware that we are humble. How does it feel to be truly humble? It feels very good. In what way does it feel very good? There is no anxiety; it is peaceful; it is intelligent; it is extremely attractive; and it is joyous and beautiful—and "all things work together for good" to them that are truly humble. It just IS. Most problems in life are accompanied by the idea that we can make or do something; we want to be in control of everything. If we are not in control, we are considered a wimp. Actually, a wimp is just a devious guy who controls you by pretending not to control you—a snake can twist itself in a million ways. Now today, we are unmasking the altogether human weakness of arm-wrestling; it is a great weakness. There are physical forms of arm-wrestling, and there are mental forms of arm-wrestling. Ruminations are a form of arm-wrestling in which the opponent is not there. It is an extremely frustrating condition.

Student: Does humility mean trying to give up trying to think or trying not to think?

Dr. Hora: Humility does not think. Humility is aware of gratitude, of love, of life, of laughter, and of listening. That is what humility is—it is beautiful, and it is wonderful, and it is of God.

Nobody can do it; it cannot be done.

Student: If we don't perceive that we are listening, if we don't hear anything and we think that we are not thinking, does this mean that we are secretly thinking?

Dr. Hora: "We think that we are not thinking, but secretly we are thinking"—this is the statement of an intellectual. We are not thinking—we just think that we are thinking. Man is a divine consciousness, and consciousness does not think—consciousness is awareness. What are you doing when you are aware? You are just listening. The more you are listening, the more you are aware of the truth of divine Perfection and of man as a perfect spiritual idea of God. Perfect God and perfect man are one in the universe, that is, the universe of Mind, which is another name for God. If you understand that God is infinite Mind, you won't have to worry about what the feminist movement will do to God. I hear they are putting God into dresses now for equal rights— another fantastic idiocy! It is important to know that God is not a human person: "he" does not need to wear clothes; "he" does not have to be male or female. God is infinite Wisdom and Love and Power and fills the whole universe. You don't have to go to church to see God. God is everywhere and always present, and we have to be aware of God so that we can see the good of God everywhere. And then we can say: "Everything, everywhere is already all right" [Prayer of Beholding]. And if it isn't, then it is just "what seems to be," and if it seems to be bad, we can replace it with the good, and then it is all right—then it is healed.

Student: I experience some of my thoughts as bad, and then I try to replace them with a Principle. But if I have, so to speak, the power to have these bad thoughts, then how can that same ignorant thought be replaced by a valid thought? I know it can be done, but how can I be doing two things at the same time?

Dr. Hora: That is an operational distortion of tonight's entire class discussion. We do not do anything. We are not really thinkers—we have the illusion of producing thoughts, but we cannot produce thoughts. Bad thoughts are impressions coming to our awareness from the "sea of mental garbage," which does not exist. So when we listen to God, God gives us valid thoughts which replace the invalid thoughts, right where those invalid, bad thoughts seem to be. The invalid, "bad" thoughts do not really exist. Only the valid thoughts have reality. Spiritual blessedness is Reality; physical cursedness is an illusion.

Student: Then "thinking" is really just thoughts that are coming into our awareness?

Dr. Hora: Right. Is our awareness focused on evil, or is it focused on God's good?

Student: So no thought is my thought . . .

Dr. Hora: Right, you aren't even there.

Student: Actually God is always talking to us, but we are not always listening.

Dr. Hora: We almost never listen. It is the greatest thing when we are in communication with God. It is interesting that we cannot tell God anything; communication is a one-way street—it is coming from God to man. If we are distracted by the illusion of communicating from person to person, it is good to know that this is not communication: this is manipulation. Unenlightened people are forever manipulating each other and thus multiplying the evil and the "bad" and the invalid thoughts in the world. God says: "Be fruitful, and multiply, and replenish the earth" (Genesis 1:28), and man has done it. Tragically the earth seems to be "replenished" by an infinite number of bad ideas, "thinking" bad thoughts.

Student: These thoughts are not valid, and yet they have the power to destroy us.

Dr. Hora: They seem to have the power to destroy us. And who is being destroyed when we are being destroyed? A fiction. Unenlightened man is a fictional character. The only Reality is God and His perfect universe. If we could see this clearly all the time, it would be wonderful—there would be no problems. "Because thou hast made the Lord, which is thy refuge, even the Most High, thy habitation; there shall no evil befall thee, neither shall any plague come nigh thy dwelling" (Psalm 91:9-10).

The Eleven Principles
of Metapsychiatry

These eleven principles are guidelines that, when contemplated regularly and applied to our everyday lives, are intended to increase receptivity to divine grace and to ensure progress on the spiritual path to enlightenment.

First Principle: Thou shalt have no other interests before the good of God, which is spiritual blessedness.

Second Principle: Take no thought for what should be or for what should not be; seek ye first to know the good of God, which already is.

Third Principle: There is no interaction anywhere; there is only Omniaction everywhere.

Fourth Principle: Yes is good, but no is also good.

Fifth Principle: God helps those who let Him.

Sixth Principle: If you know what, you know how.

Seventh Principle: Nothing comes into experience uninvited.

Eighth Principle: Problems are lessons designed for our edification.

Ninth Principle: Reality cannot be experienced or imagined; it can, however, be realized.

Tenth Principle: The understanding of what really is abolishes all that seems to be.

Eleventh Principle: Do not show your pearls to unreceptive minds, for they will demean them.

Published Works
of Thomas Hora, M.D.

BOOKS

Encounters With Wisdom (Multi-Volume Series)
Beyond the Dream
Dialogues in Metapsychiatry
Existential Metapsychiatry
In Quest of Wholeness

BOOKLETS

Forgiveness
Healing through Spiritual Understanding
A Hierarchy of Values
The Soundless Music of Life
Can Meditation Be Done?
Compassion
God in Psychiatry
Marriage and Family Life
Commentaries on Scripture
Right Usefulness
Self-Transcendence
What Does God Want?

For more information on Metapsychiatry and the works of
Dr. Hora go to:

www.pagl.org

Index

289
lesbianism, 108, 270-71
liberation, dynamics of, 9 -16
living in the context of God,
   289-90, 293,350
love
   and communication, 17-18,
and compassion, 333
         conditional, 34-35,45-
         46,63,225,317
      desire for, 86
      God as, 13,135,147,240
      human, 34,45,226,272,317
      nonconditional, 34-36, 45,
         209,293,316-17
      nonpersonal,
         34,50,102,225,273,293,31
         7
      parental, 34
      and paying attention, 173
      spiritual, 45
      unconditional, 34,46,64
Love-Intelligence,
      2,14,43,54,102,104,113,11
      8-19,143-44,146,161-
      62,190-
      91,211,217,225,230,268,2
      96,298-99,300,317,333-
      34,340-41
   God as, 14,147,325-26
   manifestation of, 144,161,
      omniactive 13,190,217,299-
      300,341
   participation in, 134
      See also God
Maharishi, 4
marriage
   meaning of, 80
meditation and attention, 4
   and belief in many minds, 8
         and ceaseless prayer, 6
      contemplative, 10 - 11
      and one Mind, 1, 2
      perfect, 27
      and
      prayer,6,11,82,125,174,212,
      purpose of, 120,212
megalomania, 2
Meher Baba, 61
mental contagion, 215-17
Metapsychiatry, 12, 30-31
      On awareness, 167-70
      and belief in metal power,
         2,8,28,172
      on compassion, 317
      definition or,30,34,45

and existential validity, 147
on experience, 45
and functioning, 251-52
on gratitude, 132
and healing, 10,14,109,136
and healing the past, 10
on the human condition, 197,
   199-200
on humility, 23
and illness, 271
on marriage, 29,87,322
and motivation, 236,274
and operationalism,
   67,91,145
and perfect Love, 34,45,209
on performance, 88
principles or, 256-7,355,376
on progress, 343,346
and psychoanalysis,
   14,197,262,303,348
and receptivity, 71-78
on relationships,
   168,189,272
and righteous judgment, 272
and science of knowing, 105
on self-esteem, 88
on social-justice issue, 313
and spiritual birth, 65
students of, 12,72,155-
   6,211,355
on symbolic structures, 330
on thinking, 109,169
on wanting, 268
millennial vision, 189-95
mind-fasting, 163-64,287,
morality, 149
mother
   and attachments, 319-25
   fixation, 84,87
   relationship with, 75, 285-86
   separation from,
      85,101,109,186,329,33
      1
motherhood, 24
motivation invalid, 29,157
motivation (cont.)
   love as, 30,59,62
   right, 217-18
   and self-confirmation, 52-53
mystical union, 322

naming, 38
Nasrudin, 119-20, 123
natural man, 45,72-73,75, 77-78
Ninth Principle of
      Metapsychiatry,

213, 349
nonbeing fear of, 113,198,200
nondimensionality, 146,315
nonpersonal, nonconditional
   benevolence, 34,
   293,317,361
   as perfect Love,
      35,45,209,317,361
nonpersons, 209

observation, 92,154,197,339
Omniaction, 4, 189-
   92,226,259,280,290,3
   26,329
one Mind
   and consciousness,

      3,5,7,14,67,82,110,155,
168,175,192,211,232,302,
   and harmony, 7
   and individuals, 3
   and meditation, 1-8
operationalism, 67
   as manipulation, 31,145,380
   meaning of, 70,104,250
   and performance, 83

PAGL,
      5,14,67,69,76,81,83,92,
      109,148,155,157-
      8,162,168,180,192,212,
      220,222,232,302,328-
      9,344,360
   Consciousness,
      67,83,148,155,168,180,
      192,212,233,302
   and envy, 162
   and glowing, 81
   and interaction, 186
   and motivation, 109,157-8
   and self-esteem, 93
   and spiritual freedom, 180
   as supreme good of life, 105
   as treasure, 76
pain, 196-206
   and anger, 185-6,232,267
   as distraction from God, 268
   and Freud, 274
   and gratitude, 134-35
   and illness, 260-62
   and interaction thinking, 260
parents, 20,22,
   fear of, 3,5-36
   neglectful, 85
past
   death of, 151,156

Made in United States
Troutdale, OR
09/28/2023

13250578R00224